DATE DUE

Be Careful Who You SLAPP

Michelangelo Delfino

&

Mary E. Day

MoBeta Publishing
Los Altos, California

MoBeta Publishing
P.O. Box 571
Los Altos, CA 94023-0571
www.mobeta.com

SAN 254-9050

Library of Congress Control Number 2002113798

ISBN 0-9725141-0-4

Printed in the United States of America
First Edition 2002

Dedicated to

Mike's dad, Cosimo Armando Delfino, who was born in Italy and became an American citizen in 1943 while fighting the Nazis under Generals Bradley and Patton.

&

Mary's uncle, Frank Evan Mackey, Jr., an 82nd Airborne paratrooper who paid the ultimate price for freedom at Normandy on June 7, 1944.

CONTENTS

AUTHORS NOTE

A California Judge has permanently banned the publication of this book on the Internet.

God Bless America!

PREFACE

"We'll post until we're dead!"

This is the real-life story of a vicious confrontation between two self-employed research scientists and one of Silicon Valley's founding companies over the right of all Americans to express caustic criticism in a public forum. Indeed why would a corporate conglomerate spend millions of dollars trying in vain to "silence, bankrupt, and incarcerate" us for simply speaking out? Labeled "cyber terrorists" by our corporate adversaries, and claimed "wrong morally" by the United States government, we unwittingly became embroiled in four years of "remarkably acrimonious litigation" that continues to this very day.

This book is a personal account and a scathing commentary of American jurisprudence in both State and Federal courts at the turn of the new millennium. Our story takes place in California's Silicon Valley where the near-perfect Mediterranean climate does little to mellow the frantic pace of everyday life. In this high-technology capital, work hours are often deliberately long and loneliness and divorce are a frequent accompaniment to one's career. For so many, the fear of losing far outweighs the joy of achieving and the disparity between society's two halves is all too apparent and ever widening. Reality is questioned as home prices rise far beyond the absurd and homeownership takes on an investment fund mentality.

Amidst the feeding frenzy of obscene wealth and ever-evolving technology is the Internet, an open and free communication medium with an unprecedented ability to instantly deliver an author's opinion and the raw truth to the world. And within this World Wide Web of the Internet, is Yahoo! and its financial message boards – a public information forum, so easily accessible, it was bound to be viewed as a threat to the disproportionately rich, the recklessly powerful, and the dispassionately influential. And so they SLAPP.

A SLAPP[1] is an underhanded and vicious tactic used mostly by those with sufficient resources to expend an inordinate amount of money to manipulate the system against an adversary. It is a tool of legal oppression that is fast becoming a pervasive part of corporate America and its executive greed – the all too autocratic accompanied by an army of legally trained ruffians. Typically, SLAPP's are civil complaints[2] alleging defamation, unfair business practice, conspiracy and related claims[3] filed against a critic who has raised an issue of public concern. SLAPP plaintiffs purposely avoid public discourse while intending to silence a public commentator into oblivion. The SLAPPed defendant is immediately overwhelmed and threatened with the loss of huge sums of money as motivation to cease and desist their public outcry. The SLAPPer, like the Nazi, is seen as the invincible aggressor. If a SLAPP blitzkrieg is effective, the unsuspecting victim is quieted and the public is never made aware of it.

"Companies have a free hand to tout their organizations ... A little guy like me comes along and says 'I disagree' or 'the CEO is ignorant,' and I'm squished. It's a free-speech issue."[4]

This book is a simple exposé about being SLAPPed and how a couple of unintentionally inspired leftover anti-war activists, since turned responsible parents, research scientists, and now business partners, relentlessly fought back. We refused to be censored and

---

[1]SLAPP, an acronym for Strategic Lawsuit Against Public Participation was coined in 1988 by George W. Pring and Penelope Canan, the authors of *SLAPPs Getting Sued for Speaking Out*, Temple University Press, Philadelphia, 1996.

[2]The first court paper filed in a civil lawsuit outlining the alleged facts of the case and basis for seeking a legal remedy.

[3]Lawsuit demands for money or other relief.

[4]Delfino quoted by Stephanie Armour, *USA Today*, January 7, 2002.

give up our Constitutional Rights no matter what the cost. The Varian SLAPP is a lawsuit fought not only in the court of law, but also in the internationally accessible World Wide Web. Yahoo! and other Internet Web sites were used as tools to fight back and defend. Like the slingshot so ably used by David to fell Goliath, the Internet likewise is well-suited to the task of bringing not one, but two oppressive corporate giants to their knees. However, this confrontation far more resembled the decisive Battle of Stalingrad[5] circa 1942-43, where an estimated two million souls were lost, than the one-on-one biblical confrontation. Before Stalingrad, the Nazi invaders considered themselves superhuman. After this SLAPP, jurisprudence and Silicon Valley would never be the same.

Our struggle is no different than any other war of attrition. We had no choice – the decision whether to fight was made before we entered the world. Born with principles and the will to defend our families for as long as we breathe, we were committed to the end. Our story carries a simple message back to fascist bullies:

Be careful who you SLAPP!

---

[5]William Craig, *Enemy at the Gates*, Readers Digest Press, E.P. Dutton & Co. Inc., New York, 1973.

CHRONOLOGY

Oct 8, 1998 – Delfino fired from Varian Associates after 10 years

Oct 12, 1998 – Delfino posts his first Internet message

Dec 21, 1998 – Day resigns from Varian Associates after 15 years

Feb 11, 1999 – EDD rules Delfino was wrongfully terminated

Feb 25, 1999 – Delfino is SLAPPed in Cal Superior Court

Feb 26, 1999 – TRO issues against Delfino

Jun 21, 1999 – Delfino placed under preliminary injunction

Jul 22, 1999 – Day is SLAPPed in Federal Court

Aug 13, 1999 – Delfino resumes & Day begins posting

Nov 19, 1999 – Day placed under preliminary injunction

Apr 7, 2000 – Delfino & Day win partial summary judgment

Sep 21, 2000 – U.S. 9th Circuit Court dissolves injunction

Oct 22, 2001 – Superior Court trial begins

Dec 17, 2001 – Trial ends and jury renders verdict

Feb 13, 2002 – Delfino & Day placed under permanent injunction

Mar 8, 2002 – Delfino & Day appeal SLAPP trial

Apr 16, 2002 – 6th DCA grants a temporary stay of all proceedings

Jun 25, 2002 – 6th DCA stays all proceedings

- 1 -

HAPPY BIRTHDAY

For me, the SLAPP began at 7:40 a.m. on February 25, 1999. It was my practice to begin my weekday morning hypnotically watching the Bloomberg stock show ticker tape scroll across the bottom of the TV screen, while listening to some sacred polyphony: a wonderful juxtaposition, I think, between high- and low-tech. Not needing to peruse through my near 1000 CD's on the shelves that morning I selected Missa Maria Zart.[6] My canine-like cat, Rana, finally getting accustomed to sharing the patio with an unwitting dove seemed more anxious than usual as her day's adventure was about to begin. With a cup of thick black coffee in hand, I answered an unexpected knock on my front door. Too early for strangers, the man politely asked if I were Mike Delfino, I said "Yeah" and he handed me a sealed envelope with this letter inside:

"Dear Mr. Delfino:
This letter will serve as notice pursuant to California Rule of Court 379 that Varian Associates, Inc. Susan B. Felch, and George Zdasiuk ("plaintiffs") will be filing an Application for Temporary Restraining Order[7] ("TRO") and order to show cause re preliminary injunction[8] on Friday, February 26, 1999, between 8:30 a.m. and 9:00 a.m., in the Santa Clara Superior Court, located at 191 N. First Street

---

[6]Literally, "Mass for Gentle Mary," a choral piece by the Franco-Flemish composer Jacob Obrecht (1475/8-1505).

[7]An immediate prohibition of an action that is likely to cause irreparable harm. It lasts until a court hearing is held at which time it may become permanent.

[8]A court order that requires one to act or to refrain from acting.

1

in San Jose. This TRO is being filed against you in response to your harassment and interference with the business relations of the plaintiffs and seeks to enjoin you from 1) impersonating Varian employees while on the Internet; 2) ceasing your anonymous defamation of the plaintiffs; and 3) ceasing to engage in unfair competition in relation to plaintiffs.

Additionally, Varian will be seeking from the Court an order for expedited discovery from you and third parties, including production and inspection of documents and things, interrogatory responses,[9] and depositions.[10]

Contemporaneously with plaintiffs' application for TRO, the plaintiffs will be filing a Complaint against you asserting the following claims for relief: Unfair Competition, False Advertising, Libel, Slander Per Se, Lanham Act, California Penal Code Section 637.1, Invasion of Privacy-False Light, Invasion of Privacy-Appropriation of Name, Intentional Inference With Advantageous Business Relationships, and Conspiracy.

Very truly yours,
Joseph C. Liburt"

Scanning over mostly unfamiliar words, I had no idea what this was and to be perfectly honest wasn't awake enough to understand. Half read, I put the letter aside and went back to being mesmerized by the passing stock-ticker, while letting the coffee and music do their work.

Soon enough, Mary, my partner in business and in life came by, her usual effervescent self. She was far more alert than me as she always got up earlier and had her four cups of coffee. Even her dog Lucy was fast asleep, recovering from their morning walk. We kissed hello and discussed our plans for the day; it was her 43rd birthday. We planned to take off from our work for most of the day, maybe head for the beach, have a nice lunch, hike a bit, basically party in the unassuming way that characterized our seven-year relationship. I hadn't mentioned the letter, in fact, I had forgotten about it when the phone rang. As I picked it up, Mary went back home to get ready. It was now around 9:30. The caller first identified himself as Peter C. McMahon, an attorney with

---

[9] Written answers to questions made under oath.
[10] Recorded sworn testimony of a witness with no judge present.

Orrick, Herrington & Sutcliffe who I would later discover was willing to pay $725 just to have lunch with his boss.[11] With a far too combative tone, this lawyer demanded that I acknowledge having been served with a letter from his firm, the letter from his colleague Joseph C. Liburt. After quizzically answering him in the affirmative, McMahon began trying to intimidate me with a follow through right out of a film noir,[12] emphasizing my newly announced troubles and throwing out all sorts of wild accusations. Coming to life, and raising my voice, I interrupted him with a "Slow down," suggesting that I didn't appreciate such unfounded accusations. I cautioned him "You'd better know what you're talking about" and if he wished to continue along these lines, "Contact my business attorney, a Mr. Glynn Falcon." Finding him growing more contentious with each response, when he wanted to know Falcon's number, I told him, "Look it up ... his office is in Palo Alto," and hung up.

Orrick, by introducing themselves so belligerently, was giving a first clue that they had no idea who they were dealing with. Perhaps it is my Sicilian-Calabrian-German heritage: I taught my children to always treat people better than they treat you, but if, they purposely mistreat you then make sure they never forget you.

Before Mary returned abuzz with our plans for the day, I faxed off Liburt's letter to Glynn. A precaution, despite my flippancy and dismissing all that had gone on that morning as utter nonsense.

I was unaware that McMahon faxed this same letter to Glynn at that same time, eerily, almost as if he knew about Glynn before I had even mentioned his name:

"Dear Mr. Falcon:
    As I detailed to you this morning in my voice mail to you, Varian Associates Inc., Susan B. Felch, and George Zdasiuk ("Plaintiffs") ... As I mentioned, Varian will be seeking from the Court an order for expedited discovery from you and third parties, including production and inspection of documents and things, interrogatory responses, and

---

[11]Renee Deger, *The Recorder*, July 18, 2002.
[12]Films with characteristically disorienting visuals like, *Citizen Kane* (1941) and *The Maltese Falcon* (1941) – menacing and oppressive, anything could go wrong.

depositions. Contemporaneously with plaintiffs' application for TRO..."

Mary and I were continuing with our original plan for the day and walking out the door when the phone rang again. It was Glynn, cryptically asking that I contact him so that we could meet as soon as possible. On listening, Mary inquired as to what could be so urgent, obviously concerned about how our day might be affected. I didn't really acknowledge her question except to say that I felt I should call him back before we left. I called him back sometime after 10 a.m. while Mary bounced between our condo units taking care of some last minute details for our day's outing. I was surprised at how concerned Glynn sounded, more so than in his message, and per his request, I agreed to be at his office around noon. Our telephone conversation was short. I got off the phone and apologetically told Mary about an unforeseen annoyance that had come from Varian, the company we had together worked collectively at for more than 25 years. While I had been fired in October, she in fact had just voluntarily resigned from Varian in mid-December, having accepted a fifteen-week paid severance package. Neither one of us had been expecting to leave, but the company was in the process of separating into three separate companies and our future and that of the soon to be defunct corporate research laboratory of Varian, the Edward L. Ginzton Research Center (GRC) where we had worked was not clear. Varian Associates had, since its inception in 1948 maintained a reputation as one of the world's premier places for technical innovation, ranking third on the list of Silicon Valley patent assignees behind Hewlett-Packard and ahead of Intel. Varian's GRC was named in honor of Dr. Ginzton (1915-1998), a Ukrainian émigré, later founder and former CEO of Varian Associates, and a Stanford University Professor of Electrical Engineering. He was a remarkably pleasant man who, despite a debilitating stroke, remained remarkably bright until his last days. He was a frequent visitor around the two Silicon Valley laboratories bearing his name, using his walker to move about. Times were changing, and the kind of hands-on materials science research jobs that Mary and

I did to earn a living were getting more and more difficult to come by as manufacturing moved out of the area and the dot.com's were then emerging as the career of choice in Silicon Valley.

It seemed like so many months ago that I had left Varian. It was a less than an amicable separation, but the severance agreement that I had reluctantly signed on October 29, 1998, the last day allowed by the terms of the contract, did not seem to end it. Nor did it end my interaction with Jane Crisler, Varian's less than stellar Senior Human Resources Representative.

Crisler was someone who, after a drink or two, might confess that she was once *that* Catholic nun who could never believe that the "grinning little boy" in her classroom might be innocent of causing some not-so-innocent lil' girl to cry. The teary-eyed little girl in this story was a middle-aged Dr. Susan B. Felch, a bantam-like former colleague, who complained to Crisler about me harassing her during my last years of employment. Although Felch's harassment accusations were never substantiated, they were believed by Crisler and acted upon by Varian, which ultimately led to my termination on October 8, 1998.

Felch's accusations seemed to originate with the previous year's change in her title from individual contributor to Laboratory Director. The change did not bring about any financial benefit to her nor did it in any way affect her responsibilities. It did, however, cause her to be more isolated in the relatively chaotic GRC of the time and this did not sit well with her need to socialize during normal work hours. Her propensity to engage in loud gossip with just about anyone and about any personal business was suddenly in jeopardy. Fortunately by this time, Mary and I had no need to interact with her technically, so ignoring her came easy despite the proximity of our offices. Felch's claims that I directed profanities at her in GRC, despite documented witnesses accounts to the contrary, were considered by Crisler to be the only truth. Raising the stakes, and I'm not making this up, she alleged that I was making facial and/or hand gestures at her often mimicking her incessant talking on the telephone. Thus, she created her so-called "telephone gesture." Not knowing how to deal with this lunacy, I had sought assistance from Crisler and then Crisler's supervisor, arguing that Felch's unfounded allegations were in themselves harassing. Coming to work was getting more and more difficult as I came to fear Felch and her growing list of bizarre accusations. Felch's recurring charges finally caused my boss, Dr. George Zdasiuk, a most disinterested manager of marginal technical competence, to ultimately fire me quite unexpectedly in the middle of me pursuing Varian's well-known company policy – "The Fair Treatment Plan."

So, even though I then received ten-weeks of salary, one for each year of employment, I found the thought of accepting Varian's dismissal distasteful. In any event, some battles are not worth fighting, and with Glynn's legal advice, this did not appear to be one of them. I decided to move on with my life and not pursue another wrongful termination lawsuit. Fired for misconduct once before, I had engaged in one such a legal battle with Glynn as my attorney and found the winning, albeit satisfying, not worth the effort. The victory was sweet, the vindication important, but the money was insignificant as I only lost two months' wages and got a higher salary and more interesting work in my new position.

But Varian was not so quick to let go and leave me alone. After I had left the company, it took almost a month for the return of my personal office possessions: things like books, photographs, a dried out dracaena and some family memorabilia that I had collected over the years. Getting a release on my retirement money so that I could roll it over into a personal IRA took even longer.

Almost immediately, Varian violated the terms of their agreement with me by challenging my right to collect unemployment. They subsequently lost a court hearing that took place in the Employment Development Department's Menlo Park office. On February 5, 1999, Judge D.J. Soviero ruled I had indeed been fired from Varian without cause:

> "The claimant appealed from a Department determination which disqualified him for benefits based on a finding he was discharged for misconduct... A notice of ruling relieved the employer's reserve account of benefit charges ... The burden of proof is on the employer to show that the claimant's actions were tantamount to misconduct. The claimant's corroborated testimony indicated that the claimant did

not engage in any harassing, threatening or offensive behavior. For this reason, it must be found that the claimant was discharged for reasons other than misconduct....

The Department determination and ruling under code section 1256 are reversed. The claimant is not disqualified for benefits. Benefits are payable provided the claimant is otherwise eligible. The employer's reserve account is subject to benefit charges...."

Varian never appealed this EDD ruling even though they had a right, in my mind, almost a duty to do so if they believed there was any truth to my misconduct. Instead, less than three weeks later there was this intimidating letter from Orrick and this unforeseen threat of a lawsuit. Today was Mary's birthday and we had plans, plans that were unexpectedly in jeopardy. We were in no mood for suddenly acting pensive. Before Mary had a chance to ask me about my conversation with Glynn, I told her that I didn't yet have enough information to understand it myself, no less explain it to her. There was no reason to believe anything ominous was happening. I suggested we go for our usual morning trek and delay our partying to the evening.

During our twice-daily neighborhood walk Mary further inquired if I thought any of this had anything to do with my unemployment victory over Varian or our newly created business and not really thinking, I answered, "No, not that I was aware." But I was more tense than usual with my mind already preoccupied with the morning's letter and phone call. I couldn't get the TRO notion out of my head either as it brought back painful memories of how my divorce had begun and how my inadvertent violation of a previous TRO caused me to spend a night in jail back in 1991. Then, separated from my soon to be ex-wife, I had returned to our house of ten-years after she had failed to attend a prearranged meeting with me only to find her at home with a police officer next to his police car in our driveway. Unbeknownst to me, I was supposed to have been served a restraining order by her attorney, who was later found to have lied when he stated to the police that he had just delivered it to me. After two hours or so of me pacing about, the house was soon occupied by no less than six male police officers. In full view of my children, I was arrested for allegedly violating this TRO, handcuffed and escorted outside to one of three waiting police cars, indeed a sobering experience with half of the Los Altos Deodara Drive neighborhood in attendance. I spent the one night in jail and was arraigned in shackles the next morning. Set free on $7,000 bail, sometime later the district attorney learned the truth – I hadn't been served. She did not prosecute the attorney who had lied and she did not exonerate me. Instead, she tried in vain to get me to plead to a lesser charge, first vandalism and then trespassing. But I don't compromise on the truth. I maintained my innocence and the alleged TRO violation was dropped the day before I was to appear in court.

Now, eight years later I was not going to contribute to whatever nonsense Varian, Felch and Zdasiuk were fabricating to obtain a TRO. At least this time, I already had an attorney, and a good one. Trying to hire an attorney from inside a jail is challenging, even in Palo Alto. It was probably good that I would not see Orrick's proposed TRO until the next day, February 26:

> "Defendant Michelangelo Delfino is ordered to refrain from impersonating, by name or otherwise, Kevin Felch, Ronald Powell, James Fair or any Varian employee, manager, or executive, including, but not limited to, Susan Benjamin Felch, George Zdasiuk, Jane Crisler, or others until the trial of this matter is concluded; ...
>
> is restrained from posting on, or emailing to, any Internet message board, chat room, stock page or any other similar publicly accessible Internet posting page....
>
> is restrained from using any pseudonym to discuss, in any way, any aspect of Varian's business, stock price, or employees until after the trial of this matter; ...
>
> is furthered ordered to refrain from destroying, deleting, erasing, altering, changing, obfuscating, eliminating, wiping, formatting, or otherwise tampering with, and from instructing or asking any other person to destroy, delete, erase, alter, change, obfuscate, eliminate, wipe, format, or otherwise tamper with, any data or information contained on any and all computers, computer peripherals and accessories, computer hardware and software, floppy disks, hard drives, back-up tapes, ZIP drives, compact disks, and other electronic storage media owned, operated, used, possessed, worked on, or utilized by Michelangelo Delfino or Mary E. Day until after the trial of this matter; ...

is furthered ordered to refrain form conspiring with, encouraging, requesting, or otherwise contacting others to engage in any of the actions specified ...

must not strike, threaten, or injure any current or former Varian employee for three years ...

must not keep any current or former Varian employee under surveillance for three years ...

must not follow any current or former Varian employee for three years ...

must not block any current or former Varian employee's movements in public places, or thoroughfares, or places of work for three years ...

must not send any message or materials by facsimile, electronic device, e-mail, or by any other electronic means to Susan Felch, George Zdasiuk, Jane Crisler, James Fair, and Ron Powell and/or their families for three years ...

must not telephone Susan Felch, George Zdasiuk, Jane Crisler, James Fair, and Ron Powell and/or their families for three years ...

must stay at least 100 yards from Susan Felch, George Zdasiuk, Jane Crisler, James Fair, and Ron Powell and/or their families for three years from the date of this Order, except that Mr. Delfino may lawfully operate a motor vehicle on public streets ...

must stay at least 100 yards from Susan Felch's, George Zdasiuk's, Jane Crisler's, James Fair's, and Ron Powell's children's schools or places of child care for three years from the date of this Order, except that Mr. Delfino may lawfully operate a motor vehicle on public streets; ...

is restrained from posting on any Internet message board any message mentioning the name Susan Felch or George Zdasiuk for three years from the date of this Order; ...

is furthered ordered to refrain from conspiring with, encouraging, requesting, or otherwise contacting others to engage in any of the actions specified in this order..."

Still reflecting on this TRO notion, I considered what had happened since I left Varian. On ending my career as a research scientist at GRC, I was now at home, not contributing to the economy, and getting $230 a week in unemployment benefits for the next half year. Being unemployed at end of 1998 was most definitely an unusual state to be in Silicon Valley. Nonetheless, I had gotten tired of all the games that seem to have characterized my last days at Varian and was enjoying the rest. Maybe it was blessing, I thought, having this opportunity to decide what I was going to do for the rest of my life. Individualistic, I was still a typical baby boomer, who was dealt a lucky 94 lottery number during the Vietnam War, then went on to achieve fame and fortune beyond what I dreamt or deserved. I was born in the Bronx, a New York city borough, worked my way through school as a laborer, married at 21, and later returned to the Bronx to get my Ph.D. in chemistry from Fordham University. Life's decisions were more often made for me than by me. Now, being almost 50 with three grown children, more distant than I ever wanted, I had time to explore options outside my 25 years of work experience as a research scientist. I could be or do whatever I wanted: a gardener, a lawyer, and a chef. However, no matter where my fantasies ran, my thoughts always returned to doing science. In some ways, winning that first science fair in the sixth grade was a lasting curse.

Just before my unexpected departure from Varian, Mary and I had come to realize a fatal flaw in an invention that we had been working on our last year together at the GRC. Its unwelcome recognition came about on doing that one "next" experiment that didn't give the expected result. Before it could be resolved or alternatively become a scientific downer I was fired. No longer my problem and now faced with an abundance of free time, I had the opportunity and solitude to reflect on it without being distracted. I needed to know why the invention failed. Soon enough I found myself putzing around and relearning chemistry long since forgotten and discovering science that I never knew. While Mary remained at Varian, she and I made a conscious effort not to discuss any of the company's business and I did not disclose to Mary what I was exploring in terms of technology. This kind of arrangement was not uncommon in Silicon Valley, where technically employed living partners often worked at competitors. Besides, Mary and I were very much aware that exchanging information was not only unethical, but risky as well.

As it turned out she was now finding her days at Varian to be a more and more political and distressing. Felch was now targeting her as well, claiming that she was directing profanity at her and doing the soon to be infamous "telephone gesture." It was a stressful and frustrating time for us both. We were, for the first time in memory, not having regular scientific discourses limiting our conversations to just about anything but science. Working by myself, I soon came to an understanding as to why our Varian invention didn't work. Excited, it was extremely difficult not being able to share this with my co-inventor. In some ways, I believe, that knowledge was the impetus for me developing a solution to the invention's fatal flaw. But would my thinking be practical?

Not until a few days after the 21st of December, when Mary giving up any hope of being treated fairly by Varian, sadly resigned her position, did I first tell her about my new idea. Almost immediately, Mary and I happily returned to those intermingled days of lively talking and reading and researching and arguing, and like a few ideas, it evolved into something more tangible. How appropriately festive for Christmas. We ended up inventing something special, something worth pursuing and in a big way. We envisioned being one of those surrealistic Silicon Valley success stories, like Apple or Intel or Adobe. Besides, even if we were overly optimistic, we benefited working together, once again relishing each others highly opinionated views on just about everything. What to do next? We were certainly not going to revisit the bureaucracy and politics of working for big business, so we decided to be our own boss and start our own company.

We named our new company MoBeta, Inc. and incorporated on January 4, 1999 with Glynn as our business attorney. Mary was President and CEO. I was Vice President and CFO. It was a welcome and challenging opportunity for us. Virtually all of our professional years had been spent working for relatively large high-tech companies as part of their corporate research teams. This was different: no more distracting meetings, time cards to track, and no more paltry stock options. There were just the two of us; we worked efficiently with self-imposed time constraints and we owned everything. For the most part we had little idea what we were doing but found the whole process incredibly exciting. We loved the freedom, the control of our own destiny, and of course, the accountability for success or failure. We were MoBeta!

The two of us are both blessed with attention deficit disorder, and being hyperactive made it good that there was so much to do: open a checking account; buy a fax/answering machine; search out and purchase lab equipment, chemicals and supplies; meet with an accountant; establish purchase order agreements with vendors; and the most fun of all, do experiments. We immediately expanded on the makeshift laboratory I had set up in my one bedroom condominium flat. Now, we found ourselves often working into the wee hours of the night in our flannel bathrobes while sipping wine and listening to Schubert and Schumann. Mary and her daughters lived in a two-bedroom unit, one door away in the same building, so our working arrangement was especially convenient. She owned a Mac computer equipped with an Internet account that I would come to use now and then. I did not own a computer myself, finding them at the time to have no more than a perfunctory personal benefit. Wherever I had worked before, including Varian, I used my office computer for my few personal needs like tax returns. Relishing family life, I made a point of doing as little work as possible at home, which was more often than not, nothing.

My home, once filled only with dozens of 19th and 18th century and earlier oil paintings and watercolors, and multi-colored oriental rugs made of silk or wool often lying atop each other, was not so gradually taking on the clutter of laboratory equipment that included a battleship gray Zeiss optical microscope and bubbling temperature controlled reaction vessels. The hooded electric stovetop in my kitchen, a place reserved for preparing our favorite risotto and pasta, was now home to our experiments and the sound of clicking relays and flashing LED's. Nearby was a red fire extinguisher, just in case our mutual clumsiness emerged. Scientific results were almost immediate and nearly always positive, thankfully especially when using the $200/hr outside analytical services of Charles Evans and Associates. Work went so well with Mother Nature being unusually cooperative that we filed our first United States Patent Application on February 4. Roberta Robbins, our newly recommended patent attorney, completed the filing in record time, a refreshing contrast to our experience with Varian bureaucracy. Ordinarily, a provisional filing might have been expected from our small operation, but we had demonstrated feasibility with a non-radioactive isotope and unlike the Varian patent we had invented – it actually worked! We assigned the rights to this, our first invention, to MoBeta, Inc. It was entitled, "Radioactive Transition Metal Stents."[13]

We were extremely enthusiastic about our science and excited for the future. MoBeta, Inc. now owned a biocompatible-radioactive technology that on the anticipated issuance of its patent would be valid for 20 years from the filing. Of course, a lot of things can happen on the high-technology front over that period of time and far more patents are useless than not. But with more than 20 patents between us, we were sufficiently versed in the patent arena to have a good idea how valuable the MoBeta, Inc. patent filing might eventually be worth. And we had some close, technically trained and trusted friends with whom we enjoyed sharing bits of our work and got that all too necessary reality check. Unfortunately, our technology with its practical requirement of a radioactive phosphorus source could only be implemented in practice by relatively huge companies like Guidant, Johnson & Johnson, Medtronic, and Boston Scientific. Los Altos, as I liked to put it, was a nuclear free zone; ours was a beta-emitting technology. So until then, all experiments were done using naturally occurring, non-radioactive, phosphorus. Soon after filing our first patent, and with confidential disclosure agreements in place, we began to contact the major medical device manufacturers with our business plan. We hoped there would be sufficient interest for us to present our technology in person.

Just before noon on Mary's birthday I headed over to Glynn's office, about 10 minutes away. On meeting, Glynn, less than his usual cheerful self, suggested that I might be in serious trouble. Before I could utter my dismissal of the morning's events he interrupted to say, "You are facing a civil lawsuit with criminal

---

[13]Stents are tubular structures usually made of metal and inserted into bodily vessels to keep them open. The most common type are placed inside arteries following a balloon angioplasty procedure.

charges ... initiated by Varian, and this Felch and Zdasiuk ... they are represented by the Orrick, Herrington & Sutcliffe law firm, an international legal conglomerate with hundreds of lawyers in offices all over the world and having a formidable reputation...."

I shrugged. I still didn't get it. None of this made any sense coming from a company like Varian, where more often than not, it didn't seem to matter if you even showed up for work. Besides, Felch and Zdasiuk were hardly ever taken seriously by anybody other than perhaps Crisler. Nonetheless, Glynn was duly concerned and focused on the content of Liburt's letter. "They're accusing you of defamation," Glynn said. "Hold nothing back from me," he added, "you could go to jail ... make like I'm you're priest if you want me to help you." I wasn't quite sure what to say, except to confess that I had indeed posted messages about Varian on the Internet. Some of these messages specifically critiqued Felch and Zdasiuk, who were directly responsible for my wrongful termination. Looking a bit annoyed, he asked me why the hell did I do it? He said, "You won the unemployment dispute. I thought you were finished with Varian and busy working on your business!" I told him that I was and that posting took almost no time since I was checking in on my stocks on Yahoo! anyway. It was at best a momentary distraction. I added that I was just having fun, and that it was more or less prompted by events following my October 8 wrongful termination and recent vindication of any wrongdoing by Judge Soviero. I didn't then give him any details other than to say it was an emotional release for me, an innocuous way to vent some frustration at having been mistreated by Varian. In any event, I still didn't understand what the problem could be with an Internet posting. And, I wasn't alone:

> "Lawyers say defamation lawsuits against message board posters by companies wanting to silence their online critics are on the rise. "It's not unusual," said Lee Tien, a lawyer with the Electronic Frontier Foundation, a cyber-rights group. "We hear about people being sued for online posts -- and getting into crazy situations -- about once a week.""[14]

---

[14]Jeffrey Benner, *Wired.com*, March 1, 2002.

I had posted 60 messages, on the Yahoo! financial message board for Varian Associates (VAR) beginning with this one on October 12, 1998 in which I even identified myself as the author:

> **disclaimer** by: <u>MANUFORTE</u>
> Dear former employees and anyone else who might be interested, I loved reading the two jane crisco postings. I'm still smiling. Unfortunately for those who think otherwise, I did not post them. Can't even take credit for the content. Can't even validate what is said. Whoever you are, God bless you and your thoughts.
> I am doing fine. Thanks for the visits, the phone calls, etc. For those of you who know me, rest assured anything I have to say, and there will be plenty at the appropriate time, will be signed by me. For those who don't yet know me, you will enjoy the experience. In the interim, I applaud any and all comments made on this message board as freedom is most important.
> Regards, Michelangelo Delfino

It was my attempt at a public response to a quickly spreading GRC rumor that I had already posted two messages using an alias that satirized Crisler. She complained about the Yahoo! VAR postings in a declaration[15] dated February 25, 1999:

> "Following my involvement in the discipline of Mr. Delfino, and his termination, I learned that e-mails were posted on the Varian Stock Board on Yahoo by someone supposedly named "Jane Crisco". Attached hereto … are true and correct copies of those emails. I was not aware that anyone ever posted e-mails under this name prior to my involvement in Mr. Delfino's discipline and termination. I have never posted any of these e-mails. The e-mails are extremely insulting. I believe that these e-mails are attempts to impersonate me because there are references to my husband, my weight, and a variety of other factors, which I believe are designed to encourage people to believe that I was the person who posted the e-mails. I find these e-mails to be distressing and disturbing. I ask the Court take action to help stop this harassment of me...."

---

[15]A signed and dated statement of facts that is admissible as evidence under penalty of perjury.

Indeed Crisler had been backhandedly referred to as "jane crisco" by others and me at Varian. Although I can not take credit for the postings or first calling her "jane crisco", as I remember it, the name originated in part from her dough-boy shape and her preoccupation with Varian social events, like picnics catered by her husband's JazzFoods. Mary and I thought this was a conflict of interest and had formally complained about it. When brought to her attention, nothing changed. Inattentive in her less than two-year tenure as our worst HR representative ever, she placed a higher priority on JazzFoods than enforcing company policy. Employee complaints about annual performance reviews being more than two years late did nothing to prevent year after year from lapsing by as Varian's corporate practices became more and more irregular and less and less consistent on her watch.

Under my attorney's advice, my then short-lived tenure as a message board poster ended on February 24, 1999 with this:

> **Sue Felch blows local mtg!!!** by: <u>ah_michelangelo</u>
> Susan B. Felch, Manager of the Ion Implantation Lab, gave what must be one of the most fascinating talks ever at a local ion-implanter user meeting in California. It was amazing how many people seemed to know that the so-called expert has no implanter. Not a good sign for Varian; it sure put a big smile on the Applied Materials implant people. By the way, she does not look good in red, and someone please tell her how important particle generation is in the latest technology!

a somewhat more brazen posting, where I commented on a technical presentation Felch gave in a publicly attended meeting. Perhaps I was a bit too sarcastic about how she dressed, but it was true. This undersized female, who I had grown to dislike more and more, had a propensity to wear some of the most garish attire imaginable, which made for some unsolicited entertainment at the GRC. The next day Felch elaborated in her next day declaration on how sensitive she was to being critiqued by me on the Internet:

"I believe that these emails were written by Michaelangelo Delfino for the following reasons. ... I am not aware of any emails posted about me before I complained of Mr. Delfino's harassment. ... Mr. Delfino has shown himself capable of acting in a bizarre way through his harassment of me at Varian. ... my coworkers George Zdasiuk and Jane Crisler, who were also involved in the investigation of Delfino's workplace harassment, are also viciously attacked.

Moreover, the emails refer very significantly to the workplace at Varian, where Mr. Delfino was one of my coworkers. They describe not only work issues that only someone who had worked in the GRC would be likely to know, but also clothing which I have worn to work, such as a corduroy skirt....

I am not aware of anyone else who has animus against me such that they would attack my husband, my family, and impersonate me in a forum which is likely to cause ridicule...."

While nothing I had said about Felch in any posting was less than true or was no more than my opinion, I hadn't then posted anything about her family. Her husband, Dr. Kevin Felch, I knew by sight as he too was once a Varian employee, but I don't even recall ever having spoken to or about him. Glynn didn't care about my entertainment needs when he told me to immediately cease posting. I would not post again for the next six months, not until August 13, 1999. Glynn's argument was simple: do not give them any more ammunition to use against you. Reluctantly, I followed his advice, but complained as frequently as I could by interjecting a protest into our all soon to be too frequent and consequently costly conversations on the subject.

Glynn needed to get acquainted quickly with the unfamiliar world of Internet message boards. Had I impersonated anyone on Yahoo! or any other message board? Answering, "No, I hadn't," I added that I had not even visited any other message boards. Besides, I explained, it wasn't obvious to me how anyone could impersonate someone even if they wanted to since the posters are anonymous and have to first sign on and access a pre-approved Yahoo! alias in order to post a message. I made it clear that although I always posted using one of these Yahoo! aliases, I sometimes identified who I was by signing my name or adding my initials to the message. His expression grew somewhat perplexed as I told him that Yahoo! encouraged users to have as many as seven aliases per email address and in taking advantage of their rules I had posted using more than one. I had used aliases such as "ah_michelangelo", "MANUFORTE", "morerumours", and "GINO_IN_TORINO".

> **WHATSA A GO ON HERE**
> by: GINO_IN_TORINO (101/M/BELLA FIRENZE)
> IMA JUSTA MAKA PUMP FOR THE COMPANY BUT I
> DONTA UNDERSTAND WHATSA HAPPINEN TO THE
> COMPANY ANDA THISA POSTING BOARD. ARE WE
> SUPPOSTA MAKA MONEY OR WHA? THISA BOARD
> ISA DISGRACA TO OUR ORGANIZATION AND WE
> THINKA YOU AMERICANA ISA NUTS. I MEANA TAKA
> FELCHA. KEEPA FELCHA. DO ONE OR DE OTHA SO
> WE CAN MAKA SOME MONEY. THJE MONEY SHES
> FOR THE KIDS EH. COME ON LETS A MAKA GOODA
> PUMP AND MOVE ON. THE STOCKA SHES ATA 38
> EH.YOU SONNA MA GUNS.

"GINO"? I told him how Varian had a vacuum pump factory in Torino, Italy, and so I found the notion of a happy employee posting in an exaggerated Italian-American accent statements like "Ima justa maka pumpa forda companee" and "Varian's vacuum pumps ah sucka" to be funny; he laughed louder. Wanting to see the postings for himself, we accessed the Yahoo! VAR message board together using his office lap top computer. I introduced Glynn to my favorite Internet alter ego:

> **IMA A STILL COM**
> by: GINO_IN_TORINO (101/M/BELLA FIRENZE)
> GEEZA THATSA A GOODA NEWS! IFA SOMEBODY
> GONNA GETA RICH IT MIGHT AS WELL BE ME ANDA
> YOUA. I BE THEREA TOMORROW MAYBE STARTA
> TUESDAY OR WEDSDAY. FIRSTA IMA GONA HAVA
> SOMA YOUR GLOUCESTER LOBSTER FRA DIAVOLO
> ANDA LOTA CHIANTI! GOODBYE TO DA DAMN
> PUMPA ANDA TO HELLA WITHA DOSA HOURLY
> PEASANTS! SUZY YOURA MY KINDA GUY.

A stand-up kinda guy, Gino when not discussing eating and drinking wine just loved to talk about the Gina in his life:

IMA THINKA IMA GETA SCREWDA
by: <u>GINO_IN_TORINO</u> (101/M/BELLA FIRENZE)
Me anda mya Gina wea thinka the compania, shesa screwa
usa. Howa com now da dooe dicks changa da policy? No mora
stocka options! No mora stocka purchase! My Gina shesa a
ona smart cookie. Shesa tella me hey gino, no mora stock
purchase plan, I beta youa the price shesa gonna go up, up, up.
My Gina seza, I beta ya da Dicks gonna get it up! And by
golly, my Gina shesa right! When it coma to gettin it up, sheza
know wat she talkin about. And onea a mora ding, isa Georgio
anda Suzie a ding or waa? I meana are theya gettin ita up too?
Fuhgeta about it.

The Gino character I had created hailed from Firenze, home of
Michelangelo's David. His critique of Varian mismanagement
always struck me as humorous and would probably have even been
laughed at by my Italian-speaking mother and Aunt Jenny had they
been made aware of him. I remember as I posted sometimes
laughing so hard that I couldn't hit the damn "enter" key to post it.
Gino came to be affectionately imitated on the message board, and
as such "he" posted for quite awhile and generated a popular
following. Glynn, on reading the postings, jokingly asked if Mary
was Gina and had Mary ever posted. Noting that Mary had no
Italian heritage, only a voracious appetite for pizza and pasta, I
answered, "No!" When I told him that "manuforte" was actually
created by Mary, his face dropped and he blurted out "I thought
you said she hadn't posted ... you said you used ... you ..." I
quickly interrupted, "What I meant is that I first used Mary's
"MANUFORTE" alias to post ... it was her only one ... she used it
to create a Yahoo! personal account, which she used exclusively to
monitor her stocks. We had them at Varian too ... nobody posted ...
didn't even know about posting ... at Varian mine was
"oh_michelangelo"" I told him I was just too lazy to create my
own account, as Mary and I monitored the same stocks. He seemed
to believe me. Before leaving, I added that to my knowledge, I was
not sure that Mary even knew that I had posted, although I had
always only used her computer to do so. In fact, Mary's computer
was the only one other than rental station computers that I had used

to access the Internet. I emphasized to Glynn how I had nothing to hide in posting and was proud of the messages I posted, and never gave them much thought.

Many months later, during my December 7, 1999 deposition, Orrick would probe into Gina. To this day, I don't know *any* Gina and certainly no Gina's were named as "Does" in this lawsuit.

> LIBURT: Mr. Delfino, in several of these postings ... there's mention made of Gina? Who is Gina?
> DELFINO: Who is Gino?
> LIBURT: Were you referring to a specific person when you -- when you made some references to Gina?
> DELFINO: No. gina is the Italian of Gino.
> LIBURT: Oh, I see. So were you essentially referring to yourself or to the -- Gino, the author of these postings?
> DELFINO: You mean when I created the GINO_IN_TORINO alias, you're asking me what I was thinking of?
> LIBURT: Actually, I'm going to get to that, but I actually was just wondering -- In many of these postings you use the word Gina, G-I-N-A, and I was just wondering who that referred to, if anybody.
> DELFINO: No.
> LIBURT: Doesn't refer to anybody?
> DELFINO: Not that I'm aware of.

Reality was setting in, albeit with me always ever so slowly. As Glynn redirected the conversation to my attendance at tomorrow's February 26 "TRO/Show Cause for Preliminary Injunction Hearing," now less than 18 hours away, he reminded me to be properly attired, "Look a bit more conservative ... you know, dress nice." He was long accustomed to my mostly Teva and t-shirt wardrobe. While we are both liberal minded and the same age, Glynn has a pleasant smile and the benefit of a full head of hair, a trait I believe makes him more suited to these kinds of court appearances than my balding, hardened-look. In hindsight, I think he was already attempting to make me appear more respectable should a jury trial be in my future. As we got up from our chairs in his office, he wondered aloud, "No one called about this before today ... no one from Varian or Orrick had ever contacted you ... this is the first you've heard about any of this?" Nodding, I left as

Glynn shook his head, and suggested that either the matter was already overblown or that we would be greeted with an especially large stack of paperwork tomorrow: "an Orrick trademark," he said. Glynn reminded me that everything we had discussed was confidential[16] and asked that I not disclose any of it with Mary, not something I was not accustomed to doing. Like most couples, we didn't keep secrets from each other. Knowing this about us, Glynn was duly concerned about keeping Mary out of it, although he confessed that she was probably already in it. Indeed, he was right, as I would see for myself soon enough.

On the evening of March 4, Mary would be served at home with her first subpoena,[17] a deposition notice and a production of documents request.[18] As soon as she received it, she came over to my place to discuss it. It was just before 8 p.m., the time at which we would usually get together for the evening. Laughing to myself,

---

[16]The attorney-client privilege prevents the disclosure of information to outside parties. Once waived it is waived for all purposes.

[17]An order directing an individual to appear and produce documents on a certain day. Failure to comply may result in being held in contempt of court.

[18]"REQUEST FOR PRODUCTION ... All DOCUMENTS and electronic files REFERRING OR RELATING to VARIAN.... FELCH.... ZDASIUK.... to Kevin Felch.... to any contract, agreement, or COMMUNICATION between YOU or DELFINO and YAHOO.... to web postings made by YOU or DELFINO on any YAHOO message board, including but not limited to the "Yahoo! Message Board about Varian Associates Inc (NYSE:VAR)," under any user name or alias, REFERRING OR RELATING to VARIAN, FELCH, ZDASIUK, any other officer, director or employee of Varian Associates, Inc., or Kevin Felch.... to web postings made by YOU or DELFINO on or in any Internet or World Wide Web message board, bulletin board, chat room, or other forum, under any user name or alias, REFERRING OR RELATING to VARIAN, FELCH, ZDASIUK, any other officer, director or employee of Varian Associates, Inc., or Kevin Felch.... to any contract, agreement, or COMMUNICATION between YOU or DELFINO and any Internet service provider.... to any user name or alias under which YOU or DELFINO have COMMUNICATED during the last year with any PERSON....

REQUEST FOR INSPECTION... All computers, computer peripherals and accessories, computer hardware and software, floppy disks, hard drives, back-up tapes, ZIP drives, compact disks, and other electronic storage media in YOUR possession, custody, or control."

I handed her my deposition notice as I, too, had just been served again. Looking at her subpoena, but not really reading it, I smirked and said, "Maybe time for you to call Glynn ... I think you should give him a call tomorrow." All she said was "Well, I guess they really are going after me ... let's have some wine." Seemed like a good idea, especially since I was about to pop the cork on a cooled '75 Chateau Branaire – we both love Bordeaux. Somewhat bemused, I could only wonder why such a well-staffed law firm like that of Orrick, Herrington & Sutcliffe would take nearly a week to contact both of us. Turning down Antar[19] a bit, I couldn't believe that the law firm described with such reverence by Glynn would operate so haphazardly. Picking up the tweezers, I returned the tiny metal foil to its plastic box and turned the light off the microscope. Now, we faced a different kind of work.

---

[19]Symphony no. 2 by the Russian composer Nikolai Rimsky-Korsakov (1844-1908).

- 2 -

SO MANY COMPLAINTS

Here I was, the morning after Mary's birthday, driving to the Santa Clara County Superior courthouse in San Jose, the first prescribed activity I had done in months. With the lunacy of the empty car pool lanes that characterize Northern California, I was suddenly forced to deal with mainstream society. After paying $9 to park my vintage 1987 Peugeot turbo sedan in a nearby lot, I met Glynn in the surprisingly crowded Santa Clara County Superior Court house lobby, having successfully traversed their metal detectors. It was Friday the 26th of February 1999. He seemed more relieved to see me than I expected. He greeted me with a wry smile holding, and I'm not exaggerating, a near half-foot thick stack of legal documents. Herding us both toward a corner, he handed me some of the documents and cautioned me to be non-expressive and careful, as we were in the midst of a dozen-strong legal entourage of Orrick attorneys, paralegals, and God knows whom else in their service. I casually flipped through the hundreds of pages with what seemed like my name stamped everywhere. At the top, was Orrick's proposed TRO. What I read was unreal. Almost before I could react, Glynn whispered "It's what they're asking for ... don't get upset ... don't show any emotion." On looking up at him, he pointed me to another document. I started reading through "Varian's Memorandum of Points and Authorities in Support of Application for Temporary Restraining Order:"

"Plaintiff Varian Associates Inc., ("Varian") urgently needs a temporary restraining order and order to show cause why a

23

preliminary injunction should not issue enjoining Michelangelo Delfino ("Delfino") from impersonating Varian employees online and from posting defamatory, harassing, and fraudulent information on "message boards" on the Internet. Varian also requests leave to take expedited depositions of Delfino, Mary Day, and other relevant persons regarding the matters in this application and to obtain documents and other written discovery from defendants and third parties on an expedited basis."

It sure didn't take long to see that Mary was indeed already involved. Thankfully, her name seemed to be the only other one included, besides mine of course. Not being a fast reader, and having dyslexia I found myself scrolling down the page retaining less and less of what was there as none of it made any sense.

"Plaintiffs believe that Delfino and Does 1-20 are responsible for posting over 200 messages on two Internet investment message boards. Approximately 50 of those messages are expressly directed at Felch and/or Zdasiuk, while the remainder are designed to damage Varian's goodwill and induce investors to sell their Varian stock."

This first sentence left me confused: 20 people? 200 messages? 2 message boards? Well, they had the wrong guy. Sure I had posted, but only on one message board and certainly not with any intent to harm anyone. It all seemed so silly. The notion that investors would rely on my postings to trade stock was certainly flattering. You decide just how compelling I am in this January 28, 1999 Yahoo! VAR message:

> **This one's for you Bud...** by: <u>ah_michelangelo</u>
> SELL as if your life depended on it!
> SELL and don't look back!
> SELL if you already haven't done so!
> SELL for God's sake!
> SELL and SELL some more!
> SELL and SELL again!
> SELL before it's too late!
> SELL today and SELL tomorrow especially if you didn't
> SELL yesterday!
> ...are you getting the message? See you on the 18th at the Dick
> and Dick et al. Stock Show. p.s. SELL!

"Delfino has engaged in a two-pronged assault against Felch and Zdasiuk. The first prong consists of his misappropriation of their names and his impersonation of them while on line. In this facet of his attack, Delfino signs on as Felch or Zdasiuk and then disparages high-level Varian executives and makes crude and derogatory comments.... The second prong consists of postings under anonymous aliases, flagrantly defamatory material about each individual, including but not limited to statements suggesting adulterous affairs between Felch and Zdasiuk and between Felch and other company executives, including the suggestion that Felch gives oral sex to Varian Executive Vice President Richard Aurelio on the company airplane; statements suggesting that Felch and Zdasiuk are incompetent and are not qualified to perform their jobs; statements that Felch and Zdasiuk are "liars"; and statements suggesting that Felch and Zdasiuk improperly misuse company resources."

The thought of Felch giving head to anybody and to doing it at 30,000 feet actually did make me chuckle. When Glynn wanted to know what I found so funny, I shrugged and declined to answer. Humor has its time and place and this was neither. As for calling someone a liar, well who hasn't lied? Felch and Zdasiuk are liars and they would confirm this fact over and over again in their declarations, their exhibits, and their testimonies. I have no knowledge whether any of these characters are adulterous or not and find the visuals of any of them doing something sexual rather repulsive. Regarding their incompetence and misappropriation of company resources, well, I believe the SLAPP speaks for itself.

"Delfino's method of revenge against Varian is equally insidious. Delfino has posted misleading, derogatory, and false information under at least 15 different aliases while on-line. Delfino hides behind the aliases to spread rumors and misinformation about the company and its stock while implying that he is a Varian employee."

Sure I had exposed some of Varian foibles, but this assertion of me seeking revenge was right out of Verdi's Rigoletto. I happen to immensely enjoy this Italian opera about a royal jester exacting justice. However, I do not relate to this singing hunchback in motivation or form. My joy in using multiple aliases allowed me to act out different characters befitting my mood changes and vivid imagination. But, fifteen? While I am a Gemini, I was not the *Sybil*[20] character, at least not yet. In any event, since Yahoo! allows each user to have seven aliases, why not sue them and leave me alone if Varian found their message board policy bothersome?

> "Delfino's campaign of harassment against Felch and Zdasiuk is nothing new. In fact, while Delfino was a Varian employee he engaged in schemes of harassment against Felch and other Varian employees."

Who were the other employees? I never heard of anyone other than Felch complain that I had harassed them. Well, I was wrong. On March 12, three days before the preliminary injunction hearing, Glynn called me with another one of those urgent requests to meet and confer; Orrick had delivered another stack of under seal documents. I first read a declaration by Dr. Ron Powell, a former Varian supervisor who bears an uncanny resemblance both in look and manner to the Woody Allen[21] movie character who laments his Jewishness but lacks his innocence and universal appeal:

> "I am seriously concerned what attacks Mr. Delfino might make on me following my providing of this declaration. If there are preventative measures that could stop him from harassing, defaming, or attacking me in any way, I ask that the court try to protect me...."

and then another declaration, this by his former subordinate, the inept Dr. Jim Fair, a somewhat effeminate yet bearish man in his 50's who when later videotaped under oath would confess, "I would stipulate that I'm a big boy," but on this day, try to paint a different picture of himself:

> "I make this declaration with extreme trepidation and fear, given what I believe to be Mr. Delfino's extremely vindictive tendencies. I am

---

[20]The title of a 1973 book by Flora Rheta Schreiber about a real-life woman having 16 different personalities. It was made into a TV movie in 1976.

[21]The Brooklyn, New York born, 1935, actor-director of tragicomedic movies: *Sleeper* (1973), *Everything You Always Wanted to Know About Sex* (1972), *Bananas* (1971), *Take the Money and Run* (1969). ·

concerned that he may harass, defame, or otherwise attack me as a result of my making of this declaration. I am confident that he is likely to attack me in some violent, particularly if the Court includes my name in any Order instructing him not to harass, defame or come close to me. I ask the Court to include me its Orders preventing Mr. Delfino from harassing, defaming, or otherwise attacking the plaintiffs. I also ask that he not be allowed to contact me or come to my home or place of business."

Fair and Powell were now working for Novellus Systems, a huge semiconductor equipment manufacturer located in San Jose. I had not seen either of them since July 1997 when Novellus purchased the Varian division in which they supported.

Fair had been my Varian hiring manager and first year supervisor. Powell, the equivalent in position of Zdasiuk, was my first supervisor in the GRC. Certainly we had our share of technical difference of opinions, and yes, some evolved into heated exchanges, but no more. And I had never received anything less than a stellar performance review from either of them. In fact, I had never received anything less than a positive review in my entire technical career. Moreover, the only "warning" I ever received in my near 30 years of professional life was this absurd document:

"DATE: May 21, 1998
TO: The file of Mike Delphino
FROM: George Zdasiuk
RE: Written Warning

Since I have spoke to Mike last week about the gestures he has been making to Sue Felch, Mike has written e-mails to me regarding a hostile work environment. Although he denies that he has been making these gestures, the complaints have continued. This warning to advise Mike that he needs to stop any adverse interaction including gestures, face-making, inappropriate conduct such as singing in the hallway, etc. with Sue Felch or any other Varian employee.

Although Mike indicates that he is being harassed, he only makes this announcement after he has been spoken to about the gestures he has been making toward Sue Felch. If Mike feels he is being harassed, he should pursue his complaint with Jane Crisler of Human Resources then Jim Hennessy. This means he should follow the normal channels for a formal complaint prior to involving senior management. This is according to written policy. If there is another complaint made by any employee regarding Mike's behavior, the next step will be a second written warning, up to and including termination.

Mike Delphino
George Zdasiuk (*signed*)
Jane Crisler (*signed*)"

At a meeting called by Zdasiuk, Crisler forced this memo on me when she trapped the three us in his office. After I read it they demanded I join them in signing it, thereby affirming its contents. Crisler scribbled on it that I "refused to sign and make a comment." Actually I never uttered a single word the whole time. Notwithstanding all this Varian lunacy and the misspelling of my surname, her wresting speech and his badgering did little to encourage me to comment on this absurd mischaracterization of events. The idea of me making gestures at anyone including Felch was truly unbelievable, but being reprimanded by these oversize fools for singing at work?

While I did occasionally hum or sing in my private office or the building's outside atrium, never once did anyone ever bring it to my attention as bothersome. In fact it always seemed to bring smiles and laughter. Later, when Zdasiuk was first deposed in March 1999, he couldn't reconcile having signed this ridiculous document with his testimony:

> FALCON: Am I right to assume that one of the grounds of complaints against Mike Delfino was that he sang in the hallway?
> ZDASIUK: No.

So what was all this nonsense really about? I had never posted any message about Powell or Fair, nor had I made any reference to them in any posting. And The Orrick had produced none either. But that would change as I would later post messages about their less than honorable past in an attempt to discover what had first motivated them to interject themselves in a lawsuit that was of no apparent benefit to either of them.

Returning to the TRO, I continued to read through my list of alleged Internet crimes:

> "Delfino's harassment against Varian is specifically designed to spread misinformation about the company in a forum where a large number of Varian employees, Varian customers, and Varian investors turn to find out information about the company. In his particularly insidious scheme, Delfino signs on to the message board under a variety of aliases and then spreads misinformation about the company. Then, under one of his other assumed names Delfino answers himself posing as another Varian employee who can confirm the misinformation."

I posted these two messages about Varian's brachytherapy[22] business:

---

more brachytherapy by: MANUFORTE

Actually I'm quite sweet. My intent as a stockholder with a rather large Varian holding is to make money. If you think this Zdasiuk is the right person to make our brachytherapy product a winner then that's great. I hope you are right! All I'm doing is expressing some doubt about what appears to me to be a non-technical person attempting a highly technical and challenging job. If you have some insight as to his rather special qualifications, please share them with other investors. You can only make us money.

BRACHYWHAT?

by: morerumours (62/F/washington, canada)
WHATS THE BIG DEAL?MOST OF OUR MANAGERS
ARE NOT TECHNICAL AND WERE DOING JUST
FINE.IN FACT THE STOCKS ALOT HIGHER NOW THEN
IN THE DAYS WHEN THE ENGINERES RAN THE
COMPANY.BESIDES IBET THIS THING IS NOT A BIG
DEAL PRODUCT ANYWAY MR INVESTOR.

Taken together, I am quite legitimately questioning Zdasiuk's ability to lead a particularly challenging product line given his lack

---

[22]Radiation therapy in which the radioisotope is placed in direct contact with, for example, the tumor.

of qualifications. And I was right! It took three years of disappointing a number of us VAR stockholders, but on October 2, 2002, that particular division was finally taken away from him and put under a more experienced and hopefully adept executive.

The other "insidious" dialogue I had with myself:

> **Can the DICKS et Al Get it UP?** by: <u>ah_michelangelo</u>
> I certainly hope so, but judging by the performance of the stock I am less than optimistic.

> **VARIAN NEEDS VIAGRA**
> by: <u>morerumours</u> (62/F/washington, canada)
> LUV THE POSTS MICHAELANGELO DUDE.COME ON DICH AND DICK AND AL LETS GET THE PRICE WAY UP>I REALLY LIKE THE IDEA OF VIAGRA AS OUR NEW LOGO! KINDA GIVES MEANING TO THE WORD TOOL.

In this second pair of postings, I am poking fun at the three executive vice presidents of then Varian Associates, whose first names are Dick, Dick, and Al, or as I so cleverly parodied, "Dick, et al.," or et alia. Sexual innuendos and bathroom humor may be juvenile, but for people like me, not only is it legal, it is also funny. Hyperbole in the form of a joke such as this is most definitely constitutionally protected speech.

In exercising my Constitutional Right to anonymity, I used my "morerumours," alias to intentionally misspell my name as, MICHAELANGELO, thereby exploiting the "comical-dumb" personality I had assigned him.

> "Delfino and Does 1-20 have concocted a nefarious scheme to undermine the public's confidence in Varian, while also attributing false, derogatory, and defamatory statements to its employees, thereby harassing them..."

I had no nefarious scheme. All I had done was author 60 Yahoo! messages over a 20-week period. If this alone could reduce this Fortune 500 Company to rubble, then just imagine what should have happened with the 20,000 plus postings Mary and I would eventually publish to expose Varian's truly nefarious deeds and Orrick's fascist acts. No posting was ever shown defamatory.

> "Delfino and Does 1-20 will suffer no harm whatsoever by being enjoined. The order would not prevent Delfino from posting messages on the Internet under his own name, nor would it impact his ability to post truthful information critical of Varian, thereby preserving Delfino's First Amendment rights. The scope of the order would limit only Delfino's impersonation of Varian employees and his practice of anonymously posting libelous and deceptive information on the Internet -- neither of which he has a lawful right to continue to do...."

How dare Orrick assert that restricting my free speech would not be harmful to me and that I would not suffer. Since when did it become permissible in this country for a large corporation like Varian to decide what is or is not acceptable public commentary?

For those unfamiliar with our Federal system of government, the right to free speech is not an absolute right. I can not post messages, for example, that cause someone injury or that incite criminal activity or that advocate actions for overthrowing the government by force. I can, however, lawfully express myself in a most bigoted, intolerant, racist and offensive manner imaginable and if the target of my speech is as a result, emotionally upset – too bad.[23] None of my postings would ever be proven to be false. And none would ever cause injury. Varian, Felch and Zdasiuk are not above the law. They had no basis whatsoever to preenjoin my right to post the truth, hyperbole, and opinion. Moreover, they had no basis for challenging this American's the right to do so anonymously on the Internet.

My partner, who honors these same Constitutional privileges as much as I do was on February 9, 2000 given a welcome opportunity to express her sentiment:

> LIBURT: Okay. What did you mean when you said "I will post until I'm dead"?

---

[23]http://ombudsman.binghamton.edu/freespeech.html

DAY: I can tell you what I would mean today if I said that.
LIBURT: Okay.
DAY: I'm never going to quit exercising my First Amendment right.
LIBURT: Does it matter to you whether or not a court orders you not to post certain things?
DAY: I will never give up my First Amendment right as long as I live, and that's - if a judge is mistaken in enjoining my First Amendment rights, I'll respect it until I fight it, and then I will keep fighting it and I will keep exercising my First Amendment rights till I'm dead. Nobody is going to stop me.
LIBURT: Okay. And if you ultimately lose and remain enjoined permanently, will you - do you have an intention to post in violation of the injunction.
DAY: That won't happen.

I can only add that I was beaming from ear-to-ear that late afternoon when, at the end of a tiring six hours of questioning, she raised her voice to respond that way. I watched a somewhat exasperated Liburt fade back in his chair, and Mary's attorney grin contentedly. Once again, I knew we could never lose.

Although I was truly overwhelmed on reading Orrick's argument for a TRO, I was not especially distraught. I did not believe that such a constraint on free speech could ever be imposed in this country. After all, this whole new electronic medium[24] was in fact created by the United States Government as an open-public communications forum for everyone. Thoughts like this only made the unfounded accusations in the TRO seem all the more outrageous.

I tried to catch my breath and looked about the progressively crowded courtroom lobby that February 26 morning. My eyes caught a sinister smile on one overfull face in particular. I was intrigued and glanced back. It was my first encounter with Lynne C. Hermle, an Orrick partner, and the lead attorney in this case. It would not take long for me to view her as utterly despicable. My amazement would grow at her lack of ethics. This officer of the

---

[24]In 1969 the Department of Defense created ARPANET, an open public network linking the government to several universities. It retired in 1988 leaving in place the Web. In 1993, Marc Andreesen's software allowed the Web to be viewed by the world.

court took herself all too seriously. She had written an on-line article entitled, *"Avoiding the Multi-Million Dollar Mistake,"* an Orrick advisory note to corporations on the why-nots of "investigating sexual harassment complaints:"

> "Because the investigation may form the foundation of the employer's defense to subsequent claims by the alleged victim (or the alleged harasser) it must be conducted thoughtfully and carefully.... the company will not retaliate against employees who truthfully participate in an investigation.... the investigator must determine whether the witness's knowledge is based on first hand knowledge as opposed to rumors, hearsay or speculation...."

Physically large and out of shape, she was the embodiment of a bully. This Grand Dame of SLAPP, was uninterested in the truth: a sexist, a management partisan who would prove to be more concerned with her career than the interests of her client. Even as the facts unfolded in this case, she remained entrenched, determined as ever not to lose her SLAPP case no matter how untenable her circumstance. She would not abandon her position even when faced with ugly facts that proved her clients guilty of invading privacy and repeatedly lying under oath. Her plan to eliminate me as a voice on the Internet was simple – SLAPP me, blitz me with an avalanche of damaging assertions so vile and comprehensive that I would never be conscious enough to reply. If by some fluke I survived the first barrage then she would attack again, bringing on wave after wave until I would be so discredited that no one would ever believe me. Once publicly disgraced and disfavored, even the most democratically minded would be willing to strip me of my Constitutional Rights. And very much like Hitler's unforeseen *blitzkrieg* invasion of Russia in 1940, her fascist plan of destruction almost worked.

As late as March 8, 2000, this Orrick partner resorted to "hearsay" in a declaration intended to obtain yet another TRO against me and ultimately have me incarcerated:

> "One mediator who was acceptable to all the parties expressed to me during a telephone call that he was extremely reluctant to become

involved in the case, stating that he was concerned he might become the defendants' latest victim on the Internet...."

Who was this mediator, and why didn't they make their own declaration? If there were such a person, they could have even signed it anonymously, something Orrick would certainly do when it suited them.[25] As it would turn out, no such person existed.

Leaving the courthouse lobby, Glynn and I now headed upstairs and exited the elevator toward Judge John Herlihy's courtroom. Glynn looked over at me gesturing, "Nice jacket." I guess he didn't like my purple linen sport coat tailored when I was in Bangkok. We entered the courtroom where I was to sit and wait, while Glynn faced Hermle and Liburt in the judge's chambers. He took the stack of documents with him.

The time alone gave me a chance to reflect on events. It seemed I could still not rid myself of Varian. I had spent a scientifically productive decade there and I enjoyed a lot of freedom, and in spite of Felch's dogged harassment, there was little to complain about. It would be a couple of weeks at Felch's March 8 deposition that I would to begin to understand just how much more scary this yenta really was and how calculating her scheme of fabricating bizarre harassment claims. I was surprised by the firing, perhaps even shocked, not a good thing for the Varian GRC and certainly not for Mary as she and I were collaborating on all our scientific projects. Almost immediately, Felch began fabricating the same harassment charges against Mary, ultimately forcing her to resign. Mary and I had been doing some promising work for Varian and the organization was benefiting from our effort. We had even received a number of Varian's so-called Exceptional Contribution Awards for patents generated and for improving manufacturing efficiency. Each award was not necessarily a big financial prize, but it was a message that we were clearly appreciated despite Zdasiuk's apathy, as he

---

[25]Orrick later twice represented an anonymous Varian employee who used the pseudonym "jazzun" to post on Yahoo! and Raging Bull message boards defamatory statements and threats against Mary and I.

generally left us alone to do science and willingly took credit for being our supervisor.

The hours passed all too slowly when Glynn rather abruptly came out of the judge's chambers. He called over and hurried me out of the courthouse, afraid that Orrick would immediately try and serve me with a subpoena. Before departing he said Mary would probably be deposed as well. I was still bewildered. What was her involvement? Glynn really didn't know, but kept muttering I should stay low. He said he needed time to understand the consequences of what had happened and above all, he warned me not to violate the TRO that Judge Herlihy had just signed:

"Defendant Michelangelo Delfino is ordered to refrain from impersonating, by name or otherwise ...

is restrained from posting on, or e-mailing to, any Internet message board, chat room, stock page or any other similar publicly accessible Internet posting page or location on the Worldwide Web ... any emails or electronic messages of any kind defaming or presenting false information ...

is restrained from telephoning, faxing, mailing, or otherwise sending any letter or other form of communication for any purpose to Susan B. Felch or George Zdasiuk until after this Court rules ...

is restrained from using more than one pseudonym or email address to discuss, in any way, any aspect of business, stock price, employees, officers, or executives of Varian ...

is further ordered to refrain from destroying, deleting, erasing, altering, changing, obfuscating, eliminating, wiping, formatting, or otherwise tampering with, and from instructing or asking any other person to destroy ... any data or information contained on any and all computers, computer peripherals and accessories, computer hardware and software, floppy disks, hard drives, back-up tapes, ZIP drives, compact disks, and other electronic storage media owned, operated, used, possessed, worked on, or utilized by Michelangelo Delfino or Mary E. Day ...

is further ordered to refrain from conspiring with, encouraging, requesting, or otherwise contacting others to engage in any of the actions specified ..."

This judge never met me, yet he wasted no time taking away my Constitutional rights and limiting my freedom. Herlihy's TRO was essentially forbidding me to use any computer since I was sure to use the backspace key and violate his order. As nonsensical as that was it made the one alias restriction seem almost reasonable. While it was a watered down version of what Orrick had requested, at least there was no stay away order. And although I hadn't had any contact with the people in question, there was always concern since we all lived and worked in relative proximity of each other, and sometimes frequented the same retail establishments.

Nonetheless, Glynn got the time he needed. And yet for several days, nothing happened. It took almost a week for Mary and I to be served with deposition subpoenas. Before leaving me in the parking lot, Glynn smirked, "Great jacket, if you're trying to get shot," and handed me a copy of the "Complaint for Damages and Injunction:"

> "Plaintiffs are informed and believe, and on that basis allege, that commencing immediately after Delfino's termination from Varian Associates, defendants began a pattern of unlawful conduct described below and which is the subject of this Complaint....
>
> defendants have committed a variety of wrongful conduct.... includes but is not limited to, the actions by defendants in impersonating various Varian employees, including but not limited to, Susan Felch, George Zdasiuk, Dick Aurelio, Jane Crisler, and others, and posting on various Internet web pages mails allegedly from the impersonated Varian employees, which contain false and defamatory statements....
>
> defendants have defamed both Varian Associates and its employees through a variety of false allegations, including by contentions that employees "cause some trouble," that nobody at Varian Associates "is working," that Varian employees are having affairs with other employees and executives, that Varian employees are engaged in projects that waste money, and that Varian Associates has engaged in actions including, but not limited to "corporate rape.""

Around February 1990, Varian's culture forever changed with the Board of Directors hiring J. Tracy O'Rourke, the first outsider to run the company. His seemingly endless greed may have been good for the stockholders in the short term, but it was not good for technologists like me. When I posted this message, one of my original 60 Yahoo! VAR, I most certainly did and still do believe that some in Varian management, like O'Rourke were indeed guilty of "corporate rape:"

> **GIVE IT TO THE VARIAN BOARD...**
> by: ah_michelangelo
> Apparently they cannot read, or at least they choose not to see what is obvious to everyone else. Besides, they have done one hell of a job helping to rape the resources of this once proud organization and reward the Varian's Executives for going from a Fortune 1000 Company to a Misfortune 100 Mess.

And I was far from alone in expressing that view when I was an employee. Although, I have socialist ideals I am a practicing capitalist who enjoys caviar and champagne as much as a warm bagel. I find the disproportionate distribution of wealth and accompanying disinterest in the plight of those disenfranchised absolutely revolting. When is enough money enough? My compassionate side just does not understand titles like *Die Rich and Tax Free*.[26] A year and a half later, I would return to this theme of "corporate rape" within Varian with a renewed sense of credibility in this Yahoo! Varian, Inc. (VARI) posting:

> **J. Tracy O'Rourke = $20,037,435= RAPE?**
> by: dr_michelangelo_delfino
> Can Investor Relations explain why the former Chairman, CEO of Varian Medical received such a total compensation for 1999? (ref. San Jose Mercury, Business F3, 18 Jun '00) Does this explain the SLAPP?

On reading through the complaint, I was beginning to feel a certain pissiness that would be sustained for many years to come. I am a scientist, highly trained, and proud of my ability to analyze information, and draw a painfully objective and sometimes even correct conclusion. I was always, I thought, able to defend the soundness of the argument and was receptive to changing a

---

[26]A popular book by Barry Kaye, one of the nation's foremost experts on estate planning outlining techniques for preserving and creating wealth.

deduction as the events warranted. My messages were no different in that they were intended to stir up a dialogue, and with some luck, do so humorously. Provocative, some call it. What little factual information I included about Varian or its employees, was to the best of my knowledge always accurate. If this lawsuit were really just about some misrepresentation made by me, then there really was nothing to worry about, so I reasoned.

> "Defendants have published on the Internet numerous emails regarding Susan Felch. In many cases, defendants have impersonated Felch by posting emails that appear to be authored by Felch but were in fact authored by defendants. In addition to the wrongful appropriation of Felch's name, the contents of the emails are defamatory and invade Felch's privacy in several different ways. Examples ..."

This thing about impersonation kept coming up. What was Orrick talking about? They did include in the complaint, copies of hundreds of postings including a sampling of a dozen or so that appeared on a message board called Stock-Talk, in which some of the aliases used the word Felch. However, I had only posted on Yahoo! where there were no such postings. In any event, the notion of impersonating her was totally incomprehensible to me. She was too short, and I had no cross-dressing tendencies, and I hadn't a clue where to find such outfits if I did. Her clothing was often tasteless, and at times clown-like. She even wore, and I'm not making this up, a heavy red, white and green Tyrolean sweater covered with a bunch of dancing reindeer.

> "In addition to the emails in which defendants impersonate Felch, defendants have also published on the Internet numerous additional emails in which defendants have defamed Felch and invaded her privacy. In these additional wrongful emails, defendants have either (a) impersonated other Varian employees by giving the emails the appearance of having been authored by such other Varian employees, or (b) posted the emails under aliases (such as "go_get_help," "ah_michelangelo," and "bite_me_now") such that the true authors of the emails cannot be determined without obtaining information from the operators of the Internet web site pursuant to subpoena. Examples ..."

. Maybe I was getting somewhere; two of those aliases listed by Orrick were not mine or associated with anyone I knew, nor did I even share the sentiment of their postings. Apparently, others were involved in this mess – strength in numbers.

> "Defendants have published on the internet numerous emails regarding George Zdasiuk. Defendants have impersonated Zdasiuk by posting emails which appear to be authored by Zdasiuk but which were in fact authored by defendants. In addition to the wrongful appropriation of Zdasiuk's name, the contents of the emails are defamatory and invade Zdasiuk's privacy in several ways. Examples ..."

While there were Stock-Talk postings with some variation of the name Zdasiuk as author, the idea that he was impersonated was not only incomprehensible, but down right silly.

In retrospect, I was not aware of Stock-Talk until it was mentioned in this lawsuit. When I would later post, I did post on it and its associated People-Talk and College-Talk message boards. I had intended on memorializing Varian, Felch and Zdasiuk there forever. But like most things in life, fame is fleeting, and in the winter of 2001 all three boards disappeared from the Internet.

> "In addition to the emails in which defendants impersonate Zdasiuk, defendants have also published on the Internet numerous additional emails in which defendants have defamed Zdasiuk and invaded his privacy. In these additional wrongful emails, defendants have either (a) impersonated other Varian employees by giving the emails the appearance of having been authored by such other Varian employees, or (b) posted these emails under aliases (such as "ah_michelangelo," "go_get_help," and "manuforte"). Examples ..."

There were literally dozens of Yahoo! and Stock-Talk message board aliases scattered throughout the complaint, including the six that I had created on Yahoo!, but I still couldn't understand how any of them might have invaded someone else's privacy no less impersonated a Varian employee whose name I did not know. If there was an employee named Michelangelo or Manuforte, they were certainly never brought to my attention.

> **brachytherapy business** by: <u>MANUFORTE</u>
> As a stockholder, I wonder if George Zdasiuk, the newly appointed vice president and director of Varian's Ginzton Technology Center, is the right person to run the Varian's brachytherapy product line. Checking Mr. Zdasiuk's background using one of the available patent web search engines shows he coauthored but a single patent, #4,642,587. And that was back in 1987 and on a microwave device! I would think that someone truly technical, someone who knows the medical field, perhaps someone having both an M.D. and a Ph.D. would be better suited for this business challenge. Should I be concerned?

This was my opinion, and Zdasiuk did indeed have but one patent, which had no relationship to anything happening in Varian.

"Defendants have published on the Internet numerous emails in which defendants have defamed Varian Associates and engaged in unfair competition. Defendants' emails regarding Varian Associates are part of a scheme to harm Varian Associates and its successors-in-interest, including Varian Medical and Varian Semiconductor, by falsely portraying Varian Associates as poorly managed, having employees with no work to do because the company's business is deteriorating, having overpriced stock, and having quality problems with its products.

Defendants have furthered this scheme by posting on the Internet a slew of emails which are not only defamatory and unfair, but in which defendants impersonate Varian managers and employees so as to give the impression that the defamatory and unfair representations are based on knowledge of highly-placed Varian employees and that these extremely negative views are widely held throughout Varian.

Defendants have also furthered this scheme by posting on the Internet numerous emails authored by aliases such as "manuforte", "bite_me_now'", "go_get_help", "'gino_in_torino", "dick_et_al", "halperthal", "lickamea," "ah_michelangelo", "jane_crisco", "ernesto", "aronaldo", "Giveemdx", "ramrod_fishguts", "FSUfanNORcal", and having these aliases respond to each other on the internet, thereby creating the impression that there is a multitude of people who have inside information about Varian which reflects badly on Varian's business and which could drive down Varian's stock price. In addition to defaming Varian Associates and being unfair, this scheme is likely to deceive consumers, stockholders, and potential consumers and stockholders regarding Varian ..."

I was happy to take responsibility for any of my postings. In this one I elaborated on already public information and everything written was in fact true:

> **go stock** by: MANUFORTE
> A least one reliable source tells me no more than 20 people will be layed off in the Gloucester plant. The layoff is to be completed before the end of the next quarter with all 15 to 20 so-called middle manager types. As has been the case so far, no one will be layed off from the ion-implantation lab in Palo Alto. Early next year, the lab in its entirety will relocate to a less expensive facility somewhere in the South Bay. This news, if accurate, may account for the recent rise in our stock price

However, the assertion that I was the only critic in the world posting on the Yahoo! VAR message board was at best ludicrous. I had not used, nor had any idea who might of used the aliases: "bite_me_now", "ramrod_fishguts", "go_get_help", "dick_et_al", "halperthal", "lickamea", "jane_crisco", "aronaldo", "ernesto", "Giveemdx", and "FSUfanNORcal".

Later in the year, Glynn, Mary and I visited Orrick's Menlo Park office to review their discovery files. We were amused to find that their never ending subpoenas had discovered the true identities of several of these aliases some of whom were to no surprise, Varian employees. None of these aliases were ever identified as Mary's, mine, or those of anyone who might have been deemed a conspirator. In fact, no other Does were named, or defendants added to the Varian, Felch and Zdasiuk lawsuit:

> **You think so....**
> by: FSUfanNORcal
> Most people here are not happy with their jobs. Instead of posting crap, they should be updating resumes.

> **Rumor has it...**
> by: bite_me_now1313
> Varian will announce the break-up of the company into three distinct companies. My connections have never let me down.

> **Time frame for Aurelio's house hunting?**
> by: Giveemdx
> Does anyone know whether Aurelio's house hunting began
> before or after the emergency board meeting?
> This may have some significance as far as splitting up the
> company is concerned, or it may just be that Aurelio wants to
> be closer to the action. If splitting up the company is now a
> good idea, it was certainly a much better idea a year ago. Now
> it will look like an act of desperation, whereas a year ago it
> would have looked like an act of corporate statesmanship.
> Why should we (the stockholders and employees) have to
> point such things out to O'Rourke and the Board? They are the
> ones being grossly overpaid to anticipate events and come up
> with the brainstorms, not us.

The latter two allegedly damaging postings that Orrick attributed
to me were done prior to my termination from Varian. As a Varian
employee I had never visited any Internet message-board. Now, it
was somewhat amusing to see that I had engaged in a message
board dialogue with this same "bite_me_now1313":

> **please don't bite me** by: MANUFORTE
> Going up?
> The price was $39.62 on Jul 6th, and $53.29 on Apr 6th.
> I usually attempt to buy low and sell high.
> You should give it a try, it works.
> Michelangelo Delfino

The assertion that I then had some ulterior motive, beside
enjoyment for posting on Yahoo! VAR is of course utter nonsense.

> "One of defendants' objectives in posting the messages has been to
> drive down Varian's stock price. This is evidenced by the fact that
> defendants have posted all of the messages on stock-related internet
> sites, and defendants have specifically stated in several of the
> messages that Varian Associates' stock is extremely overvalued...."

Where else would I post a message about Varian stock other than a
stock-related Internet site like the Yahoo! VAR message board?
Then and now a Yahoo! financial message board is by far the most

popular forum to discuss a company's performance and to vent frustration at buying or selling at the wrong time. And so what if I did believe the stock was overvalued, and said so in my postings? I was then, and still am, a Varian stockholder. And no, I have never been contacted by the Securities and Exchange Commission although I have written them several times suggesting they might wish to investigate the goings on at Varian. Lastly, there is, of course, a therapeutic value to posting, which I believe is better than "going postal."

Thereafter followed the complaint's ten claims for relief.[27] I was the only defendant. The conspiracy claim, however, allowed

---

[27]**"FIRST CLAIM FOR RELIEF** (Unfair Competition Against All Defendants) Varian ... reallege ... acts described above constitute unfair competition in violation of the common law of the State of California and Cal. Bus. & Prof. Code §§ 17200 et seq.... and were and continue to be unlawful, unfair, and fraudulent.... unlawful in that they violate California Business and Professions Code §§ 17500 et seq., California Civil Code § 45, California Civil Code § 46, California Penal Code § 502 (c), California Penal Code § 637.1, California Penal Code § 653m, 18 U.S.C. § 1341, 18 U.S.C. § 1342, 18 U.S.C. § 1343, and 15 U.S.C. § 1125 (a), as well as California common law relating to false light invasion of privacy, appropriation of name invasion of privacy, and interference with business relations.... unfair in that they offend established public policies and are immoral, unethical, oppressive, unscrupulous and substantially injurious to consumers, and the gravity of the harm caused by defendants' acts far outweighs their utility.... fraudulent in that members of the public are likely to be deceived as to the authors of the emails and as to the quality of the products and the value of the stock of Varian.

SECOND CLAIM FOR RELIEF (False Advertising Against All Defendants under Cal. Bus. & Prof. Code §§ 17500 et seq.) Varian realleges ... have attempted to make or disseminate or caused to be made or disseminated before the public in California, statements concerning Varian's business and services which are untrue and misleading, and which are known, or which by the exercise of reasonable care should be known, to be untrue and misleading.

THIRD CLAIM FOR RELIEF (Libel Against All Defendants) Plaintiffs reallege ... published on the internet ... emails contain false information regarding Varian, its products, its business practices, and its employees.... libelous on their face because they impute a lack of chastity to Felch, have a tendency to injure Felch in her occupation, charge Felch with improper and immoral conduct, charge Felch with dishonesty, and subject Felch to hatred, contempt, ridicule, and obloquy.... they have a tendency to injure Zdasiuk in his occupation, charge Zdasiuk with improper and immoral conduct, charge Zdasiuk with dishonesty, and subject Zdasiuk to hatred, contempt, ridicule, and obloquy.... they have a tendency to injure Varian in its business, charge Varian with improper, immoral, and illegal conduct, and charge Varian and its officers and directors with dishonesty.

FOURTH CLAIM FOR RELIEF (Slander Per Se Against All Defendants) Plaintiffs reallege ... emails ... slanderous per se because they tended to injure and did injure Varian in respect to its business, by imputing managerial incompetence and mismanagement and poor quality goods, that have a natural tendency to lessen Varian's profits.... they accuse Felch of a lack of chastity and have a tendency to injure her in her occupation.... they have a tendency to injure Zdasiuk in his occupation.... they accuse Varian of committing crimes such as serving alcohol to minors.

FIFTH CLAIM FOR RELIEF (Lanham Act, 15 U.S. Code § 1125a, Against All Defendants) Varian realleges ... made on the Internet false and misleading factual representations concerning the nature, characteristics, and quality of Varian's goods, services, and commercial activities.... representations that ... deceive or are likely to deceive a substantial segment of the intended audience.... have caused injury or are likely to do so.

SIXTH CLAIM FOR RELIEF (California Penal Code Section 637.1 Against All Defendants) Plaintiffs reallege ... without the consent of Plaintiffs or Varian employees, fraudulently represented Felch and other Varian employees and thereby procured to be delivered to defendants emails addressed to such Varian employees, with the intent to use such emails....

SEVENTH CLAIM FOR RELIEF (Invasion of Privacy - False light - Against All Defendants) Felch and Zdasiuk reallege ... without Felch's consent, invaded Felch's right to privacy by publishing on the Internet emails that falsely identified Felch as the author of the emails and that thereby attributed to Felch actions that she did not take and statements, opinions, and beliefs that were not her own and that she did not have.... Without Zdasiuk's consent, invaded Zdasiuk's right to privacy by publishing on the Internet emails that falsely identified Zdasiuk as the author of the emails and that thereby attributed to Zdasiuk actions that he did not take and statements, opinions, and beliefs that were not his own and that he did not have.... In making the disclosures ... defendants were guilty of oppression, fraud, and malice, in that defendants made the disclosures with the intent to vex, injure, and annoy Felch and Zdasiuk, and with a willful and conscious disregard of the rights of Felch and Zdasiuk. Felch and Zdasiuk therefore seek an award of punitive damages....

44

the plaintiffs room to add to their list of SLAPPed victims. All ten claims were based on California law except for the fifth claim, the Lanham Act. In the third, fourth, sixth, and tenth claims, all three plaintiffs, Varian, Felch and Zdasiuk, asserted damages. In the first, second, fifth, and the ninth claim, damages were alleged only

---

EIGHTH CLAIM FOR RELIEF (Invasion of Privacy - Appropriation of Name - Against All Defendants) Felch and Zdasiuk reallege ... invaded Felch's right to privacy by appropriating Felch's name by publishing on the Internet emails that falsely identified Felch as the author of the emails.... invaded Zdasiuk's right to privacy by appropriating Zdasiuk's name by publishing on the Internet emails that falsely identified Zdasiuk as the author of the emails.... appropriation was unauthorized and without the consent of Felch or Zdasiuk.... appropriated Felch's and Zdasiuk's names because the use of their names furthered defendants' malicious scheme to harm Felch, Zdasiuk, Varian, Varian's employees, and reputations.... appropriation was for defendants' advantage in that it furthered defendants' scheme to have revenge upon Plaintiffs and Varian's employees in retaliation for the circumstances relating to Delfino's termination of employment ... As a proximate result ... Felch and Zdasiuk were exposed to contempt and ridicule, and suffered loss of reputation and standing in the community, all of which caused Felch and Zdasiuk humiliation, embarrassment, hurt feelings, mental anguish, and suffering ...

NINTH CLAIM FOR RELIEF (Intentional Interference With Prospective Business Advantage Against All Defendants) Varian realleges ... An advantageous business relationship exists between Varian and its customers, investors, and prospective customers.... Defendants ... were aware of the advantageous relationships that existed and presently exist ... Defendants' false representations, misappropriation of identities, and other wrongful conduct constitute an unfair trade practice in violation of California Bus. & Prof. Code § 17200 ... interfered with, and continues to interfere with Varian's economic relationships and causing disruption of various other interests ... interference was intentional, unlawful, improper, and unjustified.... As a direct and proximate result of the wrongful conduct ... Varian has suffered immediate and irreparable harm for which there is no adequate remedy at law and will continue to suffer immediate and irreparable injury unless defendants are restrained by appropriate injunctive relief ...

TENTH CLAIM FOR RELIEF (Conspiracy Against All Defendants) Plaintiffs reallege ... defendants ... knowingly and willfully conspired and agreed among themselves to engage in the wrongful conduct set forth above.... Doe Defendants allowed Delfino to use their computers to accomplish the wrongs set forth above and/or themselves posted some of the emails ..."

by the corporation, whereas in the seventh and eighth claim, damages were alleged by Felch and Zdasiuk alone.

The restitution demanded was spelled out in the last section of the complaint, the Prayer for Relief,[28] a wish list of sorts. It began with the unconstitutional demand of permanently restricting my free speech rights:

> "Preliminarily and permanently enjoin defendants … and all persons acting under, in concert with, or for them, from directly or indirectly continuing to … [p]ublish messages on the internet whose content relates to Varian and/or any of its employees, officer, or agents, or which relates to Varian's business or stock price, under any name other than defendants' true names…."

The words were an early motivational tool that made it impossible for me not to fight back.

It was interesting too, the emphasis the Varian plaintiffs had placed on money. For me, money has never been a very high priority, despite having before this lawsuit a considerable amount with which to play. A Ph.D. almost always guarantees a fine income, but this was not the reason I earned my degree. My advisor in graduate school, Professor Phil Gentile, had often said it was a "union card." It would best allow me to pursue my hobby – science – while enjoying a comfortable lifestyle. He was right. Glynn later explained my enviable situation by saying that if I had no money I probably wouldn't be sued – there would be no answer to the plaintiffs' prayer. I replied, that I would willingly spend all

---

[28]"Plaintiffs pray that the Court ...

Enter judgment in favor of all Plaintiffs and against all defendants, jointly and severally, on all claims for relief....

Order defendants to pay Plaintiffs the general damages sustained by Plaintiffs as a result of defendants' unlawful acts ... pay Plaintiffs the special damages sustained by Plaintiffs as a result of defendants' unlawful acts ... pay Plaintiffs punitive damages ... pay Plaintiffs their attorney's fees incurred in this action and all other costs of the action ...

Order such other relief as the Court deems just and equitable."

my money if that were the price to be paid for the right to express myself. As it would turn out, I would spend even more than money.

Even then, I could have told them it would not be quite so easy. Long an agnostic, I was brought up with a strong Catholic ethic of paying for one's mistakes, but born with stronger principle of not yielding to threats. Worse yet, it seemed I was being asked to pay money for privileges already guaranteed me by both my State and Federal Constitutions. What were they really thinking?

I had worked with these people at Varian for more than ten years. They should have known all too well that I was not easily intimidated. A typical New Yorker, I am outspoken and assertive not aggressive. I had a reputation at Varian as an accomplished project leader unafraid to step on toes. Whoever, or whatever was behind all this lunacy just hadn't done their homework.

This first complaint was assigned case no. CV 780187 in Santa Clara County California Superior Court, and filed under seal on February 25, 1999. Filing a document under seal, a characteristic of this SLAPP, restricts the readership to the clients, their attorneys and the court. Thus, the complaint is not generally accessible and its merit or lack thereof cannot be publicly evaluated. It was to be the first of four different complaints filed by The Orrick, and was supported by exhibits and declarations also filed under seal. The public, as a potential critic of the SLAPP, remains in the dark. How strange, I thought, a lawsuit whose exhibits were almost exclusively Internet messages appearing on a free public forum accessible to the entire world and with no restrictions whatsoever, even viewable by our children, was being labeled secret.

Orrick first amended the complaint on April 15, 1999 as a result of the April 2 break-up of Varian Associates into three separate companies, thereby doubling the number of corporate plaintiffs: Varian Medical Systems Inc. (VAR) and Varian Semiconductor Equipment Associates Inc. (VSEA). Varian, Inc. (VARI) was inexplicably not included in the lawsuit even though I had very clearly critiqued their vacuum product line and had made remarks about Al Lauer, their Executive Vice President turned

CEO, in my postings. Was Lauer simply a less sensitive guy and not a Dick?

> FALCON: Of the three splinter organizations from the original
> Varian Associates, Inc., there's your company, the other co-plaintiff
> in the case, but one of the three is missing in this lawsuit. And that's
> by the stock symbol Vari, V-a-r-i. Do you have any information other
> than through counsel why that company is not part of this lawsuit?
> AURELIO: No.

The complaint was amended again on March 25, 1999 when Glynn moved the case from Superior court to Federal court because it had Federal claims. He also thought, he would be able to use my favorable EDD ruling by Judge Soviero, which might bring some redemption to my already shattered character.

A so-called second amended complaint was filed by Orrick on June 22, 1999 naming Mary as "Doe #1." Mary was not named in the original complaint and when finally included, she was not served until mid-July. It appeared that her addition to the complaint was intended to put more pressure on me to settle. The focus then changed from me as a single defendant, to a more conspicuous attack on our business MoBeta, Inc. now the subject of Orrick subpoenas. This was followed by interrogatories and document requests of MoBeta, Inc.'s proprietary intellectual property and financial records. Perhaps a little more meaty than its predecessor, this amended complaint was authored by the Grande Dame herself, Hermle. Besides being a bit more antagonistic than the all too prosaic Liburt, she increased the number of claims from 10 to 11, with the addition of a new one alleging "breach of contract against all defendants." She restricted this claim to Yahoo! and did not include Stock-Talk where the allegedly impersonating postings had appeared. Basically, this claim asserted that before I posted I had read and understood the Yahoo! Terms of Service, and soon thereafter posted messages that defamed and impersonated the plaintiffs, thereby violating a contractual obligation with Yahoo!, and in so doing, caused Varian, Felch and Zdasiuk to suffer. As a result of their suffering, they argued that they were third party beneficiaries of this contract. Of course, I dare say, hardly anyone whoever posted on Yahoo!, had read any Terms of Service, least of all agreed to them. I certainly had no idea what Orrick was referring to. Going back to the Yahoo! message boards circa March 1999, I really encountered this for the first time:

> "Reminder: This board is not connected with the company. These messages are only the opinion of the poster, are no substitute for your own research, and should not be relied upon for trading or any other purpose. Please read our Terms of Service ...
>
> You understand that by using the Yahoo! message Boards, you may be exposed to content that is offensive, indecent, or objectionable....
>
> ...YOU EXPRESSLY AGREE THAT USE OF YAHOO! MESSAGE BOARDS IS AT YOUR OWN RISK...DONE AT YOUR OWN DISCRETION AND RISK AND THAT YOU WILL BE SOLELY RESPONSIBLE ...
>
> SPECIAL ADMONITIONS TO PARTICIPANTS IN INVESTMENT RELATED MESSAGE BOARDS
>
> ... the watchword should be "Let the investor beware."... Never assume people are who they say they are, know what they say they know, or are affiliated with whom they say they are affiliated with. This service is being offered for entertainment purposes only ..."

How could Varian attach such credibility to anonymous words on a Yahoo! message board? Even if I had inadvertently violated a contract with them, the ramifications to the rest of the message board community would be far-reaching. In effect, any publicly traded company could argue they had been defamed on Yahoo! message boards and subsequently claim they should be awarded damages because the message board poster had made a contract with Yahoo! not to defame. Yahoo! lured the public into a false sense of anonymity – feel free to express yourself, but if you inadvertently annoy one of our corporate clients you will pay.

Much later in November of 2001, Yahoo!'s Cathy McGoff testified that the Terms of Service had undergone at least nine modifications since December 1997, the inauguration of their message boards. Each time the poster was supposed to be somehow aware of these changes, understand what legal rules were then in effect, and post messages accordingly.

Mary always had her own way of dealing with Orrick's lunacy and Yahoo!'s speciousness. She introduced her own Terms and Conditions on December 10, 1999 with this Yahoo! VSEA message:

WRONG: We won't end up with nothing, by: <u>dantecristo</u>
at least not based on all the testimony and evidence that has been presented in this case. The plaintiffs continue to go down with the truth coming out about all their dirty deeds while the defendants continue to soar. Funny how when you are innocent it can work that way. The one thing I will definitely walk away with from this trial is my freedom to exercise my first amendment right to it's fullest, i.e. I will post until I am dead. Believe me, the plaintiffs have given me plenty of motive and material to do so.

<u>TERMS AND CONDITIONS</u>
By posting this message, you agree to the following terms and conditions:
1. You will not collect or archive any personal data from me such as my email address, my name, the IP numbers associated with my message, my internet service provider, or any other information that could be used to identify me or my computer;
2. You will not deliver this information to a third party. If subpoenaed, you will notify me 15 days prior to delivery informing me of the subpoena;
3. You will not delete my messages without first notifying me as to the specific reason;
4. You will not block my messages due to URL's that are in the body of the message without first notifying me as to the specific reason;
5. If you violate these terms and conditions you are responsible for any and all costs incurred, including but not limited to litigation, damages and loss of good will.

The third amended complaint, in reality the fourth in this case, was filed in Federal Court on February 18, 2000, but never ruled upon. Amazingly, it was submitted almost two weeks after the trial had been delayed in Federal Court for the second time, with us all awaiting announcement of a new date. The Orrick, apparently frustrated with trying to prove their malicious case, was hoping to extend their search for that one defaming message board posting right up and through the trial. They needed but a single defaming posting authored by either of us to win this lawsuit, but hadn't yet found it. The truth is there never was one to find.

Finally, Orrick filed a fourth complaint on August 21, 2000. The filing came almost five months after the case had been transferred back to California Superior Court. Their complaint was trimmed down considerably: there were no remaining Federal claims; the unfounded criminal claim was inexplicably dropped and so was the slander per se claim; and finally we were no longer accused of intentionally interfering "with Varian's economic relationships." There was no explanation given why these claims were dropped. Clearly the accusation of me having committed a crime had served its purpose – a preliminary injunction was in effect.

Just as importantly, this fourth amended complaint and its remaining seven claims would no longer be governed by the June 24, 1999: Federal "Protective Order."[29] The Superior Court judge

---

[29]"This order shall be applicable to and govern all documents, discovery, information, testimony adduced at trial, matters in evidence, and other things that contain or repeat any allegedly false statement regarding any party or any family member, officer, director, employee, or former employee of any party, or that contain or repeat any statement that allegedly is falsely attributed to any party or any family member, officer, director, employee, or former employee of any party. Such documents and things, which collectively are referred to herein as "CONFIDENTIAL MATERIAL," include, but are not limited to:

All postings from the Yahoo! Inc. message board for Varian Associates, Inc., that contain or have been identified by plaintiffs in their Complaint, First Amended Complaint, other pleadings, correspondence with Delfino's counsel, or oral argument as containing such statements ...

All postings from the Stock-Talk message board for Varian Associates, Inc., that contain or have been identified by plaintiffs in their Complaint, First Amended

recognized allowing Varian to file under seal would only give them another weapon for placing us in contempt. He wanted to avoid bogging down his court with contempt proceedings. Perhaps he also realized the benefit of public scrutiny.

None of the allegedly damaging messages that I posted were removed from the Internet at this time. If I *had* defamed Varian and its employees wouldn't there have been some attempt to communicate their concern to the message board community before filing a lawsuit?

Alternatively, I believe, an official Varian posted rebuttal would have been more credible than the message of an anonymous poster or a non-anonymous me. Instead, Varian acted furtively in choosing to pursue a costly lawsuit without public scrutiny. They were determined from the onset to silence me, all while constantly fighting the exposure of the truth.

Glynn never stipulated to this Confidentiality Order, and as such, it was an ongoing point of contention that ultimately resulted in the public release of virtually all documents.

Complaint, other pleadings, correspondence with Delfino's counsel, or oral argument as containing such statements ...

All documents and things that accuse defendant Michelangelo Delfino of responsibility for any such statement, or that relate to Delfino's employment history..."

- 3 -

VARIAN'S TOXIC GAS

Less than a week had passed since I had been SLAPPed, and I was already starting to feel like I was the Will Smith character in *Enemy of the State*.[30] I was accused of conspiracy, and charged with committing all sorts of horrible acts, and yet I lacked an understanding of why I was being selectively targeted. I had never received any letter, complaint, or notice that my Internet postings were being viewed as disruptive or threatening, from anyone, including Yahoo!. Instead, 60, mostly anonymous, often sardonic, and sometimes funny messages on a computer screen were being portrayed as an affront to a corporate giant. There had to be much more to this massive legal onslaught, if for no other reason, the cost, time, and publicity to Varian. Why?

It was now about a week away from my preliminary injunction hearing before the Honorable Catherine A. Gallagher. It was scheduled for March 15 in a different Superior Court house building than the meeting with Judge Herlihy. Glynn had responded to Orrick's threat by immediately noticing Felch, Zdasiuk, and Crisler for as he put it, shortened depositions. A deposition compels one to testify under oath for the purpose of preparing for trial. As it is exploratory and no judge is present it permits a wider range of questioning than generally occurs at trial. These then central figures involved in my firing from Varian were sequentially scheduled for deposition on the afternoon of March 8.

---

[30] A 1998 movie in which the protagonist is unknowingly in possession of evidence related to a politically motivated crime.

Glynn and his white-haired office partner, Tom Kotoske, worked out of a non-descript industrial prefab office building adjacent Highway 101, the major auto conduit through Silicon Valley. The depositions would occur in their small, windowless, conference room library.

First came Felch, represented by the business-like Hermle, and now formally introduced to me. On this day Frau Felch was dressed conservatively and rather reserved, but as always, cautiously prepared. Glynn wasted no time in ardently getting to what he then perceived to be the heart of the matter:

> FALCON: There is also a claim that somehow Mr. Delfino sabotaged your lab? Have you in your own mind come to the conclusion that Mr. Delfino somehow sabotaged a lab at Varian?
> FELCH: I believe that in someway Mr. Delfino was responsible for the incident with our pumps.
> FALCON: And this had to do with toxic gas lines or something like that?
> FELCH: The exhaust line for toxic gas.
> FALCON: And I think that that would be a very serious occurrence in the lab, would it not?
> FELCH: Yes.

I believe Glynn was already finding her too much the victim, a role she had mastered well into her mid-40's, when quite unexpectedly she exposed a bit of herself on surrendering several pages from her so-called logbook, a recorded compilation of alleged work incidents. This handwritten journal offered a glimpse of her twisted view of the world:

> "   *from Los Altos Town Crier*
> *4/97 Copy of Los Altos Hills House Transactions (including mine with sales price) was posted on bulletin board outside Silicon White Room. Bulletin Board contained many Delfino articles. Jane Crisler removed it. Delfino is a Los Altos resident who gets the newspaper and told others that he knew about our new house. A few weeks later another copy was on the same bulletin board. Juanita Sonico removed it.*
> *Susan Felch*

6/4/97 I was walking through a set of double doors by the auditorium where M. Delfino and D. Cheatham (TFS) were talking and playing with the doors. Dayton saw me, opened his door for me, and said to Mike, "Open the door for her." Mike replied, completely within my earshot, "Not on my fucking deathbed."'

Susan Felch

1996(April?) - I knocked on the door to Mary Day's - office to ask her a question (about take your children to work day, I believe) and opened the door. Mike Delfino and Mary were talking. I started to ask my question and was interrupted by Mike, who said that Mary was busy and could not talk. Mary never had a chance to say anything. I just left. Mary came to me later to answer the question.

Susan Felch

8/7/97 10:10 am - I was walking into Bldg. 7 through a side door, and M. Delfino, Mary, and D. Humber also were. D. Humber was beside me, so I started a conversation with him about his upcoming vacation. Delfino immediately went into a tirade, saying to the wall (not a person) in a loud voice "Were we having a technical conversation? Yes, we were having a fucking conversation and we were fucking interrupted..." Susan Felch

12/2/97 On 12/1/97 I was told that Mike Delfino would be moving in to the office next door "to be closer to his lab," instead of remaining in his office on the other hall. I talked to Jane Crisler (HR Rep) about my discomfort with this move. First, every time I see or walk by Mike he is annoying. He makes annoying gestures (pretend telephone if I'm on the phone, talking hands if I'm talking to someone) frequently. Having him next door will only increase the number of annoying incidents each day. In addition, I have some fear that Mike could crack some day and his low-level harrassment could turn into something physical and possibly dangerous. Jane ~~will~~ agreed to look into the situation and get advice on how to handle it.

Susan Felch

12/16/97 After being informed on 12/2/97 of my concern regarding M. Delfino's office move, George Zdasiuk told

Delfino by e-mail to put a hold on it until further notice. George and I had scheduled a meeting for 4:00 on ~~that~~ 12/16/97 ~~day~~ to discuss the issue. Nevertheless, at 2:30 I discoverd that Delfino was in the office next door to mine, helping Novellus people clean it out, assuming that it was his. Ron Powell also told me that he had received an e-mail from Delfino earlier that day asking when the office would be available ~~from~~ for his moving in.

When I talked to George at 4:00 ~~he asked me to consider moving to another office to defuse the problem. I said that I would only agree if the move could be done~~ we agreed that Delfino would not move his office now. When I move to an Admin. office in 2-6 months, then he can move into my office if he wants.

Susan Felch

12/17/97 I was asked by George Zdasiuk if I would consider moving to another office to defuse the problem. I said that I would only agree if the move could be done completely during the Christmas shut-down.

Susan Felch

12/18/97 I discovered that the proposed new office for me is not large enough for all of my desks, book shelves and file cabinets. Also, there is no laser printer in that part of the building. I also heard that any such move would be very costly. So, I told George that I would not move my office at the present time.

Susan Felch

2/20/98 Today I found a blown-up copy of the Los Altos Town Crier announcement of my home purchase (from 2/97) on a table near the Bldg. 7 second floor copier/laser printer. The article was in full public view. I took the article and sent it to Jane Crisler.

Susan Felch

5/12/98 Over the last few months Mike Delfino has frequently made a "talking on the telephone" gesture (hands like a telephone by ear and mouth) when he passes my office and sees me on the phone. This is definitely annoying and can interrupt my conversation and train of thought, often with customers and colleagues.

I informed Jane Crisler (HR) last week, who said that Mike was asked by his manager to stop. Today I was walking down the hall toward my office, and he was at the other end of the hall with Mary Day. I smiled at them and nodded "hello". Mike just did the telephone gesture toward me.

Susan Felch

6/30/98 At about 12:55 pm I was talking on the phone to my husband. Mike Delfino walked down the opposite hallway (by the drinking fountain), saw me through the window, and made the telephone gesture toward me. As it happened, I mentioned the incident to my husband.

Susan Felch

7/30/98 During a presentation by Brad Friedman (Legal) on 7/21, Mike Delfino asked a question that began "Aside from cases of lab sabotage" and then continued with the real question on confidential information exchange. Matthew Goeckner told me that he heard Mike ask Adeline Shrewsbury before the meeting "What is the JO number for sabotage?" About 1 hour after the meeting Mike and Mary Day were near me in the hallway outside my office and joked about lab sabotage.

Susan Felch

9/17/98 On either 9/9 or 9/10 Mike Delfino walked down the opposite hallway past the bathrooms, looked back toward my window, saw me talking on the telephone, and made the "telephone gesture."

Susan Felch

9/21/98 At about 8:10 am today I was walking down the hall toward my office. Mike Delfino and Mary Day came around the corner at the other end of the hall, heading toward the stairs. Mike made the "telephone gesture" toward me - very clearly and for 2-3 seconds. I appeared to be quite deliberate.

Susan Felch

November 17, 1998 - At 2:30 I was on the phone talking to Matthew Goeckner. Mary Day came walking down the hall toward my office. She saw me through the window and caught my eye. She then made her version of the "telephone gesture" and made an ugly, distortion of her mouth. This is the first time that she has ever made any inappropriate gesture in my presence. I immediately told Matthew what I saw.

Susan Felch

December 3, 1998 - At 8:05 am I was walking down the second - floor hallway toward my office from the rear of the GRC building. I opened the door from the new part of the building into the old and immediately saw Mary Day walking toward me. I smiled and said "Hi." She replied in a quiet voice, "Stay the fuck away from me." Afterward we both continued in the directions that we were walking. No one else was in the vicinity to witness the incident.

Susan Felch"

The dwarf-like Felch even signed each entry as if it were historically significant. While it appeared that she had long ago attempted to seal Mary's and my fate in her secret logbook, the events in it were largely unknown to us.

FELCH: ...What is copied here is the complete log for Mr. Delfino and Ms. Day.
FALCON: And you keep a log regarding other employees also?
FELCH: If there are incidents that need to be recorded, yes.
FALCON: And have you found need to record other incidents with other employees other than Mr. Delfino and Ms. Day?
FELCH: Yes.
FALCON: How far back does this log go?
FELCH: I believe early in my employment.
FALCON: So somewhere near 1985?
FELCH: Um-hum.

Susan B. Felch scares the bejesus out of me! I had made a deliberate effort to avoid her only now to find out that she had been marking "incidents that need to be recorded" in a book for over thirteen years – and this wasn't even the whole book. Frightening! Later, on the 1st of December, Felch not expecting any follow-up on this subject, apparently thinking it closed, gave answers to Mary's attorney that contradicted this day's testimony:

WIDMANN: All right. What was your purpose in recording the
incidents in the logbook?
FELCH: To have a written document recording exactly what had
happened.
…
WIDMANN: Okay. And I take it when you recorded the incidents
concerning Mr. Delfino and/or Ms. Day, that you recorded them
accurately.
FELCH: As best as I could remember, few minutes after they had
occurred.
WIDMANN: That was my next question. What was your practice in
recording them, and by that I mean did you record them as soon as
possible after the incident, or did you wait days or hours to do so?
FELCH: I would try to record them, you know, within 10 or 15
minutes. Although there were times when I had to go off and do
something immediately after they happened and I couldn't get back
for hours.

Indeed, a perusal of her logbook shows that her handwritten entries
are not chronologically entered. Two of them have an incomplete
date and another is entered a year later, as an after thought, as if
she was instructed to document some long-ago event. This was
strange. Was the commandant simply following orders?

Felch was typical of that breed of so many Stanford physics
Ph.D.'s we had come to know, who like Zdasiuk, are often
remarkably book smart with an uncanny ability to regurgitate very
specific material, but not so quick as to be able to analyze new turf
and react to the unexpected. Felch's logbook was not the
contemporaneous diary she purported it to be. She was too
technical, too anal, to make such a blatant blunder.

After Felch, came a rather blustering Zdasiuk, whose
deposition that afternoon was fairly uneventful. Characteristically
like a bull in a china shop, he did provide a nonsequitur:

FALCON: Well, anything that made you feel that he had ill-will
towards you?
ZDASIUK: During the process of disciplining Mr. Delfino for the
problems surrounding the Sue Felch incidents, I think Mr. Delfino at
times would describe things in a very sort of -- I'm trying to use the
right words because I realize I'm under oath, and I am trying to be
able to express the feelings I have in a very legalistic -- I can't quite

describe the right words, but rather saying let's sit down and talk about this, I got the impression at times, well, this must happen here, there, then in a very overly precise manner, I suppose. But the definite incidents of hostility were during his review and the time he made a face at me in the laboratory.

FALCON: And what face did he make at you?

ZDASIUK: I don't -- I mean it was a some sort of a funny grimace the unusual expression on his face.

or two:

ZDASIUK: ... The fictitious incidents of laboratory sabotage, ...

FALCON: Accused of?

ZDASIUK: Yes. Some involvement with.

Surprisingly, he also surrendered a noteworthy deposition exhibit – a long forgotten nine-month-old Varian email from a Matthew Goeckner that he had forwarded to Crisler.[31] Dr.

---

[31]"Date: 6/2/98 3:06 PM   From: Matthew Goeckner

George:

As per our conversation:

1)This morning (~9 or 10 AM) Ziwei found that someone had come into the PLAD lab over night and turned several of the knobs on the BF3 system. This resulted in the BF3 in the regulator being dumped to the scrubber. Fortunately the person who did it did not open the gas bottle. Ziwei is the only one currently using the system and he knows which knobs to turn. He was last using the system ~ 5PM last night.

2) It appears that someone put acid on the exhaust hose from our rough pump to the scrubber. I discovered that this morning. I do not know when it occurred. The pump, however, is almost out of pump fluid so it probably occurred at least several days ago. As you know, the pump is outside in what we call the "dog house". The old lock on the dog house has been broken for a long time so anyone could have gotten into it. It now has new lock. I have the only key. The pump was just rebuilt in April. It is now full of garbage and it is likely that it will have to be rebuilt again. I have completely shutdown the PLAD system until we can fully assess the damage.

3) We have had Tygon hoses "break" three times in the last 3 months. These hoses carried either N2 or compressed air, both <+ 80 psi. The hoses are rated to ~120 psi. Old hoses can and do break but usually not at this frequency.

4) I have asked all of the members of the PLAD group to lock all of our labs whenever they are not there...."

Goeckner was a recent graduate and Felch hire who I hadn't even met. How was Zdasiuk, my immediate supervisor and responsible for a different department in the GRC laboratory, involved in Felch, her people, and her equipment? He was not even versed in her group's technology, and not in any way knowledgeable about the laboratory equipment in question. I doubt he had ever even been in that laboratory. Yet on September 25, 1999, two weeks before he was deposed, he declared:

> "In May 1998, an act of sabotage subsequently occurred with respect to the lab run by Ms. Felch. The exhaust line coming out of a pump suddenly developed holes. It appeared that the holes were formed by application of chemicals as opposed to normal wear and tear. Subsequent examination of the pump strongly suggested that chemicals had entered the pump. The damage to the pump was not consistent with normal wear and tear and sabotage was suspected. The holes in the line were dangerous because the pump is used to pump toxic gases, and holes in the line would allow toxic gas to escape into the ambient air and potentially harm people...."

When questioned about this again by Falcon on November 11, 1999, Zdasiuk was unmistakably baffled about the whole affair, now answering, "What do you mean by sabotage?"

The exhaust line referred to in Zdasiuk's declaration was, like all our vacuum pump-lines, made of stainless steel and so highly resistant to corrosion that I have never ever seen one develop holes. Unfortunately, I never saw the evidence in question even though I was the one who originally installed the equipment, including the pump-lines nine years earlier, and would have been uniquely qualified to comment on the "sudden" appearance of holes. Inspector Crisler, recorded an interview with Goeckner:

> *"Very concerned about escalation of violence. Personally feels threatened. Change locks on the lab. Please get rid of this person. I'm more than willing to tell anyone that I feel physically threatened ..."*

She also met with Felch's frumpy middle-aged technician, Juanita Sonico, who regularly moonlighted at Stanford "20 hours a week:"

"Definitely would testify. I was there. The way he's acting, there is something wrong. I'm afraid, too. Something could happen over there. What happened with the gas? I'm a little afraid. The monitor was off. I had Mike's name in mind when I heard about what happened...."

An hour or so after Zdasiuk had begun his deposition, an unusually well-dressed Crisler arrived, just bubbling to testify, and help sink me deeper, if at all possible. She was accompanied by Orrick's Joseph Liburt, the primary author of the complaint and the proposed TRO. The two waited together outside while Zdasiuk finished testifying. After the requisite introductions, Glynn first queried her about Felch's sabotage claim:

FALCON: Was this in regards to a sabotage claim that Sue Felch had made?
CRISLER: I believe so.
FALCON: And was an independent investigation conducted of that sabotage?
CRISLER: Yes, there was.
FALCON: And was a conclusion reached in that?
LIBURT: Objection. Vague and ambiguous. Conclusion as to what?
FALCON: Was the investigation concluded?
CRISLER: The investigation was concluded.
FALCON: And what was the finding of that investigation?
LIBURT: Objection. Vague and ambiguous. You can go ahead and answer if you can.
CRISLER: We concluded __ that's the question? What did we conclude?
FALCON: Well, the investigation. If it's you then __
CRISLER: What did we deduce from the investigation?
LIBURT: He's asking about the independent investigation. What was done? What was the conclusion of the independent investigation?
CRISLER: That there were certain evidences that made it clear that whomever had done the sabotage knew exactly what they were doing and knew a lot about the labs and the chemicals and the hazards of it, and we knew that Mr. Delfino had that knowledge.
FALCON: And did Mr. Delfino deny any knowledge of how the incident occurred?
CRISLER: He said something to the affect of he had no idea what

had happened.
...
FALCON: Who conducted the independent investigation?
CRISLER: I did.

Was she being evasive? Crisler, no longer a Varian employee returned to resume her deposition later that year on the 10th of November, this time represented by Orrick's ex-cop turned barrister, Peter McMahon who was smaller than I imagined. Seeming less confident than in her February 25, 1999 declaration:

"In August or September of 1998, an incident of sabotage occurred in the lab for which Ms. Felch was responsible. The person who committed the sabotage was someone who clearly understood what to do in order to create a problem. It is my understanding that the exhaust line coming out of a pump suddenly developed holes. It appeared that the holes were formed by application of chemicals as opposed to normal wear and tear. Subsequent examination of the pump strongly suggested that chemicals had entered the pump. The damage to the pump was not consistent with normal wear and tear and sabotage was suspected. The holes in the line were dangerous because the pump is used to pump toxic gases, and holes in the line would allow toxic gas to escape into the ambient air and potentially harm people...."

she would become a most memorable deponent:

FALCON: Now after your deposition that I took here in this office of March of this year are you aware of whether or not any outside law enforcement agency was contacted regarding the claim of sabotage occurring in Sue Felch's lab?
CRISLER: No.
FALCON: What I am trying to do is quantify subsequent acquired knowledge, okay. At the last session you said there was a final report.
CRISLER: I need a break.
FALCON: Please.

Following a rather typical 15-minute break, only her attorney would return, and then only to sheepishly pick up Crisler's purse. Another 5 minutes would pass before a surprisingly timorous McMahon would reappear once again, but without his witness:

McMAHON: Let the record reflect that the witness was not able to continue with the deposition. I encouraged her to take extra time. We did so. She felt that she was not able to continue with the deposition and is extremely reluctant to come back, and so this deposition is I guess concluded at this point and I would like to under the terms of the protective order -

FALCON: Well, before we get to that, what's the basis for her inability to continue?

McMAHON: She's physically unable to continue the deposition.

FALCON: Okay. I mean I didn't see any signs of it. All of a sudden she just said I need to take a break. There wasn't any crying. There wasn't emotion. Is she claiming that I did something to her?

McMAHON: She's just physically unable to continue the deposition.

FALCON: That's what we need to have said.

McMAHON: Yeah. Well, she's gone.

FALCON: Did you come together in the same car?

McMAHON: No.

FALCON: I mean I can't - we have still got several areas to go into, and I was just getting into them: The sabotage issues, and she is saying she's not coming back?

McMAHON: I understand that. You know, this was somewhat of a surprise to me, as well.

FALCON: I mean did you observe any impropriety here?

McMAHON: I would - I did not, otherwise I would have objected. I think that Ms. Day and Mr. Delfino were within their bounds of their ability to participate. That's my opinion. I believe that Ms. Crisler did not feel that way, and that she became very upset - very, very upset and has left not able to continue.

KOTOSKE: My name's Tom Kotoske. I'm co-counsel for Mr. Delfino. This process is unheard of. The deponent is not even here - apparently has been excused by counsel or left on her own and has never made a statement on the record of why she can't continue this deposition. This is extremely improper and I dare say this is certainly grounds for sanctions, and that will be addressed at a later time. For counsel to just unilaterally come in here and announce that the deposition is quote concluded which it is not is extraordinary, and we're deprived of vital testimony at a crucial time, and discovery is about to close, and under those circumstances we believe that the conduct is clearly sanctionable and we'll pursue those remedies at a later time.

McMAHON: Let the record reflect that I observed my client in a state which was one of physical inability to continue and -

FALCON: Well, physical - I mean was she throwing up or passed out? What do you mean by that? She walked out of this room and just said she needed to take a break.

McMAHON: She was very emotionally distraught is the way I'll put it, and I don't - I'm not saying that the deposition is concluded absolutely. However, I am representing that she is unable to continue today and I cannot physically compel her to come into this room.

FALCON: I'm not requiring to force somebody to come in.

McMAHON: Let the record reflect I attempted very - for a long time to get her to come in.

FALCON: I think to protect yourself on the record he doesn't want to say on advice of counsel she left.

McMAHON: No. I attempted to get her to come back into the room. She was adamant that she would not, and as a result she has asked me to retrieve her briefcase so she could leave and I did, so I will on her behalf explain for the record that she was extremely distraught.

FALCON: Did she understand that she could be sanctioned? Was she aware of that?

McMAHON: I explained to her that she could be compelled to come back and that -

FALCON: Was she going to the doctor?

McMAHON: That's a possibility.

KOTOSKE: Is she driving her car?

McMAHON: Yes.

KOTOSKE: Well, the lawyer's statements as to physical condition of this deponent are just not acceptable. The witness has voluntarily for whatever reason refused to go forward with the deposition and that's grounds for serious sanctions. Do you have anything else?

FALCON: No. You were going to talk about confidentiality regarding the employment matters. My client doesn't desire in effect since his reputation has been ruined, destroyed, trampled on - what have you. The only way that he's going to ever get a fair trial is if the truth comes out and is recognized in regards to his employment at Varian, and her deposition he doesn't desire that any of it be confidential.

This was as Tom had put it, the most outrageous occurrence he had ever witnessed during a deposition. This, coming from a 10-year veteran United States attorney, who had put away some of the more heinous characters around, like those involved in the Las Vegas Frontiers Hotel case and the shooting of the bespectacled gangster getting a massage in Coppola's movie, *The Godfather*.

I was deposed by Orrick on March 9, the morning following the Varian trio. I met Glynn with his usual calming self right outside the Orrick, Herrington & Sutcliffe office, their Silicon Valley headquarters in Menlo Park, California. The building was a gleaming monolith, with a heavy double-doored glass entry clearly meant to impress. Once inside the lobby, we were escorted to a sterile conference room crowded with video camera recording equipment, and the requisite transcription recording paraphernalia. After accepting Hermle's offer for some quite good coffee, I was asked to sit in front of a huge gray backdrop screen and clip a microphone to my tie so that the videographer could make the necessary adjustments. While the room was expansive, it was somewhat claustrophobic, with me facing Hermle and the camera, the court reporter to my right and Glynn ever so close to my left. I had been deposed a number of times before, perhaps as an add-on to living in California, being too principled or just an idiot. I was still a co-plaintiff with Mary in construction defect litigation against our condominium developer; I had made a fruitless effort in a most contentious divorce custody battle; and I had won a wrongful termination lawsuit against Philips Signetics, my employer before Varian. However, this case was different. It was my first time being videotaped and now, I was the defendant. Making matters worse, I was accused of breaking the law – committing crimes that I had no idea of the basis. As is so often said in the movies, I would "plead the fifth."[32]

---

[32]On March 9, 1999, Glynn explained his reasoning to the Judge pro tem Special Master Thomas H.R. Denver:

"... it is self evident from the face of Varian's complaint that multiple felony violations are being alleged therein, punishable under both state and federal law.... it is patently obvious from the complaint that Mr. Delfino is targeted by plaintiffs with criminal conduct and conspiracy....

plaintiffs charged that defendant criminally sabotaged a toxic fume pump in one of the Varian laboratories which allegedly "created a substantial risk of injury and death to Varian personnel!" ... Such accusations raise fear of prosecution for California Penal Code § 375(a)... Plaintiff also alleges that Delfino violated the Lanham Act according to Penal Code §350, a person who, without the consent of the registrant, willfully manufactures, intentionally sells, or knowingly possesses for sale at the point of sale a counterfeit of a mark registered with the Secretary of State and registrable under the Lanham Act, is subject to fines and imprisonment.

Ordinarily in a civil action, taking the Fifth is presumed evidence of guilt. After all, it's only money at stake – no jail time. However, here, Varian had filed a civil lawsuit against me and meretriciously included serious criminal accusations cleverly integrated into the complaint. It took Special Master Denver less than a day to see their lawsuit was more than just about Internet message board postings. He wrote Judge Herlihy and all counsel:

> "Plaintiffs' complaint charges defendant with violation of no fewer than five criminal statutes, State and Federal. While the complaint is clearly civil, it sets forth, in elaborate detail, allegations of criminal conduct on the part of the defendant.... I have carefully reviewed each of the discovery devices here involved, including all of their questions or subparts. I reluctantly conclude that the Fifth Amendment/California Constitution is appropriately asserted as to virtually all of them...."

Even though Glynn is not a criminal defense lawyer, he justifiably recommended I not expose myself to any criminal liability, even if the allegation was without merit. Very simply, until things became clearer, he could not risk my incarceration. Having witnessed my veracity in the Signetics case and knowing my unwavering character, he assured me that it was the only choice. Reluctantly, I agreed to remain silent.

> HERMLE: As we proceed through the deposition today, I will be asking you questions and you will be answering those questions, or as I understand it, taking the Fifth Amendment. Do you understand that?
> FALCON: Or making other objections.
> ...
> HERMLE: So then, it would be true that the court could infer based on your taking the Fifth Amendment that you perjured yourself in that

---

This is just a small sampling of the criminal offenses that the pleadings and discovery requests seek to explore. It appears that most of plaintiffs' allegations are focused in the period of the last several years, well within any criminal statute of limitations that might apply. No immunity has been accorded Mr. Delfino. Mr. Delfino's exercise of his Fifth Amendment Privilege to prevent compelled incrimination is neither feigned or trivial. Mr. Delfino has "demonstrated a reasonable fear of prosecution."

deposition?
FALCON: Improper question. Counsel, you are way overstepping
your bounds on this. You know that no inference can be taken by
asserting the Fifth Amendment privilege.
...
HERMLE: Were you ever employed by Varian?
FALCON: Counsel, you know the answer to that already. That's the
allegation in the complaint. And when he goes into--he's not going to
answer that question because once he answers questions regarding
employment with Varian, it will tend to go into areas where you are
claiming that he violated certain criminal statutes and he has a real
apprehension and fear that in your pursuit of this civil case he may
tend to incriminate himself in possible criminal conduct. He therefore
asserts the Fifth Amendment.

Taking the Fifth is a bit of a surrealistic trip in itself.
Questions are directed at you and are answered by someone sitting
adjacent you. Bringing me almost to laughter, Hermle reading
from her computer screen would periodically grimace as she
mouthed aloud her question, and attempt to coax me into
responding. If I uttered even a single word, Glynn warned, I might
have forfeited my Fifth Amendment privilege. The five hours or so
of questioning went something like this:

HERMLE:....Do you have a romantic relationship with Mary Day?
FALCON: That's completely improper. Fifth Amendment, invasion
of privacy.
...
HERMLE:....did you hope to manipulate the stock price of Varian's
stock?
FALCON: Same series of objections.
...
HERMLE: Were you attempting to encourage the audience which
read this e-mail to sell Varian stock?
FALCON: Same series of objections.

My days were getting more and more bizarre. While I was
increasingly fascinated with how all this worked, I didn't
understand why, if Orrick knew I was not going to answer after an
hour, then why not call it a day and send everyone home?
Relatively early in the deposition, Frau Felch sauntered into the

conference room and sat opposite me. As she sat down I happened to be staring straight at her. Hermle immediately demanded I turn my head away from Felch. I continued to stare coolly in the same direction while Glynn defended my right to position my eyes as I saw fit acknowledging that my head hadn't moved despite the staged entrance of Felch. The camera pointed at me and the microphones recorded it all, much to Hermle's chagrin:

FALCON: Same series of objections. Shall we put on the record who just entered?
HERMLE: Yes. Ms. Felch entered the room. Were you intending to imply that Ms. Felch is a bitch in that P.S.?
FALCON: Same series of objections.
HERMLE: Were you intending to disparage her reputation?
FALCON: Same series of objections.
HERMLE: Were you intending to harm her reputation for professional conduct?
FALCON: Same series of objections.
HERMLE: There is no need to stare at Ms. Felch that way, Mr. Delfino, and it's not appropriate conduct. Please don't do it anymore.
FALCON: I'm not sure what you are saying he is doing?
HERMLE: I think if you take a look at him, as it's borne out by the tape, he has switched his position so that he is staring in an intimidating way towards Ms. Felch.
FALCON: Well, I understand the staging and theatrical nature of this deposition was designed to, perhaps, cause some reaction by Mr. Delfino when he saw Mrs. Felch come in here.
HERMLE: Oh, that's just nonsense.
FALCON: I don't think there has been any reaction. I think your comments on her --
HERMLE: I'm going to ask you again to tell him not to do what he is doing.
FALCON: Let me finish, Counsel. You are interrupting here. He has a right to look in any direction that he wants. Your conclusion of what you think what Mr. Delfino is or is not doing, I don't think, unless you want to be a witness in this case, is irrelevant.
HERMLE: I don't need to be. I got it on tape.

The Orrick inquisition quickly resumed with a now flustered Felch moving to a more distant seat. Her presence had no effect, and so she soon left, disappointed, I suspect. The morning's dramatic display gave me insight into Hermle that I don't think would benefit her clients as the SLAPP evolved. For one, it suggested that she had underestimated me as an adversary. While definitely emotional and expressive, I am above all self-controlled. Hermle struck me as already personally involved, perhaps convinced of my brutish antics long before this lawsuit began.

Glynn explained that Orrick needed to establish a record:

HERMLE: Did you sabotage equipment in the lab that was run by Sue Felch?
FALCON: Objection, Fifth Amendment.
HERMLE: Did you do that in order to cause her serious harm?
FALCON: Improper form of the question, objection, Fifth Amendment.
HERMLE: Did you do that with the idea that there would be a serious accident in the lab?
FALCON: Same objection, as on the previous lack of foundation, and on this one, lack of foundation.
HERMLE: Do you know of any one else who sabotaged equipment in the lab run by Sue Felch?
FALCON: Again, improper form. The question, no foundation, and Fifth Amendment.
...
HERMLE: Did you sabotage equipment in the lab run by Sue Felch because of your personal feelings about her?
FALCON: Objection, it -- no foundation, it's an improper form of the question and Fifth Amendment.
...
HERMLE: Did you conspire with anyone to sabotage equipment in Sue Felch's laboratory?
FALCON: That's same objections and improper form of the question.
HERMLE: Did you communicate with anyone else your intent to sabotage equipment in Sue Felch's laboratory?
FALCON: Same series of objections.
HERMLE: Do you know of anyone other than yourself who would have a motive to harm Sue Felch?

Crisler's supervisor, a now retired and even more disinterested Jim Hennessy, the former Director of Human Resources at Varian Associates, was deposed on November 4, 1999. Soft-spoken and direct, he testified that Crisler had made him aware of the incident.

FALCON: Who undertook the investigation to head up the investigation?
HENNESSY: It was conducted by Kathy Hibbs, our in-house counsel, and Jane Crisler.
…
FALCON: Was Mike Delfino a suspect in that lab sabotage?
HENNESSY: Yes.
…
FALCON: And were you aware of the outcome of the investigation that Jane Crisler was performing in conjunction with Kathy Hibbs?
HENNESSY: Yes.
FALCON: And what was the outcome?
HENNESSY: I believe it was inconclusive.
…
FALCON: What does "inconclusive" mean to you when you say that?
HENNESSY: I don't believe there was any one person identified as the person who caused the incident.

It is my belief today that the so-called sabotage was just normal laboratory equipment failure brought on by irregular maintenance or operator error. Crisler's investigation was a scam. Shogo Hikido, the knowledgeable and experienced technician who long had maintained that allegedly sabotaged vacuum pump before this episode and who was then working with me, was never even interviewed. Neither was Mary, who could best attest for my time and whereabouts. In hindsight, it appears that Goeckner and the less high-strung Ziwei Fang, the two new employees then involved with the equipment, were simply used by Felch to incriminate me. Although their inexperience was brought into question during the laboratory sabotage interviews, it was not considered relevant. Felch too seemed to manipulate the relatively simple-minded and easily intimidated, Sonico, who along with Goeckner collectively convinced an all too gullible Crisler to believe that something sinister had occurred and I was responsible. Was Zdasiuk just as susceptible?

Soon after Zdasiuk emailed Crisler Goeckner's memo, all seventy or so of Varian's GRC employees were told to attend a mandatory meeting in the company auditorium. As no topic was given, this was indeed an ominous announcement.

Kathy Hibbs, a corporate attorney who was not known to the GRC, hyperventilated that "Felch's lab had been sabotaged," and by someone with "special knowledge."

> FALCON: Did anybody discuss at this meeting the possibility that toxic gases could have been released injuring or killing people?
> McMAHON: Same objection.
> CRISLER: Yes.

She added it was serious enough that an outside law enforcement agency may get involved. As GRC did a significant amount of government contract work, alerting the FBI would have been probable. At this meeting, there would be no questions taken and the subject matter should not be discussed by anyone. On adjournment, interviews would immediately begin as the pasty-white Hibbs exclaimed, "It was an inside job!" Some of the two dozen or so Novellus Systems employees then sharing building with Varian, while not at the meeting, would be questioned as well.

> FALCON: Do you know whether any Novellus employees were interviewed regarding the lab sabotage in Sue Felch's lab?
> McMAHON: Same objection. You can answer the question.
> CRISLER: Yes.

Felch and others in her sphere of influence had made a concerted effort to cast me as a villain without any supporting evidence whatsoever; the story was good, the truth was irrelevant.

I was back working in my laboratory when Zdasiuk told me I would be the first to be interviewed. What a surprise.

> FALCON: And were Mr. Delfino's fingerprints in the lab?
> CRISLER: Not that I'm aware of.
> FALCON: Okay.
> CRISLER: "... I will do lie detector tests, hypnosis, DNA, fingerprints."
> FALCON: Mike is saying that?
> CRISLER: Yes.
> FALCON: Did you take him up on that?
> CRISLER: No, we did not.

The only people to allude that anything untoward had happened in the "dog house" were Felch's Goeckner and Sonico. None of the other twenty-plus people who were interviewed by Crisler and Hibbs suggested that I could have sabotaged any equipment. No one said they believed that I would actually try to harm anyone. Was there another possibility?

Crisler's June 4, 1998 handwritten interview notes have Dave Humber, a conscientious and talented Varian machinist, proposed that Frau Felch herself might have committed the dastardly deed:

> *"I was asked by Susan if I would testify against Mike. No. I won't. If she took it that way, that's her problem... Mike felt harassed by her pushing in on the conversation. I can't imagine would escalate into violence. She's got two new engineers working for her. If Susan wants to get rid of Mike, then she might sabotage her own lab...."*

Dr. David Hodul, who supervised her for many years, reminded:

> *"... worried that she's unstable."*

While I was never vindicated of any wrongdoing, beginning on August 13, 1999 I would relentlessly post messages about Felch's alleged laboratory sabotage:

Did Varian disregard employee safety? by: ima_posta2
Dick, Dick, Dick, have you no shame? Why weren't the police or the FBI or the CIA called in to investigate the alleged laboratory sabotage at Varian - sabotage referred in depositions to be so dangerous that toxic gasses could have been released killing people!
Why no police, Varian?
Did no one care?
Ahhhhh, I'm sickened by this stuff!
Dick, are you there?

I was determined to get the whole story about this incident in the public as my professional reputation had been permanently damaged. It is important to understand that as a chemist who would often need to handle dangerous and toxic materials, it would impossible to be trusted to do this kind of employment again. Varian, of course, declined to make any public statement that would have provided closure to this most unusual event. They even refused to acknowledge subsequent chemical analysis that proved there was no sabotage, only Varian ineptitude.

Mary was deposed two days after me on March 11, and she, too, was videotaped. Glynn, as her business attorney, made a special appearance to represent her. I did not attend on Glynn's advice. Mary's testimony was a bit more interesting than mine, as she was not yet a defendant and, of course, had no reason to take the Fifth. Nonetheless, the intimidating and invasive tactics of the Orrick attorney was just as apparent during her questioning:

> LIBURT: Okay. Do you have a friendship with Mr. Delfino?
> DAY: Yes, I do.
> LIBURT: All right. Do you have a romantic relationship with Mr. Delfino?
> FALCON: Objection. Ambiguous, vague and over broad and invasion of privilege -- I mean, invasion of privilege -- invasion of privacy. Not calculated to lead to discoverable and inadmissible information. You don't have to answer that question presently phrased. No foundation.
> LIBURT: You're instructing the witness not to answer that? ... Is Mike Delfino's mother still alive?
> DAY: As of this morning, I think she was.
> LIBURT: What's her first name?
> DAY: Mary.

My mom, Mary Delfino, having heart problems throughout the time of this deposition, died on August 3, 1999 at age 80. I never understood the reason for this line of questioning. My mom and dad lived 3,000 miles away in Florida. She had never posted on the Internet, and as far as I knew, had never even touched a computer. I suspect she didn't know the Internet existed. Later, when I resumed posting, message board attacks on us and our families, including the all too frequent death threats, were a fairly regular occurrence. Responding to this Yahoo! VARI posting:

> **DUH!** by: rube47 (50/M)
> If you care not what equita or anyone else thinks, why on earth
> then do you post? Little flaw in logic, Mr. Scientist.
> It appears that the time that you don't care what people think
> only when they think you are a self-centered, selfish bore.
> You can choose to ignore the facts, but it seems the population
> of this board think you rude and narcistic. Take comfort
> though, i'm sure your mom still thinks her little boy is really
> somebody!!
> you make sure that you use dem damages to get help, you
> hear? And then maybe you get mom a home with indoor
> plumbing. By the way, if she is still of an age to bear children,
> you can buy her "Child Rearing for Dummies". Her next
> product might not be any smarter but it will have better
> manners. Unless she sleeps with her brother again

I posted with a link to Mary's deposition:

> **My mother died August 3, 1999**
> by: dr_michelangelo_delfino
> An Orrick SLAPP attorney 'investigated' her too back on
> March 11, 1999 (see p.201):
> http://www.geocities.com/SiliconValley/Hardware/8784/slapp
> /daydepo.html
> She didn't post. I do. She would most assuredly tell you that
> when I decide something, you can take it to the bank. I'd say it
> in Italian, but I suspect you wouldn't get it.
> (in English) I'm here - I will post whatever and whenever I
> want - there's nothing that will stop me - nothing.
> Are you still confused?

Mary had no reason to be concerned during her deposition.
And having no knowledge about what my lawsuit was all about
she had no call not to be forthcoming. Liburt, apparently
dissatisfied with her sense of righteousness, requested a short break
to meet outside the conference room with Hermle. He returned to
pursue a more focused line of questioning:

LIBURT: Okay. What other computers have you used in the last six
months?
DAY: Other than at work?

75

LIBURT: Yes.

DAY: I don't know. I've used that one. I had a Performa that I used. Gosh. I don't know. When I go to friend's house, you know, use their computers. I don't know.

...

LIBURT: What happened to the Performa?

DAY: I gave it to Goodwill.

LIBURT: When did you do that?

DAY: Recently. 25th, 26th, something like that.

LIBURT: Of what month?

DAY: February, 1999.

LIBURT: Why did you give that computer to Goodwill?

DAY: It had a -- It had a long history of problems, and I finally just got so frustrated with it. The drive -- The zip drive was kind of acting up, and I just said pppp. I'm not -- I'd taken it into Computerware at least four times and I wasn't going to do that again.

...

LIBURT: Okay. Has Mr. Delfino ever used that Performa computer?

DAY: Yes.

LIBURT: Okay. Do you -- Do you know what he was using that Performa computer for?

DAY: No. I don't know specifically.

LIBURT: Okay. Well, do you know generally?

DAY: Were job searches. Basketball is a big thing for him.

LIBURT: He's a basketball fan?

DAY: Yeah.

LIBURT: Professional basketball?

DAY: No, I don't think so. I don't think it's professional basketball.

LIBURT: College?

DAY: Yeah. Is it NCAA? Is that college?

LIBURT: Yes.

DAY: Okay.

LIBURT: Yes. Okay.

DAY: I don't know. Probably, you know, to look at patents and things like that.

LIBURT: Okay. To look at patents, would he have to get on the Internet?

DAY: I don't know if he has to, but in my system, that's the only way I know how to get on --

LIBURT: All right.

DAY: -- to do patent searches.

LIBURT: Okay. Do you know if Mr. Delfino accessed the Internet on that Performa?

DAY: Do I -- When you say know, I mean, I assumed he did, but I don't know because I didn't stand over his shoulder.

LIBURT: Okay. Did he ever say anything to you that indicated that he had accessed the Internet on the Performa?

DAY: Yes.

LIBURT: Okay. What did he tell you that indicated to you that he had accessed the Internet on the Performa?

DAY: He would discuss what the -- I'm trying to think what they're called, the box scores for NCAA. He would -- You know, most of the time when he watched a basketball game he'd go on the computer because these things called like box scores, I guess they're called. You know, there's something that comes up on the Internet that is interesting to him.

I attended Saint John's University in Jaimaca, Queens from 1968-1972 and have been a rabid Redman basketball fan ever since.

LIBURT: Did Mr. Delfino encourage you to give the Performa to charity?

DAY: No, he didn't.

LIBURT: Do you know if the hard drive on the Performa was wiped or completely deleted before it was given to charity?

DAY: I don't know that.

LIBURT: Okay. Do you know if Mr. Delfino, in the last six months, has had any Internet access accounts?

DAY: Do I know? I can't say that I know.

LIBURT: Okay. I'm sorry, I've forgotten what your answer was. When I was asking you about computers that were at Mr. Delfino's home, you mentioned that your Mac TV, you thought, was over there now, and you mentioned a Mac that you believe he returned to Varian. Did you mention any other computers that you have seen in the last six months of Mr. Delfino's home?

DAY: You can't look at the record thing.

LIBURT: I can't -- it's -- It would take longer.

DAY: I can't right now think of any other computers.

...

LIBURT: Okay. Yeah, I may have asked you this before, and if so, I apologize.

FALCON: Then asked and answered.

LIBURT: Great. When you donated the Performa computer, which charity did you donate that to?

DAY: I think you did ask it. Goodwill.

LIBURT: Okay. Located where?

DAY: You did ask that. I believe it's Meadow and El Camino, you know -- East Meadow, I think it is. It's Palo Alto.

LIBURT: Okay. Did Goodwill give you a receipt?
DAY: Yes.
LIBURT: Okay. Is the receipt in your name?
DAY: No, it is not.
LIBURT: Whose name is the receipt in?
DAY: It's actually blank.
LIBURT: Okay. They just gave you a blank receipt for it?
DAY: (The witness nods her head.) Yeah.
...
 LIBURT: Correct. Correct. Did you drive the Performa to Goodwill yourself?
DAY: Yeah.
LIBURT: Okay. What time of day did you go there?
DAY: Oh, I don't know. I don't know. I don't know.
LIBURT: Do you remember morning or afternoon, night?
DAY: I -- It probably -- I don't know. I would guess it's morning, midday, something like that.
LIBURT: Okay. Do you -- Do you have a receipt for the iMac that you bought recently?
DAY: Yes, I do.

Mary's decision to rid herself of her problem Performa computer and get a new one as a birthday present to herself, courtesy of our business, was certainly hers to make. Her computer literacy, coupled with my lack of interest in computer hardware in general, made such decisions fairly unilateral. The next day Hermle would file yet another declaration this time in which she appears to be talking to herself:

> "Amazingly, she admitted getting rid of the computer on the day (or day after) Mr. Delfino received notice of the lawsuit and the TRO...."

This then missing computer, the one Mary had donated to Goodwill charities, would be continually used by Orrick as an argument to support their conspiracy theory. Orrick believed that this one computer held information that would, in fact, establish us as having collaborated on posting. Why they never sought to examine any of the more than 30 other computers we acknowledged using seemed to suggest that the Performa was simply a ruse to make us look bad. Orrick contended from the beginning that I, or someone in concert with me, had authored approximately a hundred postings on Yahoo! and another financial message board, Stock-Talk, using *someone's* computer. In truth, I had only posted 60 Yahoo! messages and all of them I had authored using the Performa. All Orrick ever needed was one defaming posting by me to win this lawsuit and obtain their prayer for relief. And of course, they could have named Mary a defendant right then if they really suspected something amiss, but they didn't.

Mary and I have never understood what incriminating evidence Orrick's attorneys believed could have been found on her donated computer. As many computer users do, Mary employed Norton Utilities, which automatically rewrote over files that had been deleted on the hard drive, thereby defragmenting and increasing its efficiency. In addition, she had set up her AOL account not to place "cookies," those small files placed on a user's computer to tag their Web site visits, on her computer. Once The Orrick heard Mary testify that America OnLine (AOL) was her Internet provider, her account was immediately subpoenaed on the 12th of March.[33]

---

[33]"Plaintiffs ... issue a subpoena ... America Online ... INFORMATION BEING SOUGHT:

... "DOCUMENT" means the originals and any copies of any written, printed, typed, or otherwise recorded matter, however produced or reproduced, of every kind and description, in whatever form ... including but not limited to, all writings, diaries, notes, journals, photographs, video or audio tapes or recordings, computer generated DOCUMENTS, computer disks or data tapes, or any other tangible things ...

REQUEST FOR PRODUCTION ... All DOCUMENTS REFERRING OR RELATING to the IDENTITY of any PERSON to whom the email address "susyfelch@aol.com" is or was registered or assigned at any time from June 1, 1998 to the present ... to any correspondence, contracts, agreements, registration forms, or billing materials REFERRING OR RELATING to the email address "susyfelch@aol.com"

... to the IDENTITY of any PERSON to whom the email address "mday101619@aol.com" is or was registered or assigned at any time from June 1, 1998 to present ... to any correspondence, contracts, agreements, registration

It was truly amazing that Varian was asking to have access to all of Mary's and my emails including those belonging to her two daughters. We had all shared the same AOL account. Thankfully, AOL was unique at the time in that it notified its customers of any subpoena. At least then, the victim had an opportunity to challenge the invasion of privacy.[34] On the 22nd of March they wrote Mary:

> "Dear Ms. Day:
> America Online ("AOL") has received a subpoena duces tecum...commands AOL to produce information relating to your AOL account.... It is AOL's policy to require service of a valid subpoena before it will disclose Member identity information. Upon receipt of a valid subpoena, it is AOL's policy to promptly notify the Member(s) whose information is sought. In non-emergency circumstances, AOL will not produce the subpoenaed member identity information until 14 days after receipt of the subpoena so that the Member whose information is sought will have adequate opportunity to pursue any legal remedy that may be available...."

---

forms, or billing materials REFERRING OR RELATING to the email address "mday101619@aol.com" or to any person to whom said email address was registered or assigned at any time from June 1, 1998 to present.

... to DELFINO, including but not limited to all DOCUMENTS REFERRING OR RELATING to any email accounts assigned to DELFINO or registered in DELFINO's name at any time from June 1, 1998 to present ... to DAY, including but not limited to all DOCUMENTS REFERRING OR RELATING to any email accounts assigned to Day or registered in DAY's name at any time from June 1, 1998 to the present.

... to the IDENTITY of the PERSON to whom the identifier "spider-tp072.proxy.aol.com" was assigned at 22:01:45 hours on January 5, 1999, including but not limited to documents containing account information (name, address, telephone number, email address, type of computer used, etc.), billing information, and payment information for such PERSON ... to the IDENTITY of the PERSON to whom the Internet Protocol address "152.163.194.203" ... was assigned ... on November 23, 1998 ... on February 15, 1999 ... on February 12, 1999 ... on February 24, 1999 ... on January 19, 1999, including ... PERSON ... All DOCUMENTS REFERRING OR RELATING to Delfino. ... to DAY"

[34]A Motion to Quash is a legal brief that requests the court nullify, void, or declare invalid a subpoena.

By now I had spent upwards of $10,000, approximately half my Varian severance. It seemed like a lot of money for just 60 message board postings. Needless to say, our newly founded MoBeta, Inc. was suffering from a lack of attention and dwindling funds. Worse yet, none of our interested potential business partners were talking to us anymore about our promising, patent-pending radioactive stent technology. While we always introduced ourselves as former Varian research scientists to any prospective business partner, and noted our work history in our business plan, we didn't know if Varian had been in recent contact with any of them. But now we had our suspicions as the mood of our business contacts seemed to change. To our knowledge, Varian appeared to make a concerted effort to keep their participation in this lawsuit out of the public eye but may well have alerted the business community. As the weeks went by, less and less of our time was spent doing MoBeta technology, while my legal bills were coming in fast and furious. Little did I know then how much time and money we would both wind up expending and how many more times we would both be deposed in the next months. Fighting Varian's SLAPP was to become our full-time job, and the focus of MoBeta, Inc.'s business.

In the middle of all this chaos and quite unexpectedly, Varian offered to compromise. On April 5, 1999, the first business day after the break-up of Varian Associates into three independent companies, Hermle forwarded this settlement offer to Glynn:

"I am writing to give you one final opportunity to enter into a permanent injunction[35] designed to resolve this matter. As you know, we are now in federal court. We have been assigned an extremely intelligent and hard-working judge. Judge Whyte, we believe, fully understands the influence that will arise from your client's assertion of the Fifth Amendment.... The spoliation of evidence will gravely hurt any chances your client has to prevail in this matter. As should be obvious from the hearing before Judge Gallagher, the evidence and arguments in support of Varian's case are overwhelming. Moreover, your attempt to seek immunity is meritless and, in fact so frivolous as to warrant sanctions...."

---

[35] A court order forbidding certain speech activities, e.g., prior restraint.

Varian has incurred significant attorney's fees in an effort to stop the despicable conduct of your client. It will continue to incur these fees. Your client has no interest whatsoever in continuing to harass or defame Varian, Sue Felch, or George Zdasiuk. It would certainly be in your client's interest to put this case behind him through a permanent injunction.

If you choose not to resolve this matter through a permanent injunction, Varian will at no time be willing to settle this case prior to the recovery of significant damages against your client. We will then seek all of our attorneys' fees.

Please let me know your response."

No, I did not agree to shut up. Varian, Felch and Zdasiuk were offering to stop harassing me in exchange for me giving up my right to speak. This fascist notion of acquiescing for any reason, of denying me my right to free speech was not an option at any price. I would die before I would ever agree to a permanent injunction limiting what I can say on the Internet, or anywhere else for that matter.

Glynn seemed to see it quite differently, arguing as MoBeta's business attorney that I couldn't survive financially, and my company was certain to fail if I tried to fight this powerful corporation and its internationally-based army of Orrick attorneys. Going a step further, he warned that Mary would unnecessarily be brought into the fray.

Mary, when told of what was going on, grew even more irate, and was extremely supportive. Even if I agreed not to post messages on the Internet, she concluded, Varian would come after our business. Once silenced by an injunction, how could we defend ourselves and our company in the public arena?

Instinctively, we both believed that Varian's attempt to destroy MoBeta, Inc. was one goal behind their SLAPP. Glynn, seeing her point, added that I would be unable to fend off any future allegation that I had violated this injunction. Any message board posting could then be attributed to me, since the reliable tracing of a positing from source-to-viewer was virtually impossible, as shown later by Orrick's so-called expert witness. Nonetheless, Glynn asked that I put in writing my determination to fight. He was now understandably concerned about his own liability. Even Glynn was intimidated. On April 9, I wrote my attorney and my friend:

"I have read and understand the consequences of the Orrick, Herrington & Sutcliffe letter dated 5 Apr 1999. Contrary to your advice, I will not enter into a permanent injunction to resolve this matter. Per our 8 Apr discussion, I will do my best to have fairness and justice prevail over their fascist acts and despicable tactics despite the financial and legal risks that I face. Therefore, please proceed with the documents subpoena and the Levy, Aurelio and Hennessy depositions.

If Varian elects to cease this harassment, they must comply with the following: (1) acknowledge my first amendment right to voice my opinion anywhere and by whatever means I choose including the Internet; (2) apologize for wrongfully terminating my employment contract, for subsequently violating my unemployment rights, and for continuing to perpetuate false and misleading statements of misconduct; (3) pay all my legal fees and a substantial penalty for bringing forth this frivolous lawsuit fraught with unsubstantiated accusations; (4) agree to drop any and all claims against MoBeta, Inc., its technology and its officers."

Silence was inconsistent with both my temperament and my metabolism. On May 20, 1999 I made my first declaration:

"1. Contrary to the assertions of the plaintiffs and their lawyers, the only postings that I have made ... are those made under the "aliases" of 1) "ah_michelangelo," 2) "GINO IN TORINO," 3) "MANUFORTE," 4) "manufortetoo," and 5) "morerumours." ... I signed my actual name to some of the postings ... I have posted ... 60 messages on the Yahoo! Varian stock message board.

2. I have never posted on the "Stock Talk" Internet web page.

3. I have never posted under the "aliases" referenced in the amended complaint as "aronaldo," "bite_me_now" "go_get_help," "go_gat_help," "dick_et_al," "halperthal," "jane_crisco," "ernesto," "giveemdx," "ramrod_fishguts," "FSUfanNORcal," ...

4. To my knowledge I have never harassed Susan Felch, James Fair or anyone else at, or with Varian. .

5. I have not impersonated Susan Felch, Susie Felch, Susan B. Felch, Kevin Felch, George Zdasiuk, Jane Crisler (or any variations of those names) nor have I used their names or identities to post ...

6. For the ten years that I worked for Varian, my office was kept open and unlocked and I had a sign on my office that said "Do Not Lock." My personal information, computer and desk files, and access to my office computer was there for anyone ... My office networked computer was left on 24 hours ...my access codes for Yahoo!, timecards, Internet access, mainframe access, and expense reports were pinned to my bulletin board ... Varian employees had regular access to my office ... including Steve Henderson, Dave Baie, Ferdinand Engayo, and Gary Virshup. Managers and MIS at Varian had access to the computer and my log-in codes, ... Since my personal data, including tax information, birth date, family information, social security number were available to just about anyone at Varian. ... they could have easily obtained any or all of my personal information to use for whatever purpose they might pursue.

7. I have never sabotaged, or attempted to sabotage, a laboratory or anything else at Varian. I offered to take a polygraph exam when I learned that Varian might be claiming I had "sabotaged" Ms. Felch's laboratory. Varian did not accept my offer.

8. I filed a harassment claim with Varian against Susan Felch. Susan Felch then retaliated against me for doing so by making false charges to HR and to my manager, George Zdasiuk. The e-mails reflecting my attempts to stop her harassment of me are attached ...

9. The issue of whether I had ever harassed Sue Felch was raised by Varian and litigated at my California Unemployment Insurance Appeals Board trial ... Administrative Law Judge [D.J. Soviero] at that hearing found that there was no evidence of any such harassment and found in my favor on those issues....

10. I am not a computer nut, nor am I even computer literate, At Varian, I counted on the computer technicians to keep my computer updated and running. after this lawsuit started ... I discovered that I had even listed my Yahoo account password ("Bobo") in my account ("profile") information, which anyone looking at my account profile (which is open to the public) could then pick up and use the password to gain access to my account with Yahoo!...."

I really did include my password on my Yahoo! profile so that anyone could access my account and create an alias and use it to post messages without my knowledge. Bobo is a Spanish buffoon, in effect a clown, a sobriquet given me by my sophomore high school teacher, Brother Emiliano, and a label that is deserved. While my declaration did nothing to dissuade Orrick that I was really just a clown having fun, it did wonders for my state of mind.

- 4 -

A FAT LIAR

It was the spring of 1999 and the only thing clear to me at this point was that I had in fact posted 60 Yahoo! messages over a period of less than five months. My postings were no less protected by the United States and California Constitutions than those of anyone else. This posting I admitted making on the Yahoo! VAR message board on February 15, 1999 and included in the complaint epitomizes my right to publicly comment on Felch and her maiden name, Benjamin:

> **Susan B. Felch** by: <u>ah_michelangelo</u>
> If you know Susan B. Felch and as you put it, think she's o.k., then you must be George Zdasiuk or someone else of similar character. The mere thought of hearing the name Felch is enough to make one vomit.
> p.s. Those who really know her don't think the B is for Benjamin.

Orrick relied on its clients' false declarations to vilify me and misrepresent the words in my postings and thus gave me motivation to post. In Zdasiuk's February 25, 1999 declaration, he fails to recognize that our country allows my speech to upset him:

> "I am not aware of anyone else who has animus against me such that they would attack and impersonate me in a forum which is likely to cause ridicule... I fervently believe that Mr. Delfino is seeking to harm me professionally and personally through a vicious campaign of hate email. These emails have been upsetting to me both personally and professionally..."

Zdasiuk tries to paint the picture that only I would be so inspired to criticize him in a public forum. In truth, my view of Zdasiuk, Felch, and Crisler as being less than ethical was shared by many others at Varian. Almost immediately, more than one person who reacted unfavorably to my wrongful termination was reprimanded and made to believe that their jobs were in jeopardy should the issue be discussed further during work hours. This in part, left the anonymity of message board postings the only avenue thought to be safe for venting. Was I alone?

Prior to my wrongful termination, the discussions on the Yahoo! VAR message board was often heated. Much of the focus was on the poor performance of the stock and the recently announced breakup of the company. The talk of layoffs was in the air. Something had to be done. A diabolical plan was required. I would be singularly portrayed not just as an opinionated message board poster venting his less than favorable opinion of management, but a former disgruntled employee hell bent on seeking vengeance on those who wronged him -- the Dr. Phibes[36] of Silicon Valley. I was accused of posting messages on Yahoo! that I did not do, accused of using Yahoo! aliases that were not mine, and in the case of Stock-Talk, posting on a message board that I wasn't even aware existed. Orrick had, in fact, subpoenaed Stock-Talk on February 26 requesting all 22 messages posted on their financial board for VAR from the first one on November 16, 1998 to the last two on February 25, 1999. Obviously this was not a popular site. While none of the 25 "Requests for Production" contained in the Stock-Talk subpoena ever produced any evidence linking me to any of these postings, Orrick vehemently argued I did them all or at least that I conspired with their authors.

Admittedly, most every Stock-Talk posting did mention directly or indirectly Felch or Zdasiuk, but so what? Neither was especially well respected. Couldn't another be upset with my rather unexpected departure from Varian and protest? Or might I have

---

[36]One of Vincent Price's better known roles was Doctor Phibes, the deranged surgeon, who seeks revenge for the accidental death of his beautiful wife, in the 1971 classic, *The Abominable Dr. Phibes*.

even been set-up by someone? What made Stock-Talk postings so different than those on Yahoo! was the ability to post without logging in – true anonymity! Here, the allegedly defaming postings were attributed to the aliases: "Susan B. Felch," "Vice President Zdasiuk," "SB Felch," "ernesto," "Sue B Felch," "Susan Benjamin Felch," "murphy," "Doctor Kevin Felch of CPI," "Georgio Zdasiuk, b.s.," "I need help, by Susan Benjamin Felch," "Associate Director Susan b. Felch, B.S.," "Jane," "Vice Prez George A. Zdasiuk," "Another Investor," "Director GEORGE ZDASIUK," "Susan Kevin Felch," and "Associate Director Susan B. Felch, b.s.". Were these the basis for Orrick's impersonation claim?

To be a valid claim, the appropriation or exploitation of someone's name or likeness must have been (1) done without their consent, (2) for my financial benefit or advantage, and (3) have resulted in injury to them. It would be easy for me to refute such absurdity, except that Orrick did it for me, never once arguing I gained *any* advantage nor had either Felch or Zdasiuk been injured.

Looking with some detail at the postings and the aliases associated with authoring them, I found myself laughing aloud. I read nothing in them that I thought offensive. I would easily have accepted responsibility for expressing the sentiment made in almost all of them. Communicating my empathy with the anonymous authors of these postings would always cause Glynn to wince and cringe.

Perhaps the coupling of ego with integrity did not allow me to take credit for something I did not do. While I had knowingly fathered three children, if I had adopted another, I would have nurtured all of them with the same parental love and vigor without distinction. But I would never have said I had created four children instead of three. I make no attempt to explain the origin of any Stock-Talk posting that Orrick ascribed to me or anyone I know.

Felch complained about these Stock-Talk postings in her February 25, 1999 declaration:

> "Several of the postings were extremely offensive and caused me very serious distress. ...emails suggest to Varian employees and investors reading the Stock Board that I am mentally deranged....

emails that I found the most hurtful and offensive were those which impersonated my husband.... Kevin Felch, is a physicist who works at CPI, a company previously owned by Varian. We have two sons [Collin & Trevor].... This email, I believe, seeks to imply that my husband does not know my sons or their names, that my sons are not his children and that I need professional psychiatric help."

> **Posted by Doctor Kevin Felch of CPI on January 15, 1999 at 21:30:34:**
> In Reply to: Re: varian associates sucks posted by Susan Benjamin Felch on January 05, 1999 at 22:01:45:
> Damn it Sue you're not OK!! You're too short. You talk too much. You cry when you don't get your way. You dress silly. Ron thinks your nuts, and Dave thinks you're anal. For God's sake, sue get some help! I'm going skiing with your kids in the meantime. By the way, what's their names? They are boys, aren't they?

I did not post this Stock-Talk message, which was included in the complaint. Yet, I certainly do believe Susan B. Felch needs professional help. I knew her husband's name was Kevin and she had children, but then I did not how many, or even if they were boy or girl. Besides, I think many people at Varian and elsewhere had that knowledge. Her propensity to gossip was legendary as was her emotional neediness to be liked. When later deposed, she was asked how frequently she found it necessary to cry at work:

FALCON: Have you ever cried at work in front of others?
McMAHON: Objection, vague, overbroad. You can answer the question.
FELCH: I believe there were probably a few occasions, yes.
...
FALCON: The crying at work, did you ever cry during a performance review or salary raise -- lack of salary or raise of salary in front of either Dave Hodul, Burleigh Cooper or Ron Powell?
McMAHON: Objection, vague, overbroad, private. You can answer the question.
FELCH: That might have occurred, yes.

Drs. Hodul, Cooper III, and Powell – three accomplished scientists, each with a distinctly different personality, were her only supervisors before she reported directly to Levy, and then her next boss, Reuel Liebert, another Varian manager with a Ph.D. He, however, had the advantage of working at the main plant in Gloucester, Massachusetts and not having to deal with Felch on a regular basis. Clearly the distance did not prevent him from surfing the World Wide Web:

> FALCON: Do you know of anyone other than the persons that you're complaining or the person that you're complaining against from Varian that has posted on that particular web site?
> FELCH: Reuel Liebert.
> FALCON: And how do you know that?
> FELCH: He told me.

If she cried in front of her first three supervisors, it is reasonable to presume she did so with Levy and Liebert too. Such sensitivity to receiving bad performance reviews is touching. But isn't there something a bit peculiar about a 45-year-old wealthy professional crying at work, and with such frequency, over money?

> "... an email posted on January 5, 1999 stated that I was starting to feel okay "no more voices, no more talking behind my back, no more of those damned whispers and dirty looks from old men." Others suggested that I was engaged in sexual affairs with my coworkers. Still others made derogatory remarks about my family, criticizing my husband and mentioning our sons...."

Posted by Associate Director Susan b. Felch on January 17, 1999 at 21:26:33:
Dear Varian employees,
I have worked for Varian in Palo Alto for more than 15 years and have yet to put a full day's work. I mean, who really cares anyway. The man who used to be in my life, Kevin, also used to work here, but now he's gone, so now I play with George Zdasiuk. George is alot heavier than Kevin, but alot less demanding. For one, he doesn't make fun of my squeaky voice and how I dress. So there. I just wish he'd stop making faces at me...

"A friend of mine who works for Varian also told me that she received a telephone call from a non-employee of Varian who had seen the postings supposedly written by me. She was asked "Who is this woman?", referring to me. I ask that the Court please stop this ...

emails not only included my full name, but my supposed title and job duties.... one email which was not written by me, I supposedly state "I am an Associate Director of the Varian Technology Center responsible for future breakthrough technologies." ... goes on to suggest that "me and my people are always looking for new opportunities, hopefully ones that will bring us money" and goes on to state that "we're always home by five o'clock ..."

Certainly her office light was never on past five. When deposed later that year on the 1st of December, Felch understatedly admitted that she didn't always put in a full days work:

> FALCON: Did you ever have arrangements with Varian where you would leave work by 4:30 on a routine basis?
> McMAHON: Objection, vague, overbroad as to time. You can answer the question.
> FELCH: At one point I had arrangements where I was working seven-hour days.
> ...
> FALCON: Where you were quoted to that effect?
> FELCH: Possibly.
> FALCON: That you're always home by 5:00 o'clock?
> FELCH: I don't think those were the words.
> ...
> FALCON: When you were working, I think you said seven-hour days, did you have to make that time up, say on weekends or after hours or anything like that?
> FELCH: No.

Interviewed in *Varian Magazine* in 1994, she seemed proud to say:

> "Could I get more done at the lab if I worked a 40-hour week? Yes, but not much."

Zdasiuk, eager to enter the fray, tried to sound as distressed as his SLAPP cohort when on February 25, 1999 he declared:

> "Several of the postings were extremely offensive and caused me considerable distress. Many of the emails suggest to Varian employees and investors reading the Stock Board that I was engaged

in sexual affairs with my coworkers. Several others made derogatory remarks about my weight...."

> **Posted by I need help, by Susan Benjamin Felch on January 15, 1999 at 21:49:15:**
> In Reply to: Re: NO MORE LAYOFFS posted by Vice President Zdasiuk on November 19, 1998 at 14:39:06:
> My wonderful ever so chubby George. Some may think you really, really fat and ugly. Not me. I do think your tummy is starting to get a bit on the large side, but for the most part that's ok by me cause you're the only vice president who still listens to me talk and talk and talk and talk and talk and talk and talk... Sometimes I wish I could stop, but I gues I cn't stop talking cause I keep on seeing those faces, those gestures, those whispers...Oh, George I'll never get rid of that dress! And forget about the red corduroy skirt I got from Sears!

While I did not produce this message, I applaud everything the author refers to, and in particular, think it is an excellent descriptor of Felch. She did talk and talk. Her perpetual talk was often about nothing and as best as could be determined, no one was listening. At Varian, my office was adjacent hers, and for the last four years my primary laboratory was positioned almost directly across from her office. And so I quickly learned not to be distracted by her babble as well as the poster of a half-naked Fabio that she plastered on the outside of her office door.

In only one of my original 60 Yahoo! VAR postings named in the complaint, did I refer to Zdasiuk's propensity to gain weight:

> **...headed for bottom** by: ah_michelangelo
> The Varian you know had offered technology and quality because it spent R&D money to make it happen. What will remain after the break-up will be a joke. Their so-called research center will house, I'm told, 19 people somewhere in the East bay. VP George Zdasiuk is supposed to come up with 'breakthrough' technology for medical. The only thing I have seen him do is gain weight. The Oncology folk think so highly of him that they prioritized their inventory space over his operation! As for x-ray manufacturing, it's a good operation getting more and more squeezed. You don't have to be a rocket scientist to know what's gonna happen.

The first complaint listed two postings critiquing Zdasiuk's chronic weight problem. The Stock-Talk posting was best:

> **Posted by Susan B. Felch on February 23, 1999 at 02:13:00:**
> In Reply to: Re: NO MORE LAYOFFS posted by Vice President Zdasiuk on November 19, 1998 at 14:39:06:
> George, I love you as much as I love Dick. I only wish you weren't so fat.

Zdasiuk asserted that I had defamed him and asked in the preliminary injunction that I be forbidden from implying he was "overweight." Thus, this rather ridiculous line of questioning:

FALCON: Has anybody ever told you that you were overweight?
ZDASIUK: Yes.
FALCON: And who told you that?
ZDASIUK: My mother.
FALCON: When did she tell you that?
ZDASIUK: I don't remember.
...
FALCON: Anybody else other than your mother mention to you or tell you that you were overweight within the last two years?
ZDASIUK: Explicitly that statement?
FALCON: Words to that effect.
ZDASIUK: Can you explain what you mean by "words to that effect"? And verify that?
FALCON: "Words to that effect" means anything other than being of normal weight.
McMAHON: Overbroad. Vague.
FALCON: It's not a tough question.
ZDASIUK: My wife.

And his little friend who had also claimed it was defamatory:

FALCON: Has Mr. Zdasiuk ever made any comments to you regarding his weight?
McMAHON: Objection, vague. You can answer the question.
FELCH: Yes.
FALCON: On how many occasions?
McMAHON: Overbroad.
FELCH: Maybe five to ten times.

Steve Henderson, a 40-ish year-old ingratiating subordinate of Zdasiuk, cursed with a similar body, noted on November 30, 1999:

FALCON: Did George Zdasiuk ever discuss his weight with you?
HENDERSON: His weight? His physical weight?
FALCON: Physical weight, yes.
HENDERSON: Yes.
FALCON: And generally what was he saying about his weight?
HENDERSON: Complaining that he needed to lose weight.
FALCON Did he joke about that?
HENDERSON: It was a joke.

Returning to the joke, Zdasiuk declared on February 25, 1999:

"... another email which purports to have been written by me but which was not, I am purported to address laid off Varian workers in Massachusetts and reports about the huge company Christmas party that the Company is having in Palo Alto, and also state that the Company will be serving alcohol to minors...."

> **Posted by Vice President Zdasiuk on November 19, 1998 at 14:39:06:**
> In Reply to: NO MORE LAYOFFS posted by Varian Extrion Employees on November 19, 1998 at 13:51:01:
> I am very sorry for what is happening to you Varian workers in Massachusetts. But let me assure you that the Varian workers in Palo Alto are doing quite well. This year, while not as good as the recent past years, is good enough to warrant our biggest Christmas celebration ever. If you had been fortunate enough to have been at our 50 year anniversary party you would know that the employees in Palo Alto sure know how to have a good time. Our party plans include the usual multicourse meal and free drinks for everyone including the kiddies. In recognizing our responsibility, I think we should be prepared to pay for taxis or busses for all employees and their guests who may have had too much to drink. of course, we might not be able to pay if the stock continues to drop in which case I would ask my people not to drink and drive. If any of you people happen to be here the night of the party feel free to drop in for a drink or two. But remember, don't drink and drive and may next christmas be better for you than this one.

And the only posting on the same subject made by me.:

> **PLEASE...don't drink and drive!** by: ah_michelangelo
> It is certainly great to read that the Company is paying for its folks to 'booze it up' especially with the stock dropping like a rock. Party hard, if that is your thing, but don't drink and drive. Varian can ill afford to be the Silicon Valley drunk driving poster child. Spend some of those hard earned profit sharing dollars on a cab or bus ride home. Who knows, maybe Dick will be your designated driver.

While I did not author the former, both seem to deliver the same message: don't drink and drive. Neither posting makes any reference to the serving of alcohol to minors. Zdasiuk, if indeed he did not author the Stock-Talk message, should at least not so blatantly distort the truth. Later, his apparent sensitivity to being caught intoxicated would be traceable to his own behavior.

Arguably, the most controversial of my 60 Yahoo! postings:

> **CONGRATULATIONS!!!!** by: ah_michelangelo
> Clearly you are too smart to work at Varian. You deserve to work at a Company that one, makes money, and two, knows how to treat its employees. If you think things are silly in Gloucester, you would be amazed to see the goings on in Palo Alto. The so called research center, building 7, looks like a ghost town, with the IIS manager Sue Felch doing as much as she has ever done. Ask Reuel about her. I'll bet you big money that Dick had nothing to say about her and her so-called operation in Palo Alto. The only thing that makes any sense, and I'm gropping, is there is a dress with a stain on it somewhere...find the dress and you might make money!!!

Felch first referred to it in her February 25, 1999 declaration:

"Other emails that relate to supposed affairs seem to mimic the Monica Lewinsky[37] dress issue, stating things like "oh, George I'll never get rid of that dress!""

---

[37]The young intern who proved she had an affair with President Clinton in the White House by preserving her semen stained blue dress.

and then again that year on September 10 in another declaration:

> "I have never been involved in any extramarital sexual or romantic affair. In particular, I have never had sexual or romantic relations with any of my colleagues at Varian, including but not limited to Dick Levy, Richard Aurelio, and George Zdasiuk. I do not own and never have owned a dress with a semen stain on it, as implied in one of Mr. Delfino's admitted Internet messages."

Reference to it even made the November 12, 1999 *San Francisco Daily Journal's* front page "Delfino denied that his comment referred to the Monica Lewinsky scandal, and he stood behind his claims that the manager is a liar and hallucinator." Here again, was this rather revolting visual of Felch giving head, or at least having a mouthful of semen spill onto her God-awful clothing. Questioning about Felch's supposed affair continued as late as early February 2000, clearly a major discovery topic for Orrick:

> LIBURT: Okay. Do you believe that George Zdasiuk and Sue Felch have ever had a sexual affair?
> DELFINO: I don't have any idea.
> LIBURT: All right. Do you believe that Sue Felch has had sexual relations with Dick Levy, L-E-V-Y?
> DELFINO: You'd have to ask him.
> ...
> LIBURT: Okay. Do you have any -- Are you aware of any facts that suggest that Sue Felch has had sexual relations with Dick Levy?
> DELFINO: I don't know anything at all about Sue Felch's sexual relations with anything.
> LIBURT: Okay. So -- So if I ask you the same questions about Sue Felch and Dick Aurelio, would your answer be you don't have any idea whether she's had sexual relations with Dick Aurelio?
> DELFINO: You'd have to ask those people.
> LIBURT: Okay. But I want to know what your belief is.
> DELFINO: I don't have a belief one way -- I don't think about them -- certainly not sexually.

On January 9, 2001, Megan E. Gray, then an attorney with Baker & Hostetler LLP in Los Angeles wrote the following about us in a legal brief intended to protect the identity of an anonymous Yahoo! message poster alias that we had twice tried to subpoena:

"Defendants often posted messages implying, if not outright stating, that Plaintiff Felch is a female executive who acquired semen stains on her clothes from oral sex with a supervisor, which was supposedly the reason she still had a job, etc...."

There were no such postings. It was a blatant lie. But her attempt to inflame the case and prejudice the court against us worked, as our subpoenas were twice denied. We comforted ourselves with our loss and dealt with Gray's lie by posting her words for more than a year thereafter. Our fun would come to an end when a judge who, to our amazement, would say it was untrue "that Megan Gray said that Susan Felch had a semen stain on her dress or other clothing or had sex with a supervisor." I knew all of her supervisors quite well and none were rumored to have been a Felch sex partner. No postings said otherwise.

Despite this, and the judge not having met Gray, he went on to say that it was untrue "that Megan Gray is or was a liar," I posted this on Yahoo! VSEA on January 25, 2001 at a time when I was legally allowed to do so:

> **"Felch is a female executive who**
> by: dr_michelangelo_delfino
> acquired semen stains on her clothes from oral sex with a supervisor..." was stated by Megan Gray the famous LA lawyer. Now I ask you, where does Megan get her information from?
> In all the years of having to be around Susan B. Felch, I did find her to dress somewhat garishly but I can't for the life of me recall any blotches on her clothes that I would have associated with semen stains. Besides with who?
> AAAAAAAAAAAAGH!

Felch's preoccupation of being perceived of having sexual affairs with other Varian executives and in engaging in carnal acts with the company's highest-ranking officers on the Varian Associates corporate jet, which by the way I was never a passenger, has its obvious origin in her mind.

There is some basis, perhaps, in these two Stock-Talk postings that I love reading but did not author:

> **Posted by Associate Director Susan B. Felch, b.s. on January 28, 1999 at 01:31:56:**
> In Reply to: Re: I LIKE DICK TOO posted by Vice Prez George A. Zdasiuk on January 27, 1999 at 02:32:31:
> I LUV DICK!!! I LUV BOTH DICKS!!! IN FACT, CHUBBY, I GET TO FLY WITH THE BIG DICK!!! YOU ONLY GO WITH LIL DICK!!! SO THERE GEORGIE!!!

and

> **Posted by Susan B. Felch on February 25, 1999 at 13:57:48:**
> In Reply to: I LUV DICK MORE THAN SUE!!! posted by GEORGE ZDASIUK on February 23, 1999 at 02:14:36:
> No you don't George! No one loves Dick more than I.

Zdasiuk took Felch's fantasy a step further in his declaration:

"In another email ... I supposedly state "No one likes Dick more than I do. No one, not even you Sue" thereby implying that I am homosexual...."

in referring to the words in this Stock-Talk posting:

> **Posted by Vice Prez George A. Zdasiuk on January 27, 1999 at 02:32:31:**
> In Reply to: I LIKE DICK posted by Susan B. Felch on January 27, 1999 at 01:50:39:
> No one likes Dick more than I do. No one, not even you Sue.

Zdasiuk was apparently so troubled that a Web surfer would conclude he was a homosexual that he felt it necessary to voice his concern as a matter of record. When later questioned on November 11, 1999, about his revisited adolescent sexual insecurity he protested a bit too much:

FALCON: Are you in any way homophobic?
ZDASIUK: No.
FALCON: Have you ever made disparaging comments regarding people that you suspected to be homosexuals in or about the Ginzton

Research Lab?
ZDASIUK: Not that I'm aware of.
FALCON: Does that sound like something you would do?
ZDASIUK: I don't think so.

You don't think so? When deposed again on July 25, 2001 the ever-reticent Zdasiuk was even more confused:

FALCON: [A]re you claiming that it is a false statement that you were asked at a deposition whether you were homophobic or not?
ZDASIUK: I'm not claiming it was a false statement. I am claiming it is defamatory.
FALCON: Okay, and the basis for your claim that it was defamatory, in your mind, is?
ZDASIUK: The way the statement is made carries the implication that there is some reason to suspect that I was homophobic.

While Mary and I never implied Zdasiuk was homophobic in any posting, his preoccupation with sexual orientation, was in itself, fascinating. Not until February 13, 2002, was the matter resolved, when the same self-righteous judge who appeared to know so much about the origin of semen stains stated it was untrue "that George Zdasiuk is or was homophobic." But I think his, adding that Zdasiuk "has [not] stared at or regularly stares at female employee's breasts or chests in the course of his employment" didn't help the image of this Varian executive either.

I had vented, pure and simple. I told the truth or expressed my opinion in ways similar to my everyday speech. I had defamed no one, no less impersonated anyone. I did not then use anyone's name as an alias, other than my own. The more juvenile Stock-Talk postings seem no more harmful than the ones I so proudly did on Yahoo!. I admire the authors for poking fun at Felch and Zdasiuk. Stylistically different, I gleefully admit sharing a similar theme. I think I am more witty and direct, perhaps because I have had more interaction with the players involved.

> **Can the DICKS et Al Get it UP?** by: ah_michelangelo
> I certainly hope so, but judging by the performance of the stock I am less than optimistic.

This was another of my puerile Latin references to Varian Associates' Executive Vice Presidents: Dick Levy, Dick Aurelio, and Al Lauer. It was hard to resist exploiting a certain insinuation with alpha-males referring to themselves as Dick. Orrick would see it differently, and with the help of their rather dumb declarants raise the stakes far beyond what they may have imagined. The diminutive Levy and Aurelio were always called and signed their names Dick. While both men are short, one abnormally so, they were known as "Big Dick" and "Little Dick," a reference not to penis size, but to their presumed power position within Varian.

> FALCON: Have you ever heard any, oh, comments from any
> employees that referred to you as either Big Dick or Little Dick?
> AURELIO: No.

When I was an employee, I sometimes debated with my boss, Dave Hodul, which Dick was in fact larger. I revisited this theme in a few Yahoo! postings, but nothing compared to what I was accused of posting on Stock-Talk, and a far cry from what this SLAPP would later motivate me to post over the years to follow.

It was disappointing to see how easily Orrick was able to dupe Judge Whyte with this nonsense. Referring to postings, Whyte wrote "... identical on tone and diction to messages that Delfino has admitted authoring, included repeated use of the nickname 'Dick' for men named 'Richard'." Of course, that was before any evidence was presented, and I just loved proving this judge wrong.

> FALCON: And what first name do you use for Mr. Levy and Mr.
> Aurelio?
> McMAHON: Compound question.
> FELCH: I call both by the name Dick.
> FALCON: Do you know anybody that addresses them by first name
> using the -- using Richard?
> ...
> FELCH: No, I can't recall anyone.

Felch and Zdasiuk's twisted assertion that the Dick innuendo exclusively implied a sexual impropriety when appropriately phrased ("I like Dick") would motivate us to use it in literally hundreds of messages. It would be a hot topic throughout this whole lawsuit. Here, Mary in her February 9, 2000 deposition justifies her use of the "Dick" heteronym in Internet messages:

> LIBURT: Okay. Looking at the title of this message which says "Your Dick can't come," question mark, when you wrote that title, what did you mean to convey by your use of the word 'Dick'?
> DAY: It appears here that it's referring to the quote in which they are discussing Dick Aurelio.
> LIBURT: Okay. Can you tell me what you were intending to convey at the time that you wrote this?
> DAY: I'm guessing that it's in reference, that Dick Aurelio was delaying his deposition, or something to that effect.
> LIBURT: Do you have any recollection of what you intended to convey when you wrote "Your Dick can't come" at the time that you wrote this?
> DAY: I don't recall specifically.
> LIBURT: Okay.
> DAY: I can tell you what I think it means by the text there.
> LIBURT: Okay. Do you think that it has - do you think that the word "Dick" has two meanings, one of them being that Mr. Aurelio can't come to a deposition, and the other meaning being a reference to a penis?
> DAY: I don't see "penis" in the text.
> LIBURT: Please answer my question.
> DAY: I would say that other than Orrick's obsession with sex, it's referring to Dick Aurelio, which is his first name, as long as I have known the man.
> LIBURT: Okay. Did you intend this message to be a reference to a penis as well?
> DAY: No, I did not.
> LIBURT: Okay. Have you ever heard the word "Dick" used to describe somebody in an un-flattering manner similar to words like "jerk" or "nasty person," something like that?
> DAY: I have heard "dickhead."
> ...
> LIBURT: Okay. So have you ever heard anybody refer to someone as a "Dick" with some sort of derogatory meaning?
> DAY: Well, I guess a detective is often known as a Dick, right? Dick Tracy.
> LIBURT: Have you ever heard anyone use the word "Dick" to refer to someone in a derogatory sense?

DAY: I can't recall a specific time.

LIBURT: Are you familiar with the word "Dick" is sometimes used to refer to someone in a derogatory way?

WIDMANN: Assumes facts not in evidence, calls for speculation.

DAY: I have never heard anyone say "Dick Aurelio" and meant that he was a derogatory statement. So when I am referring to Aurelio and his first name being Dick, I don't know if other people when they say Dick Aurelio and they are insulting him. I have not seen him react in that fashion that he was insulted when someone said "Dick Aurelio."

LIBURT: Okay. My question was more general than asking about Mr. Aurelio. I want to know if you are aware, however you became aware, that the word "Dick"' is sometimes used to describe people in a derogatory way.

DAY: I - it doesn't come into my repertoire. It's not a -

LIBURT: What do you mean, it doesn't come into your repertoire?

DAY: The people I associate with don't use that term in a derogatory fashion. As I said I called Dick Aurelio "Dick Aurelio" and Dick Levy "Dick Levy." My dad's name was Dick. I didn't insult him when I called him Dick, so - I hope I didn't.

...

LIBURT: What do you mean when you wrote "The CEO of MoBeta, Inc. is not a Dick"?

DAY: My name is not Dick.

LIBURT: That's the only meaning you intended?

DAY: I mean, that's - yeah, that seems to be an obvious.

WIDMANN: The record should reflect that the spelling of "Dick" is with initial cap "D-i-c-k," by the way.

LIBURT: Okay. Well, I didn't ask you whether it's obvious. I asked you what you intended. Was the only meaning that you intended to express was that the CEO of MoBeta's name is not Dick?

DAY: I can answer what I interpret this today, and that is that I'm the CEO of MoBeta, and my name is not capital D-i-c-k. And that's what the statement says, so I have no problem with that statement.

LIBURT: At the time that you wrote this, was that the only meaning that you intended?

DAY: As far as I can recall, that would be consistent with my - I don't know why I would change that, my name is not Dick. It's never been Dick. So I have no problem with that.

LIBURT: Okay. I don't believe your answer is responsive. What I want to know is, at the time - at the time that you wrote this, was the only meaning that you intended to convey that the name of the CEO of MoBeta, Inc. is not Dick?

DAY: That would make sense to me today.

LIBURT: Move to strike, non responsive. I'm not asking you about whether it makes sense to you today. I'm asking what your intent was when you wrote this. When you wrote this message, was the only meaning you intended to convey that the name of MoBeta's CEO is not Dick?

WIDMANN: It's been asked and answered. You can ask it one more time.

DAY: Based on my interpretation of this today, I would have to say that I was making the statement that my name is not Dick.

LIBURT: Do you -

DAY: Which it is not.

LIBURT: Do you have any recollection of what you intended to convey at the time that you wrote it?

DAY: I don't know what I was thinking October 26 at 10:03 Eastern Standard Time, if that's the correct time.

LIBURT: Okay. So at that time, you don't recall what you intended to convey when you wrote this?

DAY: My guess is that I was stating my name is not Dick, which is what I would say today, probably I said it in October, that my name wasn't Dick.

LIBURT: I'm not asking for your guess, I'm asking for your recollection.

DAY: I can't recall when I made this specific posting what my intent was.

Another truth I was preenjoined from expressing was Felch and Zdasiuk's lack of veracity. Knowing them well, I expressed my opinion about her in one of my very early postings and made no bones about who I was:

---

ms. susan b felch is going away by: ah_michelangelo

First the good news: I hear Felch is going away, relocating several miles away from what's left of the Palo Alto bldgs. It is my hope she will then be able to carpool with George Zdasiuk, who is also relocating.

Now the bad news: I also hear she won't be leaving Palo Alto for 6 months. It is my concern that she will continue to disrupt the Company during this time. In my experience, I believe she has acted as a manipulative liar, or worse yet, as a neurotic hallucinator. Hopefully, the Company will resolve which characterization is correct before the stock drops further.

By the way, this post is for those who are bothered by anonymity. You know who I am, let's see who you are. I'm waiting...

A FAT LIAR

In her September 10, 1999 declaration Felch disagreed:

> "I am not a chronic liar, a manipulative liar, or a liar at all. I value and respect the truth, and hold myself to a high standard of truthfulness. I speak the truth as a rule even when doing so may be difficult. I am truthful in all my personal and professional relationships, including with my family, my friends, my colleagues, and others."

Less than three months later on the 1st of December:

> FALCON: On a truth scale of one to ten, one being completely untruthful and ten never telling a falsehood, white lie, where would you fall on that chart --
> ...
> FELCH: Do you mean that the nine would mean that I tell the truth 90 percent of the time? Or does nine mean almost never tells a lie, just even a little white lie? I mean, you have to define the scale.
> FALCON: Let's say that nine says almost always tells the truth, but an occasional white lie.
> McMAHON: Objection, vague, calls for speculation, incomplete hypothetical, overbroad. You can answer the question.
> FELCH: I would say that when it comes to matters at work, I'm very close to a ten. And probably general life, between a nine and a ten.
> FALCON: What's the most troublesome white lie or untruth that you've ever had to make?
> McMAHON: Objection, overbroad, vague, calls for speculation, foundation. You may answer the question.
> FELCH: I would rather not divulge details, because it involves personal family things, but small little things related to my children's habits that I may be telling my mother.

Felch was now by her own admission, a liar. Of course, no one always tells the truth, and it would be most annoying if they did. But only someone as far from reality as Felch would be smug enough to make such an absurd assertion, do it in a declaration, and immediately get caught on it in her deposition. Mother Theresa, she was not. But more amazing, as the lawsuit continued to drag on and the years passed, she showed no signs whatsoever of seeing herself for what she was – a fascist liar.

I was accused of having defamed both Felch and Zdasiuk in this Yahoo! posting when I described them as "chronic liars":

> **YES, some VARIAN Managers are dishonest!**
> by: ah_michelangelo
> Without question, Susan B. Felch, Manager of the Ion
> Implantation Laboratory in Palo Alto and Vice President
> George Zdasiuk of the Ginzton Technology Center are chronic
> LIARS. Company policies like annual salary reviews and so
> called fair treatment policies are enforced at the whim of the
> supervisor. Fictitious incidence of laboratory sabotage are
> perpetuated to justify incompetent work habits. Go to the
> stockholder meeting ask Executive Vice President what his
> Biosynergy operation actually does, when his Brachytherapy
> line will be competitive, when Varian Imaging will be
> profitable, etc. The answers are there if you are interested!

Before I posted that message, I distinctly remember looking up the word "chronic" in my *Merriam Webster* and finding it to mean "marked by long duration or frequent recurrence."

Zdasiuk, not to be outdone by his accomplice's effrontery, mimicked her falsity in his September 10, 1999 declaration:

"I am not a chronic liar or a liar at all. I value and respect the truth, and hold myself to a high standard of truthfulness. I speak the truth even when doing so may be difficult. I am truthful as a rule in all of my personal and professional relationships, including with my family, my friends, my colleagues, and others."

And when deposed for the second time:

FALCON: Mr. Zdasiuk, do you always, and I mean always, tell the truth?
ZDASIUK: I don't recall ever not having told the truth.
...
ZDASIUK: I repeat, I do not recall ever having lied.
...
ZDASIUK: I repeat, I do not recall ever having told a lie.
...
ZDASIUK: I can't give a digital answer to your question.
...
ZDASIUK: Simply because I stated to you earlier that I did not recall ever having told a lie.
FALCON: Does that mean it's a possibility that you told a lie but you just don't recall it as you sit here now?

ZDASIUK: I repeat, I do not recall ever having told a lie.
FALCON: Well, let me get specific. What do you mean you don't recall? Do you mean that you have absolutely no inclination in any of your thought processes that you have ever told a lie to anybody?
McMAHON: Objection. Argumentative. Asked and answered. Vague. Overbroad. You can answer the question.
ZDASIUK: I don't remember.

I would often tell my children that when you can't recall, it is often a way to avoid telling the truth about some misdeed. Zdasiuk brought my simple admonition to new heights. On those seemingly rare occasions when he could recall events, he all too often contradicted the testimony of other witnesses.

First, on March 8, 1999, an unprepared Zdasiuk claimed having conversations that his subordinates denied:

FALCON: ...apparently you've come to a conclusion that there were others at Varian that believe like you do that this was all done by Mr. Delfino.
LIBURT: ...Varian that the postings were by Mr. Delfino? And you mentioned Crisler, and Felch, and yourself so far?
ZDASIUK: Marcel Marc, Steve Henderson.

Vs.

FALCON: Did you ever tell George Zdasiuk that you thought Mike Delfino had posted messages on the internet?
HENDERSON: No.

Then on November 11, 1999 Zdasiuk said he had conversations with a boss who remembered differently:

FALCON: Who's the top guy in your company?
ZDASIUK: Richard Levy.
FALCON: And did you ever talk to Mr. Levy about this lawsuit?
ZDASIUK: Yes.

Vs.

FALCON: Did you ever tell Mr. Zdasiuk at any time that you thought the postings that you have been seeing on these chat room message boards were those of Mr. Delfino? By that I mean authored by Mr.

Delfino.
POPPE: Objection. Lacks foundation.
LEVY: I'll answer I don't recall discussing any of this with George Zdasiuk.

Why? Perhaps Zdasiuk never thought that nine months later his obscenely short boss would be deposed, no less videotaped:

FALCON: Any others?
ZDASIUK: Dick Levy.
FALCON: Who's he?
ZDASIUK: Actually, strike that. Strike that from the record. I am just trying.

Being truthful did not came easy to this Varian executive.

FALCON: Did you ever tell Jane Crisler that Susan Felch's lab sabotage was just like Jim Fair's lab sabotage?
ZDASIUK: Not that I recall.
FALCON: Did you tell Jane Crisler that Sue Felch's lab was sabotaged?
McMAHON: Objection. Vague as to time. Overbroad. You can answer.
ZDASIUK: I don't recall who told Jane Crisler that Sue Felch's lab was sabotaged.

Vs.

CRISLER: *"George Z. [Zdasiuk] call at 3:40. 6/2/98. Tuesday. Sue's exp has been sabotaged. Twisted. Vents gas. Lab is locked. Clearly sabotaged. Poured acid on one of the pipes. To vacuum system. Acid etched through and hole. Someone came in last night. Matt G. [Goeckner] reported it today at 3:10 p.m. He called Sue and he called me. Release of toxic gases into system from time to time. The air hoses would be cut. This is exactly the sort of thing that happened with Jim Fair. Repeat of same pattern. Clearly sabotaged. Hold meeting and give blow_by_blow what's happened in concern. If anybody knows anything, strangers in the building, risk/dangers."*

FALCON: Was there a meeting held?

CRISLER: Yes, there was. This is just the notes that I took prior to the meeting was the initial notification of the sabotage.

FALCON: And as I understand it, George Zdasiuk is being quoted here?

CRISLER: That is what it looks like.

The false-hearted Zdasiuk even contradicted Levy's recollection of the events occurring in their weekly staff meetings:

FALCON: Do you know of anybody that's taken any of these internet postings seriously? Seriously believing them to be true?

ZDASIUK: I have no way of reading somebody's mind.

FALCON: Who in upper management have you talked to?

ZDASIUK: The supervisor Dick Levy. It was mentioned at staff meetings. Tim Guertins, I believe were some. These sort of hallway discussions. Personally it has been brought up at Dick Levy's staff meetings.

FALCON: Who was present at the staff meeting?

ZDASIUK: His direct reports includes me and a number of other vice-presidents, our soon-to-be chief financial officer. His immediate staff.

Vs.

FALCON: Other than counsel, have you discussed this matter with anybody?

LEVY: My wife, maybe one or two other employees who happened to see it and asked me about it - what's going on.

FALCON: Does this come up in weekly meetings or strategy sessions or anything like that?

LEVY: No.

As the testimony of both witnesses suggests, Zdasiuk was not only fat, he was a fat liar:

FALCON: And what if anything did you do about that when he [Delfino] made references to you as a liar?

ZDASIUK: People call -- I mean.

LIBURT: The question is, what did you do, if anything?

ZDASIUK: I shrugged it off. People do this all the time to managers. Call them liars ...

Really, I didn't know that. Felch and Zdasiuk had the distinction of being the first managers I ever called liars, and that was only because they turned it into such an art form. They didn't just distort the truth; they created untruths and continued to perpetuate them even when proven to be a lie – chronic. Perhaps lying was so pervasive at Varian that even the CEO didn't know what is the truth. More than once, Levy's testimony left us all speechless:

> FALCON: And did you ever observe Mr. Mike Delfino engage in that conduct towards Sue Felch?
> POPPE: Objection. Vague.
> LEVY: No. I was never in that building. I don't even know where Sue Felch's office is.

Unless impersonated, Levy interacted with us in the GRC building at meetings and laboratory demonstrations over the years. He had in fact visited me in my office which was next to Felch's. Much to my dismay, we even used a GRC company restroom together. Moreover, Mary and I worked in the GRC building. So in what Varian building did this gnome imagine this "intimate encounter?"

> "Two things. On one occasion, I walked into an instrument lab or a semi-conductor lab and they [Delfino & DAY] were sitting head to head and knee-to-knee having a very, very private conversation. it appeared to me it did not look like a business meeting...."

In marked contrast to the sentiment expressed in this Stock-Talk posting that Orrick attributed to me, I never viewed Felch or Zdasiuk as cunning or clever and in my opinion, the Dicks have long fooled themselves about the whole lawsuit:

> **Posted by Director GEORGE ZDASIUK on January 28, 1999 at 20:33:13:**
> In Reply to: Re: Three Varians are better than One posted by ernesto on November 30, 1998 at 02:09:33:
> Susan Felch and I are not the most talented employees at Varian, but we are the most devious. Some people think we are sick when in reality we are very, ver clever. Fooled the Dicks didn't we.

Ten months into the Varian SLAPP lawsuit, Levy's December 15, 1999 testimony established him as a bigger fool than I surmise "ernesto" might have ever imagined:

> FALCON: Okay. Are you aware that Varian Medical Systems is a plaintiff in this lawsuit?
> LEVY: I was informed of that today.

At the March 15, 1999 Superior Court preliminary injunction hearing, Judge Gallagher had refused to issue an harassment order against me. Harassment would have meant that my postings had served no useful purpose. She did, however, keep Judge Herlihy's TRO in effect until she decided on the injunction itself. After all, it was an issue of free speech that even the Canadian born Zdasiuk seemed aware of that when first deposed back on March 8, 1999:

> "I was told that the Internet boards are a freedom of speech issue and that there is nothing much that could be done."

Two weeks later on March 25, while Judge Gallagher was deliberating, Glynn moved the case to Federal Court based on federal question jurisdiction, i.e., the Lanham Act Claim. Federal Court was always a far less crowded affair than I experienced in either of the State Court buildings. It was still quite hectic, and the presence of Federal Marshals gave it that special movie set appearance. The judge assigned my case, the soft-spoken Honorable Ronald M. Whyte, moved ever so slowly. First, on April 16, he extended the TRO. Then, on June 21, 1999, after what seemed like years of Glynn and I strategizing, he granted the "Order Granting Plaintiffs' Motion for Preliminary Injunction."[38]

---

[38]"Plaintiff's motion for a preliminary injunction was heard on Jun 11, 1999. The court has read the moving and responding papers and heard oral argument of counsel.... the court grants plaintiffs' motion....

A party seeking a preliminary injunction may establish its entitlement to equitable relief by showing either (1) a combination of probable success on the merits and the possibility of irreparable injury, or (2) serious questions as to these matters and that the balance of hardships tips sharply in its favor....

Defendant does not dispute that many of the messages that were posted on the various bulletin boards would constitute violations of unfair business practices and represent invasions of plaintiffs' privacy rights.... defendant primarily contends that plaintiffs cannot prove that defendant posted the alleged defamatory and harassing messages.... defendant admits to posting 60 messages on the Yahoo! bulletin board, he denies posting messages on the Stock-Talk board, impersonating any Varian employees, or posting messages under certain aliases.... messages that defendant admits to posting reveal a pattern of abuse directed at plaintiffs Felch and Zdasiuk and repeatedly discuss the poor performance of Varian and its stock price.... similar in theme and content to the messages posted on the Stock-Talk bulletin board and the messages posted by the person impersonating Felch and Zdasiuk.... court is permitted to draw an adverse inference against defendant due to his assertion of his Fifth Amendment privilege throughout discovery... in light of the postings that defendant admits he authored and his assertion of the Fifth Amendment privilege, the court finds that plaintiffs have established a strong likelihood that they can prove that defendant posted the alleged defamatory and harassing messages and that they will succeed on the merits of their claims.... court finds that the continued posting of allegedly false materials designed to harass and defame plaintiffs and effect Varian's stock price would constitute irreparable injury.

Defendant also argues that plaintiffs' motion for preliminary injunction should be denied due to the doctrine of laches. Defendant appears to contend that plaintiffs' delay of five months before filing their lawsuit prevents them from arguing that they will suffer irreparable injuries.... court observes that the complexities involved in tracing the source of internet bulletin board postings, especially when the author uses various aliases, would necessarily delay bringing action.... plaintiffs argue that the number and severity of the postings escalated in the months just before plaintiffs filed their complaint.... court finds that plaintiffs are not estopped from pursuing a preliminary injunction based on the doctrine of laches.

The court need not address defendant's objection to the evidence submitted in conjunction with plaintiff's motion, since the court primarily relied upon the messages that defendant admits to authoring ...

The court did not consider the contents of defendant's declaration, except for his admission of postings, since he asserted his Fifth Amendment privilege and refused to meaningfully respond to plaintiffs' discovery.... after plaintiffs have had an opportunity to perform discovery in light of defendant's recent waiver, defendant can seek reconsideration or modification of the preliminary injunction.... the court did not consider the evidence offered in support of plaintiffs' petition for an order to show cause regarding criminal contempt proceedings and the proffer submitted in support of plaintiffs' motion to permit live testimony at the preliminary injunction hearing. Plaintiffs can seek modification of the preliminary injunction and can offer such evidence after defendant has had reasonable opportunity to review it....

The court finds that the balance of hardships greatly favors issuing the preliminary injunction. Defendant would suffer little or no hardship if required to post messages regarding Varian under one alias and if he is enjoined from impersonating Varian employees and from publishing false and misleading information about the individual plaintiffs and Varian.... plaintiffs would continue to face serious irreparable injuries if the posting of such information is not enjoined....

The court finds that defendant is not entitled to First Amendment protections for false statements of fact or defamatory materials.... to the extent that his speech is deemed commercial, defendant does not enjoy First Amendment privileges over commercial messages that do not accurately inform the public of the nature of a business' activities.... the reasonable manner restrictions placed on defendant's postings do not violate First Amendment free speech rights.

The court finds that plaintiffs are likely to prevail on the merits, that they may suffer irreparable harm ... balance of the hardships favors plaintiffs, a preliminary injunction is hereby issued against defendant, his officers, agents, servants, employees, attorneys, and those in active concert or participation with him who receive actual notice of this order by personal service or otherwise, until trial, from:

(1) Impersonating, by name or otherwise, Kevin Felch or any Varian employee, manager, or executive, including but not limited to, Susan B. Felch, George Zdasiuk, Jane Crisler, Ronald Powell, Jim Fair, and/or their families;
(2) Posting on, or e-mailing to, any internet message board, chat room, stockpage or any other similar publicly accessible internet posting page or location (including but not limited to any Yahoo or Stock-Talk page), any e-mails or electronic messages of any kind defaming or presenting knowingly false information about Varian or any Varian employee, including, but not limited to, Susan B. Felch, George Zdasiuk, Jane Crisler, Ronald Powell, Jim Fair and/or their families, and including, but not limited to, statements substantially similar to or implying the following:

(a) That Susan B. Felch is having or has had a sexual affair with George Zdasiuk, Richard Aurelio, Dick Levy, or any other Varian executive or employee;

A United States Judge had taken away my First Amendment privileges using a spurious Lanham Act claim as justification. I found Judge Whyte not only unfair, but also downright oppressive, especially since unlike Judge Herlihy, he had the time and the

---

(b) That Kevin Felch is having or has had an extramarital affair with any person;

(c) That Susan B. Felch or George Zdasiuk is a liar;

(d) That Susan B. Felch is neurotic, insane, or crazy;

(e) That Susan B. Felch hallucinates or imagines voices, faces, or gestures;

(f) That George Zdasiuk is a non-technical person;

(g) That George Zdasiuk is overweight:

(h) That nobody at Varian Associates, Inc. and/or any of its successor companies is working; and

(i) That defendant Michelangelo Delfino is a current Varian employee;

(3) Telephoning, faxing, mailing, or otherwise sending any letter or other form of communication for any purpose to Susan B. Felch or George Zdasiuk;

(4) Using any pseudonym or e-mail address to discuss, in any way, any aspect of Varian's business, stock price, or employees on the internet, except that a pseudonym may be used after identifying the pseudonym to plaintiff's counsel and the court in writing;

(5) Destroying, deleting, erasing, altering, changing, obfuscating, eliminating, wiping, formatting, or otherwise tampering with, and from instructing or asking any other person to destroy, delete, erase, alter, change, obfuscate, eliminate, wipe, format, or otherwise tamper with, any data or information contained on any and all computers, computer peripherals and accessories, computer hardware and software, floppy disks, hard drives, back-up tapes, ZIP drives, compact disks, and other electronic storage media owned, operated, used, possessed, worked on, or utilized by Michelangelo Delfino or Mary E. Day;

(6) Conspiring with, encouraging, requesting, or otherwise contacting others to engage in any of the actions specified in this order under paragraphs (1) - (5) above.

This order should not be construed as enjoining defendant from expressing his opinion, negative or otherwise, about Varian, its management or employees.... as a condition of this preliminary injunction, plaintiffs shall give security within five (5) days of this order in the amount of $10,000 for the payment of such costs and damages as may be suffered by defendant if he is found to have been wrongfully enjoined."

resources to properly read and understand the consequences of the constraints the injunction imposed. How could I be expected to use a computer and not format or change or erase a floppy disk? And if I asked someone to do any of these things for me, were they then part of some conspiracy? And all because of bogus criminal accusations, corporate lies that forced me to invoke my Fifth Amendment privilege and not defend myself.

Listening to my attorney's advice, I continued not to post during this most difficult period. And I tried to ignore what was happening behind the scenes. I felt like an American trapped in a foreign land without a passport. With Mary I continued to try and make MoBeta, Inc. succeed, but all this legalese was distracting When I would finally resume posting, I would never stop again.

- 5 -

KINKO'S AND A BAD COPY

I continued to backspace using my computer despite risking a keystroke being construed by Orrick as a possible violation of Whyte's preliminary injunction. At least I was trying to get some work done. My temporary absence as a message board poster did not end the SLAPP and it did not stop others from expressing their opinion about the company's many problems. Aside from a few very close friends I did not yet tell anyone about the lawsuit. For one thing, I did not want to inadvertently involve anyone else as a Doe. Nonetheless, postings continued on Yahoo! VAR that were just as critical of Varian mismanagement as ever:

> **FSU: Compensational excellence III.** by: Giveemdx
> Probably because O'Rourke cashed in a few more thousand
> shares in preparation for the 200,000 new options he will grant
> himself on April 2. This is called "compensational excellence
> III". ("Compensational excellence II" is the $7 million
> severance package he is awarding himself in exchange for his
> assuming the less demanding position of COB of SEB.)
> Giveem dx dx dx,
> Giveem dx dx dx,
> Giveem dx, giveem dx, giveem dx, where?

While O'Rourke remained the prime target of the VAR message board posters, it was always refreshing to see an occasional message reference Zdasiuk or Felch's incompetence or the more frequent appearance of an alias that Orrick had repeatedly said in their complaint was me, or someone supposedly conspiring

114

with me. And it was even more delightful to see new Yahoo!
aliases appear that I would be accused of hiding behind:

Outrageous compensation. by: gusdusted
Over $31,000,000 paid out to the top 4 execs in the past 3
years for a company with sales of $1.4 b is unbelievable. I
hope the Board of Directors has good liability insurance. A
company like H-P which is 30 times as big does not pay its top
execs like this. I will not put money into this company as long
as it retains this Board. Who are these people? What world do
they live in?

DON'T BUY THIS STOCK by: dutchjo
THE REASON FOR THE THREE WAY SPLIT IS THAT
NOW THE BOARD AND IT'S MANEGERS WILL BE
ABLE TO MILK THREE CO. DRY, INSTEAD OF
ONE.SAME OLD PEOPLE, SAME OLD COW.JUST LOOK
AT THEIR SALARIES AND LOOK AT THEIR
RECORD.OLD COW DIVIDED BY THREE EQUALS BAD
MEAT.CHEW ON THAT BEFORE YOU BUY.NO
WONDER THE STOCK DID NOT MOVE ON THE
BARRON'S ARTICLE.

Then on March 10, 1999, a posting appeared on Stock-Talk
VAR, the first on that board since the lawsuit was filed. Three days
later, two more messages followed, this being my favorite:

**Posted by SUSAN B. FELCH on March 13, 1999 at
15:10:47:**
In Reply to: poison postings posted by investor on February
23, 1999 at 08:59:07:
DICK IS MY LIFE. HASNT ALWAYS BEEN THAT WAY.
ACTUALLY MY LIFE CENTERS AROUND TWO DICKS.
OH HERE COME THOSE VOICES. IS THAT YOU
GEORGE? GOTTA GO.

The SLAPP was not working. Varian had failed to censor the
message boards. Orrick tried a new twist based on our regular use
of Kinko's computer rental stations, a fact first disclosed by me
when the SLAPP started. For some time now and for a variety of

reasons I visited Kinko's stores in neighboring Mountain View, Cupertino and Palo Alto. I explained why on December 14, 1999:

> LIBURT: Taking all of those Kinko's stores together, can you list for me the different activities that you have done in those Kinko's in 1999?
> DELFINO: Sure, ... Fed Express drop-off and, ... of course, copying and, ... buying stuff, ... especially in the May time frame ... the web sites, was the creation of the Web pages and differences -- on different machines at PC versus a Mac... accessing the Internet...look up basketball scores, eBay -- in particular, JPG, I think it's what we call it. Images that are generated on a PC would not be view able on our Mac for reasons that aren't clear...zip drive or floppy, and looking at that and loading the image, and, in particular, things to do with art.
> LIBURT: Okay. May I interrupt you for a moment?
> DELFINO: Sure.
> LIBURT: I understand you're not done. I want to ask you one question right now. Have you ever posted a message on any Internet message board from a Kinko's computer?
> DELFINO: No.

Two years later we discovered that Varian had us placed under surveillance[39] even before filing the SLAPP. Although Glynn was sufficiently paranoid to periodically remind us how easy and inexpensive it was for Varian to spy on us, unfortunately, the advice was taken all too lightly.

The Orrick was unable to connect me with certain Yahoo! postings that I denied doing or knowing anything about and with any Stock-Talk postings. Now, Orrick claimed I violated Whyte's April 16, 1999 temporary restraining order. They asserted I had impersonated Felch and Zdasiuk in a number of Internet postings. These alleged impersonations were made only on Stock-Talk, which unlike Yahoo!, does not require any kind of sign-in process and allows the user to enter a name, a subject, and a message, any of which may be as cryptic as an alphanumeric character, even a

---

[39]Tal Global, an International Security Management, Investigations and Consulting Corp., advertises itself as the largest investigative agency in Silicon Valley, California. Mr. Tal, the founder, served as a European based anti-terrorist security specialist for the Israeli government.

punctuation mark as innocuous as a period. But I never posted on the Stock-Talk VAR message board because it was removed prior to August 13, 1999. When I finally did post on Stock-Talk, I was forced to restrict myself to other companies. Orrick never cited any of more than 1000 Stock-Talk postings that I did author in any legal brief, perhaps because of the accompanying disclaimer:

> "**Warning**: Please read this disclaimer - Stock-Talk.com is an unmonitored free-for-all of un-restricted free speech. Much of the information presented here may prove to be total fabrication, rumor or hype. Do NOT make financial decisions based on any information contained in this forum without first checking with your licensed financial advisor. No effort has been made to determine the validity of any statement presented in this forum, nor has any effort been made to ensure that those posting here are who they say they are. Stock-Talk Partners reserves the right to remove (or not remove) any information it feels is disruptive to the operation of this forum. To see our full disclaimer, click on ..."

The Orrick, was only interested in Stock-Talk postings that were not mine. Even though the Stock-Talk VAR message board was long since removed and the postings had been accessible to the public for no more than three months total, Orrick was determined to destroy me, now going so far as to urge the court to put me in prison – for words on the Internet! They put together a rather convincing argument and as usual, filed it under seal:[40]

> "Based on the foregoing facts, Plaintiffs ask this Court to issue an order to show cause why Delfino and Day should not be held in criminal contempt. Plaintiffs hope that this Court, after a hearing, will put an end to Delfino's harassing and criminal behavior by punishing him with an appropriate prison sentence and fine.
>
> I declare under penalty of perjury under the laws of the United States of America that the foregoing is true and correct. Executed on June 11, 1999 at Menlo Park, California.
>
> Matthew H. Poppe."

---

[40]"Petition for Order to Show Cause Why Michelangelo Delfino and Mary E. Day Should Not be Held in Criminal Contempt for Violation of Order Dated April 16, 1999"

This overly zealous Orrick attorney, who we would hereafter come to refer to as "POOP," even have the audacity to include Mary, who was not yet named a defendant and not under any such court order, as a co-conspirator. Her attorney would later write the following in our defense:

> "... they must show that she acted in pursuit of a common plan or design to commit a tortuous act, actively took part in it, furthered it by cooperation or request and aide or encouragement to the wrongdoers or ratified and adopted the acts done for her benefit.... A Defendant in a conspiracy must share a common purpose with another person, not merely suspect or have knowledge of the other person's private purpose.... She must have united or cooperated with another in inflicting a wrong on the Plaintiffs....

> Mere knowledge by one party of what the other is doing is not sufficient concert to make her liable for the acts of the other since one person ordinarily owes no duty to take affirmative steps to interfere with another's activities in the absence of some special relationship.

> Thus, in seeking to impose liability on the co-conspirators as joint tortfeasors, it is essential that each Defendant charged with responsibility should have been proceeding tortuously, that is, with intent to commit a tort or with negligence, because one who innocently does an act that furthers the tortuous purpose of another is not acting in concert with him/her."

My wrongful act, according to Orrick, was willfully violating a court order and perjuring myself when at the time I denied ever posting on Stock-Talk. Judge Whyte wasted no time believing Orrick's plea, and on the 24th of June, without hearing a single word from either so-called conspirator, granted their request.[41]

---

[41]"On June 11, 1999, plaintiffs' filed a petition for an order to show cause ("OSC") why defendant Michelangelo Delfino and Mary E. Day should not be held in criminal contempt for violating this court's April 16, 1999 order extending the temporary restraining order issued by the Santa Clara County Superior Court. The court hereby refers the petition to the United States Attorney's Office to consider whether it wishes to present to the court an application for an OSC as to why Delfino and Day should not be held in contempt."

Criminal contempt is serious stuff and The Orrick smelt blood:

> "Plaintiffs have established a direct link between the May 5 posting and the Cupertino Kinko's store.... evidence demonstrated that (1) two Stock-Talk messages from March 13, 1999 that impersonated Felch were traced to the Cupertino Kinko's store, (2) on May 5, 1999, Delfino and Day were in the Cupertino Kinko's store when a third message was posted on Stock-Talk, and (3) the Stock-Talk messages were almost identical in tone and content to each other and to many of the messages that Delfino admitted posting on the Yahoo! message board for Varian ..."

Their argument was entirely developed by Poppe following his pre-subpoena raid on a Kinko's store in Cupertino on May 26. An Orrick paralegal, Jessica Niehaus, who according to Poppe, was there to identify Mary and me on a supposed May 5 video surveillance tape, accompanied him. However, Mary and I had never met either of them before.

The so-called "mountain of evidence," as Hermlé would annoyingly refer to over and over again would be immediately suspect as she and her SLAPP team would never establish a uniquely direct connection between the Stock-Talk postings and Mary or me. There was, in fact, no contiguous chain of Internet events connecting a posting with *any* computer, no less a person. Not until December 8, 1999, when Orrick deposed two Kinko's experts, Don Rollings and Ray Short, were Mary and I exculpated of any criminal wrongdoing.

First, the accuracy of the time stamp on the video was flawed, and not as claimed by Poppe in his OSC declaration:

> POPPE: Is it Kinko' policy that the time on the multiplexer should be changed on the day of the switch to or from daylight savings time?
> ROLLINGS: No it's not a policy. We would like it to be done, though. It's a guideline.
> POPPE: In your experience, is that guideline followed?
> ROLLINGS: Out of a thousand branches, about 50/50.
> POPPE: Okay, In the 50 where the guideline is not followed, what does that mean? It's never switched?
> ROLLINGS: Typically, it will be an hour off.
> ...

FALCON: In your experience in the diligence of each individual
store to reset their surveillance recorders to current time after a switch
either from daylight savings or savings to daylight has been about
50/50?
POPPE: Daylight to standard?
FALCON: Yes. Daylight to standard.
ROLLINGS: Yes.

Next, and not too surprisingly, both Rollings and Short
testified that they were unable to identify us in the Orrick
reproduced Kinko's videos, even though we were both sitting in
the same room with them and their attorney. At one point, Mary
quite comfortably redirected the deposition:

DAY: Can you tell tell whether he was again using floppy disks or
keyboards or whether the computer was --
SHORT: No, I can't. I speculate that he did begin or she -- I can't
even tell if it's a he or she, began working as his arms seemed to be
bent at the level of the desk but that's, again, speculation.

Poppe was not amused by Mary's venture as a barrister. He
was, in fact, not amused that whole day. First, it was never clear
how many video surveillance tapes Orrick had obtained from
Kinko's. Poppe made it clear that at least a half dozen original
video surveillance tapes were in his possession as of October 1999,
yet only two were proffered in support of his case:

"The full set of Kinko's videotapes in our possession is as follows:
videotapes from the Cupertino Kinko's store dated May 5, May 18,
and May 21, 1999; videotapes from the Mountain View Kinko's store
dated May 5, May 10, May 13, and May 18, 1999...."

Yet, there were no Stock-Talk postings on some of these dates, and
on all but two of the dated videos corresponding to Stock-Talk
postings, there was no Mary or Mike. Why were so many tapes
acquired in the first place and from only those two stores? How
many videos were actually viewed?

Orrick alone procured, edited, and copied the two Kinko's tapes
that were presented as evidence. Rollings, Kinko's security expert,

highlighted the Orrick problem when he testified: "Law enforcement of course has a chain of custody that they have. We have no chain of custody, and I have none on these tapes."

We would never view any original Kinko's tape because they required playing on a special machine to which we had no access. Incredibly, we were told Orrick was unable to purchase or rent one either. On first watching their May 5 videotape, I discovered that the date stamp abruptly changed to May 7 and then back again to May 5. No one, not even Rollings could explain this one when he testified: "I've never seen it before." Even Poppe, who secured the original tape and later supervised the editing and copying, was unable to explain this second date stamp on what was deemed a uniquely dated 24-hour, multiple camera video surveillance tape. There was no accounting for Orrick's disturbing "evidence." Nonetheless, this exculpatory flaw did not deter a heedless Judge Whyte from finding us in contempt.

One of the more humorous moments came when I was deposed on December 14, 1999 and asked questions about what I was viewing on Orrick's Kinko's tape as it was being played in a Federal Court House. As if impersonating the Keystone Cops, Poppe operating the VCR was supposed to bring his edited Kinko's videotape to the point at which someone, presumably me, entered the store as Liburt readied his next question:

> LIBURT: Yeah. Matt, can you please speed up to when the
> gentleman enters that we believe is Mr. Delfino?
> POPPE: He's in.
> LIBURT: Oh, he is? I missed it?
> ...
> DELFINO: I didn't catch it either, so don't feel bad.
> ...
> LIBURT: Have you -- Mr. Delfino, have you recognized anybody so
> far watching this tape?
> DELFINO: No.
> LIBURT: Okay.

I wasted no time exploiting this latest fault with Orrick's fabricated Kinko's video. That evening, I posted this Yahoo! VSEA message:

> **Orrick SLAPP attorneys were speechless** by: <u>ima_posta2</u>
> again as an alleged incriminating Kinko's 24 hour video
> surveillance tape was played that shows two non-sequential
> date stamps! And how does that happen? Duh!
> Then an Orrick SLAPP attorney was unable to recognize the
> alleged presence of a Defendant in another 'created' video - so
> where is he? Where is he hidding[sic]? Hello?
> DAMAGES? You betcha!

as my message to the world that I was being wronged. Nowhere else, other than the Internet, could I have such a voice.

Whyte, a former corporate lawyer and George Bush appointee, was enamored with the Orrick attorneys from the beginning. As Glynn would say, "He sees you as puerile ... he doesn't like you." He was unable to acknowledge that two publicly traded corporations represented by such a prestigious law firm could behave so unscrupulously. Whyte never scrutinized the "mountain of evidence." If I were trying to be deceitful, why didn't I simply make some effort to disguise myself, or use an Internet rental outlet without a surveillance system, or at least go to a Kinko's further away from my neighborhood?

On November 19, 1999, I was found in civil contempt for allegedly impersonating Felch: "Order Holding Delfino in Civil Contempt, Submitting Sanctions Motion, and Modifying Preliminary Injunction."[42]

---

[42]"Varian's motions for sanctions and civil contempt against Delfino were heard by the court on November 12, 1999.... the court holds Delfino in civil contempt, submits the sanctions motion for consideration at the close of trial, and modifies the preliminary injunction ....

At the hearing ...Varian displayed a videotape from the Kinko's store showing Delfino renting a computer, together with co-defendant Mary Day.... Varian has now produced affidavits from several Internet service providers that appear to establish that the message impersonating Felch was sent from a computer at the Kinko's store at the exact same time that Day and Delfino were renting a computer there.

Since the preliminary injunction issued, Delfino has continued to post hostile messages to Varian on the Internet. With regular frequency, Delfino has changed his username on the Yahoo! bulletin board, although he has always notified Varian's counsel of his intent to change his username. Delfino claims that the injunction only requires him to post under one username at any given time, while Varian contends that the injunction requires Delfino to use the same username for the duration of the preliminary injunction. Varian now moves to hold Delfino in civil contempt for his alleged violations of the preliminary injunction. Varian has also moved for sanctions ... based on the allegedly false declaration submitted by Delfino.

... the court held a hearing, at which Delfino was afforded the opportunity to present evidence and legal argument why he should not be held in contempt. (Delfino presented no new evidence at the hearing.) The court has thoroughly reviewed the evidence relating to the alleged May 5, 1999, Kinko's posting and hereby makes the following findings of fact, all of which are supported by clear and convincing evidence:

1. On May 5, 1999, Michelangelo Delfino was subject to a specific order of the court, namely the TRO originally issued by the Santa Clara Superior Court, which this court extended on April 16, 1999.
2. On May 5, 1999, the TRO contained certain definite prohibitions on Michelangelo Delfino's conduct, including a prohibition on online impersonation of Susan Felch.
3. On May 5, 1999, a security camera at Kinko's location in Cupertino was trained on the area of the store containing computers available for rental....
4. The security cameras were equipped with an accurate time/date stamp mechanism. Varian's ... (noting inspection of cameras).
5. In response to a subpoena from Varian, Kinko's produced video recordings that were taken by its security cameras on the morning of May 5, 1999....
6. The recording made by the camera trained on the computer area shows Delfino and Day entering the computer area at approximately 9:35 a.m. Pacific Daylight Time. The same recording shows Delfino and Day sitting at a computer terminal together until approximately 9:48 a.m., when they get up and leave the area under surveillance.
7. The recording made by the camera trained on the cash register shows Delfino and Day approaching the cashier and placing money on the counter at approximately 9:48 a.m. The cashier retrieves a single sheet of paper, which he briefly examines and then throws away. He then takes the money from Delfino and Day, who promptly leave the store. Delfino and Day do not appear to be carrying any papers.
8. Based on the recorded evidence, it is clear that Delfino and Day did not visit Kinko's to make photocopies or to print documents from the printer.
9. The sole purpose of their visit to Kinko's on the morning of May 5, 1999

was to use a computer for purposes other than printing documents.
10. At 12:46 p.m. Eastern Daylight Time, a message was posted to the
Stock-Talk computer bulletin board that read as follows:

> **Posted by SUSAN BENJAMIN FELCH on May 05, 1999
> at 12:46:34:**
> In Reply to Dicky Aurelio removed from Novellus Board!!!
> posted by Sue B Felch on December 01, 1998 at 20:35:52:
> OK SO NOW WHOS LAUGHING I MEAN WERE DOING
> ALOT BETTER THAN NOVELLUS I MEAN DICK WAS
> RIGHT ALL ALONG TO GET RID OF THAT BUSINESS
> AND KEEP ME BESIDES HE MADE ALOT OF MONEY
> OH FOR THAT MATTER SO DID I AND SO WHAT IF I
> DIDN'T DO SO WELL AT THE INTEL PRESENTATION I
> MEAN THEY'RE NOT BUYING FROM NOVELLUS
> EITHER SO THERE MIKE ITS NOT SO BAD THE
> PRESENTATION I GAVE I MEAN SO WHAT IF SO FEW
> PEOPLE SHOWED UP BY THE WAY DICK THINKS IM
> OK ESPECIALLY WHEN IM ALONE IN THE PLANE
> WITH HIM YOU KNOW BACK AND FORTH BACK AND
> FORTH HERE TO GLOUCSTER HERE TO GLOUCSTER
> BACK AND FORTH SOMETIMES I GO ON I JUST WISH
> I COULD STOP AND YOU KNOW I CAN BUT I WAS
> JUST GONNA SAY THAT INTEL WELL MAYBE I
> DON"T KNOW WHY WAS DICK REMOVED

11. Assuming that it was not written by Felch herself, this message is an
impersonation of Susan Felch, as it states, "Posted by Susan Benjamin
Felch."
12. Stock-Talk's records show that the message purporting to be from Susan
B. Felch was posted from Internet Protocol address 208.250.189.41....
13. IP address 208.250.189.41 is registered to the Kinko's location in
Cupertino....
14. The court takes judicial notice that Eastern Daylight Time is three hours
ahead of Pacific Daylight Time.
15. The Stock-talk message was posted at the same time that Delfino and
Day were in the Kinko's store.
16. The Stock-Talk message is identical on tone and diction to messages that
Delfino has admitted authoring, included repeated use of the nickname
"Dick" for men named "Richard".
17. Delfino has offered no credible evidence (admissible or otherwise) that
he and Day did not author the message in question. At best, his declarations

consist of bare denial and argument that other pieces of evidence that hypothetically might establish his posting of the message in question do not support such a finding. These arguments are inadequate in the face of the videotaped evidence.

18. The court therefore finds Delfino, in concert with Day, authored the Stock-Talk posting, which was an impersonation of Susan Felch on the Internet.

These facts establish, by clear and convincing evidence, a violation of a specific and definite order of the court. The court therefore holds that Delfino is in contempt of court.... the court has two goals: (1) to remedy the wrong caused by Delfino's contempt of this court's order, and (2) to coerce Delfino's future compliance with this court's orders. The contempt is therefore civil in nature.... Delfino shall pay Varian's costs, including attorney's fees, incurred in investigating Delfino's Kinko's posting.... reminds Delfino that this matter has already been referred to the United States Attorney's office for possible criminal prosecution, and notes that this order holding Delfino in civil contempt does not preclude future criminal prosecution....

Delfino's May 20, 1999 declaration statement that he did not impersonate Susan Felch appears to be entirely lacking in evidentiary support.... because, the court has just held Delfino in contempt, it would be more appropriate to consider the sanctions motion at the close of trial.... the likelihood that it will assess some sanction for the submission of a false declaration to the court.

The court's clear intent ... was to prevent Delfino from using multiple usernames on one bulletin board to create the false impression that multiple people were involved in Delfino's campaign of harassment against Varian and its employees. The language of the injunction was ambiguous, however, allowing Delfino to employ several usernames seriatum. The court now issues a modified injunction, which restricts Delfino to the use of one username, which he must maintain for the pendency of the preliminary injunction.... the court now amends the injunction to include Day by name.

...the court holds Delfino in contempt of court and orders him to pay Varian's costs incurred in investigating this contempt of court. Varian is to submit within fifteen (15) days an itemization of its costs supported by declaration and appropriate evidence. Delfino will have ten (10) days thereafter to respond to Varian's submission on costs... The court defers consideration of the motion for sanctions until the close of trial. The court will issue an amended injunction consistent with this order. Finally, the court will also forward a copy of this order to the U.S. Attorney's office for it consideration as it decides whether to institute criminal contempt charges based upon the previous referral."

Judge Whyte's civil contempt finding was just plain wrong. The three attorneys representing us at the hearing were all flabbergasted when later informed of his decision. Glynn confessed that he never imagined a finding of contempt, as the evidence, while at first overwhelming, was on inspection, inconclusive at best. When Kinko's was eventually deposed, Orrick's entire argument was simply destroyed. And the Stock-Talk depositions that took place in Jupiter, Florida on December 13, 1999 weren't useful either. Moreover, Orrick presented no witness who believed that Felch or Zdasiuk had in fact ever been impersonated. Yet, none of this dissuaded the court, and on April 3, 2000, Judge Whyte issued his "Order Granting Costs Against Michelangelo Delfino for Contempt of Court:"[43] I was ordered to pay $22,000 for his mistake.

Fortunately for me, the bill was not due until the "conclusion of this matter." This was far from realized, and so I was not required to make any payment. Was this judge actually making amends for his faulty contempt ruling, now seeing Orrick's "mountain of evidence" as just a valley of lies? On December 10, 2001, the entire matter was summarily dismissed by a California Superior Court Judge, who exclaimed in open court, "There is no Federal contempt," thus ending this painful stage.

The Orrick did not get the expected response. They were completely frustrated by our repeated denials of any involvement in the Stock-Talk postings. They had to establish us as liars first,

---

[43]"The court has received plaintiffs' itemization of costs pursuant to the court's order holding defendant Michelangelo Delfino in civil contempt of court. Plaintiffs claim $25,960.85 in costs attributable to their investigation of Delfino's responsibility for the May 5, 1999 Stock-Talk posting. They provide ample declarations, receipts, and billing records to substantiate these costs.

For his part, Delfino spends a great deal of time arguing that he should not have been held in contempt of court in the first place, and making accusations of misconduct against plaintiffs and their counsel....

The court therefore will deduct $4,019.11 from plaintiffs' itemized costs, resulting in a final award of costs in the amount of $21,941.74. Such costs shall be payable within thirty days of the conclusion of this matter...."

and Internet defamers second. Attempting to make this argument more convincing, The Orrick hired Dr. Stephen W. Melvin, a self-proclaimed computer expert. He was, according to his curriculum vitae, from "August, 1998 - present, a Court Appointed Expert, *Cadence v. Avant!* assisting Northern California Federal District Court Judge Ronald Whyte in understanding issues and technology relating to CAD design software and its alleged copyright infringement and trade secret misappropriation." So much for objectivity, I thought. Glynn thought it clever. Billing Varian $210/hr, Melvin attended the Kinko's deposition:

> "Mr. Rolling's testified that the times stamped on the video tapes are generally kept accurate and are adjusted for daylight saving time."

Perhaps he heard things a bit differently than the rest of us. Later, I am told, Melvin listened in on a speaker telephone to the Stock-Talk depositions. The now defunct, two-person Stock-Talk operation was deposed by Poppe and Glynn in Florida, while Mary and I waited to hear that the outcome was uneventful. This highly profitable, low-budget dot.com company had no firewall or authentication protocol, thereby making the identification of the message source ambiguous.

Now, it was Melvin's job to technically tie Mary and me to the Stock-Talk postings, using the supposedly incriminating Kinko's videos and related Internet evidence. Stock-Talk had surrendered copies of its Varian postings that were no longer accessible to the public, having removed the VAR board altogether. Four postings were in question. A May 5 posting was supposed to have originated from the Cupertino store at 9:46:34 PST. This is the time stamped on the Stock-Talk message, adjusted for the then three-hour time difference. A May 18 posting was at 15:28:19 PST, and the two May 21 postings were at 19:04:38 and 19:08:23, both PST and both supposed to have come from Mountain View.

Melvin provided a rather wordy legal report concluding:

> "... on May 5th, 1999, a user named "bud" used a machine named "Mac 2" for 11 minutes ... based on printed times of 8:37 and 8:47..."

on May 18, 1999 ... a user named "bud" used a machine named "Macintosh Workstation #1" for 11 minutes on that day. The time indicated is from 14:23 and 14:34 ... on May 21, 1999 ... a user named "bud" used a machine for 18 minutes on that day. The time indicated is from 17:54 and 18:12"

First problem: the user name was "bud" and the computer-user log times were consistently an hour before the alleged postings. And this was true in the two different Kinko's locations. How did Melvin explain this hour discrepancy?

"... a hand-written note which states '57 minutes behind actual time.' The hand-written note appears to be a calibration of the times on the Monthly Machine Summary."

Whose calibration and when was it done? Of course, such information was not addressed in his report.

Second problem: why only user records for Mac machines:

POPPE: How many computers are in the Mountain View store for customer use?
SHORT: Approximately 12.
POPPE: You say approximately. Is there some --
SHORT: Forgive me. I was not aware that I would need to know this information. As I mentioned, as a senior manager, I represent so many branches with differing numbers, I can't give you the exact number without looking it up. We rent access to both Macintosh-based computers and Windows-based computers in that branch. It is approximately an even number of both. And, as I recall the layout of the branch and the space available for rental computers, there is approximately, I would say, 10 to 12 computers, total, for -- for customer access.
POPPE: Your recollection would be that they're split about half and half, Macintosh versus Windows?
SHORT: Yes.

Periodically throughout 1999, I had rented both Mac and Windows machines at Kinko's. On September 24, I declared:

"I can't say whether I was in fact at a Kinko's on May 5, 1999 since I visit Kinko's regularly. I was especially likely to visit Kinko's in early May as MoBeta, Inc. was about to "publish" the MoBeta, Inc. web site on May 11. Ms. Day and I were also working on another (Original Art) web site and this particular site contained many "jpeg" pictures which we wanted to ensure were available to both Mac and PC buyers. Moreover, Kinko's has laser printers that will print higher quality images of artwork than the printer available at MoBeta, Inc. This is also important to the MoBeta web site development. I am a regular eBay participant, where I buy/sell paintings, antiques, etc. Apparently, if a "jpg" image is generated with a pc, I sometimes cannot get an image on MoBeta's Mac. So I rent time on a pc at Kinko's, sometimes printing out the images. I still do not understand technically why this happens, but it does. I would have to view this alleged videotape in order to ascertain what day I was at any Kinko's and which of the many possible activities I might have been engaged in on that day. None of those activities ever involved posting on the Stock-Talk message board for Varian Associates, Inc. web page. I didn't post on it; I didn't assist or aid anyone to post on it, nor did I ever witness Ms. Day or anyone else post on it...."

In general, I only restricted myself to the least expensive, the 20 cent-per-minute computer stations. Whenever I rented time on a computer at Kinko's, I had to enter a user name, or more properly, have a Kinko's employee do it.

POPPE: On Exhibit 4 there is a column for user I.D. I believe you testified that the user I.D. may be entered by the customer or by a Kinko's employee; is that correct?
SHORT: Correct. Kinko's instructions, which are sometimes followed, sometimes not followed, is to -- is to have the co-worker ask the customer what their name is, both first and last name, and enter that on behalf of the customer. As you can see from this log, and backed by my personal experience, most co-workers do not do that. They allow the customer to enter their name. As you can see from this log, most enter only their first name. Before we had the password restriction -- correction. Before we had the password requirement, co-workers -- customers could come in and enter their own name without co-worker involvement, and we found a lot of customers by the name of Mick I mouse, snoop I, dog wonder, all sorts of things. We don't find that today.
POPPE: When was the password requirement implemented?
SHORT: About a year and a half ago. To clarify, we don't find that abuse of the system today because of the employment of this password restriction. Customers are not likely to enter bogus names

right in front of a co-worker such as Mick I mouse or something. But, for example, mat, you could come in and say your name is Brian. I'm not going to check your I.D. I don't know if you're Brian or mat or whomever. If it seems like a realistic name, customers -- co-workers generally do not question.

I only used "Mike" or "MoBeta" as a user name at Kinko's. My choice depended on usage and was irrespective of whether or not Mary accompanied me.

Third problem: who appears on the Kinko's 24-hour videos? The Orrick had obtained at least 7 original videos, each with as many as 12 camera views, yet was able to show Mary and me in no more than one short sequence.

> "It is my opinion that either Mr. Delfino or Ms. Day, or both Mr. Delfino and Ms. Day, are personally responsible for two postings on May 21, 1999 to the Varian area of the Stock-Talk Web site."

Melvin's statement was somewhat entertaining. For one, Orrick never showed any May 21 Kinko's videotape. Refusing to explain its absence, one can only presume that they were unable to find anybody resembling either Mary or me on any tape other than Orrick's so-called May 5 videotape.

Fourth problem: what proves the Stock-Talk postings came from any Kinko's?

> "The information that machines at these two locations were responsible for posting these messages comes from logs of IP addresses on the Stock-Talk Web server and from connection logs from GTE, not based on any information recovered from the actual machines at Kinko's."

Here again, all Melvin had to do was presumably examine the computer that the Kinko's video showed as the alleged source of the Stock-Talk postings. But The Orrick never subpoenaed any such computer. Why?

We all knew, of course, that having the computer hard drive examined would in no way guarantee the presence of relevant information like, cookies. In fact, their likely absence would then be viewed as exculpatory, something Orrick could ill afford. How ironic to see the same Orrick, who steadfastly accused Mary of destroying evidence because she donated *her* computer to Goodwill, caught in their own web of deceit.

So who is this "bud"? The third of the 60 Yahoo! VAR postings I did and signed MD, very specifically referred to my former colleague Dr. Bud Buttrill who was suddenly and quite inexplicably terminated from Varian's GRC:

> **GARY VIRSHUP** by: <u>MANUFORTE</u>
> Mr. Virshup,
> Please stop making disparaging remarks behind my back. First, I am told, you tell my former colleagues at Varian, Salt Lake City that I was hoping to get laid off. Now, I am told you are telling my former coworkers in Palo Alto that I should not be on Varian premises. Why my interaction with Varian and/or Novellus employees would bother you is especially troublesome. Should I assume that you are singing me out on your own volition or is the Company encouraging your behavior? Are you doing this to other former employees, like Bud Buttrill for example? Rest assured, Mr. Virshup, you will most certainly get the opportunity to explain yourself. Sincerely, MD

Was this the "bud" in question, or was it Gary Virshup, a weasel-like, overly ambitious computer savvy former coworker who reported to Zdasiuk, now inclined to give The Orrick some extra assistance? None of us in GRC knew why Buttrill was fired except that he was an outspoken critique of Varian Associates management, and O'Rourke, the CEO, in particular. His familiarity with message boards coupled with his displeasure of the Varian Board of Directors and the poor stock price performance was so pronounced that I was convinced he was the "Giveemdx" alias. So convinced, I replied to him as "bud" in several more of my 60 Yahoo! postings.

Again, the credibility of Orrick's case came into question. Almost two weeks after the trial was to begin, Poppe apparently realized that two critical depositions had been neglected despite Judge Whyte's contempt ruling based on "clear and convincing evidence." Both of these crucial depositions were essential to demonstrate a contiguous Internet path from Kinko's to the alleged impersonating Stock-Talk postings. Magistrate Trumbull did not buy Poppe's pleas, and on March 23, 2000, issued this "Order Denying Motion for Relief from Scheduling Order."[44]

Found guilty of contempt without ever being allowed to speak in court is un-American. Whyte simply listened to Orrick's false and deliberately incomplete arguments, questionably produced affidavits, and edited videotape. Compounding his irresponsible ruling, he modified the preliminary injunction[45] on November 19,

---

[44]"On February 25, 2000, Plaintiff filed a Motion for Relief from the Scheduling Order to Take Telephonic Depositions of Third Parties UUNet Technologies and GTE Corporation. Defendants opposed the motion. Having reviewed the papers filed by the parties, the court finds it appropriate to issue a ruling without oral argument....

IT IS HEREBY ORDERED that Plaintiffs' motion is DENIED....

Plaintiff fails to establish good cause for leave to take post-discovery depositions of Mr. Marino and Mr. Lebredo. Plaintiff argues that these two witnesses had "indicated their willingness" to travel to California for trial, but that later their employers would not allow it. Plaintiff was well aware of witnesses' employment status when it made the decision to forego deposing them. Yet it did not bother to confirm, before the close of discovery, whether or not their employers would allow them to take time off to attend the trial....

Plaintiff contends that decided not to depose the two witnesses in order to avoid "considerable expense." However, Plaintiff admits it envisions only a one or two hour deposition for each witness. Given the witnesses' willingness to voluntarily travel to California, it would have involved little added expense to depose them in California during discovery. The travel costs would be the same either way - whether they traveled here for trial or for deposition. Thus, deposing these witnesses would not have put any significant burden on Plaintiff."

[45]"A modified preliminary injunction superseding the injunction filed by the court on June 21, 1999, is hereby issued against defendants Michelangelo Delfino and Mary E. Day, their officers, agents ...

(4) Using any pseudonym or e-mail address to discuss, in any way, any aspect of Varian's business, stock price, or employees on the Internet, except that each defendant may use only one pseudonym for the duration of this injunction. Each defendant is specifically enjoined from changing his or her pseudonym...."

1999, to include Mary, thereby violating her Constitutional rights too.

I often consider the evening that Mary and I were informed of the contempt ruling to be the turning point in the case. Not ten minutes after getting a copy of Whyte's order faxed over from Glynn, I got an afternoon phone call from Craig Anderson, a reporter with the *San Francisco Daily Journal*. Having attended the court hearing, he was seemingly delighted with the ruling and wanted me to comment on the contempt order for another story. He had done a front-page story on us back on November 12, entitled "Web Guerillas," in which he painted us in a less than favorable light. Describing me as "unfazed," I responded to his inquiry, "We're still in a position to fight that [ruling] and prove our innocence." "We put on no evidence," "I don't think Judge Whyte has heard what I've got to say."

Less than convinced, Anderson wrote "... a victory for Varian Medical Systems against its World Wide Web antagonist, Michelangelo Delfino ..." and quoting Hermle, "The company incurred significant costs, all to track down somebody who was sneaking around violating court orders and then lying about it." It was not a pleasant night. Our personal life was suffering. News like this was certainly not conducive to love making.

On December 6, 1999, Poppe fired off this plaintive letter to Judge Whyte:

> "At the civil contempt hearing on November 12, 1999, you instructed the parties to attend a second mediation session. The plaintiffs and Mr. Delfino had attended a prior, unfruitful settlement conference with Magistrate Judge Infante on August 12, 1999. On behalf of the plaintiffs, we expressed a reluctance to expend time and money on a second mediation session due to Mr. Delfino's expressed unwillingness to compromise. However, Mr. Delfino's counsel claimed that further mediation would be worthwhile because "the battlefield has changed." You then ordered us to mediate, with the costs to be split among the parties (1/3 - 1/3 - 1/3) unless one of the parties failed to mediate in good faith.
>
> Based on recent statements made by Mr. Delfino in the press and on the Internet, we ask the Court to reconsider its mediation order. A November 26 article in the San Francisco Daily Journal ... And while

[Judge] Whyte urged both sides to settle the case during the Nov. 12 hearing, Delfino ruled that out. "There will be no settlement conference," he said. "We are not interested in pursuing that."

A copy of the article is enclosed with this letter. Mr. Delfino also continues to post messages proclaiming his intention to post "forever and ever" and "till the day that I die (exactly how I'm quoted in the news)." Copies of two of these messages ... are also enclosed.

It is clear from these statements that further mediation attempts would be futile. We therefore ask that the Court withdraw its mediation order. At a minimum, we ask for an order providing that any party that fails to mediate in good faith must pay the attorney's fees of the other parties in addition to the costs of the mediation."

I always rejected the notion of a free speech compromise and demanded a jury trial as the only acceptable resolution. On August 5, 1999, Glynn translated my need for American justice into a characteristically more American demand for money:

"Defendant, by way of his counterclaim to be filed, seeks past wage losses and benefits estimated at $70,000; future wage and benefit losses estimated at $500,000; pain, suffering, and emotion distress damages of $500,000; and punitive damages of $1,000,000. Dr. Delfino also seeks recovery of his costs and attorneys' fees...."

A so-called settlement conference that August 1999 with Magistrate Judge Edward A. Infante in the Federal Courthouse in San Jose was another one of those unexpected turning points. It became a truly inspiring moment as this slight man inadvertently became, for me, an anti-SLAPP motivational speaker extraordinaire. Tom Kotoske memorialized the event:

"The settlement conference occurred on the morning of August 12, 1999 before Federal Magistrate Judge Edward Infante. I was present with Glynn Falcon, as well as Mike Delfino and Mary Day. The regular defense counsel were present. The conference proceeded and the Judge expressed despair as the parties were too far apart for any attempts at settlement.

The conversations went round and round and got nowhere. Ultimately, the Judge called Delfino into his chambers and explained to him that he was on a course of financial destruction. He told him that he could probably lose the case. If he lost he could probably be liable for attorney fees, court costs in astronomical sums. On the criminal referral for contempt of the preliminary injunction, he faces the possibility of a federal prosecution by the US attorney's office and maybe some jail time.

Delfino on the other hand, very calmly, told the Judge that he didn't think that he was right. He told the judge that no matter what the Judge says he's going forward with the case. He finds that it is a matter of integrity and principle with him and that Varian is not going to grind him down with an eye towards stealing his patent from him.

The Judge looked quite astounded and abruptly ended the conference and says: "March on to your drummer Mr. Delfino.""

Outside Infante's chambers, I told Mary that perhaps I had made a mistake even though I felt wonderful. A few minutes later Glynn and Tom appeared. Tom shook my hand, and said, "Let's go get the bastards." I said to Glynn, who was still shaking his head in disbelief that I wanted to post. And I said that I wanted to start immediately. No offense to his considerable legal skills, but our resources were just no match for Orrick and its two corporate plaintiffs. Glynn reluctantly agreed to allow me to begin posting the next day, as soon as he alerted the court and Orrick of my alias, in accordance with Whyte's order. All too excited, I told him I was ready and my alias would be "stents4me2". Tom, chuckling, warned me to limit my postings to generalities about Varian and not mention any names, at least for now. Glynn asked that I email him a sample posting before it hit the Web.

Mary, who was then pro per,[46] did not need anyone's approval to post. When she exclaimed her intent to begin, both Glynn and Tom smirked. Whyte had made it clear he would not allow either of them to represent her because it would be a conflict of interest.

However, Mary's tenure in pro per was short lived and beginning on August 20, 1999, she was represented by Randall Widmann, a pleasantly plump, soft-spoken Palo Alto attorney. Always impeccably dressed and meticulously organized, Randy was a long-time colleague of both Glynn and Tom.

August 13, 1999 was one of those special days. It marked Mary's first day as a poster and my return to the Internet with the

---

[46]To represent ones self in court without assistance of an attorney.

debut of my 61st posting. It was fun for us and the beginning of a nightmare for the Varian plaintiffs and their Orrick attorneys. In no time at all, 60 postings by me alone became literally thousands of postings with two very distinct authors with very similar motivation. No longer content to post on the Varian Yahoo! financial message board alone, my words began to appear on other Yahoo! company boards, and other message boards like those operated by Raging-Bull, Motley Fool, and Silicon Investor, actually any board that could be found. Non-investor related message boards like the Yahoo! JohnDoes Club and FindLaw were posted on too. Not a day went by, that both of us did not post something about the Varian plaintiffs and the SLAPP. Admittedly, Mary had a bit more fun because, like everyone else on the Internet, she was able to use an unlimited number of aliases such as "stents4me2", "post_like_a_bunny", "maceliza", "nitemayor", and "yamdayo". However, unlike me, Orrick had no idea what her aliases were, and so she could use any or all of them as she chose. Not until November 19, 1999, when unlawfully restricted by the same injunction, did Mary share my single alias restriction.

As time passed, the inability of the SLAPP to stop us from posting messages about the lawsuit on the Internet, day in and day out, became ever more apparent. Intentionally or otherwise, Orrick was motivating us to post and to further raise the stakes in this war without compromise. Mary and I couldn't wait to oblige them, never intending to disappoint fascism. Poppe was Poppe.[47]

"Delfino engaged in an egregious course of underhanded conduct in violation of the Court's authority and orders throughout the pendency of this litigation. First, immediately after receiving notice of the TRO application, Delfino and/or his girlfriend Mary Day disposed of the computer from which the e-mails had been spent, despite a provision in the TRO issued by the superior Court prohibiting such destruction of evidence by Delfino or people acting in concert with him.

After disposing of the computer, Delfino continued to post, despite the TRO. In the most egregious and undisputed incident, Delfino

---

[47]"Plaintiffs' Notice of Motion and Motion for Sanctions Against Michelangelo Delfino," filed September 10, 1999.

went into Kinkos on May 5, 1999 with Mary Day. He then rented a computer and posted another e-mail impersonating Sue Felch....

Delfino appeared to be empowered. He escalated his conduct... Although the Court has found that plaintiffs are likely to prevail in this action, Delfino loudly proclaims this to be "SLAPP lawsuit" designed to oppress free speech (although the Court has also rejected all of his First Amendment arguments throughout this litigation). He describes defendants as "despicable corporate bullies" in conjunction with the SLAPP allegations ...

Delfino's dishonesty in impersonating Plaintiffs is for the purpose of harassing and defaming them. Delfino continues to violate the Order by transferring among different aliases despite this Court's order that he post only under one alias, and despite the prohibition against continued defamation, posting e-mails describing Varian corporate plaintiffs as "despicable corporate bullies." Indeed, Delfino has now broadened his attack to plaintiffs' counsel, posting their names, bar numbers and addresses and disparaging their efforts in this action....

Delfino has shown that he will not stop regardless of the consequences. He will not obey the TRO or Preliminary Injunction, and it would be a triumph of hope over experience to believe that Delfino will obey any permanent injunction that this Court issues. Delfino has demonstrated that he will go to great lengths...

Delfino is incorrigible. Indeed, he seems empowered ... Delfino persists in describing this as a frivolous "SLAPP" suit designed only to oppress defendants and to impair their First Amendment rights. His co-defendant Mary Day has entered the fray, stating that plaintiffs are "unscrupulous" and "despicable.""

Another Orrick entreaty for sanctions had failed. Thus, the plaintiffs' efforts turned out to be quite counter-productive in terms of silencing both Mary and myself. In fact, the very fascist nature of illegal censorship only served to inspire our strong sense of integrity and principles. Deposed on February 8, 2000, I had plenty to say about Poppe's fascist tactics:

LIBURT: Okay. If you look down at the next-to-last sentence on this message, which says, "Hopefully the whole truth behind the despicable fascist tactics at work will come out during the trial --

February 14th." Who were you referring to when you used the phrase, "despicable fascist tactics"?

DELFINO: That under seal document in which Poppe lies to the Court and then does not have the courage to come forward and sign it under -- under the threat of -- of perjury, is absolutely unbelievable. If that's not despicable and fascist, then I am looking very forward to my day in court.

LIBURT: Okay. So when you use the term, "despicable fascist tactics," you were referring to Mr. Poppe?

DELFINO: I'm referring to a tactic in which a so-called attorney has the audacity to try and put me in contempt, claiming that I did something wrong, when he's purposely hid, snuck behind this document, is absolutely disgusting.

LIBURT: So the tactic that you're referring to is this tactic of Mr. Poppe's that you've just described?

DELFINO: Yes. It's so despicable that I would love to see the Orrick SLAPP firm come forward and release that document and -- and let it become public and let the public draw their own conclusion.

LIBURT: Okay. Were there any other -- anybody else that you were referring to when you used the phrase, "despicable fascist tactics"?

DELFINO: The letter is signed Matthew H. Poppe.

LIBURT: Okay. Are there any other despicable fascist tactics that you're referring to in this posting?

DELFINO: The man not only did Yahoo!, but then he sent a similar message to Stock-Talk, and, as you know, Stock-Talk has closed down their board in its entirety, and this man had the audacity, the despicableness, to go to Florida, talk to the Stock-Talk people and ask them why they removed their board. I wish I had such nerve.

Poppe wrote Yahoo! on May 27, 1999, the day after his first Kinko's visit, and at a time when neither of us were even posting. He asked them to immediately remove 60 "illegal postings" on their VAR financial message board that had been authored by me and other posters:

> "... the author fraudulently impersonates various Varian employees, including Susan B. Felch, George Zdasiuk, Dick Aurelio, Jane Crisler, and others.... the author has defamed Varian and its employees through a variety of false allegations, including by contentions that employees "cause some trouble," that nobody at Varian "is working," and that employees are having affairs with other employees and are engaged in projects that are wasting money."

He also wrote Stock-Talk, requesting they remove "26 messages allegedly appearing from Nov 16, 1998 to May 18, 1999" from their VAR message board, none of which were authored by me. Stock-Talk responded by deleting the Varian message board altogether.

Notwithstanding all this, the foolhardy Poppe submitted an October 19, 1999 brief asking that Mary and I be found in civil contempt for suggesting in our postings that messages were being ominously deleted:

"Defendants' Internet Messages Clearly (and Falsely) Accuse Plaintiffs of "Evidence Tampering" by Causing Messages to Be Removed from Yahoo! Message Boards.... These messages leave no question that the authors are accusing Plaintiffs, falsely, of having caused the removal of the postings. The dozens of other messages posted by Delfino and Day on this topic convey the same defamatory meaning ...."

His request was denied by Judge Whyte, who this time, may have actually looked at the evidence. It was a lie to refer to the messages in question as unlawful. Facetiously crowned, "Orrick's 2001 grand champion of deceit," and praised by his SLAPP mentor Hermle as, "the person you'd least like to meet in a dark alley,"[48] to us, he was simply a malevolent magician:

WIDMANN: Okay. That's all we can ask for. So your recollection now is is that you saw the Kinko's video about the time you were signing the first declaration which is Exhibit 2, correct?
FAIR: Correct.
WIDMANN: Back in March of 1999.
FAIR: That's my best recollection.
...
WIDMANN: That's okay. Give me a second to check my notes, I think I might be finished, and let Mr. Falcon ask you some questions.
POPPE: Just so you know, the videotape he's referring to has a date and time stamp on it that says May of 1999. So he's asking you if you think you signed it -- or think you saw it when you signed the declaration dated March of 1999.

---

[48]Krysten Crawford, *The Recorder*, August 20, 2000.

FAIR: Like I said, I'm not sure.

WIDMANN: Move to strike counsel's comment and ask him not to coach the witness or supply him with information while the deposition's pending. If you want to have a private conversation and do that, which I think would be unprofessional, improper, go outside, don't do it on the record, because I think it's coaching the witness.

How else can you explain this key SLAPP witness previewing a purported May 5, 1999 surveillance video at Orrick's Menlo Park office two months before it was supposed to have been produced?

No posting, by either of us, was ever shown to have violated any law. The blatant removal of these postings was censorship, pure and simple, and his letter to Yahoo! and Stock-Talk proved that he was responsible.

However, Poppe's speciousness was but a preview of Orrick's penchant for censorship on behalf of its clients. It would reach new heights after that fateful August 13, 1999 day when in the years that followed, literally thousands of messages authored by us and other anonymous posters would be deleted on Yahoo! alone.

- 6 -

A BATHROOM WITH A VIEW

While we were doing our part to keep the Yahoo! VAR message board readers entertained, occasionally someone else would lend a helping hand. This, my all time favorite Yahoo! VAR posting done by a unknown poster was not even ascribed to me by The Orrick:

Yes... varian YOU SUCK FOR SUING THESE
by: <u>voltaire_is_here</u> (412/M/In my time machine of co)
people SUE ME YOU WORMS. HOW DARE YOU A PUBLIC COMPANY TRAMPLE ON OUR FIRST AMMEDMENT RIGHTS... HOW DARE YOU. Your company is dirt to me now and forever. SHAME ON YOU VARIAN EXECUTIVES SHAME ON YOU, YOU ARE DISGRACES TO HUMANITY. These people have posted this message all over yahoo and now the whole net will come here and tell you what they think... I hope your stock is 20 cents in the next year. Free speech extends to every place residents of america reside in whether its here or on the hard drive that resides at yahoo hq. Your lawsuit is breach of all that is dear to americans on this coming labor day and not one employee of your company who works for you and stays on during this dishonorable act is worthy of his citizenship. I urge all real americans at varian to stand up and revolt and charge into your board meeting all at once and tell them WHO REALLY RUNS THIS COMPANY AND ITS US YES US AMERICANS REVOLT VARIAN EMPLOYEES REVOLT LIKE THEY DID IN 1786... STAND UP FOR YOUR FREEDOM. How else will you look at yourself if the company bathrooms mirrors? with honor or disgrace? WE ARE AMERICANS STAND UP !!!!!

I recognized my Constitutional right to post my opinion with my very first message back on October 12, 1998. The first time I realized that the Varian, Susan B. Felch and George Zdasiuk lawsuit was a SLAPP came after watching the Bloomberg station on TV, one August morning in 1999. With the television sound off, and listening to Palestrina's Missa Nigra sum[49] I saw a news brief about Total Renal Care Holdings (later DaVita, Inc.), a company in the midst of its own Internet message board lawsuit. On mentioning this to Mary, she followed up on it and quickly got into the story. As the saying goes, a little bit of knowledge is a dangerous thing. This Yahoo! VAR posting by her soon appeared:

> **VARIAN, FELCH & ZDASIUK SUE SINGLE MOM!**
> by: siztheday (43/F/Los Altos)
> I am a single mother with two small children who is being sued by Varian (VAR & VSEA), Susan B. Felch and George A. Zdasiuk for alledged internet postings. In my opinion, this is just another frivolous SLAPP suit aimed at suppressing free speech.
> "Integrity is an island without a beach; once you leave it, there is no return."
> Note: This is in no way intended to advise anyone to buy VAR & VSEA stock.

It was our first public reference to the lawsuit as a SLAPP. Later, viewing the Yahoo! message board for Total Renal Care (TRL), we were amazed at the similarities it had to our Varian case and intrigued by this SLAPP phenomenon. SLAPPs were not new, but were in fact on the rise with regard to Internet message board postings in particular. Now, one could reach a relatively large audience while remaining anonymous, and do so with little or no effort. This reach was immediately perceived as a threat by the power brokers who controlled the usual voice boxes: the newspapers, television, and radio. These are two Yahoo! TRL postings that prompted our interest in SLAPPs:

---

[49]Literally, "I am black mass," a beautiful choral work by Giovanni Pierluigi da Palestrina (1525-1594).

A word of caution!!!!
by: fredumb4all (76/M/Saint Paul, MN)
My Personal opinion with regard to these silly SLAPP suits is that companies first see how some of the early cases play out before they start intimidating and harassing posters with flim flam acccusations.
Well, here is where ITEX vs. Les French (John Doe #2) (this case really is the one which began SLAPP suing) is at: http://lesfrench.com/legal/html/answer1.html
As I posted earlier, ITEX decided they didn't like posts which were appearing on their board. The problem was - anywhere where opinion was stated as fact - it appears that the fact was truthful! They tried to intimidate Mr. French into not posting - the result was Mr. French fought back. It appears Itex hoped posters would just "go away". Mr. French supoenaed numerous SEC and corporate documents (per a post by Mr. French at www.clubs.yahoo.com/clubs/itexgroup) and in fact, ITEX refused to produce many of the items Mr. French asked for to prove the truth. The bluff has been called! My bet is Mr. French is a damned good chess player as he finessed this SLAPP suer right into check mate! It appears he may get damages for the harrassment! Check the link out for yourselves!
To the Does who have been named here - I bet Mr. French would be happy to tell you how he has pulled this off (my understanding is he has done this without an attorney! Stating to judges that the case is so weak and frivolous that he doesn't need representation!!!). I know that you can e-mail him at either the John Doe site or the Itex Group site. This guy deserves a medal.
FREDUMB

Info for those being sued by TRL by: ibc96 (42/M)
I assume that the lawsuit has been filed in California which has a very strong "anti-SLAPP" statute. Check out the following link http://www.casp.net which offers good info on slap back suits.
Having been sued and served in a similar suit filed by ITEX Corp earlier this year, my advice is to sit tight, don't panic and do nothing until you are actually served with a lawsuit - which is extremely unlikely as the purpose of these lawsuits is twofold; to chill free speech and to uncover the identity of anonymous posters. I am not an attorney, however I was able

to get myself dismissed from the lawsuit without hiring an attorney or taking any legal advice. These lawsuits are usually so frivolous that the judges hearing them want to wash their hands of them as quickly as possible. Several of these lawsuits have been filed this year and the companies filing them usually seem to have one thing in common - their stock price has plumeted, management is in disarray (or incompetent) and they are trying to deflect attention from their own considerable problems. I know nothing about TRL but I wonder if it falls into this category?

In no time at all, Mary and I were becoming well-educated about this despicable legal practice of SLAPPing. The more we learned about SLAPPs, the more obvious it became that the Varian lawsuit was a SLAPP. On October 29, 1999, a *San Jose Business Journal* headline read: "Ex-Varian employees cry "SLAPP.'" Therein, I said, "We are calling it a SLAPP. It clearly is a SLAPP." I explained, "It has nothing to do with the Internet postings. It's an attempt to use the Internet to go after our business. ... What we think they're trying to do is go after our patents." Orrick's Hermle responded that the SLAPP charge was "ridiculous" adding, "We never asked the court to prevent him from posting, ... All we asked was: Don't impersonate, don't defame, don't harass." And, "In trial we're going to ask for damages," "You bet."

This story by Erik Espe was the first news article about our lawsuit. Its publication was prompted in part when he became aware of our message board postings and viewed our newly created Varian (VAR & VSEA), Susan B. Felch and George Zdasiuk SLAPP Web site. He seemed intrigued by our determination to speak out. When asked when the MoBeta, Inc. owners will stop posting, I replied, "We'll post until we're dead."

Mary's research into the Total Renal Care SLAPP, and the California Anti-SLAPP Project Web site [http://www.casp.net] laid out the basis for establishing our own SLAPP Web sites and for our growing devotion to message board postings. In doing so, she found a message board forum, the Yahoo! JohnDoes Club dedicated to supporting anonymous message board posters who were being sued and referenced on the Yahoo! TRL board:

> **Are you a John (Doe)** by: <u>LongCOX2</u>
> If you are please join the Yahoo John doe club chat room
> tonite at 9PM ESt- Interesting chat and news. You have to
> sign up as a member 1st. Good luck to all fellow Does
> Just opinion

This club was founded by Les L. French, an Oregonian SLAPP survivor, who from our first encounter was always extremely supportive and informative. The Yahoo! JohnDoes Club was in itself a valuable forum for educating the public about SLAPPs. Les later founded The Anonymous Internet Foundation [http://www.johndoes.org], funding it with a portion of his SLAPP settlement proceeds. Les' posting on the Yahoo! VAR board on April 4, 2002, showed what he and Varian were all about:

> **Legal Representation**
> by: <u>LesLFrench</u> (46/M/Portland, Oregon)
> Yesterday I was informed that Yahoo! has been served with a
> deposition subpoena duces tecum to discover the identities of
> persons publishing on Yahoo!'s Message Board "VAR".
> I am not familiar with the requirements of the subpoena, but it
> appears to have been served on the deponent Yahoo! without
> leave of any court of jurisdiction. Generally, such a subpoena
> is unenforceable because it is not authorized by law. I do not
> know the status of the subject subpoena.
> The John Does Anonymous Foundation represents anonymous
> internet publishers in an effort to protect their First
> Amendment rights. The Foundation maintains counsel in
> California, the venue for the subject subpoena duces tecum,
> for that precise purpose. It is our intent to file a motion to
> quash the within subpoena, however any protective order by a
> court would normally apply only to the individuals that we
> actually represent.
> If you have been notified by Yahoo! that confidential
> information regarding your account is being requested under
> this subpoena, and you are presently unrepresented in this
> case, I encourage you to contact me immediately. My email
> address is barter@johndoes.org. All information relating to
> your identity and your request to seek counsel is privileged
> and confidential.
> Les L. French

More than two years before Les' posting, at my December 7, 1999 deposition, it seems Orrick wondered if I was French or vice versa:

> LIBURT: Since October 8, 1998, have you posted on any Internet
> message board using the alias "LesLFrench", spelled L-e-s, the letter
> L, F-r-e-n-c-h, all one word?
> DELFINO: No.

And two days later, Liburt asked Mary if she could help identify who "LesLFrench" might be:

> LIBURT: Have you ever posted under any -- strike that. Have you
> ever posted on any Internet message board using the alias leslfrench,
> spelled L-E-S-L-F-R-E-N-C-H?
> DAY: No, I have not.
> LIBURT: Do you have any information as to the identity of the
> person who has posted on Internet message boards as leslfrench?
> DAY: I have no information about his identity.
> ...
> LIBURT: Do you have any idea whether leslfrench is a man or a
> woman?
> DAY: I have no -- I don't know.

Realizing I had been SLAPPed did little for my predicament. A few states, California being one of them, enacted as early as 1993, laws to protect citizens from SLAPPs. Specifically, a judge can decide at the outset if the lawsuit is a SLAPP and if it has no probability of succeeding. If these conditions are met, an unrealistic event for most victims, the judge can dismiss the lawsuit and award the defendant his attorney's fees. Unfortunately for me, Varian's bogus criminal charges, all which were later conveniently dropped by them, made it impossible for my attorneys to then argue it was a SLAPP. On October 8, 1999, Glynn explained:

> "The Varian (VAR and VSEA), Susan B. Felch and George Zdasiuk
> lawsuit is a SLAPP because the defendants' right to free speech on
> the Internet is a public issue. Moreover, the SLAPP is frivolous
> because claims of damage, such as affecting the stock prices, are and

have been, if anything, proven incorrect (check the rising stock prices) and plaintiffs' accusations, such as impersonation, are not only unsubstantiated, but also utterly untrue. What plaintiffs' are doing is to trying to stifle and thwart free speech....

Plaintiffs claim this isn't a SLAPP, but obviously that is just their opinion. The statute says it is....

As noted by that section of the law, the public has a strong and prevailing interest in protecting free speech on the Internet, and Internet free speech is a very public interest. It should never, as plaintiffs do here, be dismissed lightly.

Plaintiffs contend that since their complaint was not attacked by a motion to strike, and because the court found that the plaintiffs' are likely to prevail, that this is not a SLAPP action. Just because defendants have not (yet) such a motion, does not mean that this is not a SLAPP suit. Moreover, the court's finding of "likely to prevail" was expressly conditioned upon the fact that Mr. Delfino had asserted his Fifth Amendment Privilege in the state court and the court was therefore permitted to draw adverse inferences against Mr. Delfino because of such assertion of rights. This court stated it did not consider his declaration, except for admission, submitted in this action...."

For us, the concept of publishing the truth about the Varian SLAPP and using the Internet to report the news was born during this period. The more Orrick tried to hide the case by filing under seal and out of public scrutiny, the more determined we were to disclose the facts. With our "Internet Buddie," our audience was to be literally the entire world, or at least those with an interest, and access to a computer, and a telephone line. Without the Internet, losing the lawsuit to Varian and its legal army at Orrick was a given. In what would become a long war of attrition, we could not match their resources. We did, however, have rather lucrative financial reserves at our disposal, and a willingness to devote literally every day, and spend every dime, if necessary, lawfully using the Internet to expose their every torrid secret. We would disclose everything about the plaintiffs that was a matter of public record, and turn this lawsuit into a soap opera, if nothing else. If they tried to hide something and we thought its release would benefit our cause, we published it. Our relentless determination to post messages never abated; we both posted every single day. In fact, no more than seven hours would ever pass without our posting, even when we took time to vacation. Dr. Martin Blinder, a psychiatrist who achieved a certain amount of fame,[50] would later categorize us as "obsessed," and was curious about us hoping to someday give us a proper and full evaluation. While it never happened, it seemed as the case evolved and discovery wound down in Federal Court, Orrick still didn't get it:

> LIBURT: My question is, are you trying to post accurate information when you post on these boards?
> DELFINO: Well, show me the posting.
> LIBURT: Okay. So you can't answer that general question?
> FALCON: Same objections. Arguing with the witness; now.
> DELFINO: Well, it is a question – there's always questions, I guess, or concerns of accuracy and hyperbole and fun and humor, and as you know the Yahoo! message boards, themselves, it tells you you basically have got to be somewhat foolish to take these things literally. It also -- It also warns you that these things are opinions, so within that kind of broad envelope, unless you can show me a specific posting, I'm not sure what -- how I can answer that any more accurately than Yahoo! itself is able to answer it for you.
> LIBURT: Okay. Well, as you sit here today, can you recollect posting any message on any of these company boards about this lawsuit where you were thinking to yourself, well, I know what I'm writing is untrue?
> DELFINO: I have never made a knowingly false statement, if that's what you're asking.
> LIBURT: That -- That's essentially what I'm getting at.
> DELFINO: Never knowingly false statement, never.

Then again, maybe this February 8, 2000 deposition gave Orrick insight into how strongly we valued our free speech privilege. After hugs and kisses, what greater legacy could we leave our children other than the right and the will to speak, ever so loudly, to express themselves no matter how unpopular, even

---

[50]Known for his celebrated diagnosis of the killer Dan White, "The Twinkie Defense," Blinder, M.D. argued that eating junk food caused diminished mental capacity that *could* account for his actions.

offensive their views might be. And we were prepared to do whatever was required to preserve this right for them and for us. Mary's Yahoo! posting reflects that sentiment:

> **Hey, Dick, now THIS is integrity!** by: <u>dantecristo</u>
> "There is nothing in all the world greater than freedom. It is worth paying for; it is worth losing a job for; it is worth going to jail for. I would rather be a free pauper than a rich slave. I would rather die in abject poverty with my convictions than live in inordinate riches with the lack of self respect." - Rev. Martin Luther King, Jr.

Early on, we decided that information about our company should be accessible on the Internet. In making this a reality, Mary taught herself HTML, the language of Web site design. She became sufficiently proficient that the MoBeta, Inc. Web site made its debut early May 1999. Realizing the power and the ease of marketing news on the Internet, we decided to publish our SLAPP lawsuit Web sites as well. Showing our idea to Glynn, and watching him toss between grin and grimace as he viewed it on the computer screen, we were excited. When asked what we intended to publish, we responded in unison, "everything!" On the 2nd of September 1999 around 4 o'clock, we released the Varian (VAR & VSEA), Susan B. Felch and George Zdasiuk SLAPP Web site [http://www.geocities.com/mobeta_inc/slapp/slapp.html].

Unbelievably, 19 days later our displayed counter registered its $5,000^{th}$ hit. On June 17, 2000 this SLAPP home page received its $17,000^{th}$ hit. On February 12, 2002 the number grew to 48,000 and on October 28, 2002 it became 68,000. Our counters were set up so that they registered a hit whenever someone other than us visited the Web site. They were soon replaced with a more sophisticated tracking version equipped with an ability to disclose the referring URL and the time of the visit. Most hits came on Monday, with more than 88% of them scored Monday through Friday, suggesting that they came from the workplace. Saturday was the least frequented day. This information helped to optimize our Web site design, and even affected our marketing. We found, for example, that Yahoo! and Google were the main search engines

149

used by Web surfers directed to our site, accounting for 55% and 32% of the key-word searches respectively. The major domain to visit was commercial (.COM) at 45%, followed by network (.NET) at 30%, and that less than 3% of the hits came from educational (.EDU) and military (.MIL) establishments collectively. Organizational sites (.ORG) made up 1%. Statistics showed that our readership, while overwhelmingly American, was worldwide, and as I used to phrase it in postings, was followed in every time zone. One of our SLAPP Web sites lists the lands that had visited our home page.

We were internationally followed in Argentina, Australia, Austria, Belgium, Bermuda, Brazil, Brunei, Canada, Cayman Islands, Chile, China,[51] Costa Rica, Croatia, Czech, Denmark, Dominican Republic, Egypt, Estonia, Finland, France, Germany, Greece, Hungary, Iceland, India, Indonesia, Ireland, Israel, Italy, Japan, Jordan, Korea, Lebanon, Lithuania, Luxembourg, Malaysia, Malta, Mexico, Moldova, Netherlands, New Zealand, Norway, Panama, Peru, Philippines, Poland, Portugal, Romania, Russia, Saudi Arabia, Singapore, South Africa, Spain, Sweden, Switzerland, Taiwan, Thailand, Turkey, Ukraine, United Arab Emirates, United Kingdom, Uruguay, Yugoslavia, Venezuela, and of course, all 50 United States of America.

The worldwide interest of our Web site was not going to be out-classed by VSEA CEO Aurelio's ridiculously grandiloquent remark about his self-importance when deposed by Glynn:

> "I have no normal business hours. My business hours are twenty-four hours a day. We run a company that operates in all of the time zones in the world seven days a week."

Unlike Aurelio's provably false pomposity, we got hits from Iceland, a time zone that is without Varian Semiconductor equipment. Visits from far-away Brunei and Malta were surprising to us simply because of their small population. I even used the

---

[51]As of this writing, China refers only to Hong Kong since the remaining billion plus mainland Chinese are not allowed access to our Web sites and others, like Google.

international nature of our audience as an excuse to post messages to our non-English speaking clientele. I posted this message in French on Yahoo! France Telecom (FTC) financial message board:

> **Susan B. Felch est une chienne fasciste**
> by: poppe_is_poop (31/M/Menlo Park, CA)
> Mme Felch de VSEA est une chienne fasciste ignoble coupable d'enregistrer des hommes, les femmes, et les enfants en vidéo qui ont utilisé une salle de bains de compagnie! Ses crimes incluent le harassment résolu des employés et elle est une suspecte dans le sabotage allégué de laboratoire où des gaz toxiques pourraient avoir été libérés!
> Contrôlez-le dehors:
> http://www.geocities.com/mobeta_inc/slapp/slapp.html

I posted messages in Spanish, Italian, German, Portuguese, even Norwegian. My choice of languages was only limited by the on-line translator that I used. Of the more than 200 foreign language postings I produced, none were ever cited by Orrick.

Our first Web site, which we named "homepage" was followed by several more, all of which included a series of links and cross-links to court documents such as deposition testimony and exhibits, briefs, motions, and judge's orders. Links to the ACLU and the CASP[52] were included. We even linked to the Orrick, Herrington & Sutcliffe law firm homepage. Our intent was not only to publish the truth, but to educate the public as well. In one Web site created on October 15 and called "sloppy SLAPP," [http://www.geocities.com/mobeta_inc/slapp/sloppy.html] we used a question and answer format with links added to better inform the interested reader.

Postings that included links to one of our SLAPP Web sites were always almost immediately removed from the message boards. This early one that I posted on Yahoo! VSEA on September 6, 1999 lasted on the Internet but eight minutes:

---

[52]Mark Goldowitz' California Anti-SLAPP Project has been on the Web since 1996. It provides a summary of relevant cases in California and other states as well as Federal precedents and offers assistance to SLAPP victims.

> **Welcome! Please visit**
> by: million_dollar_mistake (000/Argentina)
> our Web-Site @
> http://homepages.go.com/~manuforte/slapp.html
> 3000+ visits so far !!! The response has truly been
> overwhelming! We will be adding to our Web-Site as
> 'interesting things' become available, so keep clicking.
> Suggestions and criticisms are always welcome.
> Note: In my opinion, the decision to buy or sell VSEA stock is
> yours to make. Good luck!

I first considered the removal of one of my postings as just a humorous event in the day of the average message board poster whose First Amendment Rights were under attack. I wanted to see it as perhaps a measure of the effectiveness of my words, but was unable to correlate a deleted posting with a particular SLAPP topic. Now being censored was certainly different than before the lawsuit, when none of my postings were deleted and no one even asked me for a retraction. But soon the removals took on a more sinister tone as more and more messages, including those of other posters, began to disappear. Much to our surprise, this one appeared on Yahoo! VAR and was deleted the next day:

> **Giveemdx** by: egamz
> I have just read the linked web page
> http://homepages.go.com/~manuforte/slapp.html concerning
> Varian's lawsuit and found that the suit names as defendants,
> in addition to the two, named people, 18 John Does, of which I
> am presumably one, since some of my postings are quoted.
> I have posted under a number of aliases, all of them in fun;
> Creanna was the first, given to me by Yahoo the first time I
> posted. My message #42 proposed breaking the company into
> 3 parts four months before management actually did it (and
> my message #300 congratulated the Board on finally taking
> that action). Some of my other messages have complained
> about the "golden parachutes" and stock options that the Board
> so generously awarded to the top four executives as a result of
> the breakup, even though three of them were, for all practical
> purposes, merely changing their titles.
> Giveemdx is the only one of my aliases mentioned in the web
> page referenced above. Let me state clearly: To my

knowledge, I have never known, nor had contact of any kind with, any past, present, or future Varian employee. My only interest in the company has been as a stockholder: Varian has been one of my largest holdings for over 30 years, and I presently hold 6,000 shares in each of the pieces, (which, not incidentally, is probably more than many of the Board members own)

Now I would like to point out some facts: I and the other shareholders own this company, the Boards of Directors is elected by us, and they are supposed to represent us and not the management that may have nominated them. I have no problem with individual Varian executives who feel they may have been wronged instituting a lawsuit against the individuals involved, but the company itself claiming to be on of the wronged plaintiffs and randomly naming 18 John Does in the suit is shameful. I suspect that what is going on here is a disguise attempt to learn the names of the Varian employees who have been posting on this board. Is there not a single Director who finds this despicable.

I feel that the management of VAR and VSEA, their Boards, and their law firm owe me and the other innocent John Doe contributors to this chat board an apology. It appears that the aforementioned groups are avid readers of this board. I shall be waiting.

Giveemdx (Any resemblance to persons living or dead is purely coincidental.)

(The name, no longer one of my aliases, comes from an old Stanford football cheer, which apparently was too lowbrow for anyone to pick up on.)

Perhaps we were not alone in our outrage. Realizing its value, we immediately made copies of this posting and alerted Glynn, who was, of course, delighted. For a while, at least, it vindicated me as Varian's sole critic. The significance of this posting was twofold: one, it was triggered by our SLAPP Web site; and two, the alias "Giveemdx" was included in the first complaint against me. Was this the alias of Bud Buttrill? We never learned who used this alias and it never appeared again.

Several months later, another of Orrick's so-called defaming message board aliases named in the first complaint came forward and posted this on Yahoo! VSEA:

> **yeah, yeah, yeah...** by: <u>Montelemar</u>
> they wanted to make sure I wasn't someone else (wink, wink). The gentleman was very pleasant, and since I wasn't the one slamming these hapless people, I cheerfully told them anything they wanted to know.
> You can't yell "Fire!" in a crowded theater, and you can't just randomly rip people apart in a public forum. You should also refrain from violating a court order.
> Free speech is not false speech.

Orrick subpoenaed Yahoo! which provided "Montelemar's" email address, birth date, postal zip code, and other private information in sufficient detail for him to be contacted by phone. He was never named a defendant. This SLAPP was not intended for everyone. It was exclusively directed at Mary and me.

Quickly, the extent of the censorship became frighteningly pervasive. The efficiency with which postings disappeared suggested more than complacency on the part of Yahoo! Yet, the more postings were removed, the more enthusiastically we posted.

During this time I tried to reactivate "GINO_IN_TORINO" but Yahoo!'s ever-changing policy no longer allowed capital letters in aliases. And so, I settled for a more soft spoken "gino_in_torino" as my voice. This September 1999 Yahoo! VAR posting I did thrice was thrice removed:

> **Will CEO DICK LEVY resign???** by: <u>gino_in_torino</u>
> I don't have any idea!
> But, in my opinion, the VARIAN (VAR & VSEA), Susan B. Felch and George Zdasiuk SLAPP is long past being just a million dollar mistake. Please visit here
> http://homepages.go.com/~manuforte/slapp.html
> and of course here
> http://homepages.go.com/~manuforte/slappshot.html
> and let us all know, if its (A) a million dollar or (B) a multi-million dollar mistake.

And while we could post faster than any message board host could delete, we thought it important to show the words that were being censored. We reproduced many of those postings, most of which were deleted from Yahoo! on our "removed postings" Web site [http://www.geocities.com/mobeta_inc/rempost.html]. It soon became necessary for us to create multiple Web sites as the number of our deleted postings grew into the hundreds. As a response, I presume, Yahoo! prohibited postings that included links to our URL's. On October 22, 1999 Yahoo!'s Karen Schuster informed us that URL's incorporating "manuforte" were permanently blocked from their message boards. She refused to explain, and so Mary simply moved our Web sites from Disney's GO.com [http://homepages.go.com/~manuforte/slapp.html] to Yahoo!'s [http://www.geocities.com/mobeta_inc/slapp.html]. Our paid-for SLAPP Web sites were never blocked again.

Later, we added public opinion polls to the Web sites. This first one was intended to prompt an awareness of how much effort was being spent trying to silence our message board postings:

Impeccable Integrity
How much has the Orrick, Herrington & Sutcliffe law firm billed Varian for this SLAPP?
$500,000
$1,000,000
$1,500,000
$2,000,000
more than $2,000,000

More than 400 votes were cast before the Web host for this polling tool failed sometime in early 2001. 87% of the votes cast was for "more than $2,000,000!" But as it would turn out, Orrick would charge their SLAPPer clients several times that.

Varian claimed we were costing them money too. On January 7, 2000, Jeff Wright, a nondescript giant, balding-man declared:

"1. I am currently employed by Varian Medical Systems, Inc. as the Director of Corporate Facilities. I have been employed by Varian

155

since approximately 1984. My duties include management of Varian Medical Systems, Inc.'s Palo Alto and Mountain View facilities for real estate, engineering, maintenance, security, and contracted services.

2. As a result of the postings on the Yahoo message board, for the period of October 1998 through approximately February 1999. Management at Varian became extremely concerned about the safety of its employees as a result of postings which I understand have been made by defendants Michelangelo Delfino and Mary Day. Some of the messages seem to suggest that those who were harassing and defaming company executives would attend, among other things, Varian's stockholders meeting in February, 1999 with the intent to disrupt the proceedings.... attached ... is one such posting [Dated January 4, 1999, it is one of my original 60 Yahoo! postings]:

> **A more educated reply** by: <u>ah_michelangelo</u>
> Dear Bud,
> It's time to let go of the past, count your losses, and buy stock in a company that has a future like AMAT and NVLS. As a former employee, you more than most, should know the state of affairs Varian now finds itself. Perhaps, if you need a more recent update you should visit what is left of building 7; thirty-four people and counting. I am somewhat surprised that you did not sell at the end of last year and take your losses, but such is life. Better luck this year and see you at the stockholder meeting.

3. ... to ensure that there would not be disruptions ...Varian incurred expenses to ensure that security measures had been taken to protect the company against the posters.... Varian hired an executive protection service TAL Global, Inc., which is an executive security firm, employing off duty police officers to protect those employees and stockholders who attended the meeting.... Varian hired another security company, American Protective Services, to provide additional security to ensure that all who attended the event were protected from any harassment or potential violent act.

4. Varian employees came forward and informed me, (and to my understanding, other people) that they were concerned about their own safety given the fact that those posters seemed to be mentally imbalanced as well as harboring an intent to do malicious harm to Varian and its employees.

5. Additional security measures were taken for the same reasons. In the site selection process for Varian's new research facility, Varian paid an increased amount of money to study site access issues to

protect occupants from those who might wish to enter the site in an unauthorized fashion. Additional security measures were taken, such as a ... a lockdown device on the front entrance, a security measure not taken with respect to other Varian buildings.... Varian spent increased time and money ensuring that it's new facility ... would be secured from attacks or invasions by persons who harbored malice against the center or the employees. Upgraded lighting was provided in parking lots to ensure that visibility was secure, and several additional security upgrade measures were also taken.

6. Similarly, at Building 4A, the Executive Headquarters building in Palo Alto, Varian increased it's security measures including, but not limited to, the design and installation of interior security doors. We continue to maintain additional security guards at the Executive Headquarters building as a result of our concern that the angry and hateful posters might pose a security threat to employees in this building as well.

7. As a result of the defendants' postings, Varian has also hired a security consulting firm, Security By Design, in response to the escalation of the message board postings...."

True, Mary and I are a formidable pair, but does our mere presence at a public meeting warrant such safeguards?

As Varian stockholders, Mary and I had attended every annual meeting except 1999. We had inadvertently missed that one because we were so engrossed in getting MoBeta, Inc. started having happily moved on with our lives. But apparently Varian missed us. VAR attorneys now argued that our intended attendance at the 2000 stockholder's meeting was of such concern to management that security had to be stepped up for the event.

WRIGHT: It's an invoice from Tal-Global for the amount of $4,164 for services they provided at our shareholder meeting in February of 2000.
...
POPPE: Solely for the additional security measure implemented due to the concern from Mr. Delfino and Ms. Day?
...
POPPE: Were you present at the year 2000 stockholder meeting?
WRIGHT: Yes, I was.
POPPE: Did you see Mr. Delfino at the meeting?
WRIGHT: Yes, I did.
POPPE: And did you see Ms. Day at the meeting?

WRIGHT: Yes, I did.
POPPE: Were they present for the entire meeting?
WRIGHT: Yes, they were.
POPPE: Was there any disruption caused at that meeting?
WRIGHT: No, there was not.

At VAR's 2000 stockholder meeting in Palo Alto, the shorter than ever Levy stood at a podium and had the audacity to look at us and proclaim that Varian was a company with "impeccable integrity!" Returning home, I posted my impression of this Internet Nazi:

> **Novice CEO Dick's stockshow highlights!** by: ima_posta2
> Impeccable integrity!
> Can you imagine, Richard 'Dick' Levy, the MAN in charge of people being videotaped as they use a Varian company bathroom, had the audacity to look me in the eye and suggest a nexus between Varian and impeccable integrity!
> Dick did confirm that his 'incubating' Ginzton Technology Center was STILL NOT making money - something that comes as no surprise to those who know George Zdasiuk, its head - so to speak!
> Craig Moro was present, even holding the door for the MoBeta, Inc. stockholders in attendance. Did he take a short break away from watching the bathroom videos?
> I didn't see Kathy Hibbs, or her socializing associate Lynne Hermle, who I assume were unable to take a SLAPP break.
> Now I know what Joseph Phair and Jeff Wright look like. I assume it is mutual.
> See you all at the SLAPP trial!

In this message, an anonymous Yahoo! poster lambastes me, I assume for *not* interrupting the VAR stockholder meeting:

> **big mouth..** by: gc72_1999
> Hey big mouth I see you didn't say a dam thing .you remind me of that dog on the taco bell commercial all bark and no bite you little *ussy.

Perhaps the best documents included in our Web sites, if not the most popular, were deposition transcripts of the plaintiffs and their witnesses. Even when excerpted they allowed us to report a story, using only the words of Varian SLAPPers. Some were better than others, and, of course, made for a more interest. To her credit, the inimitable Jane Crisler triggered a sequence of events that would ripple through this lawsuit and undoubtedly the company as well. On her first day of deposition on March 8, 1999 she blurted out a disclosure that surprised everyone, became a major source of posting material, and one claim for my cross-complaint.[53]

> FALCON: Did you ever see it on videotape - - you hesitate I wonder why?
> CRISLER: We did a video and the results of that were inconclusive. If you didn't know what you were looking for, you might not see it was a gesture.
> ...
> FALCON: Where was the camera located at?
> CRISLER: It was in Building 7.
> FALCON: And directed toward Mr. Delfino's office?
> CRISLER: Toward the rest room where he would routinely come out of the rest room he could see directly in Sue's office.
> FALCON: So you had a videotape at the rest room pointed toward the men's room? And for how long did that video surveillance camera exist?
> CRISLER: At least a week.

Even months later, on November 10, 1999, she stuck to her story improvident of how offensive this deed would be viewed.

> FALCON: Do you know where the camera was placed from that camera angle?
> CRISLER: All I know is that it was facing the men's room.

Varian's Edward L. Ginzton Research Center (Building 7) was a *Jetsons*[54] era two-story structure where Mary and I worked. It

---

[53]Tom and Glynn initiated a counter-suit based on my wrongful termination: "Answer & Affirmative Defenses, & Counter Claim of Michelangelo Delfino," filed May 10, 1999.

[54]Reference the ABC television cartoon series that premiered on September 23, 1962, and showed American family life in the future – year 2062.

had two inner atriums with balconies leading to facing windowed offices and laboratories and on the second floor an adjacent men's bathroom and women's rest room with a janitorial closet in between. As it turned out, Hibbs, totally unfamiliar with the building and its occupants, had authorized Craig Moro, a low-level Varian security employee, to install hidden video surveillance to record me allegedly harassing Felch. Neither of them spent time in GRC, and in fact, as far as I knew, Hibbs had never even visited until she gave her emotional "Felch sabotage" auditorium speech. Not understanding the building layout would prove to be more troublesome for them than imaginable.

Felch claimed that one of my most frequent harassing acts as a Varian employee was to go to the bathroom and on entering or exiting make her so-called "telephone gesture" toward her office window as it was in direct view of the bathroom door and perhaps only 30 feet away.

FALCON: Tell me about what you observed Mike Delfino doing on this one particular incident.
FELCH: I believe that it was the same phone gesture that we've described before.
FALCON: And that was putting small finger and thumb up to mouth and ear and what, wiggling a little bit?
FELCH: Yes.
...
FALCON: And during that time period, you only saw him make a gesture or a face or a hand gesture, whatever it was, that one time?
FELCH: That's correct.
...
FALCON: Now, the time that you saw Mr. Delfino make the phone gesture to you, you said you called Mr. Moro, is that correct?
FELCH: Yes.
FALCON: Did you actually talk to him?
...
FELCH: Best I can recall, I said something to the effect that at whatever time it had just been, Mr. Delfino passed and made the phone gesture.

Felch had since mid-1997 periodically subjected me to this ridiculous allegation. Every so often, Zdasiuk would make one of his rare appearances in our laboratory or my office and when alone, confront me with this almost unbelievable Felch allegation. The same conversation replayed each time – Zdasiuk saying, "I want you to stop," me responding, "I can't stop what I'm not doing," and us ending up with a "he said, she said" scenario, as Hennessy, Crisler's supervisor, testified:

FALCON: So tell me what evidence you had or you were aware of at the time that you met with Jane Crisler regarding the termination of Mike Delfino, that Mike Delfino was in fact making inappropriate facial expressions towards Sue Felch?
HENNESSY: All we had was Sue's allegations.
FALCON: And tell me what evidence, if anything, that you had at the time that you had this conversation with Jane Crisler that Mike Delfino was making rude or inappropriate hand gestures at or toward Sue Felch?
HENNESSY: Just her allegations. Sue's allegations.
...
FALCON: Is it your understanding that Mike Delfino was utilizing the fair treatment plan because he felt he was being harassed and falsely accused by Sue Felch in accusing him of doing these things?
HENNESSY: Yes.

What about witnesses?

FALCON: So you think failing to advise the Court that there were witnesses known to Varian that denied the allegations of Susan Felch was not a fact that the Court should have been made aware of?
HIBBS: I did not think any of those witnesses were credible.
FALCON: And that was your determination alone to make; is that correct?
...
HIBBS: Was that -- well, obviously I was not the primary author of the declaration. So obviously outside counsel had drafted the declaration. But I believe that the declaration is truthful, accurate, and reflects the information that the Court needed.
FALCON: You don't feel you were compressing, concealing, or denying the Court any information that it needed in order to make a fully aware and factual ruling?
HIBBS: Absolutely not.
FALCON: The -- are you doing okay?
HIBBS: I'm fine.

> FALCON: The reason I ask, you've got a rash that's developing underneath your neck there as you're testifying. Is that –
> HIBBS: That's okay. When I get mad ...

The seriously misguided Hibbs, apparently believing a picture to be worth a thousand words, decided that a camera would finally reveal the truth – it did! Obviously I was not aware of the secret video surveillance taking place back in May 1998 when the taping was done. I had not yet met Moro, had never even seen Hibbs, and of course, I never had made any such gesture.

> FALCON: And what did you review?
> MORO: The tapes of what the camera captured.
> FALCON: Would you do this on a daily basis?
> MORO: Yes.
> ...
> FALCON: And it's your recollection that on each day you saw Mike Delfino at least once on the videotape?
> MORO: I can't recall.
> ...
> FALCON: And did you observe Mr. Delfino to be making any gestures or facial expressions on the videotape?
> MORO: That couldn't be ascertained.

Following Crisler's admission, Varian was put in the awkward position of trying to cover up this whole sordid affair. No person or video camera ever showed me doing anything other than relieving myself in the bathroom.

First came the issue of how long my trips to the Varian bathroom were under video surveillance:

> FALCON: How long was it in place and in operation in Sue Felch's office?
> ...
> MORO: I don't recall the exact time frame.
> FALCON: Was it more than a day?
> MORO: Yes.
> FALCON: More than a week.
> MORO: Yes.
> FALCON: More than a month?
> MORO: No, I don't believe so.

More than a month, maybe two!

> FALCON: Do you know how many weeks the camera was located in
> your office?
> FELCH: I don't remember exactly.
> FALCON: Approximately?
> FELCH: I would say somewhere two to five weeks.

Next followed the issue of where the camera was positioned and
how the surveillance was done:

> FALCON: And where did you install the camera?
> MORO: That would go in Sue Felch's office.
> FALCON: And where in Sue Felch's office?
> MORO: On the windowsill.
> FALCON: What kind of camera was it?
> MORO: A black and white camera.
> FALCON: A black and white still camera, video camera?
> MORO: Video camera.

Then, with Hibbs' December 17, 1999 long-argued, court-ordered
deposition, came proof of just how insidious all this plotting and
invasive bathroom videotaping really was. This Varian lawyer was
obviously not concerned about her own credibility:

> FALCON: Was the entrance to the men's room visible on the
> videotape that you saw?
> HIBBS: No, it was not.
> ...
> FALCON: Were you involved at all in the surveillance camera that
> was placed in Sue Felch's office directed towards the breezeway in
> the Ginzton Research Lab?
> HIBBS: Yes.
> FALCON: What was the involvement?
> HIBBS: I approved the placement of the camera.
> FALCON: Did you ever view any of the videotapes that came from
> that surveillance?
> HIBBS: I did.
> FALCON: How many?
> HIBBS: About a forty-five seconds clip.
> FALCON: Forty-five seconds clip. Has that been preserved?
> HIBBS: In photographs.

Varian, conveniently unable to locate and produce any of the 800 hours or so of videotaping, did, after a "diligent search," have Poppe surrender at Jim Hennessy's November 4, 1999 deposition six black and white photographs that showed me going to the bathroom in the Varian Edward L. Ginzton Research Center. The disturbing photos taken from Felch's video were date stamped May 28, and had times of 2:43:41 to 2:44:53. On March 30, 2001, the frazzled Hibbs was deposed again and asked to explain:

HIBBS: Yes, the figure at the -- that is seen through the window in those photographs, I believe is Mr. Delfino.
FALCON: Okay. And do you see that figure in both photos?
HIBBS: Yes, I do.
FALCON: And where is the door to either the men's or women's bathroom located, as far as you can tell by looking at either of those two photographs?
HIBBS: Well, I never worked in that building so I certainly couldn't identify the door to the men's room. So I don't know which -- I couldn't identify the -- of the doors which is -- which is what.
FALCON: The reason I was asking you is at your last deposition, you mentioned there was a post blocking the view to the men's room bathroom, I believe was your testimony.
HIBBS: Correct.
FALCON: Is that still your testimony?
HIBBS: It is.
FALCON: And so where would that place the men's room bathroom door in either of these two photographs?
HIBBS: Behind the post that's holding up the overhang of the building.
FALCON: Okay. And you would agree that that -- if it blocks any door, it would block only the men's room door not the women's bathroom door?
HIBBS: Well, I think it depends on the angle that you're -- that you are looking at the post from.
FALCON: That I'm looking from or --
HIBBS: Are you asking me from this camera angle?
FALCON: From this camera angle, yes.
HIBBS: Yes.
FALCON: The second page on this, can you identify any person in those two photographs?
HIBBS: Again, the figure in the -- seen through the window in the photographs is Mr. Delfino.

The Orrick did not seem to be fully aware what these shocking photographs actually depicted. They were also not familiar with the bathroom layout and its relative angular positioning to Felch's panoramic office window view. Thus this entertaining dialogue during Mary's second day of deposition:

> LIBURT: Okay. Do you have any other facts to support your belief that the video camera could see someone inside the men's bathroom in the act of urinating or defecating at the urinal or a toilet?
> DAY: Yes.
> LIBURT: What other facts do you have?
> DAY: I personally used that bathroom. I used to take showers in that bathroom, and I, in fact, used to put up a barrier in the men's bathroom because I did not want a straight-line shot. I know exactly where the toilets are, and the sinks, in that bathroom, and I also used the women's bathroom over a period of 15 years.
> ...
> LIBURT: How -- how certain are you that the video camera could see inside the men's bathroom and see people actually urinating or defecating in that bathroom?
> DAY: Very certain.
> LIBURT: Okay. And that -- your certainty is based on the facts you've just been telling me?
> DAY: And having worked in that building for 15 years.

In particular, what Orrick didn't know was that because of an inner wall full-length mirror inside the men's bathroom, you could see Felch eating a banana in her windowed office when standing at the sinks or using either of the two urinals. The same was true if one of the doors to either of the two toilet stalls was ajar. The best view of a man urinating or defecating, so to speak, was best described by Felch herself:

> FALCON: Was the surveillance camera that was in your office there before or after the lab sabotage incident that we talked about last time?
> FELCH: I don't remember.
> FALCON: In your office at the time that the video camera existed, focused out toward the hallway and the janitor's utility room, where was your desk, which way did you face is what I'm trying to find out, in your office?

FELCH: My chair faced the wall, and about a 45 degree angle from that was the angle looking out the window towards that opposite hallway in that spot.
FALCON: So the camera would actually be focused at a 45-degree angle from your forward view and on your left side?
McMAHON: Objection, vague, may call for speculation. You can answer if you know.
FELCH: Yes, approximately 45 degrees.

The angle was even smaller, so much so that this Varian "urinating or defecating problem" was often joked about:

HERMLE: Now, as I understand your testimony, the way that you would see Ms. Felch's office would be that you would be standing facing the urinal looking behind you at a mirror, and you would see the corner of her office; correct?
DELFINO: From the urinal. If you were standing at the -- may I stand up? … If you're standing at the urinal doing what you've got to be doing and you turned around looking in the mirror, you could see the corner of the office, that's correct.
FALCON: Was it common for you to be turning while you were standing at the urinal and looking at the mirror behind you?
DELFINO: Yes. One of my colleagues who -- we seem to have similar urinary tracts -- actually, my supervisor, Dr. Dave Hodul, we used to joke about that, because I used – the answer is yes, because I'd tell him, "I can't pee, Dave, if you keep talking to me." He'd stand there with the door open.

The camera in Felch's office most definitely recorded private moments, at least as long as the bathroom door was open. Sometimes a water leak or janitorial maintenance caused the bathroom door to be held fully open, occasionally for consecutive days. Perhaps to disguise the fact that the camera captured the inside of the bathroom, Moro actually produced an engineering diagram that was conveniently not drawn to scale and depicted an unfamiliar building layout. His schematic showed a bathroom without the shower Mary and others so often used. A toilet stall was missing altogether. And an inner bathroom door was added. No such door or traces of a doorway were present at any time during my ten-year tenure using that bathroom. Mary testified that she couldn't recall any such door either. Varian's apparent cover-up was developing like Watergate, this time, with another Tricky Dick in charge.

Incredibly, Orrick first argued that Varian secretly videotaping its employees and customers going to the bathroom was not at the time an illegal act:

> "... violation of California Labor Code section 435.... bars employers from videotaping employees in a rest room unless authorized by court order ... was enacted in September of 1998 and therefore did not take effect until January 1, 1999 ... Delfino cannot complain about alleged conduct that did not become unlawful until a later date."

Orrick was not embarrassed about any of this invasive bathroom videotaping as my February 4, 2000 testimony suggests:

> LIBURT: Okay. Do you have -- Do you have a belief as to whether it's a crime to videotape someone using a bathroom?
> DELFINO: It should be.
> LIBURT: Okay. Do you -- I under -- I appreciate your answer. Do you have any idea whether it is?
> DELFINO: I would hope it is.
> LIBURT: Okay. I believe you said before, you certainly -- and correct me if I'm wrong, but you believe it's a despicable thing to do?
> DELFINO: What do you think?
> LIBURT: I'm asking you.
> DELFINO: I think anybody in just about any civilized part of the world would think that videotaping somebody going to the bathroom is about as low as you can go.

Deposed on March 29, 2001, Felch seemed to disagree with this commonly held sentiment:

> FALCON: Now, forgetting the particular instance of the video camera allegations in your office and where it's pointed to and what it reveals and what have you, generally what kind of opinion do you have if you were to hear that someone has placed a video camera so that it would get people as they enter or as they leave a public restroom?
> POPPE: Objection; vague, compound.
> FELCH: If the video camera were looking at the entryway only, I

think that's acceptable.

FALCON: So as long as it did not peer to, even when the door was open, into the bathroom, that would be okay. Is that what you're telling me?

FELCH: Yes.

FALCON: Now, what if the camera peered inside when the door was open? Would you think of that as despicable behavior by whoever was videotaping that restroom?

POPPE: What part of the inside?

FALCON: Any portion of the inside.

FELCH: You'd have to be more specific on parts.

FALCON: When you use a public restroom, do you have an expectancy of privacy while you're within the confines of the restroom?

POPPE: Objection; calls for a legal conclusion.

FALCON: I don't want your legal understanding of what privacy is. Do you expect that you -- what goes on there will be private from anyone who is outside of the restroom?

FELCH: It's getting into the definition of inside. I think while one is truly deep within the bathroom and using various facilities there, then that is the expectation. If one is a half a footstep inside the door, then I don't consider that truly deeply inside the bathroom.

FALCON: Whether they're coming or leaving the bathroom? Makes no difference to you if they're only a foot or a step inside the bathroom?

FELCH: If that's all that is seen, then I don't consider that --

FALCON: Well, that's a good question.

FELCH: -- invasion of privacy.

FALCON: Some people are still finishing their -- returning to their normal attire and decorum as they're stepping out of the bathroom.

FELCH: If they do that in the doorway, that's -- that's their own problem.

Felch had absolutely no sense of right and wrong. In her February 28, 2000 declaration she had the gumption to declare under oath:

"Mr. Delfino has also gone to the Los Altos Home Page Web Site, where my neighbors, friends and colleagues are highly likely to browse and posted links to one of his Web pages, which then contains defamatory misinformation about the lawsuit. For example, the defendants accuse me of invading "people's privacy" and testifying that "employees were secretly videotaped going to and inside the bathroom at work.""

Yet, she had no shame It was not until March 28, 2001 that Felch finally admitted what everyone else already knew:

> FELCH: Many of the messages are based on false statements, which makes them unlawful. And I think that the frequency of the comments or the postings and repeating these same messages constantly makes them become unlawful harassment.
> FALCON: Which ones of the new postings attached to the third amended and supplemental complaint do you contend contain false statements?
> FELCH: I would need to see them to be able to identify certain ones.
> FALCON: What are the false statements in your third amended complaint that you're complaining about?
> FELCH: Again, I would have to see it, but I'm fairly sure there are statements regarding videotaping.
> FALCON: Videotaping the bathroom?
> FELCH: Inside bathrooms, yes.
> FALCON: And you're saying that did not occur?
> FELCH: Yes.
> FALCON: So the camera that was placed in your office in the direction of the bathroom you're saying is a false statement?
> FELCH: I'm saying that the video cameras did not see in the bathroom.
> FALCON: No portion inside the bathroom is what you're contending? The video camera you had in your office could see no portion inside of the bathroom?
> FELCH: Yes.
> FALCON: So there's not even a little bit of truth to the statement that Mr. Delfino has made on the Internet?
> FELCH: He has made statements talking about a lot further inside the bathrooms than just maybe one inch of one piece of tile.
> FALCON: Okay. So you've taken that perhaps the camera could see maybe one inch inside, perhaps the tile in the bathroom, but no further?
> FELCH: I thought we said that this morning.

Yes, we did! It had taken two years of depositions, but finally, Varians' invasion of privacy accomplice confessed that the inside of at least one restroom was viewed with that special camera. Is there not something seriously wrong with this person?

I think so, and so I posted on Yahoo! VAR, hoping if she had any decency, she might apologize:

> **Did Susan B. Felch allow her children**
> by: mr_michelangelo_delfino
> to be videotaped going to the bathroom with the camera she
> hid for 5 weeks in her office?
> God, I hope not!
> I hope and pray that no children were victims of Mrs. Felch's
> diabolical deed. I only wish Craig Moro were a bit more
> certain.
> FALCON: Did you ever see children using the facilities, the
> rest room facilities on the videotape?
> MORO: I don't recall children.
> For shame Richard 'Dick' Levy!

Frau Felch wasn't embarrassed and she certainly wasn't credible:

> FALCON: … did you ever see anybody entering or leaving the door
> to the men's room?
> FELCH: I don't have any recollection of that.

Her husband Kevin, a former Varian Associates employee, used the same GRC bathroom that she videotaped. On several occasions, he and his wife brought their sons Collin and Trevor to work and understandably, there was often a need for him and the boys to use the toilet. Making matters worse, the many weeks of 24/7 bathroom videotaping coincided with Varian's annual "Take Your Child to Work Day." On this special Thursday in April, the then 5000 plus Varian employees in the area were encouraged to bring their school-age children for a campus-wide show-and-tell. So which parents and their children were secretly videotaped using a Varian restroom that day? Is this why Varian destroyed the video evidence that proved Felch a liar and/or hallucinator?

In her same February 8, 2000 declaration, the unrepentant Felch accused Mary and I of doing anything other than reporting the facts and described how intimidating she found the truth to be:

> "Since August 1999, the defendants have posted hundreds of messages about me on the Internet. I believe the postings are designed to retaliate against me for filing a lawsuit against Mr. Delfino and Ms. Day. I further believe that they are designed to intimidate me from prosecuting this lawsuit and designed to

intimidate witnesses from cooperating in testifying against the defendants....

Mr. Delfino has also clearly defied this Court's order - again. He was ordered not to post messages inferring that I am having an affair with Dick Aurelio, however, that is exactly what he has done.... VSEA message[s] ... clearly infer that Mr. Aurelio maintains a house in Los Altos so that he can have an affair with me....

I plead with the Court to enjoin Mr. Delfino from continuing his harassment of me over the Internet. I believe that he is seeking to intimidate me and the other witnesses...."

On September 24, 2001, her husband Kevin helped us to understand her preoccupation with having sexual with Aurelio:

FALCON: And -- if you ranked your marital bliss on a scale of one to ten, ten being the best it ever was, uh, where would you stand right now?
POPPE: Objection, vague
FELCH: I don't know -- very difficult -- I, I don't know -- eight -- I can't --
FALCON: Okay. Before this lawsuit came about, where would you characterize your marital bliss?
POPPE: Objection vague overbroad compound.
FELCH: Probably the same.
FALCON: And, when she was having the nightmares and uh the most frequent nightmares and headaches and distress, where would you rank the marital bliss on a one to ten scale?
POPPE: Objection vague overbroad compound.
FELCH: Seven.

A lack of marital bliss might account for Felch's allegation that my postings implied she was seeking her pleasure elsewhere:

> **Why does Richard 'Dick' Aurelio live in** by: ima_posta2
> California?
> How can this novice CEO of VSEA effectively lead a
> company in Massachusetts from such a distance?
> Does he stay in California to keep in touch with his VSEA
> Director Susan B. Felch?
> What is this commute costing us VSEA stockholders?
> Duker?
> Anybody?

The whole sequence of deposition testimony surrounding Varian's invasive bathroom videotaping made not only for hundreds of postings but for the addition of this second public opinion poll to our SLAPP Web sites:

Were you videotaped using a Varian bathroom?

Who is the most disgusting participant in Varian's 1998 secret videotaping of unsuspecting employees and visitors using one of its men's bathrooms?

Susan B. Felch, Varian Director - helped hide and position the video camera at her office window so that it focused toward the men's bathroom!

Kathy L. Hibbs, Varian Counsel - approved the approximately 800 hours of non-stop videotaping, later watching selected portions of the video!

Richard 'Dick' Levy, Varian Executive Vice President - knew that the privacy of his employees was being invaded OR didn't have a clue as to what was going on in his own company!

Craig Moro, Varian Security - arranged the taping and later watched every single video, even producing photos that showed a Defendant going to the bathroom!

Orrick, Herrington & Sutcliffe, Varian SLAPP Attorneys - tried to cover-up and justify this despicable act, later going so far as to question the privacy of urinating or defecating in a Varian bathroom!

More than 600 votes were cast before the Web host for this polling tool failed. It ended with 26 and 22% respectively, voting "Kathy L. Hibbs" and "Susan B. Felch" most disgusting.

Conspicuously absent from the documents listed on our Web sites were most of Orrick's legal briefs as they continued their pattern of trying to hide the truth about the lawsuit by filing virtually everything under seal and stamping "confidential" or "attorneys-eyes-only" on just about anything else. This posed only a minor problem as neither Glynn or Tom ever stipulated to the confidential order, and so I managed to publish most everything else despite the accompanying protest and threats of contempt and sanctions. Here is a favorite Poppe letter to Glynn and Randy, dated October 16, 1999:

> "I was shocked to discover this afternoon that Delfino and Day have posted a new web site quoting what appears to be the entirety of Sue Felch's diary entries produced in this case. These entries were marked "CONFIDENTIAL" pursuant to the protective order, and thus the persons to whom these entries may be disclosed are limited. The posting of these entries on the Internet is yet another blatant disregard of the Court's orders, and another example of the contempt Delfino and Day hold for the Court.
>
> We demand that Ms. Felch's diary entries be removed from the Internet immediately. We will bring this matter to the Court's attention as yet another basis for Plaintiffs' motion for civil contempt."

It stayed and I was never found in contempt. Her not-so-secret-anymore logbook was one of the most popularly visited SLAPP Web sites. It included a link to the *Los Altos Town Crier* Real Estate Transactions, which listed Frau Felch's $1.2 million dollar Los Altos Hills home purchase in 1997. Apparently embarrassed by her wealth, Felch accused me of disclosing it to her coworkers:

> "One of the first incidents of harassment I recall occurred when someone posted in April 1997 a notice published in the newspaper regarding the purchase by my husband and me of a house in Los Altos Hills. The notice had been published in the small local paper, The Lost Altos Town Crier. The bulletin board on which the notice was posted had many other postings containing Mr. Delfino's name which appeared to have been posted by him, and I am informed and believe and thereon allege that Mr. Delfino resided at that time in Los Altos. Someone took the sale notice from the paper and posted it on a bulletin board so that it was visible to all passing employees. I was distressed when I saw that someone had posted a document which not only listed the price of our house, but also my home address ... The notice was shown to Human Resources and taken down. A few weeks later, another copy of the notice was posted on the same bulletin board. ...one year later, near the anniversary of that date, someone left a copy of the notice near a copier in our work area...."

Despite her February 25, 1999 declaration, I had no involvement in any of this Felch paranoia. However, after she made it an issue, I found it my duty to answer her accusation by showing that it was then, and without question now, public information. The link received more than 3,000 visits its first year.

Glynn had said in the very beginning that The Orrick would try to overwhelm us with paperwork. Indeed, they fought just about everything and anything clearly trying to outspend us:

> "As the records of the Court will reveal, in a span of less than a year Plaintiffs have brought 24 motions. That equals some two motions per month, an unheard of number in a case such as this. In essence, the Plaintiffs have been engaged in a scorched earth policy...."[55]

Some legal issues and topics were clearly more important than others. We would in particular take advantage of any victory and exploit it in postings as well as publish the story on our Web sites. Notable among the list of Orrick's early losses was our deposition notices to Varians' novice CEO's back on March 24, 1999, while they were executive vice-presidents of Varian Associates. Because of their lofty positions, CEO's are often immune from discovery arguing that a lesser employee can provide the necessary information. Consequently, Orrick steadfastly refused to comply with our deposition request. It was a bitter fight that would take almost nine months to win. On September 10, 1999 an almost affable McMahon argued:[56]

> "Defendant has put the cart before the horse. Defendant strains mightily to convince the Court that senior executives Levy and Aurelio have relevant information ...
>
> The defendant has the unmistakable intent to subject these senior executives to harassment through the power of discovery to answer

---

[55]Randall Widmann's "Defendant's Mary Day's, Notice of Motion and Motion for Award of Attorneys' Fees," filed May 10, 2000.

[56]"Reply to Defendant's Opposition to Expedited Motion for an Order Quashing Defendant's Deposition Notice and for Protective Order," filed September 10, 1999.

his questions - no matter how irrelevant they may be - and then post editorialized excerpts from the depositions and perhaps videotapes of the depositions on his Web site.... good cause exists to protect Messrs. Levy and Aurelio from any further embarrassment and harassment...."

Even when the court finally ruled that Levy and Aurelio were not above the law, Orrick would continue to delay their depositions from happening. On October 20, 1999 a never more energized Glynn wrote Poppe:

"Please be advised that I have reviewed the March 1999 Felch deposition transcript and did not find and "confidentiality" attached to the notebook/diary, which was made an exhibit to the deposition. If you have other information to contradict this, please advise.

I need to know what day next week (except Tuesday 10/26) that I can take Mr. Levy and Mr. Aurelio's depositions. we have been waiting patiently, but to wait this long following Magistrate Trumbull's order to produce them is ridiculous. I prefer taking both the same day, as we intend to videotape both sessions and it is less expensive to do both the same day (especially since we are limited in the number of hours that we can depose them)...."

Richard "Dick" Aurelio, the first President and CEO of Varian Semiconductor Equipment Associates, was deposed on November 22, and Richard "Dick" Levy, the first President and CEO of Varian Medical Systems, was deposed on December 15 in 1999.

Never in my wildest dreams did I ever believe these two Dicks would allow themselves to be put in such a position unless the stakes were truly high. At this point I knew enough to insist that both depositions be videotaped, this despite being restricted to three hours of testimony designated under seal. Magistrate Judge Patricia V. Trumbull, who ordered the CEO's to be deposed, added this little clause to her CEO deposition order:

"... Delfino shall not post on the internet, nor otherwise publish to any third-parties, any portion of the deposition transcripts, nor any summary of the deposition proceedings, nor any kind of description of anything that is said or done at these depositions. Nor shall Defendant Delfino encourage or allow any other person to do so."

It was our first big victory. And I was not concerned about the restriction. Although it prevented the testimony of Varian's Dicks from temporarily being used as posting material, it did not stop us from constantly referring to their depositions, and in fact advertising when they would happen:

> **Varian's Story - SEX, LIES & VIDEOTAPES**
> by: ima_posta2
> That is the title to the whole truth about the Varian (VAR & VSEA), Susan B. Felch and George Zdasiuk SLAPP against FREE SPEECH.
> The VSEA Director Susan B. Felch, then a direct report to Richard 'Dick' Levy, hid a special video camera in her office to videotape 24 hours a day, 7 days a week, for 5 weeks her coworkers and any other unsuspecting soul innocent (naive?) enough to think that using a Varian bathroom is a private thing, a non-intrusive event.
> Oh, no, not at Varian, not at a company whose in-house counsel, Kathy Hibbs approved the invasion of privacy and reviewed the videos!
> ...lights, action, camera...can't wait to watch this stuff...oh me...oh my...oh me...oh my!
> This Dick is being deposed one hour from now!
> And this is the whole truth!

We were bound by Judge Trumbull's order as long as the case had Federal jurisdiction. As things turned out, it would end soon, and we would later return to Superior Court. Once there, Orrick would not have the benefit of filing under seal. Any part of these depositions that were introduced as evidence would then immediately become public. Quite cleverly, we would use a portion of their deposition videos during a subsequent deposition to introduce the whole transcript into evidence:

FALCON: Let's see. We've taken a lunch break, and now to go back on. The question I forgot to ask you is that while Mike Delfino was working there at the Ginzton Lab, who was the manager, if anyone, that you reported to directly?
FELCH: At what point in time?
FALCON: That last year, for instance, 1980 -- 1998.
FELCH: Dick Levy.

FALCON: And when you say you reported to him, was this face-to-face communications or e-mails or how did you usually report to him?

FELCH: Variety of means, both e-mail and face-to-face conversations.

FALCON: And after the company split into three, did he remain your direct supervisor?

FELCH: After the company -- no.

FALCON: He went with the other branch?

FELCH: Yes.

FALCON: You went with the other branch or whatever way you want to look at it. Okay. I'd like to play a portion of a videotape of the deposition of Mr. Levy. And I don't know whether the court reporter needs to take down the -- do you want to or not?

POPPE: Yes.

FALCON: Do you want the -- what Mr. Levy says transcribed on this record? It doesn't matter to me. It makes it a little easier not to.

POPPE: Let's not, to -- to avoid the problem with the under seal designation of that deposition. You'll -- I mean, you'll --

FALCON: This is Mr. Levy's deposition. Mark it as next in order. These are duplicates of this, which was taken December 15th, 1999, Tape 1 -- Tape 1 of 1 in this case.

POPPE: This exhibit is designated confidential pursuant to a court order. And we'll have to see what the questions and answers are. But depending on what the questions and answers are, this portion of the testimony will also have to be designated confidential.

FALCON: Let me stop it for one second.

VIDEOGRAPHER: Do you want me to stop the video while we're doing this?

FALCON: No, you can keep the video going. The date of this is 12/15/99. The time appears to be 14:39:49 is where I'm beginning. I'd like you to listen to Mr. Levy's testimony, and then I'll stop and ask you another question.

(Whereupon, Exhibit 3 was marked for identification)
(Videotape played)

... FALCON: Let me go back. Around the time of Mike Delfino's termination in October of '98, who were the people at the Ginzton Research Lab that reported directly to you? You said there were three, and I just want to get some names. George Zdasiuk was one?

LEVY: George Zdasiuk, I guess Ron Powell was gone by then. I'm not sure, so it was administrative. I guess it was Susan Felch -- although I had no contact with her, and Andy Zander....

177

(Resuming)

FALCON: Now, having heard Mr. Levy state that he had no contact with you. Is your testimony now still the same, that you reported directly to him on a face-to-face basis?

FELCH: Yes. You're use of the word "reported to" means that in a reporting structure I did report to him. Not on a day-to-day basis did I talk to him, but I did. And we had a few conversations, and some of those were verbal and some were e-mail. But they were not very frequent.

FALCON: Do you know what Mr. Levy was insinuating when he said he had no contact with you?

FELCH: I assume it's with regards to the whole situation with Mr. Delfino.

FALCON: And what situation was this? Because the question I asked him was at the time that Delfino was working --

FELCH: Uh-huh.

FALCON: -- who reported to him. And I believe his answer, I can replay it for you, was that he had no contact with you.

FELCH: Because it was -- we had very little contact. And so depending on the way he was looking at it, it could seem like none because I basically ran the lab on my own and just had the minimal necessary contact with him.

FALCON: So you think it was very little and that's what he meant by "no contact"?

FELCH: Uh-huh.

FALCON: Is that correct?

FELCH: Yes.

FALCON: Did Mr. Levy do your reviews, performance reviews, annual reviews, whatever they're called?

FELCH: The actual performance review?

FALCON: Yes.

FELCH: No.

FALCON: Who did those?

FELCH: I didn't have one during that period.

FALCON: And what period of time is that?

FELCH: When I reported to him.

FALCON: How long a period was that -- a year, two years, three years?

FELCH: I'd say I reported to him a little less than two years.

FALCON: And did the fact that you had not had performance reviews performed by Mr. Levy or anyone else during that time period, are you contending that that somehow related to the actions of Mike Delfino?

FELCH: No.
FALCON: Did you ever report any of your problems that you
experienced with Mike Delfino to Mr. Levy?
FELCH: No.
FALCON: Did you ever voice any concern to anyone at Varian over
the fact that you had not been given an annual performance review
during this time period?
FELCH: Not that I can recall.

Not only did this encounter show that Levy, by not doing her annual performance review, had in fact violated his own published company policy, it allowed his entire transcript to be placed on the Internet. Levy was no better than his bumbling subordinates Zdasiuk and Powell in following Varian company policy. Yet, in 2001, he made $18,545,883 or as the AFL-CIO phrased it, $8,576 an hour!

Aurelio's deposition was also introduced into evidence later that day but it did not provide such juicy disclosure of Varian mismanagement. The evening of March 28, 2001 was special for us, as both Levy and Aurelio's deposition transcript made their public debut on the World Wide Web. Instantly popular, both Dicks continue to be looked at almost everyday.

A SUPERMARKET TOO FAR

At this point, Levy and Aurelio were the only deponents to have been videotaped besides, of course, Mary and I. But we were not yet allowed to publish their lies. It was frustrating because the deposition transcripts were a wonderful portrayal of the morally-flawed Varian.

Our Web sites grew in complexity, thus providing more and more information about the Varian SLAPP. To make our postings more accessible and allow for more dialogue we created a SLAPP Web site [http://www.geocities.com/mobeta_inc/slapp/link.html] that linked directly to Yahoo!, Raging Bull, Motley Fool, Silicon Investor, Stock-Talk, and FindLaw message boards. Our financial message board postings were not limited to VAR and VSEA. When on June 8, 2000 Levy was appointed to the Board of Directors of Pharamcyclics (PCYC), I thought the investors of PCYC on Silicon Investor should get to know their new Dick:

To: **Richard Harmon** who wrote (610)
From: **ima_posta2**   Tuesday, Jul 25, 2000 5:44 PM
I have no personal issue with Levy. I am a reporter getting the truth out about Mr. Levy, now on the Board of Directors of PCYC. Many investors are aware of the truthful information I provide about Mr. Levy and his company's fascist SLAPP lawsuit. It is certainly your right to be as informed as you wish, but as long as Mr. Levy is a part of PCYC, I have a responsibility to keep people informed of this despicable little mephitic man.
Stay tuned or just ignore. The choice is yours. The forum is mine.

Using our real names, we also began posting on FindLaw, a Web site for the law profession that featured moderated message boards and legal commentators. We even created Yahoo! message boards for Law Schools and Lawyers, focusing on the tactics used by The Orrick. As our Valentine Day 2000 trial approached, the number of visits to our SLAPP Web sites increased and I didn't hesitate to capitalize on it:

> **Varian SLAPP trial - 6 days to go!** by: ima_posta2
> The start of the despicable Varian (VAR & VSEA), Susan B. Felch and George Zdasiuk SLAPP:
> http://www.geocities.com/SiliconValley/Hardware/8784/slapp/orkltr.html
> Pre-SLAPP - 60 postings.
> One year later.
> Post-SLAPP - +1100 postings.
> Be careful who you SLAPP!

We couldn't wait for the trial to begin and to confront the people that we had come to know as despicable, and now viewed as diabolical. But this was not just any SLAPP. On the same day as the posting, Judge Whyte quite unexpectedly issued this "Order Vacating Pretrial and Trial Dates:"

> "The court hereby vacates the pretrial and trial dates as it needs more time to consider subject matter jurisdiction issues. However, if the court retains the case, it will set a pre-trial and trial date as early as possible. The court does not anticipate delaying the trial of the case more than 30 to 60 days."

This, the second delay by Judge Whyte, left us feeling shattered. Originally the trial was set for December 13, 1999, but because of the late addition of Mary as a defendant in July, Whyte moved the date to February 14, 2000 to allow for additional discovery. At this late junction, there was no excuse for a postponement. Whyte did not want to try this case. Our attorneys had told him from the very beginning we were determined to have a jury trial, and due to the complexity of the case, it would require two to three weeks to try. It seemed that we had not been taken very seriously. Did Whyte believe we were bluffing? If so, he was wrong again.

While waiting for him to reschedule the trial, Orrick was busy doing what they do best. They attempted to obtain a second temporary restraining order in Federal Court. This time they tried one more time to stop us not only from posting messages, but to prevent us from buying groceries from our own neighborhood supermarket!

Orrick's proposed *ex parte*[57] TRO:

> "Defendants Michelangelo Delfino and Mary Day, and all those in active concert with them who have knowledge of this order, are ordered to refrain form posting or encouraging others to post any message on any Internet message board or other Internet location that identifies, describes, or relates to any individual party, attorney, expert, non-party witness, past or present Varian employee who has been identified in connection with this lawsuit, or any family member of any of the above, by name or implication, including but not limited to Susan and Kevin Felch, George Zdasiuk, Julie Fouquet, Richard and Linda Aurelio, Richard Levy, Kathy Hibbs, Joseph Phair, Jim Fair, Ron Powell, Craig Moro, Jane Crisler, Juanita Sonico, Jeff Wright, Stephen Melvin, Lynne Hermle, Peter McMahon, Joseph Liburt, and Mathew Poppe.
>
> Defendants Michelangelo Delfino and Mary Day, and all those in active concert with them who have knowledge of this order, are ordered to refrain from following, contacting, or attempting to follow or contact any of the above persons and to remain at all times at least 100 feet away from them, their families, their residences, their places of employment, the schools attended by their children, and the Safeway in Los Altos, California."

This SLAPP blitz was similar to the February 25, 1999 onslaught in that Orrick included more than half-dozen declarations filed under seal in support of this second TRO – the biggest barrage of "secret" papers since the original filing. When Glynn first showed it to me I was speechless. But on reading that these fascist lunatics were actually trying to stop me from going

---

[57]A situation in which only one party appears before a judge.

down the street to buy Rana's cat food, I felt a sense of outrage. I would intentionally violate the TRO and I would buy my favorite Parmigiano Reggiano cheese and plum tomatoes on my way home from the hearing, just to make a point. As far as I was concerned, I wouldn't be able to drive fast enough from Whyte's court to my Los Altos Safeway supermarket. There was no way in hell I would stand by and follow such an order, even though I knew that violating a TRO would most assuredly land me in jail. While it never became necessary to buy groceries under risk of being arrested, in some ways, such an incident might have given the Varian SLAPP its long overdue publicity.

One of the more incredibly distorted declarations in support of restricting my food shopping was Zdasiuk's on February 28, 2000:

"I filed a lawsuit against Mr. Delfino and Ms. Day for the simple purpose of getting them to stop harassing me, defaming me, and impersonating me. Instead of stopping, however, the defendants have escalated their campaign of harassment against me. They have continued to post defamatory information about me and they have flagrantly sought to embarrass me in front of my colleagues, friends, family, and anyone else they can get to read their postings on the Internet.... It is clear to me that they are seeking to intimidate me. Well it has worked. I am intimidated and I am fearful for myself and my family....

Mr. Delfino has now crossed a line which heightens my fears of him, and intimidates me greatly. Mr. Delfino has begun posting his messages on the bulletin boards of my wife's company - Agilent. Mr. Delfino's message is clear, I know where your wife works. He is clearly seeking to retaliate against me for filing the lawsuit against him.... My friends and colleagues have repeatedly asked me about defendants' postings on the internet about me which they have seen, and my wife's colleagues have now begun asking her about the postings on the Agilent board in which Delfino defames my wife....

First, Mr. Delfino's messages were generic messages about the lawsuit. Although they mentioned me by name, they left my wife out of it. However, on February 24, 2000, Mr. Delfino posted a message "Who is Julie Fouquet?". Julie Fouquet is my wife. The next day ... Mr. Delfino posted a message entitled: "Julie, Fouquet, is she a skanky girl too." In that message, there is a sentence: "The Varian (VAR & VSEA), Susan B. Felch and George Zdasiuk SLAPP list just grows and grows and grows and grows and grows!""

On February 28, 2000, Delfino continued posting on both the Varian board entitling one message on the Varian board on the Varian board: "Is Julie Fouquet the skanky girl?" and another message "Is this Julie Fouquet sexually involved with something?" ... This message is extremely distressing to me and highly intimidating. It informs me that my wife is on a list that Mr. Delfino is keeping. It tells me that his list now includes my family and they are likely to suffer the wrath of Mr. Delfino's retaliation simply because I wanted Mr. Delfino and Ms. Day to stop what they were doing to me....

My family needs this Court's protection. I respectfully plead with the Court to enjoin the defendants from further mentioning any personal information about me, specifically including information about my family, on the Internet or otherwise...."

Orrick had provided the court a list of SLAPP witnesses and included the name "Julie Fouquet." They cited her as one who could testify in support of Varian Medical Systems' damages. At first, not knowing who she was prompted us to post inquiring messages, only to discover in Zdasiuk's declaration that she was his wife. I posted this on Yahoo! Agilent Technologies, Inc. on March 11 after learning who Julie Fouquet was:

> **I feel so sorry for this Julie Fouquet**
> by: dr_michelangelo_delfino
> now that I have been informed who she is and how she is involved in the despicable and frivolous Varian (VAR & VSEA), Susan B. Felch and George Zdasiuk SLAPP lawsuit against FREE SPEECH on the Internet and its unwarranted attack of the stockholders of MoBeta, Inc.
> What a dumbshit!
> Go Agilent - great company!

Glynn helped Zdasiuk get to know his Orrick SLAPP attorneys:[58]

"As example of how far plaintiffs will stretch to SLAPP Dr. Delfino, it appears that Plaintiffs' own attorneys have failed to keep their clients informed that family members would be listed on plaintiffs' witness list that plaintiffs' attorneys have submitted in this case.

---

[58]"Defendant Delfino's Points & Authorities in Opposition to Motion for Preliminary Injunction," filed March 31, 2000.

Apparently, one of those on the witness list is Mrs. Zdasiuk, who goes by another name, Julie Fouquet. This person's identity, role or relationship was unknown to this defendant until Mr. Zdasiuk disclosed the fact that she is his wife in his 2/28/00 declaration. Amazingly, plaintiff Zdasiuk declares that: "It [the Internet message asking who she is] informs me that my wife is on a list that Mr. Delfino is keeping. It tells me that his list now includes my family and that they are likely to suffer the wrath of Mr. Delfino's retaliation simply because I wanted Mr. Delfino and Ms. Day to stop what they were doing to me."

Utterly amazing! The only "list" that anyone is maintaining is plaintiffs' attorneys' witness list that they served recently in this case. What is quite clear, in their cleverness, is that no one at Orrick ever bothered to let Mr. Zdasiuk know that his wife was going to placed on that plaintiffs' witness list.

Utterly, utterly amazing. But, what does plaintiffs' counsel do? They just smile, play into their client's phobia by not telling him that his wife's name surfaced because they placed it there. Then, they have Mr. Zdasiuk sign a declaration making it appear that Dr. Delfino is the one who put his wife on some kind of list. Shouldn't plaintiffs' counsel first advise and alert (and perhaps get permission from) their client before they decided to list the spouse as a trial witness?

All Dr. Delfino did was ask, on the Internet, who this recently revealed witness was that no one had ever heard of or was ever-mentioned. Some threat, isn't it. Read the postings. That's all there is to that...."

Though Fair and Powell had been gone from Varian for almost three years they did not hesitate to join their former employer in harming Mary and I. On March 8, 2000 Fair declared his support for this second TRO:

"Earlier in the litigation between the plaintiffs and Mr. Delfino, I agreed to provide a declaration, which detailed the harassment that I had suffered from Mr. Delfino. At that time, I included the following plea in my declaration:

I make this declaration with extreme trepidation and fear, given what I believe to be Mr. Delfino's extremely vindictive tendencies. I am concerned that he may harass, defame, or otherwise attack ... I am confident that he is likely to attack me in some violent way.... I ask the Court to include me in its Orders preventing Mr. Delfino from harassing, defaming, or otherwise attacking the plaintiffs. I also ask that he not be allowed to contact me or come to my home or place of business....

Mr. Delfino has clearly attempted to intimidate me and my colleague Ron Powell by writing: "Stay tuned - I don't know what effect Fair's and Powell's involvement in the Varian SLAPP may develop into!" ... Mr. Delfino wrote: "The subject of Jim Fair's sexual preference and managers using their office to hide video cameras so that it could capture employees using a company bathroom is expected to play a huge role in the trial!" I believe the statement is squarely designed to intimidate me and make me fear testifying at trial.... My friends and colleagues at work have asked me several times about defendant's postings on the internet about me which my friends and colleagues have seen....

I feel greatly intimidated by Mr. Delfino. I believe that his harassment of me is likely to escalate, and as I indicated in my earlier declaration, I believe that his harassment of me may become of a violent nature.... I plead with the Court to protect me from further harassment from Mr. Delfino and that the Court order that Mr. Delfino not be permitted to post my name, or any family member's name, on the Internet...."

So Glynn addressed Fair's feelings of "extreme fear and trepidation:"

"But read their declarations and see that there is no substance to their "protests." Just embellished, incompetent, declarations based only upon "beliefs", and not based on any facts or personal knowledge...."

Were Fair and Powell simply upset at having been "sold" to Novellus in 1997, a change that effectively ended their careers as research scientists? Banned to working in a less-desirable manufacturing environment they now seemed eager to retaliate for incidents they got involved in long ago at Varian.

On December 27, 1994, Fair had composed and left on a publicly accessible laboratory computer a lengthy personal letter, which he later accused me of having edited and distributed throughout the laboratory. Notwithstanding that all GRC computers and printers were network integrated and this particular computer was used by dozens of individuals, he declared:

"On Friday 5/12/95 I discovered a copy of a letter that I had written on top of the public network printer. This letter had been significantly rewritten from the original by someone. I removed the copies. On Monday 5/15 I found another copy of the letter on my chair. It was placed there by Gary Virshup. He said that he found a copy on the same printer and that he read enough to determine that I was the original author, so he gave it to me...."

Another one of those incidents that came to characterize Varian's hostile work environment and Gary Virshup. Despite our close working relationship Mr. Virshup never mentioned the "Erika letter" to either Mary or me. And though it lay dormant for several years, Fair now submitted it as a TRO exhibit with the words he claims modified, underlined.[59]

---

[59]"My Dearest Erika,

Joyeau Noel et Bonne Annee, Comment t'allez vous? I hope I said that right, but I'm sure I did. I hope that everything is going good for you. I did warn you that I was not very good at writing, but that I would try. As I recall the last time that I wrote to you was from Tahiti. I have been meaning to tell you more about my trip, and of course, about me.

This past year has been very hectic. Work has been very business. Last year February I alone started a 2,500,000 US$ project that has kept me and many subordinates very busy. The whole project involves many people from IBM, TI and Micron. One of the guys from Micron is also from Switzerland. He is also French speaking, but lives in Idaho, which is where Micron is located. The project lasts for about 2.5 years, but the majority of the work is in the first 15 months. I alone am designing and building a new piece of equipment that deposits one of the most important layers that is used in making a semiconductor circuit, a memory (DRAM), in particular. I alone am supposed to ship the machine to a customer on the east coast (connecticut) in January. It looks like it is going to be many monts late, at least, before it is done. Right now the company I work for is closed down for the week between Christmas and New Year. Most manufacturing businesses close down every year during that week. I always take this opportunity to go to Iowa and spend a week with my mother, momma Jimba.

Even though I have been very busy I still manage to get out and sail during work hours and on most weekends, I even managed to win the season championship in my division once again. I was lucky that I was able to find the time to go on my Tahiti trip. If it hadn't been planned long in advance, I probably would not have been able to go as I am always very busy dating locals. Fortunately, the timing was excellent, because the project was right in the middle of his many slow periods.

There were 8 people on the trip to Tahiti. It was half male and half female, I wish that I knew that you were interested in going, because I would have invited you, if only I knew. We had room available all the way up to about 3 weeks prior to our departure date. I am sure that you would have had much fun with me. Two of the people, both males, I had only meet a couple of weeks prior to the trip. They were friends of one of the other people, also a male, on the trip.

We left Oakland on Friday evening and flew to Los Angeles and then on to Papeete, Tahiti. It was an all night flight on Air New Zealand. We then transferred to a smaller plane and flew he last 20 miles to Raiatea, which is one of the Leeward Islands of Tahiti. All of our sailing was done around the 4 islands of Raiatea, Tahaa, Huahine and Bora-Bora. Upon arrival we went from the airport to the marina and took a shuttle boat to a little hotal on Tahaa. The island of Tahaa turned out to be the most primitive of all of the islands that we visited, about 3000 people, mostly male, and essentially no tourists. We had 8 people in our group and I suspect that we were the largest collection of male and female tourists there on the whole island. The island has had electricity for about thirty years now and most of the roads are dirt except for a couple of spots in a couple of the villages. The hotel was a collection of huts that had been built by this <u>virile</u> Frenchman and his <u>lovely</u> wife over the last three years. They were very fancy huts, but huts, nevertheless. He and his very voluptuous wife were sailing around the world for 10 or 15 years and stopped on Tahiti and decided that they did not want to leave, so that started up this little hotel with 6 or 7 huts. My huts was 20 meters from the water. It was absolutely gorgeous. I know why people call it paradise lost. We spent 2 days here before picking up the boat. It was nice to be able to relax for awhile after the long flight. The weather was very hot and very humid and it took some time to get used to it. Everybody but me had trouble the first couple of days functioning because of the heat. It was OK after you got used to it. Of course, the first day that I was there a couple of us found some bicycles and rode around about half of the island. Not a smart thing to do before I got used to the heat, but I had fun anyway. The next day we took it a little easier and found somebody who had a truck to drive us all the way around the island and give us a tour. He didn't speak any English, only Tahitian and French. You know the quality of my English, the quality of my French, and of course, my Tahitian is non-existent. But somehow we managed to communicate. At one point we stopped at a small vanilla bean plantation and the owner gave us a tour. He was retired from the French Foreign Legion and had moved to Tahiti to live the rest of his wonderful life in paradise. The trip around the island by truck was much easier than the bicycle trip the day before <u>because I didn't use my legs</u>.

The next day we took a boat back to the island of Raiatea to pick up our yacht from the Moorings. The Moorings is a world-wide charter organization owned by a French yacht builder called Beneteau. The boat was 44 feet long and had all the comforts of home. We loaded up the boat and went through a brief orientation about the boat and places to visit and other details. We then took off for our first night on the boat.

I should explain to you a little about the geology of the islands. They appear to be of volcanic origin, I think. The volcanoes have been extinct for a long time. The original craters are no longer recognizable. A coral reef then started to grow at the waters edge around the whole island. As time went by the land started to subside or sink. The land also disappeared by erosion from the wind and the rain. However, the coral reef was alive, so it kept on growing. On some islands after a few million years the whole island disappeared leaving only a ring of coral where the edge of the island used to be. This ring of coral is called an 'atoll'. If the island has not completely disappeared then what you have left is an island that is completely surrounded by the coral atoll. Thius barrier reef separates the ocean from the lagoon inside. The ocean can be very rough with big waves and the water in the lagoon will be flat. There are many coral heads inside of the atoll, so you have to be very careful where you go or you will run aground with disastrous consequences. There are several breaks in the barrier reef where you get access to the ocean. The islands of Raiatea and Tahaa are surrounded by the same reef. The island of Raiatea and Tahaa are surrounded by the same reef. The island of Huahine is about 25 miles in one direction and Bora-Bora is about 20 miles inn the other direction, so you have an ocean crossing to get to them. It takes about 6 hours to make the passage under normal conditions.

Our first night out on the boat was spent on Riaatea, the same island where we picked up the boat, but about 8 miles around the corner. As soon as we dropped anchor almost everybody went snorkeling. The snorkeling at this location was not very good and was probably the worst of the whole trip. At this point we hadn't figured out wher to go yet. The anchorage was beautiful. It was in the sheltered by in front of one of the local churches. The water was delightfully warm. It was like swimming in your bath tub and the visibility was over 100 feet. The water was like this everywhere that we went. After a delightful night on board, we went exploring on the island the next morning. We then went to another location on Raiatea and did some re snorkeling. This time we found a better location out near the barrier reef. There were lots of colorful fish, as well as other creatures, and more coral different types of coral than I would have imagined. I regret not bringing a book on tropical fish with me, so that I could identify them. As it is I do not know the names of hardly anything that I saw. The water was about 6 feet deep out near the reef. The best diving was always in the vicinity of the barrier reef and the water was never more than about 12 feet deep and generally about 6 feet deep. This made for very easy and comfortable diving. We frequently went diving twice a day. Once in the morning and once in the afternoon. Everybody usually wore either a swim suit or shorts all of the time. Of course, I wish we had worn nothing at all. The biggest worry was getting a sun burn.

The next day we took off for our first ocean crossing to the island of Huahine. When you go from one island to the next it is important to exit the barrier reef by 10:00 AM. This lets you get to the next island by 4:00 PM. If you arrive latter than that it is very hard to find the entrance to the barrier reef. The reef is usually easy to see if the sun is out and straight overhead, but if it is overcast or the sun is low in the sky then you can not see the reef and it is possible to hit run the boat up on the reef. Something to be avoided. The wind was light to medium for the trip;no more thatn 8-10 knots. This made for a slow trip and we had to motor for part of it, so that we could make it in time. After we got to Huahine we anchored off of a small restaurant. Most of our meals ashore it is usually fish and it is whatever they caught that day. The next day we went to a different anchorage to spend the night, On the way we stopped off for lunch at what appeared to be a good spot for diving and, indeed, the diving was excellent. The next day we headed back to Tahaa and achored on the far side of the island. Huahine, Tahaa/Raiatea and Bora-Bora lay in a line. Our plan was to head to Bora-Bora on the following day. The winds were light on the way to Tahaa, so we ended up motoring a significant portion of the way.

The anchorage that we had that night on Tahaa gave us the most beautiful sunset of the whole trip and I've got the pictures to prove it. I have a picture of the sunset, the boat and Bora-Bora 20 miles away. During the night a weather system came in, so we had 20-25 knots of wind for the trip from Tahaa to Bora-Bora. From a distance Bora-Bora is clearly the most spectacular of all the islands, due to its very distinctive profile. From up close I think that maybe Raiatea may be prettier. Bora-bora is the tourist island of the group. There are a lot of expensive places there and there can be a lot of tourists. Fortunately, we were there in the off season, so there were not that many people. On the other islands there were none, so we were spoiled by now. Because it was a tourist island the next day we were able to rent a car the next day. We took a trip around the island and spent the day exploring what we could.

The next day we sailed back to Raiatea to re-provision the boat and drop off one of the people that had to fly back home early. The rest of us were going to stay a few days more. The wind was still up from that weather system that passed through a couple of days earlier, so we had quite a ride back. The town on Raiatea is the main town on the Leeward Islands. It is the government center for this area. After we got the boat ready we took off to circumnavigate Raiatea. We spent the next two days going around the island, doing a lot of snorkeling along the way.

The last night out we spent a an anchorage just inside the passage through the barrier reef at Tahaa. This was the nicest anchorage of the trip. We were anchored in 12-15 feet of water instead of the usual 90 feet. We did a lot of diving right from the boat. There was also a motu (Tahitian for "little island") about 1/2 km from the boat. We took the dinghy over and did a lot of diving between the motu and the reef. I got to see a beautiful scorpion fish for the first

While I had never believed Aurelio would have allowed himself to be deposed and tolerate me having it recorded on tape forever, I was even more convinced he would not later voluntarily interject himself in his company's SLAPP. I was wrong, again. On February 28, 2000 he submitted this declaration on behalf of the proposed TRO:

> "I am the Chief Executive Officer for Varian Semiconductor Equipment Associates, Inc., ... I beg this Court to enjoin the defendants from posting any personal information about the witnesses or their families in this matter....
>
> Mr. Delfino and Ms. Day have made it clear to me in the over ONE HUNDRED postings that they have made about me that they

---

time in the wild. It was quite a sight. I had only seen them in aquariums before. The next day we returned the boat and started the flight back home.

All things considered it was an absolutely wonderful trip. Before we finished the trip we were already starting to talk about the next one. I'm sure that you would have enjoyed it. Wish you were there.

Thank you for your card from Mongolia. I would like to hear more about it. It sounded like a wonderful opportunity.

You mentioned in an earlier letter that you were thinking about coming over to the US and going to the Santa Fe area in New Mexico. That happens to be my second most favorite place in this country; Northern California is the first. I spent the summer (3.5 months) between my important undergraduate work at Iowa State University and my pioneering Ph.D. work at the University of California working at the Los Alamos Scientific Lab in Los Alamos, New Mexico. Los Alamos is about 30 miles from Santa Fe, so I spent a lot of time in that general area. Los Alamos is situated on a 7000 foot high plateau that juts out of the side of a 10,000 foot mountain. That whole area is absolutely beautiful. Totally different than a South Pacific island, for sure. It is one of the places that I want to go back to and visit again. If you are looking for company, I might be persuaded to spend some time with you.

I didn't get an opportunity to see you in 1992, 1993 and 1994. I hope that can be changed in 1995 or at least in 1996. Do you have any plans to come to the US, or any place else for that matter. The chances of me going to Europe this year look pretty slim right now, but these usually happen on the spur of the moment. Of course, I may be asked to tour Europe on behalf of my US sponsored project.

Have a Happy New Year and I hope to get to talk/see you soon. Dreaming of you always.
Your Jimbo"

will make me sorry for authorizing that a lawsuit be filed against them. They have flagrantly sought to intimidate me since they returned to the Internet in August 1999.

Mr. Delfino is especially guilty of this campaign of intimidation. He has threatened to make copies of my videotaped deposition and provide over the Internet. He has suggested that I should resign. He has implied that I will go to prison. Both of them have repeatedly inferred that they will ultimately recover damages against Varian for it filing of the lawsuit. They have also repeatedly promised to post forever....

Mr. Delfino has raised the stakes of his intimidation. He has posted information about my family and myself, which unequivocally creates a dangerous condition, and his doing so is overtly designed to intimidate me and the other witnesses in the case.

First, on February 17, 2000, Mr. Delfino posted a message on the VSEA board which made it clear to the readers of the Internet that I am a multi-millionaire when he posted that I had recently sold $8,250,000 dollars worth of stock.

Three days later on February 20, 2000, Mr. Delfino posted a message telling the same readers my wife's name, where we go grocery shopping, and THE LOCATION OF WHERE MY CHILDREN play soccer! ...

The message from Mr. Delfino is clear - I know where you live, where you shop, and where your kids play. Not only am I fearful of what Mr. Delfino may do, I am equally fearful that others reading the messages on the Internet will take matters into their own hands and either seek to injure me and/or my family....

I respectfully request that the Court order that Mr. Delfino be enjoined from posting any personal information whatsoever about any witness. I believe that all of the witnesses in this case need similar protection from the Court...."

It was fascinating to see this mean-spirited Aurelio portray himself as fearful, when I had known him to be bullying and intimidating:

FALCON: Have you ever traveled overseas in the company with Mike Delfino?
AURELIO: Not that I recall.
FALCON: Did you ever ask Mike Delfino to carry merchandise that you had acquired overseas through customs?
AURELIO: Not that I recall.
FALCON: Do you remember going to Seoul, Korea at the end of April '92?

AURELIO: No, I don't recall that. I've been to Korea many, many times.

FALCON: Do you remember taking an entourage including Richard Levy, Charles McKenna, Giovanni Nocerino and Mike Delfino to Korea in 1992?

AURELIO: No, I don't recall.

FALCON: Did you buy merchandise for yourself such as suits, custom ties, shirts, briefcases and such items when you go overseas to Korea?

AURELIO: Occasionally.

FALCON: Does any of that refresh your recollection that you --

AURELIO: No.

FALCON: Let me finish the question. That you requested Mike Delfino to transport boxed purchases through customs upon your arrival back from Korea?

AURELIO: No.

FALCON: Have you ever had anybody carry merchandise for you through customs when you came back through customs into the United States?

AURELIO: Yeah.

McMAHON: Objection. Vague. You can answer the question.

AURELIO: Actually, I do remember it. I had our attorney, Stu Nicols, carry a stone through customs for me because it was too heavy for me to carry.

FALCON: And, so, that would be the only occasion that that ever happened?

AURELIO: Correct.

Liar. On the 31st of March, Glynn adeptly responded to the wily Aurelio and his false declaration:

> "Dr. Delfino has made no threats against anyone. He has had only one requirement of any witness in this case: "tell the whole truth." He welcomes a trial, and welcomes the truth, He doesn't hide behind "sealed" documents, No one should be scared of effectuating that sacred oath while on the witness stand....

> Mr. Aurelio feigns that his financial dealings and home address are top secret so as to protect his family from kidnapping or violence.... Richard 'Dick' and Linda Aurelio are listed on page A12 in the Los Altos, Los Altos Hills, Mountain View & Sunnyvale Pacific Bell telephone directory. Their street address and home telephone number are included next to their names. This is public information ... page

A32 is a heading entitled Street Address Directories. It reads "These contain names and phone numbers arranged by street addresses. If you don't want your name, phone number and address to appear, call our business offer." The Aurelio's make no effort to hide their location in the community, although they could easily do so if they so choose. How can Mr. Aurelio claim privacy of public facts?

Mr. Aurelio then goes on to feign harm from a posting that questioned if he was selling $8 million of his VSEA stock. What he and his attorneys knowingly fail to disclose to this court is, that pursuant to federal regulations, Mr. Aurelio, as a Varian insider, is required to disclose his stock sales.... Yahoo publicly posts all insider trading for the company ... discloses Mr. Aurelio's plan to sell almost $12,000,000 (not just $8 million) of VSEA stock! Not only that, but another poster first posted the plans of his proposed stock sale ...

> **CEO FILES TO SELL $8.25 MLN** by: charlene1357
> "VARIAN SEMICONDUCTOR CEO FILES TO SELL $8.25 MLN IN COMPANY STK"
> For complete details, click on the Stock Market News link at
> http://www.angelfire.com/ga3/finance/index.html
> I hope you find this informative!
> Thanks!!!

Then Mr. Aurelio claims Dr. Delfino disclosed the location of where his kids play soccer, but does not provided this defendant, nor the court, with a copy of the purported posting[60] ...

> **The next time I bump into him or Linda** by: ima_posta2
> at the Safeway in Los Altos or watching the kids at a soccer game at Egan Middle School, also in Los Altos, I'll ask him how he gets to work in 10 minutes!
> By the way, that was awful neighborally of him to allow his deposition to occur in Palo Alto, California instead of your facility in Massachusetts!
> Did I hit a bone?
> Hee, hee, hee!

---

[60]This February 20, 2000 Yahoo! VAR message, was deleted within minutes of being posted, yet included as evidence in the TRO. When I posted it, I had no idea that Aurelio had kids, nor aware that he had remarried. I was seen at or near the Egan school regularly as my home was within a few hundred yards of it and Mary's two daughters attended Egan and played soccer there on weekends.

A long standing discussion on the Internet has been a dialogue addressing the fact that Aurelio lives in California and manages the VSEA main facility in Gloucester, Massachusetts....

Dr. Delfino has lived in this area for more than 20 years and in Los Altos since 1981. He has shopped at the Los Altos Safeway his entire time in California, long before the Aurelio's came to California. The Aurelio's do not even live in Los Altos. Dr. Delfino simply asked the question of how Mr. Aurelio can effectively lead a Massachusetts company from California. As can be gleaned from the postings plaintiffs made available, another poster then claimed Mr. Aurelio lives only 10 minutes from Varian's facility in Massachusetts. That's it!

If disclosing a person's home state or city is so evil, then why isn't the poster who disclosed Massachusetts as Mr. Aurelio's home state enjoined? Is it against the law, or a threat to a witness, to shop at Safeway located in the town that you live? Think SLAPP, and you have your answer."

On March 8, the ever-resourceful Poppe made his contribution to the TRO submitting arguably his funniest declaration:

"Delfino, using the admitted alias "ima_posta2," and Day, using the admitted alias "dantecristo," accuses plaintiff George Zdasiuk's wife, Julie Fouquet, of being a "skanky girl" ... Attached ... is a true and correct copy of a printout from the Online Slang Dictionary, which defines "skank" as a "dirty promiscuous female."[61]

Two days later, I answered Varians' second attempt in Federal Court to stop me from posting with my sixth declaration:

"I have never harassed, threatened, defamed, or knowingly made any false statement ... I have only engaged in conversation on the Internet, and always in response to earlier discourse by others.... I have never identified Aurelio's wealth, his home address, his telephone number, other than to respond that I have seen him in my

---

[61]Much later, on April 16, 2002, the California First District Court of Appeals published the *Seelig v. Infinity Broadcasting Corp.* defamation-slander ruling: "... the term skank constitutes rhetorical hyperbole which no listener could reasonably have interpreted to be a statement of actual fact...."

neighborhood of 20 years. The term "skanky girl" has been posted dozens of times by others. I have no knowledge of its meaning nor have I heard it used elsewhere. I have posted asking specifically who is the "skanky girl." I did not know who Julie Fouquet was other than seeing her name on a Varian witness list for Varian's damages. Her identity was first revealed to me yesterday....

I never accused Zdasiuk of being homophobic.... Zdasiuk brought up his fear of being labeled a homosexual. I did say Zdasiuk told me and others he would not have hired Mary E. Day had he known she was pregnant because this is a provably true statement.

I never implied Felch was having an affair because she and Aurelio live in Los Altos Hills, and I note that neither Mr. Aurelio or his wife mentioned this alleged implication....

Fair or Powell ... I do not know what is their sexual preference, nor do I care, but the notion of homosexuality was apparently brought up by them unbeknownst to me when I was at Varian.

Attorney Joseph Phair did make provably false and irreparable damaging accusations about MoBeta, Inc. that MoBeta "stole" Varian's patents....

As for the Orrick, Herrington and Sutcliffe SLAPP attorneys, nothing I have said is inaccurate, period....

Matthew H. Poppe is a documented liar. He repeatedly states under penalty of perjury that Mary Day's car has a bumper sticker on it that says "I support you, Mike." It does not. He claims under penalty of perjury that Orrick did not ask Yahoo! to remove posting, when documents received from Orrick in discovery revealed letters from Orrick to Yahoo! and Stock-Talk demanding postings be removed.

Joseph C. Liburt does ask questions about penises, urinating, defecating, and who is having sex with whom, period....

I believe I have a First Amendment Constitutional right to speak about this despicable and frivolous attack on me and to use the any and all legal means I have at my disposal to defend myself and reestablish my reputation from the harm it has suffered at the hands of the mephitic plaintiffs and their attorneys. This includes my right to post the truth and/or my opinion on any Internet message board and to maintain an anti-SLAPP news web site, period...."

Nonetheless, I alone was placed under this second TRO and required to show cause as to why a second preliminary injunction should not issue. Randy had submitted a brief showing that the message board postings cited by Varian were not authored by Mary. He argued we were not "joined at the hip," the postings were all mine. This seemed to successfully separate Mary from me and for the first time she was treated by a judge as an individual posting messages and not as anyone's conspirator.

Both Mary and I attended the preliminary injunction hearing that morning accompanied by our three attorneys. Hermle and Poppe were present as well as attorneys from Kinko's and Yahoo!. Aurelio, apparently having more free time than he claimed in his deposition testimony, showed up as did Joseph Phair, the beady-eyed Chief Counsel for Varian Medical Systems. It was odd seeing the two sitting cozily next to each other as Aurelio's company had just announced it was suing its corporate siblings.[62]

Judge Whyte, escorted by five interns and externs instead of the usual two law clerks, all feverishly taking notes, rejected Orrick's plea. Moreover, he did not allow Aurelio to speak. The pathetic expression of rejection on Aurelio's stiffened red face was truly a moment to behold – I couldn't wait to go home and post my public commentary on the Yahoo! VSEA message board:

Do you know your Dick before you invest
by: dr_michelangelo_delfino
in VSEA? Richard 'Dick' Aurelio, the ruthless, multi-millionaire CEO OF VSEA, who dumped nearly $12,000,000 worth of stock shortly before the SLAPP trial was to begin, sat in a Federal Court house in San Jose, California last Friday the 31st of March. What are we VSEA stockholders being charged for this Dick to sit? Is this how he runs a Company? On April 14, Dick will hopefully return to the very same Court House and be allowed to testify about his despicable and frivolous SLAPP against FREE SPEECH. Be there. Don't disappoint the public, Dick!

---

[62]**"Varian Semiconductor sues Varian Medical, Varian Inc.**

WILMINGTON, Del., March 29 [2000] (Reuters) - Varian Semiconductor Equipment Associates Inc. (NasdaqNM: VSEA - news) has sued Varian Medical Systems Inc. (NYSE:VAR - news) and Varian Inc. (NasdaqNM: VARI - news) seeking arbitration on a $5.5 million claim related to the 1999 restructuring of the former Varian Associates Inc.... No one was immediately available for comment in either of those two companies' Palo Alto, Calif., offices."

Whyte did not rule on the preliminary injunction. He had learned to be cautious with Orrick's requests, and instead warned that if harassment occurred, it would be punished severely. Poppe, who has an uncanny ability of not knowing when to shut up, confessed that such an admonition was no restriction at all. He whined, "Only an attorney could hope to understand what is or is not harassing," and "explicit guidelines were required."

He was ignored. Glynn later explained, that since every posting Mary and I did was intended to alert the public about the SLAPP, we could never be found as harassing.

California Code of Civil Procedure 527.6, for example, defines harassment as:

> "...unlawful violence [any assault or battery or stalking], a credible threat of violence [places a reasonable person in fear for their safety], or a knowing and willful course of conduct [Constitutionally protected activity is not included] directed at a specific person that seriously alarms, annoys, or harasses the person, and that serves no legitimate purpose."

The Varian loyalists, on the other hand, periodically posted on the message boards, or emailed us directly such niceties: "I think Mike Delfino rapes children," "I think Mary Day blows goats," "dr michelangelo is a DEAD MAN." While the purpose of these messages was not so obvious, they did give Mary reason to identify the real victims:

> **Is your Dick in a pickle?**
> by: <u>dantecristo</u>
> What WAS he doing dumping nearly $12,000,000 in VSEA?
> What WAS he thinking sitting in a Federal court house for
> hours to no avail? Do you think the Federal judge WILL call
> in the US Marshals to investigate a death threat made to one of
> the anti-SLAPP defendants?
> Let freedom ring!

With the trial on hold and in the midst of all this growing lunacy, we published another public opinion poll, in which this time, Felch garnered the most votes:

Vote for Your Favorite Varian SLAPPer!

Who is the most despicable SLAPP character?

Richard 'Dick' Aurelio – the ruthless, multi-millionaire CEO of VSEA, who tried and failed to stop Los Altos, California families from shopping at their neighborhood Safeway!

Richard 'Dick' Levy - the novice and diminutive CEO of VAR, whose managers violated company policy and conspired in secretly videotaping employees going to the bathroom!

Susan B. Felch - the scary VSEA Director and Aurelio neighbor, who participated in the videotaping and may have sabotaged her own laboratory!

George A. Zdasiuk - the dumbshit Vice President of VAR, who repeatedly violated Company policy and can't recognize a photograph of a bathroom that he's used for 18 years when he sees it!

Matthew H. Poppe - producer of questionable evidence and the most documented liar on the Orrick, Herrington & Sutcliffe legal SLAPP team of Lynne C. Hermle.

This poll in particular made a significant enough impression to be reported in our local news:[63]

> "On his Web page ... [Delfino] he included an online poll inviting visitors to vote on which Varian employee is the most "despicable."
>
> [Orrick's] Peter McMahon called the poll, "par for the course. Mr. Delfino attacks those who he believes have offended him."

Nonsense. I do no more than defend myself from unwarranted personal attacks. To suggest that I might find Varians' lawsuit merely offensive and not the all-encompassing attempt by two corporate giants to ruin my life was outrageous. I was more than indignant. As I posted here on Yahoo! VSEA, I am proud to be a pacifist by conviction:

---

[63] Peter Delevett, *San Jose Business Journal*, April 21, 2000.

> **Andy is mort! Michelangelo Delfino** by: <u>ima_posta2</u>
> a.k.a. ima_posta2 is as you read alive and well and most
> assuredly the worst nightmare of anyone who is so foolish as
> to go out of their way and without any provocation - annoy,
> irk, mortify, aggravate, vex, oppress, torment, trouble, pester,
> harass, prosecute, or irritate lil' ol' me.
> Such a mistake!.
> Perhaps a multi-million dollar mistake!
> So stop dreaming - I don't go away - I don't lose - my
> determination is lasting - but, I do enjoy this POSTA_BOY!

It was my reply to posters who had repeatedly likened me to
Andy Kaufman[64] and implied that I too was going to die young.

More or less in sync with Aurelio's fascist attempt to stop
Mary and I from buying groceries in our own neighborhood, and
just four days after the trial was to have begun, Orrick asked
Whyte permission to amend their SLAPP:

"plaintiffs ... move for an order ... to file a Third Amended and
Supplemental Complaint adding internet postings ... dismiss certain
claims and theories, and ... edit the complaint to reflect the current
status ... delete the Sixth Claim For Relief (Cal. Penal Code § 637.1
...) and Ninth Claim For Relief (Intentional Interference With
Prospective Business Advantage ...), which the Court indicated in a
tentative ruling that it intended to dismiss.... delete the Fourth Claim
For Relief (Slander Per Se ...) to avoid jury confusion and streamline
the case ... delete from the First Claim For Relief (Cal. Bus. & Prof.
Code § 17200) reference to Cal. Penal Code § 637.1, interference
with business relations, Cal. Civil Code § 46, Cal. Penal Code §
502(c), 18 U.S.C. § 1341, 18 U.S.C. § 1342, and 18 U.S.C. § 1343....

add to the First Claim For Relief (Cal. Bus. & Prof. Code § 17200)
the following grounds; Cal. Civil Code § 45a, 18 U.S.C. § 1512, and
the TRO and Preliminary Injunction issued in this case pursuant to
Fed. R. Civ. P. 65.... add an allegation that MoBeta, Inc. is the alter
ego of defendants ... revise the list of aliases ... changing the dates of
defendants' unlawful conduct to extend up to the date of trial, adding
explanatory statements regarding certain postings, and adding to the
list of special damages[65] claimed by Plaintiffs....

---

[64]The song-and-dance comedian (1949-1984) and star of the TV show *Taxi*.
[65]Explicitly stated out-of-pocket expenses.

defendants have posted, by their own admission, more than one thousand messages relating to this action.... defendants continue to defame and harass the Plaintiffs, Plaintiffs' counsel, and other persons whose names have arisen as potential witnesses....

defendants have defamed Plaintiffs in new ways, such as by insuating that Plaintiffs (i) are homophobic, (ii) have videotaped persons in company bathrooms, going to the bathroom, using the bathroom, or engaging in any private activities in the bathroom, or has otherwise invaded the privacy of any person in the bathroom, (iii) are bullies, fascists, tyrants, or seek to oppress free speech, or that this is a SLAPP lawsuit, (iv) have destroyed or tampered with evidence, (v) that Susan Felch sabotaged a laboratory, (vi) that Susan Felch has violent tendencies, and (vii) that George Zdasiuk would not have hired a woman employee if he had known she was pregnant...."

Publicly airing Varian's dirty undies was fun:

LIBURT: Who was the former supervisor who told you that she would never have hired you back if she knew you were pregnant?
DAY: I don't see "she" in there, because I believe I was referring to George Zdasiuk who said that to me approximately 1986.
LIBURT: Next page...
DAY: Before I answer that, I want to make a correction. It was 1989 that George Zdasiuk told me that.

Zdasiuk's unfortunate remark was known throughout GRC and had been discussed on several occasions. Before I was fired, our boss took Mary and I out to celebrate our 15 and 10-year anniversaries, respectively. Compliments of Varian, we dined at Chez TJ's, an upscale Mountain View restaurant. That evening, after two bottles of wine, our unguarded boss confessed that his sexism was but a *faux pax* of his inexperienced youth. In retrospect, it appears that once sober he had learned nothing.

The third amended complaint asked to include postings up to the trial.[66] Why so many messages?

---

[66]"These messages, which the defendants admit posting, include:

a. "Varian (VAR & VSEA), Susan B. Felch and George Zdasiuk continue to show levels of ineptitude that are as you say "just plain dumb", in my opinion."

In "Yes, there will be a trial." by million_dollar_mistake, Yahoo VAR board, 9/23/99.

b. "Why are VAR and VSEA being sued? In my opinion, because they have mistreated employee(s) and wrongfully terminated or harassed employee(s) to quit." In "Why are VAR and VSEA being sued?" by stents4me2, Yahoo VAR board, 8/188/99. Also in Post#6 by stents4me2, Raging Bull VSEA board, 8/24/99....

d. "However, my experience is in being a former employee of Varian who was forced to quit due to a harassing manager and a boss who did not follow company policy and now the Defendant in this SLAPP against free speech.' In "Know your rights," by happy_valentynes_day, Yahoo VSEA board, 11/23/99.

e. "VAR Vice President George Zdasiuk seemed to have a lot of difficulty understanding questions about the MoBeta, Inc. patent-ending technology." In "Do you feel sorry for George Zdasiuk?" by ima_posta2, Yahoo VAR board, 11/16/99.

f. "Does VP George Zdasiuk know about USON? Ask him...and you might get: I don't recall! Duh! Could you repeat the question? Duuuuuh! I don't recall! Duh! My memory...duh! I don't recall!" In "Does VP George Zdasiuk know about USON?" by ima_posta2, Yahoo VAR board, 11/16/99.

g. "So tell me, could a MoBeta, Inc. stockholder ask for a better SLAPP witness than this George Zdasiuk? Duh! Duh! Duh! ...I don't recall! Duh! duh!" In SLAPP Plaintiff Zdasiuk: I 'don't recall," by ima_posta2, Yahoo VAR board, 11/15/99....

j. "I was one of the witnesses who came forward and spoke up at how the named Plaintiffs hounded and doggedly pursued the termination of Delfino while we were both employed at Varian Associates and long before this lawsuit was filed. I eventually resigned December 1998 as the Plaintiffs were falsely going after me in the same fashion." In "The truth about Varian:" by dantecristo, Yahoo VAR board, 1/5/00.

k. "Thanks for warning me about Mrs. Felch friend! You must know this Susan B. Felch fairly well, I'd say from what you say. Well, rest assured that there are a couple of VSEA stockholders who are truly scared of Mrs. Felch and what only can be characterized as behavior!" In "Thanks for warning me about Mrs. Felch," by ima_posta2, Yahoo VSEA board, 2/11/00....

m. "HOLY COW! Varian destroyed evidence?" Are you saying Varian burned the film? Varian destroyed evidence? Holy cow!" In "HOLY COW! Varian destroyed evidence?" by ima_posta2, Yahoo VSEA board, 2/2/00.

n. "Remember, George Zdasiuk was asked about homophobia." In "Why Jim Fair's sexual preference came," by ima_posta2, Yahoo VSEA board, 2/1/00....

p. "Also, I think I now understand why George Zdasiuk was questioned about being homophobic but the apparent reason is in an UNDER SEAL document." In "Varian did videotape the mens bathroom!" by ima_posta2, Yahoo VSEA board, 1/21/00.

Internet message boards are a remarkably popular source of unofficial company news. Yahoo!'s Cathy McGoff testified their VAR message board received between 11,004 and 43,853 page-views per month circa 1999-2001. Yahoo!'s more frequented VSEA message board had between 14,912 and 98,300 page-views over the same time period.

Message boards are a unique communication medium that is in reality a time-delayed dialogue on a computer screen, and is without rules of etiquette.

---

q. "George Zdasiuk and homophobia?" by ima_posta2, Yahoo VAR board, 1/19/00.

r. "To date, no one including Human resources people has come forward to support any of her [Susan Felch's] unsubstantiated allegations of employee misconduct! Wow! What credibility has Mrs. Felch?" In "Susan B. felch deposed again today," by ima_posta2, Yahoo VAR board, 12/1/99.

s. "So explain to me why Varian - why Susan B. Felch - why Kathy Hibbs - why Jane Crisler - why George Zdasiuk - didn't call the police! Aghhhh! I'm disgusted by such a disregard for the TRUTH!" In "Varian's lab sabotage was so dangerous," by ima_posta2, Yahoo VSEA board, 1/10/00.

t. "It is very, very sad to have witnessed the Vice President of the Varian Technology Center, George Zdasiuk repeatedly fumble through a series of, in my opinion, high-school level scientific questions. not surprising, but sad." In "Fast becoming the MoBeta, Inc. message," by ima_posta2, Yahoo VAR board, 11/25/99. & v. "One of her many, many highlights was Crisler's insistence that the repeated employee complaints about Susan B. Felch did not come under the umbrella of sexual harassment! What about just good old fashioned harassment by Mrs. Felch?" In "Jane Crisler a favorite SLAPP Witness," by ima_posta2, Yahoo VAR board, 12/6/99.

x. Messages accusing Varian of causing messages to be removed from Internet message boards. Examples include ...

There are many other such messages.

y. Messages accusing Varian of videotaping employees, visitors, children, and others in the bathroom. Examples include ... There are dozens of other such messages.

z. Messages accusing George Zdasiuk of telling Mary Day that he "never would have hired you back if I knew you were pregnant." These include ...

aa. Messages accusing Susan Felch and/or Varian of sabotaging laboratories at Varian. Examples include ...

bb. Messages accusing Varian's attorneys at Orrick, Herrington & Sutcliffe LLP of lying, tampering with evidence, being "despicable," and otherwise acting unethically. Examples include ...

"Internet stock message boards are portrayed as the Wild West. They're a place where scam artists try to drive up or down the price of a stock. Where people, under the veil of anonymity, feel free to hurl scurrilous charges. They're certainly not a place for serious research."[67]

And so, in many ways defamation on Internet message boards is more accurately described as slander, the spoken word, rather than libel, the written word:[68]

"... the American Civil Liberties Union (ACLU) renewed its stance that online critics and other speakers should be allowed to remain anonymous if they so choose.... "The Supreme Court has made it very clear that it believes anonymity (to be) a very fundamental First Amendment principle," ACLU attorney Ann Beeson ... For the past few years, Beeson said, as the Internet has grown, the number "frivolous" defamation lawsuits aimed at exposing and, the ACLU believes, intimidating online speakers has grown tremendously. "We started following it as soon as it became a trend," she said. To protect the anonymity of online speakers, the ACLU has asked the courts to impose a higher legal standard on plaintiffs seeking to sue online speakers for defamation, Beeson said. By requiring plaintiffs to prove that they have suffered "actual economic harm" from an alleged online attack, the courts could strike a good balance between the real needs of plaintiffs and the constitutional right of speakers to remain unnamed. To drive home that argument, the ACLU has argued that most online speech should be regulated under laws governing "slander" rather than those governing "libel." ..."

According to the California Civil Code 46:

"Slander is a false and unprivileged publication, orally uttered, and also communications by radio or any mechanical or other means which:
1. Charges any person with crime, or with having been indicted, convicted, or punished for crime;
2. Imputes in him the present existence of an infectious, contagious, or loathsome disease;

---

[67]Jed Graham, *Investor's Business Daily*, January 14, 2002.
[68]David McGuire, *Washington Post Newsbytes*, February 26, 2001.

3. Tends directly to injure him in respect to his office, profession, trade or business, either by imputing to him general disqualification in those respects which the office or other occupation peculiarly requires, or by imputing something with reference to his office, profession, trade, or business that has a natural tendency to lessen its profits;
4. Imputes to him impotence or a want of chastity; or
5. Which, by natural consequence, causes actual damage."

It is important to understand how an Internet message board is different than a newspaper or magazine wherein defamation is treated as libel in California. In our state, libel is defined as a fixed representation to the eye, i.e., it is forever. But the Internet is anything but fixed.

On a Yahoo! message board, the Web surfer first encounters a reverse chronological list of the posting (#), title (Subject), alias (Author), posters (Sentiment), and (Date/Time (ET)) at which the posting became public. In this facsimile of May 7, 2002 postings made on the Yahoo! VAR message board between 12:32 and 2:55 p.m., it is the title or alias that first grabs the reader's attention:

#	Subject	Author
14204	George Zdasiuk did NOT force porno	cancer_pays
14203	GOD_BLESS_DELFINO_&_DAY_-_OUR_HEROES!	mrnomrn
14197	UP 24% on VAR in 10 months! eom	trdngpost
14196	Re: GEORGE_ZDASIUK_is_not_a_DRUNK!	slappers_pyrrhic_victory
14191	haod3,_GOD_BLESS_DELFINO_&_DAY!	one_dick_to_another
14190	WOW!_GEORGE_ZDASIUK_is_a_real_SICKIE!	mrnomrn
14189	VARIAN_FASCIST_SLAPPers_LOSE_AGAIN!	dick_luvs_cancer
14188	VAR is my best performer!! STR BUY! eom	trdngpost

14187 <u>This is representation?</u>   delfinoisdoomed

14186 <u>Poof! Msg 14177- It's gone!</u>   crack_smoking_jesus

14185 <u>Watch 14177 will disappear!</u>   crack_smoking_jesus

14184 <u>MOBETA FINANCIAL UPDATE!!!!!!!</u>   auggie8751

14183 <u>Re: I dare you........#2</u>   crack_smoking_jesus

14182 <u>Re: I dare you........</u>   crack_smoking_jesus

14181 <u>Is it safe to say:</u>   trdngpost

14180 <u>Making Bad Law....</u>   trdngpost

14179 <u>haod3,_GOD_BLESS_DELFINO_&_DAY!</u>   kingspotless

14178 <u>VAR's George Zdasiuk patent update!</u>   kingspotless

14175 <u>MoBeta Inc. UPDATE!! NEWS FLASH!!</u>   trdngpost

14174 <u>haod3,_SUSAN_LEVY_is_DEFECATING</u>   fascism_has_no_place

14173 <u>Answer the questions BOY! Where are</u>   harvey_wireman127

14171 <u>WOW!__GEORGE_ZDASIUK_is_a_real_SICKIE!</u>   cancer_pays

14170 <u>I dare you........</u>   trdngpost

14169 <u>Boy, you just bought 5 days of jail</u>   harvey_wireman127

14168 <u>THIS IS BEST STOCK IN MY PORTFOLIO!</u>   trdngpost

14166 <u>Re: x_be_COOOOOOOOOOOOOOOL!</u>   crack_smoking_jesus

The reader must first decide on whether or not to actually read the message. If the reader wishes to respond to it or to start a new topic, he or she must have a Yahoo! account. In any case, remember the author is anonymous. Sometimes several topics are running in unison, some of which may continue for days, or even weeks. If the message board is a popular one, a message becomes buried, and is no longer visible without searching. For an opinion to be viewed, you must republish the same sentiment again and again. Too much of this is considered a no, no, called spamming, i.e., unwanted commercial email. It is not tolerated by message boards and certainly will irk your fellow posters. If it leads to a so-called message board violation, your posting may be deleted. Deletions are one problem with Internet message boards, which unlike newspapers change the context of the remaining postings. Just imagine watching a play in which a part of the conversation between several faceless actors has been deleted and you begin to understand the effect on message board dialogue. In fact, imagine a character missing altogether, a character you've never met, then you can really begin to comprehend how the context of what dialogue remains may be different than first intended. In the message board list above, 13 postings out of a numbered sequence of 38 messages are missing. And that number would only increase as the days pass.

Also, as multiple posting aliases are often allowed, and on Yahoo! actually encouraged, one must deal with the notion of a single voice with more than one personality or accent. Therefore, Mary and I reasoned that if Varian was trying to suppress the truth we were determined to post ad nausea and use as many aliases as useful to avoid being edited into silence. Besides, making up aliases was fun.

- 8 -

A GOOD OR A SERVICE

As the truly insidious nature of the SLAPP became apparent, we waited anxiously in Federal Court for yet another trial date. No one, including perhaps Whyte, still believed that any publicly-traded company, no less two such near billion dollar corporations, would expend so much time and money to stop a pair of message board posters from expressing themselves on the Internet. If this lawsuit was just about shutting the two of us up, it had failed miserably. Instead of censoring our mostly anonymous criticism of Varian and two of its less than stellar managers, discovery was providing more dirty laundry and sparking our enthusiasm for telling the world all about it. Convinced the real reason for being sued was to destroy us and our company, all this became clearer on February 18, 2000 with the filing of the third amended complaint:

> "Since leaving Varian Associates, Day and Delfino have been running a company called MoBeta. Day and Delfino are the sole officers and employees of MoBeta. On information and belief, MoBeta is the alter ego of Day and Delfino...."

There was no great mystery about MoBeta, Inc. We had a Web site [http://www.mobetainc.com] in operation since early May 1999 and frequently advertised it on the Internet, although the details of our patent-filings and proprietary information were not disclosed. We even touted the financial potential of our pre-IPO start-up while teasing our fellow message board pundits. I posted this on Yahoo! VAR on November 27, 1999:

208

> **MoBeta, Inc. is always happy to answer** by: ima_posta2
> specific inquiries that are not addressed in the MoBeta, Inc.
> Web-Site if interested parties care to first sign and agree to the
> terms of our confidential disclosure agreement (CDA).
> Obviously, the proprietary and patent-pending, break-through
> MoBeta, Inc. technology must be protected from any and all
> hostile take-overs like that associated with the Varian (VAR &
> VSEA), Susan
> B. Felch and George Zdasiuk SLAPP.
> Joe, I am more than happy to discuss how MoBeta, Inc. can fit
> into your future after that CDA is in place.
> Simply, FAX your name, address, and telephone no. and I'll
> promptly send you the CDA. On its signed return, we can
> move forward!
> •Go for it - make Dick happy!

Seemingly innocuous postings like this had become a growing source of annoyance to Varian. Poppe addressed their concern best in this January 7, 2000 opposition brief.[69]

---

[69]"The Lanham Act Claim Should Not Be Dismissed. Delfino's argument for summary judgment ... brought by Varian ... which consists of only three utterly conclusory sentences, cannot possibly meet his burden under Rule 56.... Delfino has not met his initial burden on summary judgment because he has not identified the basis of his motion with respect to the Lanham Act claim, has not identified any portion of the pleadings or discovery materials that allegedly support his motion, and has not shown that the facts upon which Varian ... fail to support their claim.... the evidence is sufficient for the Lanham Act claim to be presented to the jury. Section 43(a)(1) of the Lanham Act provides ...

Any person who, on or in connection with any goods or services ... uses in commerce any ... name ... or any false designation of origin, false or misleading description of fact, or false or misleading representation of fact, which --

(A) is likely to cause confusion, or to cause mistake, or to deceive as to affiliation, connection, or association of such person with another person, or as to the origin, sponsorship, or approval of his or her goods, services, or commercial activities, by another person, or
(B) in commercial advertising or promotion, misrepresents the nature, characteristics, qualities, or geographic origin of his or her or another person's goods, services, or commercial activities, shall be liable in a civil action by any person who believes that he or she is or is likely to be damaged by such act.

The third amended complaint was alleging MoBeta, Inc. was nothing more than just a company set up to hide our assets. How clever we were to anticipate being SLAPPed, they argued. Nowhere before was such an outlandish accusation made, even though Orrick knew about our company and its business no later than when Mary was first deposed back in March 1999:

> LIBURT: When--When was this company, MoBeta, incorporated?
> DAY: I think it was January--early January 1999.

It was apparent from the very beginning that Orrick had more than a passing curiosity about MoBeta. They seemingly already knew about our corporate functions,

---

Delfino has violated the Lanham Act in at least two ways: (1) by improperly using the name of Varian employees, i.e. Felch and Zdasiuk, in order to pass off his Internet messages as those of Varian employees and thereby to disparage them and, indirectly, Varian; and (2) by making false representations of fact about Varian, its products, and its employees....

Delfino has used the names of Felch and Zdasiuk in order to pass off his Internet postings as those of Varian employees, with the ultimate goal of enhancing the credibility of his attacks on these individuals and Varian. The Internet postings themselves are publications, and are therfore "goods" within the meaning of Section 43(a)....

Delfino's use of the names "Felch" and "Zdasiuk" is reasonably likely to cause confusion given that he is deliberately attempting to do so, and in light of direct evidence of actual confusion ... Delfino has used these names in interstate commerce is shown by, among other things, his use of the Internet to distribute his messages and his targeting of Varian employees in both California and Massachusetts as his desired audience....

Delfino, he has violated the Lanham Act by making false statements of fact regarding Varian's goods, services, and commercial activities.... Delfino's false statements were made as part of a campaign to promote his company, MoBeta, Inc. Delfino and Day incorporated MoBeta, Inc. in January 1999, less than two months after Delfino's defamatory postings began. Beginning in autumn of 1999, Delfino and Day began regularly referring to and promoting MoBeta directly in their Internet postings that viciously attacked Varian and the other Plaintiffs.... Plaintiffs are able to make out their Lanham Act claim on this theory as well...."

LIBURT: Okay. Can you tell me who the officers and directors are?
DAY: Mary Day, myself, and Michelangelo Delfino.
...
LIBURT: Okay. What's your title?
DAY: With the company?
LIBURT: Yeah.
DAY: President and CEO.
LIBURT: What's Mr. Delfino's title?
DAY: He is vice president and CFO.

and our basic financial information including the purchase of capital equipment like our first computer:

LIBURT: Was it a corporate check?
DAY: Yes.
LIBURT: Okay. What was the corporation?
DAY: The name of the -- corporation on the check?
LIBURT: Yes.
DAY: Mobeta.
LIBURT: Can you spell that for me?
DAY: M-O-B-E-T-A.

Almost two months before the lawsuit had even begun, Mary and I had spent upwards of $5,000 incorporating MoBeta. Now, to be accused of hiding behind a fictitious business front, when we could have achieved the same "clandestine" status by forming a less expensive shell of a company, such as a Limited Partnership, was simply ludicrous. After a year of hellacious litigation, Varian must have wondered if MoBeta was being funded from outside sources and in this way sustain this multi-million dollar legal war. As it turned out, we had no financial backing. It was all our hard-earned money that was being used to fuel MoBeta and keep our attorneys fed. The following year on April 24, 2001, having depleted our savings, we would sell both of our condominiums to the same buyer and use all those proceeds to sustain our struggle now as renters. More than likely, Varian was betting we wouldn't use all our wealth to fight them. They were wrong.

Despite never naming MoBeta, Inc. a defendant, Orrick constantly harassed us with discovery about our business, if for no other reason than to distract us and drain our limited resources. Glynn always successfully fended off Varian's probing of MoBeta, Inc.'s intellectual property answering yet another Orrick subpoena:[70]

---

[70]"MoBeta, Inc. (hereinafter "responding party"), responds to plaintiffs' SDT requesting production of documents and things served upon this non-party on 10/12/99 as follows:

Responding party objects to each and every demand for inspection of documents and things to the extent it requires disclosure of information protected from discovery by attorney-client privileged, the work product doctrine, Constitutional right to privacy, federal patent laws, and any other lawfully recognized privilege or immunity from discovery which might attach to the documents and/or things requested.... protected from discovery by Civil Code Section 1799.1 or any other lawfully recognized privilege or immunity from discovery which might attach to the documents requested.... protected from discovery by Civil Code Section 3295 and/or Revenue and Tax Code Sections §1746, 7056, 19542, and 26451 or any other lawfully recognized privilege or immunity from discovery which might attach to the documents requested.... responding parties does not in any way waive or intend to waive, but rather intends to preserve and is preserving:

(a) all objections as to competence, relevance, materiality, and admissibility of the responses of the responses or subject matter thereof;   ·
(b) all rights to object on any ground to the use of any of said responses, or the subject matter thereof, in all subsequent proceedings, including the trial of this or any other actions; and
(c) all rights to object on the ground to any request for further response to these or any other discovery request involving or related to the subject matter of the Request for Documents....

Responding party objects to each and every Request for Production of Documents to the extent that the documents and things requested will involve disclosure of inventions, patent-able ideas, trade secrets and other confidential and proprietary business, technical and financial information. Such documents are protected from disclosure by applicable case law and California and Federal statutes including, but not limited to, California Civil Code §3426 and Code of Civil Procedure §§2025(I)(13), 2030(e)(6), and 2031(e)(5)....

Responding party's discovery is ongoing. In agreeing to produce documents responsive to any particular request, responding party does not represent (and

A GOOD OR A SERVICE

Because MoBeta, Inc. was not named a defendant, Orrick had no legitimate way of learning about our company's financial status and to what lengths we might be able to survive this SLAPP war of attrition. Nonetheless, this self-imposed restriction did not prevent the diligent Liburt from getting caught trying by Federal Magistrate Patricia Trumbull, who had just been put on speaker phone to settle the dispute:

> TRUMBULL: My understanding is that this is a continued deposition of Ms. Day?
> LIBURT: That is correct.
> TRUMBULL: And I have a question about that. The last thing that I've looked at had continued her -- her -- set for February 9th, 2000. It's March 30th and this is still going on?
> LIBURT: Yes, your Honor. We -- I believe we actually did have a deposition around February 9th. We did not finish. We actually believe we're going to finish today.
> ...
> TRUMBULL: You can ask her how much money she has transferred to MoBeta, Inc. That's it.

Resuming Mary's deposition:

> LIBURT: Okay. In line with the magistrate's order, Ms. Day, how much money total, have you transferred to MoBeta?
> DAY: I don't know.

---

indeed, does not yet know) that such documents necessarily exist. Rather, responding party intends to indicate that he will search for and produce any non-privileged responsive documents located by diligent search and inquiry....

Request for Production No.1: DOCUMENTS sufficient to identify the nature of the products and/or services offered by MOBETA.

Response to Request for Production No. 1: Objections: 1)This information is protected from disclosure by the patent laws of the United States, 35 U.S.C. §1 et seq. including but not limited to §122 and 37 CFR §1 et seq.; 2) Calif. Evidence Code 1060 et seq.; 3) Calif. Civil Code §§ 3426-3426.11 Uniform Trade Secret Act; 4) Irrelevant to the subject matter and not reasonably calculated to lead to the discovery of admissible evidence; 5) Over-broad, burdensome and oppressive in that the question seeks information not tailored to the specific claims, alleged facts, or issues raised by the pleadings, ..."

LIBURT: Okay. Can you give me an estimate of how much money
you have transferred to MoBeta?
DAY: Sure. Despite Varian's efforts to destroy the viability of
MoBeta, I put everything I possibly can into my startup company,
because, as you know, startups are especially vulnerable to attacks by
corporations like Varian and Varian Semiconductor, so I've put
almost everything I can, except for what I need to live on.

Indeed, MoBeta was our focus, and like our children, it was
something we helped develop and grow. And like any parent we
were driven to protect it. Mary and I are a self-proclaimed happy,
rather cute, albeit clumsy, middle-aged couple. We generally avoid
conflict and are not easily riled to anger. However, we are not
ordinary looking. She is blessed with a head of thick, curly,
graying, red hair atop a radiant face that has never seen make-up.
And I have a closely cropped white beard that matches a gray,
balding, head. At first glance, seeing either of us walking about in
our heavily worn Teva's, t-shirts, and jeans does not, I suspect,
leave you with a sense of unbridled envy. Sometimes, however,
like during Mary's deposition, this look caused some attention:

LIBURT: And I note for the record that defendant, Michelangelo
Delfino, is also present wearing a T-shirt that says "MoBeta, Inc.
Anti-SLAPP Task Force."
WIDMANN: Like it.

They were bewildered. How could the two of us survive this
yearlong war with these lunatics of the corporate establishment,
but also gleefully fight back? We battled with a vigor and
creativity that was always coupled with a sense of invincibility or
marked stupidity. Either way, ignorance is bliss.

Thinking the trial would be quickly rescheduled, discovery
picked up. Orrick was now more direct in its questioning about our
business, as shown in Mary's February 9, 2000 deposition:

LIBURT: If you look down at - towards the bottom of the message
you wrote "Viciously going after MoBeta, Inc.'s patents and in my
opinion unfairly competing with its technology." Do you see that
statement?

DAY: Yes.

LIBURT: Okay. Is it your opinion that Varian is unfairly competing with MoBeta?

DAY: You mean today, do I think that?

LIBURT: Yeah, today do you think that?

DAY: Yeah. I think this SLAPP is an example of unfair competition.

LIBURT: Okay. And today, do you think that Varian is going after MoBeta's patents?

DAY: I think your own interrogatory admissions and document requests will verify that, yes.

LIBURT: Okay. Well, let me ask you what you mean by "going after"?

DAY: Asking to have rights to a company's proprietary information in the guise of a SLAPP is amazing.

LIBURT: When you say "Asking to have rights in," what do you mean?

DAY: I have no idea what Varian and your motive is.

LIBURT: Move to strike, non responsive. What I'm asking is, when you say that you believe Varian is seeking to have rights to MoBeta's patents, do you mean that you believe Varian is seeking to have some sort of ownership interest in MoBeta's patents?

DAY: I said the right to have access to our patent applications, and that I find appalling, that a company would think that they could have the right to do that. That's proprietary information.

MoBeta, Inc. was a privately owned business, without sales, and not generating any income. Yet it is a business with value, and that value, among other things, is in its intellectual property:

LIBURT: How many patents does MoBeta have?

DAY: Two.

...

LIBURT: Can you tell me when the patent applications were transmitted to your lawyer for further filing with the U.S. Patent and Trademark Office?

DAY: **NO RESPONSE!**

...

WIDMANN: This is proprietary to MoBeta, confidential, trade secret. It's also irrelevant to any issue in this case. Instruct the witness not to answer.

LIBURT: Okay. I disagree with those objections, and I'd like to have the note that Mr. Delfino wrote made an exhibit to this deposition.

WIDMANN: No you may not.

When Liburt began this invasive line of questioning, I frantically wrote a note and passed it on to Randy. I insisted Mary should not answer this probing, as the information would jeopardize MoBeta, Inc. It is nonsensical to divulge proprietary details about pending patents to a hostile adversary. Perpetually hungry, I would have eaten the note before Liburt would have come close to touching it. As far as I was concerned, too much had been said already. In her testimony that day, Mary disclosed the existence of two patents referring to our February 4, 1999, U.S. Patent filing and our January 31, 2000, Patent Cooperation Treaty (PCT) filing. The latter, in effect provided for patent filing rights in several countries other than the United States. Entitled "Radioactive Transition Metal Stents," the PCT was published on August 10, 2000:[71]

On January 26, 2001 Varian's multi-purpose SLAPPer reacted to our PCT in this under-oath interrogatory response:

> "Felch contends that Day has posted false information about her and her professional capabilities and competence, both alone and in concert with Delfino, at least in part for the purpose of attempting to advance the business interests of MoBeta, Inc. Facts supporting this contention include ... the fact that MoBeta, Inc. appears to have submitted a patent application for technology that was developed in part while Delfino and Day were still Varian employees and that is similar to and/or serves a similar purpose as technology owned or under development by Varian.... The MoBeta, Inc. patent application and any related documents, which Delfino, Day, and MoBeta, Inc. have refused to produce in this case and which Felch believes is in their possession."

How outrageous was this Felch to believe that she was entitled to have access to MoBeta, Inc. property! Our company was under no obligation to divulge this information to anyone, including her. At

---

[71]"A radioactive transition metal stent, comprising one or more transition metals, wherein the transition metal stent surface is chemically bound to a radioactive material; and a method for producing the radioactive transition metal stent wherein the radioisotope is chemically bound to, and is uniformly confined to the transition metal stent surface without affecting the metallurgical properties of the transition metal stent is disclosed."

5:51 p.m. on July 6, 2001 I posted the following message on Yahoo! VAR:

MoBeta, Inc. patent update! by: michelangelo_delfino_phd
U.S. Patent No. 6,264,595 will issue July 24, 2001

Returning from a walk, I had just played back a message on my answering machine from Roberta Robbins, our patent attorney, informing us of the good news. As soon as our patent issued we posted about it everywhere often linking directly to the U.S. Patent Office on the Internet or our company's first press release:

"MoBeta, Inc. Awarded Radioactive Stent Patent

LOS ALTOS, Calif.--(BW HealthWire)--July 24, 2001--MoBeta, Inc. a pre-IPO R&D start-up company, today announced that U.S. Patent Number 6,264,595 for radioactive transition metal stents was assigned to MoBeta, Inc. The patent is intended to address the therapeutic and diagnostic applications of implantable medical devices like stents in which the placement of transient radiation is deemed beneficial.

The MoBeta, Inc. patent claims a radioactive transition metal stent with a chemically bound radioactive surface and a methodology for forming a radioactive transition metal metaphosphate and phosphide stent surface. Radioactive phosphorus atoms chemically bound in this way ensure high activity and remarkable stability. Transition metal stents include those made of stainless-steel, the shape memory alloy nitinol, and tantalum, among others.

Michelangelo Delfino, Ph.D., MoBeta, Inc.'s vice president and co-inventor stated, "Ours is a chemically bonded radioactive surface in which the pure beta-radiation emitter phosphorus-32 is conformally distributed on the stent or alternatively confined to the distal ends, for example, to produce a more selective and localized source of healing radiation." Beta radiation has shown desirable effects in the treatment of restenosis, the regrowth of scar tissue associated with balloon angioplasty failure. Phosphorus-32 with its 14.3 day half-life is perhaps the most popular and least-expensive source of beta-radiation per dose being experimented with today. Delfino added, "We believe that beta-radioactive medical devices will improve the quality of our lives and see MoBeta, Inc.'s patents contributing."

BE CAREFUL WHO YOU SLAPP

About MoBeta, Inc.

MoBeta, Inc. is a pre-IPO R&D start-up company specializing in the creation of novel medical technology located in Los Altos, California. Incorporated in January 1999, it maintains a web site at http://www.mobetainc.com. The information contained in our web site is not incorporated by reference in this press release.

Mary E. Day, President of MoBeta, Inc. and co-inventor said, "This press release contains forward-looking statements about our technology. There are a number of important factors that could affect what is suggested or indicated by such forward-looking statements." These include, among others, a SLAPP lawsuit filed in 1999 against the company's principal stockholders and awaiting trial in the California Superior Court. While extremely optimistic of the outcome, MoBeta, Inc. cannot guarantee what will happen as a result of this and future litigation...."

Mary and I had worked together on a similar technology at Varian at a time the company had an exploratory interest in radioactive stents. Back in 1997, we had submitted an invention disclosure for making stents radioactive. However, as is sometimes the situation, we discovered our invention was flawed. It did not work and we did not understand why. Shortly after this realization, I was fired. Zdasiuk immediately took the project away from Mary, and told her colleague Steve Bandy, a 1970 Ph.D. in electrical engineering from Stanford with no experience in this type of work, to take-over the work and understand the invention. When Zdasiuk informed Mary that I had been fired and replaced by Bandy, she coolly told him he had made a big mistake. Zdasiuk later rationalized his ill-advised decision on December 11, 1999:

FALCON: ... Was there some particular incident or fact that you can point to where she was not fully participating in the lab after Michael Delfino was terminated?
ZDASIUK: We wanted to continue the work that Mike had begun prior to his termination, and Mary did not cooperate with -- at least I felt that Mary was not cooperative in terms of continuing to pursue that work.

When Mary was deposed two days earlier, she gave her version:

218

LIBURT: Okay. Please tell me all additional reasons you resigned from Varian in addition to your belief that Sue Felch was harassing you?

DAY: Yes. I believe that my boss, George Zdasiuk, was also treating me in the same fashion that he had treated colleagues, and I didn't want to be subjected to his behavior, so to speak. My projects were also in jeopardy because the lead on some of those projects had been terminated without me having any access to the files that he had which we both shared, and so I was not able to continue my work. I was getting mixed signals. My boss, George Zdasiuk, was telling me not to work on things. Other people were telling me to work on them. I was trying very hard to work on those projects, and I felt that I was being politically sabotaged at -- at the company.

Was Varian serious about radioactive stents? Just before the 1999 year-end deadline, Varian filed a PCT on the flawed invention. And they did so without ever informing Mary, the sole inventor still employed by them. Because the invention didn't work, we never imagined a PCT would have been filed and despite its publication on June 17, 1999, did not see it until October 10, 2000 when it issued as U.S. Patent No. 6,129,658, entitled, "Method and Apparatus Creating a Radioactive Layer on a Receiving Substrate for In Vivo Implantation:"[72]

How embarrassing to be named on a patent that should not exist. Needless to say, Varian Associates' exploratory stent project, like so many others, was discontinued shortly thereafter, contributing to Mary's decision to resign from the company in December of 1998. But did Varian really have no interest?

FALCON: Are you familiar with MoBeta?
AURELIO: No.

---

[72]"An apparatus and method of forming a radioactive stent having a radioactive layer. A solution containing a radioactive isotope depositing substance in solution is provided and placed into contact with the stent or any other substrate material capable of receiving the radioactive isotope. The radioactive isotope is deposited on the stent or substrate material. Preferably a phosphorous isotope is used and the solution is polymerized forming polymer chains containing the radioactive isotope. In this embodiment, the phosphorous is bonded with the substrate material in a phosphorous-oxygen-phosphorous network."

FALCON: Is your company involved at all in ion implantation
devices?
AURELIO: Yes.
FALCON: How long has the company been involved in that type of
business?
AURELIO: Twenty-eight years.
FALCON: Do you make radioactive stents?
AURELIO: No.

But the VSEA spin-off was probing into our medical device
technology. Why?

FALCON: Does Susan Felch have any corporate charter to explore
the medical device application of ion implantation?
McMAHON: Objection. Vague. You can answer the question.
AURELIO: No.
…
FALCON: Are you familiar with the acronym PLAD, P-l-a-d?
AURELIO: Yes.
FALCON: What does that stand for?
AURELIO: Plasma immersion doping.
FALCON: Is that something your company is involved in?
AURELIO: Yes.
FALCON: Has that made a profit yet?
AURELIO: No.
FALCON: Do you have any -- does PLAD have any medical device
applications yet?
AURELIO: Potentially.

A month after Aurelio's deposition, Felch testified about Varian's
PLAD project, the same project that I was accused of sabotaging in
the spring of 1998:

FALCON: Now, Mike Delfino, apparently as the sole inventor, filed
a patent application on the -- I think you used the term plasma doping
of radio -- is PLAD , p-l-a-d, the acronym for it?
FELCH: yes.
FALCON: Is that true, that he had filed individually?
FELCH: I don't know the details of his patent application.
FALCON: Were you aware, though, that generally that a patent
application had been filed by him through Varian --
FELCH: Yes.
FALCON: -- before the patent application that you and Mr. Zdasiuk

was filed? ...Whose patent application got filed first, yours or Mr. Delfino's?
FELCH: I don't actually know the dates that his was filed.
FALCON: Do you believe it to be before yours?
FELCH: Yes.

Indeed, I had submitted an invention disclosure using PLAD to make radioactive stents. It was filed as a patent by Varian on August 24, 1999, a year after my firing. Unbeknownst to me, Felch and Zdasiuk filed a competitive PLAD invention disclosure some time after mine. However, their patent was never filed after several engineers struggled in vain to make it work. I explained the technical rivalry between us as a motive for their continued harassment of me as early as my December 14, 1999 deposition:

LIBURT: Mr. Delfino, you've told me that you believe you were terminated from Varian because of a conspiracy between George Zdasiuk and Sue Felch and you've now described for me, in some detail, some of the particulars of the conspiracy regarding competition, or competitive inventions. Are there any other reasons that you believe you were terminated, in addition to what you've already told me?
DELFINO: Not that I can think of.

The Orrick instead tried to paint a picture of me as an envious Varian scientist upset by Felch's "on or about January 23, 1995" promotion. This supposed promotion to a Director in charge of three technicians was certainly not well known in GRC. Neither Mary nor I were ever aware of any change in Felch's status. Even Felch later said she got no more money as a result. Was there another explanation? Her secret logbook of work-related incidents records June 1997 as the first alleged act of harassment, a time that coincided with the partial dissolution of her group in GRC. The disruption had no effect on us, yet for two and a half years I supposedly seethed with jealousy, plotting a vengeful attack on my little foe, the yenta who had snatched the position that was rightfully mine. Zdasiuk, I think, projected his own managerial aspirations onto me in his March 8, 1999 deposition in trying to explain how her promotion devastated my all-too-fragile ego:

"Well, Sue had been essentially promoted to a position of manager of Ion Implantation Research Group, and I think that Mr. Delfino had some degree of problem with that. And that he, I believe, that he felt that perhaps Sue may not have been the most technically qualified or perhaps he felt that he ought to have had that opportunity. I don't know. These are just speculative things."

If Zdasiuk ever believed any of this, he sure as hell never communicated it to me when I was at Varian. This same absurd sentiment was stated by Orrick in the original complaint, and supported in countless declarations as if it were true. I could only guess it originated with Felch, who had repeatedly expressed her sensitivity to social status and a concern for what others thought about her. This lawsuit provided a new opportunity to accuse me of wrongdoing, and Orrick needed a motive for malice. Indeed, these were desperate folk! It didn't matter if the accusations were true or not. In reality, Mary and I were both in a different group reporting directly to Zdasiuk, and at the time, happily working on technology of great interest to the company and to us:

LIBURT: What -- Did you have any particular career ambitions when you were at Varian in terms of what career path you wanted to follow or positions you wanted to achieve?
DELFINO: Yeah, I loved doing science.
...
LIBURT: Okay. so there wasn't -- there wasn't some other position in the company that you were aware of that you wanted to do more than being the individual contributor you thought you were?
DELFINO: No, I was very happy.

I *do* love doing science, and this love may have been my undoing at Varian. Technical people like Mary and I and all are technically-trained friends tend to be somewhat nerdy, highly-focused on what we are doing, and generally lacking in political savvy. We are under-paid hobbyists. In contrast, Stanford Ph.D.'s like Felch, Zdasiuk and Powell avoid working in the laboratory and prefer spending as much time as possible not doing science. They are simply nerdy bureaucrats hell-bent on making money. The contrast between these two camps is often a source of tension, especially in Silicon Valley, but at Varian under Dick Levy, it became a one-sided rivalry that destroyed careers and gave birth to this SLAPP.

> LIBURT: Who do you believe was politically sabotaging you?
> DAY: I don't know who was all behind all of this. The key players seemed to be George Zdasiuk, Sue Felch, Jane Crisler, and now it seems like Kathy Hibbs also was part of this whole conspiracy, so I don't know who else was part of that whole conspiracy.

And when pressed just a little bit further the plot would inevitably lead back to Felch and/or Zdasiuk:

> LIBURT: ....Have you now thought of additional facts that support your belief that there is a conspiracy?
> DAY: Between Zdasiuk and Felch, at least.
> LIBURT: Okay. What are those facts?
> DAY: Okay. I remember two. One, Delfino and I had presented a business plan to Dick Levy, and it had been given to George Zdasiuk, who gave it to a Steve Bandy. Steve came up and told me that Sue Felch had stolen the business plan from him, and she had no real reason to get a hold of our work product that we were working on. So that was suspicious to me, that she would do that.
> LIBURT: Okay. Before you tell me the second thing you remembered, did Mr. Bandy use the word "steal," or some variant of "steal"?
> DAY: Yes, he did.

Mary was recalling my ill-fated September 24, 1998 meeting with Levy. Afterwards, I told her that he had asked me if Zdasiuk had seen "Betastent," and on replying "No," was it ok to pass it on? Betastent was the name given to a business plan by Mary and I which addressed how Varian might exploit our pending radioactive stent patent. I told Levy that Varian had to decide on whether to file a PCT before the December 11, 1998 deadline and that was my reason for seeing him. I was not yet aware that the invention was flawed. Zdasiuk had attempted to prevent the meeting from happening. Conspiracy?

During the course of the litigation Felch submitted a declaration in which the same Betastent business plan was inadvertently stapled to the back of it. When deposed on December 3, 1999 she explained:

> FALCON: Did you ever receive a proposed business plan for a Betastent authored by Mike Delfino?
> McMAHON: Objection, vague, overbroad. You can answer the question.
> FELCH: I was given a copy of it, yes.
> FALCON: And who gave you a copy?
> FELCH: My technician, Juanita Sonico.
> FALCON: And do you know where she got it?
> FELCH: It was in her mailbox.
> FALCON: And did it have any identification of where it came from?
> FELCH: No. She found it in her mailbox one morning.
> FALCON: Do you remember reviewing that business plan?
> FELCH: I --
> McMAHON: Objection, vague. You can answer the question.
> FELCH: I did look it over.
> ...
> FALCON: What did you do with the business plan after you reviewed it?
> FELCH: I believe that I sent it over to Human Resources.

There was only one Betastent copy, the one I handed to Levy. Apparently sometime after I was fired it wound up in Juanita Sonico's mailbox. But Sonico did not give it to Mary, the co-author on the cover, or even put it in Mary's mailbox. Nor did she give it to Zdasiuk, Mary's boss. Instead, Sonico gave it to *her* boss Felch, who also ignored the logical recipient and then sent it off to Crisler. Mary never saw it again. All this intrigue occurred while Mary was accused by Zdasiuk of being less than cooperative.

Originally, my meeting with Levy was scheduled for June 3, 1998. I had made an appointment eight days earlier with his secretary, and with Zdasiuk's knowledge. Inexplicably, Jim Hennessy, the Director of Human Resources, canceled it the day before because of the remarkably coincidental alleged Felch PLAD laboratory sabotage, in which I was immediately the suspect.

> FALCON: But how was this fair treatment plan resolved or ended from your point of view?

HENNESSY: I don't think it was ended. What I recall was that Mike had requested to meet with Dick Levy. And in and about the time that that request had occurred this lab incident, the sabotage thing came up. And I remember -- I don't know if it was directly from Dick or whether I had heard it from someone else, but I remember a comment that Dick didn't want to meet with anybody until that lab incident had been resolved. And that would have been the next step in the fair treatment.

FALCON: And do you know why the lab incident had to be resolved before he met with anybody?

HENNESSY: No.

Having given up on Crisler as being less than fair, I was now dealing with her boss regarding my never-ending harassment complaint against Felch.

FALCON: What is the fair treatment plan, if there is one, at Varian?

HENNESSY: It's a program whereby employees can escalate their complaints or concerns beyond their immediate supervisor.

FALCON: Is that a published policy?

HENNESSY: Yes.

In what seemed like a matter of seconds, I had gone from a well-respected scientist, albeit an occasional pain in the ass, seeking company help for being harassed to an alleged saboteur, who wanted to harm people. Felch's plot against me was thickening. From that point on, I was told that Levy would not meet with anyone from GRC, although he continued to interact with Zdasiuk, who explained to me that the postponement was in everybody's interest. Although my innocence was never publicly acknowledged, on September 24, 1999, two weeks before I was fired, I was allowed 30 minutes to meet with Levy alone, an unusual event. Ordinarily my interaction with him was limited to the Research Center or in the company's x-ray tube facility in Salt Lake City, Utah. A fast talker, it took me 20 minutes to make my spiel to the boss. More than a year later, when deposed in December 1999, Levy recalled that day:

FALCON: Okay. No I understand. How about did you have a meeting with Mike Delfino regarding a business plan called

Betastent.

LEVY: I did have a meeting with Mike Delfino regarding a business plan. I don't recall the name of it.

FALCON: Okay. Generally what was the nature of that business plan?

LEVY: It had to do - the nature of the business plan was a method of depositing radioactive material on a stent.

...

FALCON: That was going to be my next question. Who besides you and Mr. Delfino were present?

LEVY: Nobody.

FALCON: And what was the - what was actually discussed?

LEVY: The business plan.

...

FALCON: Are you aware of what business the company known as MoBeta, Inc. is involved in?

...

LEVY: My understanding is that it has something to do with coating of stents with radioactive material.

...

FALCON: The radioactive coating of stents, is that something that your company is currently involved in?

LEVY: No.

...

FALCON: Do you believe that MoBeta, Inc is in competition with your company?

LEVY: No.

FALCON: Why do you say no?

LEVY: We're not in that business.

FALCON: Has any company contacted you or your company to your knowledge regarding the MoBeta technology?

LEVY: No.

A few months before little Levy was deposed, on September 10, 1999, Zdasiuk had made the following declaration:

"Varian Medical conducts research and sells products related to the area of radioactive implantable medical devices. Radioactivity can serve several purposes, such as preventing undesirable tissue growth from forming around an implanted medical device. While at Varian, Delfino and Day conducted research related to radioactive stents. Stents are devices implanted inside blood vessels or other vessels in order to prevent the vessels from collapsing, such as after balloon angioplasty. I am informed that the MoBeta, Inc. web page, http://homepages.go.com/~manuforte/MoBeta.html, states that its technology can be used to apply radioactivity to stents and related devices such as wire catheters. Varian Medical also has technology and is conducting further research in the area of applying radioactivity to wire catheters and other implantable devices. Therefore, it appears the MoBeta, Inc., is attempting to compete directly with Varian Medical in this area...."

and then two months later provided this testimony when he was deposed on November 11, 1999:

> FALCON: And what did you mean that MoBeta is attempting to compete directly with Varian Medical?
> ZDASIUK: Varian Medical develops technologies for rendering objects radioactive. Those technologies that we are developing are marketed in various ways. To the extent that MoBeta claims to have a technology capable of rendering objects radioactive, in fact, is competing with Varian in our own marketing of these technologies. To partners, to customers, whatever.

It was too unbelievable to expect that Levy and Zdasiuk, his directly reporting technical guru, did not talk about their company's technology. Levy, always the marketeer, was as highly educated as Zdasiuk, and in fact, had a Ph.D. in nuclear chemistry from U.C. Berkeley. How could the CEO of a high-tech company and its Chief Technical Officer be in such opposition?

Either somebody was lying, or Zdasiuk was positively incompetent. His technical insecurity at Varian was understandably a touchy point and on September 10, 1999, he elaborated on it in this declaration:

> "I am the named inventor on at least one issued patent, and on several other patent applications, related to my technical specialty. In addition, since approximately 1984, I have been a technical manager. During this period, many other technical patents have been issued to people in my department under my supervision.... I am competent in my job. With the exception of Michelangelo Delfino and Mary Day, nobody at Varian has told me to the contrary, and my colleagues at Varian have generally treated me with respect and expressed their belief and trust in my ability to perform well at work. I have received

uniformly positive reviews during my 18 years at Varian, during which period I have received several promotions and pay raises. I am a well-trained scientist, engineer, and technical manager, and apply what I know rigorously and creatively. I am a successful manager and leader of others...."

Zdasiuk's frightening misperception of himself became even more apparent when deposed on March 8, 1999:

FALCON: Do you -- have you authored or own any patents?
ZDASIUK: Yes.
FALCON: How many?
ZDASIUK: Can you clarify patent applications?
FALCON: Well, let's start with patents actually issued patents.
ZDASIUK: I have one I am absolutely certain about. There are a number of patent applications that we are fairly far along which I do not know the outcome of because they were sold along with our gallium arsenide device business.
FALCON: My understanding when a corporation files a patent, you have to put the inventor's names down on that. How many sets of applications do you think you have been associated with whether or not you have an awareness of whether the patent was issued?
ZDASIUK: I don't recall the exact number, but it's probably in the vicinity of 20 or so.

On December 14, 1999, I simply stated the reality:

LIBURT: Generally speaking, is it to your advantage, if you're trying to get a job in your field, to have more patents rather than less patents?
DELFINO: To answer your question, Zdasiuk has one patent, and I believe he's a vice president at Varian. I have something like 15 patents, and I'm unemployed.

Although I was preenjoined by Whyte's preliminary injunction from expressing my God given opinion that Zdasiuk was "technically incompetent," I was not restrained from referring to his less than stellar performance as an inventor. I regulary posted this on Yahoo! VAR to help my fellow investors keep a watchful eye on the progress of those twenty or so applications that have yet to materialize into a single patent:

228

> **George Zdasiuk weekly patent update!**
> by: michelangelo_delfino_phd
> NOTHING!

I welcomed every opportunity to air Zdasiuk's ineptitude:

LIBURT: Mr. Delfino, why is it your opinion that Mr. Zdasiuk was less than competent as your manager?
DELFINO: Because he did not follow company policy would be one reason.
LIBURT: Okay. Before you give me the other reasons, let me ask you, which company policies do you believe that Mr. Zdasiuk did not follow?
DELFINO: Annual review, performance reviews.

And it was a popularly held point of view. Even the company librarian had complained:

FALCON: Did you ever hear Rose, Ailya Rose complain about George Zdasiuk?
HENDERSON: Yes. … Most of the people were complaining -- complaining about the management in general.

But Zdasiuk could never acknowledge his years of job neglect:

FALCON: How often are the performance reviews to be done to your knowledge of the people working for you at Varian?
ZDASIUK: They are done on an annual basis.
…
FALCON: In Mr. Delfino's case, what was the time interval between his two most recent performance reviews?
ZDASIUK: I don't recall what they were.
FALCON: Would two and half years sound about right?
ZDASIUK: I don't know if it was two and a half years. Two years and some months or something.

As is often the case, ineptitude starts at the top and has a way of trickling down the ranks:

FALCON: Before Mike Delfino was terminated was approval obtained for that from Mr. Levy?

HENNESSY: Not that I recall.
FALCON: Doesn't company policy require the vice president, in this case Mr. Levy, to approve any terminations?
HENNESSY: No.
FALCON: Did any company policy at that time require that the supervisor of the employee's direct manager, in this case Mr. Zdasiuk, give his approval or her approval for termination?
HENNESSY: In most circumstances, yes.
FALCON: How about in this circumstance?
HENNESSY: Yes.

Finally, Zdasiuk was not in conflict with someone else:

FALCON: How many people, to your knowledge, approved the decision to terminate Michael Delfino? ...
ZDASIUK: I don't know. Maybe four or five. I don't know.
...
FALCON: Dick Levy, would be another one?
ZDASIUK: I believe so.

But the little man in charge contradicted everybody:

FALCON: Did you after the fact have to approve Mr. Delfino's termination?
LEVY: No.

Firings in high-tech companies, unlike lay-offs, are generally infrequent, and with such high-liability that those involved in the process, usually Legal and Human Resources, are acutely aware of the company policy. At Varian, none of this was true:

FALCON: Is it your understanding that Mr. Levy's approval to terminate Mr. Delfino was required under company policy and procedure that existed at the time?
HIBBS: No.

Hibbs may in fact, have been too excited by the whole process:

FALCON: Were you in favor of the decision to terminate Michelangelo Delfino from employment with Varian?
HIBBS: Absolutely.

230

And she always gave more conflicting information than I suspect she intended, and for that, I will always be grateful:

> FALCON: Were you involved in the termination of Mr. Delfino?
> HIBBS: Yes.
> FALCON: And did you consult with anybody in regards to the termination of Mr. Delfino?
> ...
> HIBBS: Jim Hennessy, Jane Crisler, and George Zdasiuk.
> FALCON: And in what time frame? Were these all in one meeting or separate occasions, separate dates?
> HIBBS: They were separate meetings.
> FALCON: Just so I'm clear, was Mr. Hennessey, Mr. Zdasiuk, and Ms. Crisler ever at this one same meeting in relationship to this general topic?
> HIBBS: Actually, I don't believe so, no.

Once again, the Varian attorney responsible for so much SLAPPing[73] provided the contradictory testimony that keeps attorneys with integrity busy:

> FALCON: Was there a meeting in which Mr. Zdasiuk was brought into regarding the possible termination of Mike Delfino?
> HENNESSY: Yes.
> FALCON: And who was at that meeting?
> HENNESSY: To the best of my recollection, it was myself, George, Jane Crisler, and I think Kathy Hibbs.

Always disingenuous, Zdasiuk sometimes told the truth:

> FALCON: How many people, to your knowledge, approved the decision to terminate Michael Delfino?
> ...
> ZDASIUK: I don't know. Maybe four or five. I don't know.
> ...
> FALCON: Dick Levy, would be another one?
> ZDASIUK: I believe so.

---

[73]The 38-year-old Hibbs, later as Vice President & General Counsel of ViroLogics Inc. (VLGC), initiated another lawsuit against anonymous message board poster(s) only to have the San Francisco Superior Court Case dismissed as a SLAPP on September 10, 2002.

FALCON: Any others come to mind? Perhaps corporate counsel?

ZDASIUK: Perhaps.... Because the decision was made as a result of a meeting of some sort.

FALCON: Were you at this meeting?

ZDASIUK: Yes. I believe I was.

FALCON: And who else was at this meeting?

ZDASIUK: I don't recall exactly who was there.

FALCON: Tell me anybody you remember.

ZDASIUK: I believe Jane Crisler, I believe Jim Hennessy.

FALCON: And you believe that there may be others?

...

ZDASIUK: I don't recall exactly who was there. Beyond - I mean corporate counsel [Kathy Hibbs] may have been there; I'm not sure.

At Varian, it seemed, no one was ever sure of anything, and the issue of its highest-level managers violating published company policy would be revisited again and again.

> **Varian's hostile work environment**
> by: be_careful_who_you_SLAPP
> on Dick Levy's watch:
> -pornography forced onto subordinates;
> -secret videotaping of Varian employees, their children, Novellus employees, etc. using a Varian bathroom;
> -computer tampering;
> -thefts;
> -allegations of lab sabotage;
> -repeated violations of company policy;
> -managers harassing subordinates;
> -manager terminating employees who challenged a conflict of interest at Varian.
> Maybe there is a good reason Dick Levy states that he was never in this Varian building where all this went on.
> Damages? You betcha!

Notwithstanding all this, a judge would later threaten to jail us for saying "Varian Associates, Inc., Varian Medical Systems, Inc., Varian Semiconductor Equipment Associates, Inc. managers, past or present, violated company policies...."

Life is just full of unexpected surprises. On April 7, 2000, after having delayed the Valentine Day trial for two months, the

Honorable Ronald M. Whyte awarded us "Partial Summary Judgment" dismissing Varian's Lanham Act Claim.[74]

Winning meant the claim was so frivolous that it was unworthy of a trial. For the first time, a judge acknowledged that MoBeta, Inc. was a "pre-IPO start-up ... in the business of coating stents with radioactive material." Strictly speaking, our radioactive surface was not a coating per se, but Whyte understood enough to make the proper ruling:

> "Plaintiffs have presented no evidence of actual competition with Delfino, Day or their company, MoBeta....

> Dr. Richard Levy, the CEO and President of VMed, indicated that MoBeta is in the business of coating stents with radioactive material, and that MoBeta is not in competition with VMed.... there is no evidence that MoBeta could even potentially compete with VSemi, or either of the individual plaintiffs. Plaintiffs have presented no evidence that MoBeta currently competes with, or is likely to compete with any of the plaintiffs in the future....

> plaintiffs have presented no evidence from which a reasonable jury could conclude that MoBeta is in current competition, or is likely to be in future competition, with plaintiffs as required by the statute.

---

[74]"Plaintiffs have failed to present sufficient evidence for a reasonable jury to conclude that defendants' statement were on, or in conjunction with, goods or services as required ... plaintiffs have failed to present evidence from which a reasonable jury could conclude that : (1) defendants made a false statement of fact in a commercial advertisement about its own or plaintiffs' product; (2) the statement actually deceived or had the tendency to deceive a substantial segment of its audience; (3) the deception is material, in that it is likely to influence the purchasing decision; and (4) plaintiff has been or is likely to be injured as a result of the false statement, either by direct diversion of sales from itself to defendant or by a lessening of the goodwill associated with its products, as required.... plaintiffs have failed to establish that any of defendants' statements constitute commercial advertising because plaintiffs have failed to present evidence from which a reasonable jury could conclude that any of defendants statements were: (1) commercial speech; (2) by a defendant who is in commercial competition with plaintiff; (3) for the purpose of influencing consumers to buy defendant's goods or services, or were (4) disseminated sufficiently to the relevant purchasing public to constitute "advertising" or "promotion" within that industry, as required ..."

... If the court were to conclude that a pre-IPO start-up with two employees, no products, no funding, and no assets other than a pending patent application, was in competition for venture capital with an established, publicly-traded company, that would mean every company seeking funding of any type was in competition with every other company seeking funding of any type...."

We had beaten the Varian (VAR & VSEA), Susan B. Felch and George Zdasiuk SLAPP in Federal Court. The ruling was correct, but was the testimony upon which it was based? On August 8, 2000, after Whyte's decision was final, Glynn would ask all four plaintiffs this same question again and again without ever receiving an answer:

"**INTERROGATORY NO. 87:** Was Richard Levy telling the truth when he stated, under penalty of perjury, at his deposition (at page 37, lines 20-24) in this case that MoBeta, Inc. is not in competition with Varian?"

Was Levy guilty of perjury? Undeniably Levy is a liar, but perjury requires that he in fact *knew* that he made a false statement under oath. Indeed, this was a novice CEO who claimed he didn't know his company was a plaintiff ten months into a multi-million dollar lawsuit. Was it not just as plausible he could not tell when he was telling the truth?

We had beaten the SLAPP in Federal Court, but at one helluva a price. Mary and I had already paid our three attorneys a whopping $194,853 as of April 2, 2000. The awarding of our attorney's fees was one potential consequence of defeating Orrick's Lanham Act claim that was quickly exploited by our attorneys. On April 16, Glynn demanded an estimated $60,000 based on his billing records:[75]

"Plaintiffs have been hiding behind their non-existent Lanham Act claim in an obvious, blatant, and bad faith attempt to obtain and maintain an injunction suppressing defendant's free speech criticism

---

[75]"Defendant Delfino's Notice of Motion & Motion for Attorneys' Fees & Costs for Judgment on the Lanham Act, Points and Authorities"

of the corporate entities. Suppression, even disguised in the sheep's clothing of the "Lanham Act," is still the wolf attacking free speech with the use of illegal tactics to obtain prior restraint of free speech. It is the ultimate bad faith tactic against our single, most cherished freedom....

As there are four plaintiffs ... the fees and costs incurred by this defendant, as set forth in the attached cost bill and in the declaration of Glynn Falcon, should be apportioned 50-50 between individual and corporations, and each corporate defendant ordered to pay the 50% of fees and costs attributable to them...."

On May 10, Randy, perhaps a bit more detailed than Glynn in his accounting, submitted another bill:[76]

"DAY has claimed as attorneys' fees in this action, 1/2 of the fees she has incurred and paid in defending herself in this matter, namely the sum of $42,279.75. This amount is being claimed in light of the fact that the same wrongdoing that was claimed by Plaintiffs as against DAY for violation of the Lanham Act is the same wrongdoing that Plaintiffs claim supports their state claims. Thus, the work would have been expended whether there were state claims or not. It is appropriate that 1/2 of the fees incurred and paid by DAY to date be paid now as allowed under the Lanham Act and as is set forth hereinafter...."

Imagine Orrick's client having to pay us too? The battle heated-up and on May 26, 2000 Glynn declared:

"Plaintiffs' claim the bill for fees and costs are inflated. That can hardly be true, especially in light of the claim that plaintiffs asserted earlier in their pleading on file with this court that they had expended approximately $250,000 on this case as of the time of the conference with Magistrate Infante! That was back in August of 1999 that they made the claim, well before the bulk of any discovery, countless discovery motions, summary judgment motions, etc. This defendant's bill for attorneys' fees has been just a fraction of plaintiffs' billing, and if we were to assert a quantum merit claim, then easily the defense of Mr. Delfino on the bogus Lanham Act claims would be

---

[76]"Defendant's Mary Day's, Notice of Motion and Motion for Award of Attorneys' Fees"

worth at least $250,000. It appears that the only inflated billing done in this case may have been plaintiffs' counsel. Plaintiffs' counsel further asserts that the defense attorney was not of the same quality, reputation and experience as that of the combined forces of their firm, and therefore not deserving of such fees.

Admittedly, Orrick is one of the nation's, if not the world's, foremost and prestigious law firms, respected and feared (and occasionally loathed) throughout the country. They are able to band together different legal talents, skills, specialties and experts to generate the most scholarly briefs and dissertations on just about any legal subject. I have no such pretense about myself. I am a one-man office that does everything personally --- from typing pleadings to washing the coffee cups at night. But regardless of our respective standings and reputations, there is one thing that I know for certain, and that is: AT LEAST IN THIS INSTANCE, IN THIS CASE, I WUPPED 'EM! That has to mean that, at least as to the Lanham Act, I am due (but not receiving) at least an iota of respect from my loyal opposition. It also means I earned my fees to have beat the best of the best, and in light of Plaintiffs' enormous billings, my fees must intrinsically be worth what I charged Mr. Delfino. Fees and costs should be awarded to defendant Delfino.

... plaintiffs' have argued from both sides of their mouths. They now claim that their Lanham Act claim was not important to them, but earlier they fought like the dickens to keep that claim in. Why did they fight so vehemently? Simple. Plaintiff's injunction against Mr. Delfino was based on commercial competition and the likelihood of corporate injury. The individual plaintiffs could never have gotten an injunction against Mr. Delfino's constitutional right to free speech, as that would have constituted impermissible prior restraint on free speech....

But as this court found, both under the law and the facts of this case, there was no competition. Plaintiffs pursued, and pursued vigorously, the Lanham Act claims knowing from discovery that they had no claim and that there was no competition.

While plaintiffs voluntarily dismissed other causes of action, they flatly refused to drop the Lanham Act claims, thereby necessitating the filing of defendant's motion to dismiss. Plaintiffs understood and feared that if the Lanham Act claims disappeared, not that they would be remanded back to state court, but they feared the underpinning of their preliminary injunction (enjoining commercial speech) would dissipate also. Plaintiffs have often tried to confuse this court, by tugging on the court's sympathies for the individual plaintiffs. But this motion is not directed to the individual plaintiffs. They had no Lanham Act claims. This motion is directed to the corporate plaintiffs that misused, abused and used as a ruse, the Lanham Act claims to further their own financial interests. The corporate plaintiffs wanted the 3-way split-up of the parent Varian to go ahead smoothly, without the attacks upon the wisdom of such by Dr. Delfino over the Internet. They wanted to shut Dr. Delfino up. And the only way for the corporations to do that was to assert the bogus Lanham Act claims. Fees and costs should be awarded to defendant Delfino.

When plaintiffs realized that this court was wary of their Lanham Act claims, Plaintiffs almost immediately attempted to by-pass the adverse effects which would have been caused by that. Plaintiffs made motions to file a new complaint and TRO, alleging every possible twist to any conduct by defendant (shopping at Safeway, picking up her kids at school, etc., tampering with witnesses, etc.) under the guise that plaintiffs were fearful of the defendants.... there was almost nothing that plaintiffs wouldn't stoop to do to keep the injunction in place, given the expected dismissal of their Lanham Act claims.

Again, fees and costs should be awarded to defendant Delfino...."

While we knew that this judge would never allow us a money victory, our win made wonderful postings. Mary posted this on the Yahoo! Lawyers message board with a link to Whyte's Order:

> **Orrick loses another one!** by: dantecristo
> Yesterday, the Federal judge presiding over the VAR/VSEA, Susan B. Felch, George Zdasiuk SLAPP against free speech granted the Defendants' motion for partial summary judgment based on the Plaintiffs' mistaken Lanham Act claim:
> http://www.geocities.com/mobeta_inc/slapp/lanhamord.html
> Did I say frivolous?
> Did I say damages?
> Did I say I'd win?
> You bet!

Awarding partial summary judgment was not the only thing Judge Whyte did for us on that April 7, 2000 day. He was now in a position to get us out of his court once and for all.[77] Whyte

---

[77]"The Lanham Act claim was the only basis for this court's removal jurisdiction. It is therefore proper for the court to consider whether to adjudicate the remaining state law causes of action or remand the case to state court.... Even where the court could retain jurisdiction over the state law claims, as a general matter, "if the federal claims are dismissed before trial ... the state claims should be dismissed as well." ...

Although this case was previously set for trial and the trial date vacated to allow the court more time to evaluate plaintiffs' Lanham Act claim, any judicial economy that might result from keeping the case in federal court is outweighed by comity due the state court. Although this court is familiar with the factual issues, much, if not all, of the parties' pretrial efforts to narrow the issues in the case, along with all of the discovery conducted to date, will not have to be repeated in state court. The court does note that defendant Delfino was the one who removed the case to federal court and now seeks to remand, perhaps in the hope that he will find the state forum more sympathetic to his cause. However, it is not necessarily unfair for a defendant to seek removal of a case and then seek remand if the federal claim is dismissed. Here, the federal and state courts are equally accessible to the parties and there is no reason to believe that the state court is not the best position to fairly apply state law to the facts of this case.

... the court hereby remands this action to the Superior Court of Santa Clara County with the recommendation that the case be set for trial as soon as is practical. The court notes for the parties the pending matters that need to be brought to the state court for resolution in addition to a request for a trial date:

> 1. Plaintiffs' request for a preliminary injunction based upon Cal. Code of Civil Proc. 527.6(b);
> 2. Plaintiffs' request for an order allowing telephonic depositions of third parties UUNet and GTE:
> 3. Plaintiffs' request for review of the magistrate judge's recommendation to the district court that it be precluded from offering evidence of dollar amounts for two items of claimed damages;
> 4. Plaintiffs' motion to compel further discovery responses and production of documents by defendant Delfino and third party MoBeta, Inc.
> 5. Plaintiffs' motion to amend its complaint; and
> 6. The parties respective summary adjudication motions involving state law issues.

remanded the case and all its remaining state claims back to Superior Court. We were not happy having to continue this war elsewhere. We were emotionally psyched for a trial and now there would be none. In many ways our Lanham Act victory in Federal Court was a hollow one. We knew that we did not have the financial resources to match the Varian corporations forever if they decided to continue the SLAPP. Although we would daily use the Internet to post and publish our Web sites, a legal war of attrition lasting for years was not something we could expect to win easily and our financial shortcomings were becoming all too apparent. Some change in strategy was required as we readied ourselves for a new judge and a new set of rules.

The court notes that the magistrate judge ruled or made recommendations on items 1-4. However, plaintiffs timely appealed the rulings and objected to the recommendation. The undersigned district judge has not ruled on the matters in light of the remand...."

- 9 -

WHAT ABOUT THE CONSTITUTION

The return to California Superior Court in April 2000 was almost like going where no one had gone before. There was no legal precedent in California for remanding a civil case from federal to state jurisdiction after rulings had been made. What protocol was to be followed? Our attorneys were of the general opinion Orrick had to refile most, if not the whole case and that any existing orders, including the preliminary injunction and my contempt ruling, were no longer in effect. The virtual standstill and accompanying inactivity led Tom Kotoske to remove himself from the case at the end of July 2000. His departure coincided with ending his practice with Glynn and moving to a new office. Shortly before leaving, Tom, still elated from our victory, gave an interview in our local paper.[78] He described the state claims that remained to be heard as "a matter of great dispute," since many "questions remain as to whether or not any of these claims still survive and who would be the proper plaintiffs." Orrick's attorneys, as always, did not agree. In the same article, Hermle still hurting from her loss said, we are "pleased to be moving towards trial," adding that "judge after judge has told us that we are likely to prevail against [Delfino's] reprehensible behavior."

Still unclear what Orrick hoped to achieve with a trial other than ruin us financially, our worst-case scenario showed us, perhaps sitting at a Kinko's rental station posting messages. And in spite of the cameras, we would be able to use as many aliases as

---

[78]Shoba Rao, *Los Altos Town Crier*, May 31, 2000.

we could conjure up to preserve our anonymity. Even Glynn and Randy smirked when we projected this as our epitaph.

So while we waited for something to happen in Superior Court, we continued to post and expand our SLAPP Web sites. Up until then, we had published only deposition excerpts and some readers complained we weren't presenting the whole truth. Always eager to please, we published Felch's third day of testimony in its entirety. Almost immediately it caught Orrick's attention. On May 5, 2000 the self-inflated Hermle wrote our attorneys and we created a Web site that highlighted her letter entitled "Fascism has no place in America!":

> "Delfino and Day have posted on their web site portions of the Susan B. Felch deposition transcript from December 1, 1999, and Delfino has posted links to that site in several of his recent Yahoo messages. The transcript is designated "Confidential" in its entirety pursuant to the District Court's protective order, and the posting thereof on the defendants' web site is yet another violation of a court order. On behalf of Plaintiffs, we demand that Delfino and Day remove the deposition excerpts and any other "Confidential" materials from their web site immediately. We note that the order provides that it is to remain in effect even after termination of the lawsuit, so the Court's remand order does not render it void.
>
> Please confirm in writing when the transcript excerpts have been removed from the web site...."

Hermle was wrong again. McMahon, her Orrick apprentice tasked with representing Felch that day, had said on the record that only "... certain portions of the deposition be sealed ...." However, he subsequently failed to designate *any* "portions" as confidential. The juxtaposition of Hermle's bluster with McMahon's blunder on our Web site demonstrated Orrick's gamesmanship and the efforts made to hide the truth. Typically, when we pushed the envelope, Orrick would alert a judge screaming we had violated something, but this marked the first time they just wrote our attorneys. So we pushed harder, adding Felch's deposition hyperlink, i.e., URL, itself to postings giving her lies more exposure.

By now we were getting very good at advertising Varian, Felch and Zdasiuk's dirty laundry on the Internet. On this Web site, like a few others, we added an invisible counter to monitor our readership, optimizing the site for the most popular browsers, and, in particular, gave a profile of who was clicking. For the past nine months it showed regular, almost daily visits from an Orrick networked computer, a guest whose privacy seemed well worth violating. On June 7, 2000, I finally succumbed to the news and shared my joy on the Yahoo! VAR board:

> **Wowee! At 8:12:48 svwall.orrick.com**
> by: dr_michelangelo_delfino
> viewed the last message!
> Now that is freaking fast!
> What do you, my fellow VAR stockholders think we got charged for that peek?

It was most pleasurable, our ability to invade the privacy of Orrick just like they had done so many times to us and others, some of whom were never even made aware. It was alarming the number of innocent people who were unwittingly subpoenaed and what personal information was unveiled because Orrick attorneys believed they were me or someone acting in concert with me.

Predictably, Orrick didn't show up on our counters anymore, possibly because they were no longer accepting computer cookies that marked their visit. So I did the same thing with hits from Varian servers, e.g., [hana.cis.varian.com], announcing visits from within the corporation. If nothing else, it showed employee interest in the company's lawsuit during normal work hours.

Throughout this relatively quiet waiting period, we posted about the SLAPP on a daily basis despite the absence of any new court documents. Already we had a plethora of material to draw from, and could now link back to more than one 100 Web sites.

Around this time a mood change occurred on the message boards. This posting on Yahoo! VAR:

> **Yep , I wouldn't invest in VAR** by: dsanwmen
> or any company that sues for message board posts. Is the company hiding something? This would worry me, IMO

and this one on Yahoo! VSEA seem to best reflect that change:

Varians Viet Nam. by: harvey_wireman127

Varians dispute with Delfino+Day is a no win situation for them. If Varian wins in court, they still lose. If Delfino+Day win, Varian loses. Let me explain. If Varian gets a judgement against Delfino+Day, how are they going to collect it. I may be wrong, and I am not a lawyer, but couldn't Delfino+Day declare bankruptcy and not pay anything. If Varian wins, are the internet postings going to stop. HELL NO. In fact, the war of words by Delfino+Day against Varian will probably increase exponentially if Varian wins. Will anything have changed if Varian gets a judgement against Delfino+Day. NO! Nothing will have changed.

On the other hand, look out if Day+Delfino win. They will be cockier than Deion Sanders after he scored the winning touchdown. All the people Delfino+Day are mad at are really going to get torched on the message boards. If you think it is bad now, wait until they win.

Again, I think Varian is in a no win situation. Similar to our war in Viet Nam. Varian has superior fire power, but Day+Delfino definately have the will to fight to the bitter end. Whether its one, five, ten, twenty or even fifty years, these two are not going away soon. They are just as committed as a Viet Cong soldier.

Lastly, will all the parties involved with this dispute take me up on my offer to SETTLE. If not me, than someone else. Late.

Perhaps none of us ever realized how long this war of words would last, but our resolve never wavered – not for a single moment. Mary's June 30, 2000 reply to the anonymous "harvey" on Yahoo! VSEA showed that our position was indeed resolute:

Thanx, but no thanx! by: dantecristo

Dear harvey_wireman,

In order to negotiate a settlement the VAR, VSEA, Susan B. Felch, George Zdasiuk SLAPP plaintiffs must have something I want. Well, they don't. My rights are already protected by the laws of the United States of America. We, the defendants have .already triumphed in Federal court and we expect to be

---

victorious in both California Superior Court and in the Federal 9th Circuit of Appeals Court.

And yes, I will publish every single failure and loss of the Varian SLAPP plaintiffs. And yes, I am highly motivated to post until I am dead. And Varians' 'fire power' does not supersede the laws of this country no matter how misguided they are.

So, thank you for your efforts but I would rather beat Varian and their despicable Orrick Herrington & Sutcliffe SLAPP attorneys over and over and over and over again!

Damages?

You bet!

On another front, Randy and Glynn initiated on December 17, 1999 a "Notice of Appeal" in the United States Court of Appeals. At issue was Mary's right to a court hearing. She had been denied one when Judge Whyte imposed a preliminary injunction that prohibited us from posting certain statements on the Internet, and restricted us to a single alias that we were forced to identify to both Orrick and the court before using. Moreover, once Whyte dismissed Varians' spurious Lanham Act Claim, he had an obligation, a duty to dissolve the injunction, as it was *the* basis for preenjoining us in the first place – he did nothing!

The Ninth Circuit Court of Appeals process had been plodding along rather slowly when suddenly after Whyte's remand back to State Court it picked up momentum. Asked to meet and confer with a court-appointed mediator, Hermle expressed her concern about the return of our free speech privilege in this May 5 letter to our attorneys:

"During the conference call with Lisa Evans yesterday, the issue was raised whether Plaintiffs will take the position that the District Court's Modified Preliminary Injunction remains in effect despite the remand to Superior Court. Having reviewed the issue, it appears quite clear that the injunction remains in effect.

... when counsel convene again with Ms. Evans on May 10, 2000 at 11:30 a.m., we will inform her that it is our understanding that the Modified Preliminary Injunction is still valid and in effect. Mr. Delfino and Ms. Day should be made aware that we will seek to enforce any violations of the injunction...."

Despite Evans' forewarning that the injunction was void, Hermle refused to concede defeat and so on June 30, 2000, Randy had to respond:[79]

". it is prior restraint on free speech by enjoining DAY from, for instance, calling one of the plaintiffs "overweight".... a review of the underlying postings upon which the injunction is premised reveals, first of all, that the vast majority were posted by Defendant, DELFINO, and second that while they may be obnoxious, the postings do not even rise to the level of defamatory statements."

On that same day, Glynn filed a similar brief on my behalf:

"The Preliminary Injunction Is Unconstitutional as a Prior Restraint of Free Speech.... places prior restraints on content-based, non-commercial, electronic speech (i.e., Internet postings) in violation of the Constitutions of both the United States and the state of California.... Plaintiffs' Commercial Claims Were Found to Be Factually Nonexistent, There Was No Legal Basis for Placing Prior Restraints on Delfino Internet Postings.... the District Court erroneously considered this case to be a commercial speech case.... when the District Court granted defendants' summary judgment motion against plaintiffs' Lanham Act claim, any notion that defendant was engaging in "commercial speech" dissolved....

The First Amendment of the United States Constitution provides in part: "Congress shall make no law ... abridging the freedom of speech ...." Even broader in scope is the California Constitution .... :

"Every person may freely speak, write and publish his or her sentiments on all subjects, being responsible for the abuse of this right. A law may not restrain or abridge liberty of speech or press."

... Delfino's Internet postings involve both free speech and freedom of the press (his web site is devoted to the reporting of the events of this lawsuit).... (such as calling a person "fat"). Nowhere do plaintiffs have the right to prevent him from speaking beforehand, and this was always true ...

---

[79]"Opening Brief for Appellant's, Mary Day, "On Appeal From a Modified Preliminary Injunction of the United States District Court for the Northern District of California""

While Delfino's Internet postings may have been viewed by some as irritating, poignant, stinging, hostile, distasteful, ridiculing, offensive, insulting, humorous, and even impolite, it is the very fact that they are these things which makes this speech even more deserving of protection by the First Amendment than those statements which are politically correct, polite, tame, currently respectable and in no need of protection. The marketplace of ideas needs no court ordered censor.

... the preliminary injunction entered against Delfino, and Day, was erroneously entered and violates fundamental state and federal constitutional proscriptions against prior restraints of free speech....

The injunction should be dissolved and Delfino awarded his costs and attorneys' fees on appeal...."

Of course, The Orrick was always less than forthright and it would take another year for them to publicly acknowledge the falsity of their clients' claim. On July 25, 2001 Poppe admitted that all four plaintiffs, and not just Zdasiuk had lied when they claimed calling him "overweight" was defamatory:

FALCON: Well, let me be more general, then. As you sit here today, are you asserting that Mike or Mary falsely stated that you were fat, overweight, or words to that effect?
POPPE: I'll state that plaintiffs' claims for defamation are no longer based on postings that Mr. Zdasiuk was fat.

We had been unlawfully prohibited from speaking the truth. For the first time it was clear that not only our right to free speech on the Internet was being threatened, but that of everyone else was in jeopardy too. When in 1938, the Nazi annexation of the Sudentland went unchecked, it sent a message that such behavior was acceptable. I am amazed even to this day the United States Government forbade us from calling Zdasiuk overweight, incompetent, and a liar when in proof he was all three:

"A simple demonstration will suffice to establish the imprudence of enjoining what Plaintiffs call defamation. All the Court need do is order Plaintiff, ZDASIUK, to appear before it in order to discern the wisdom of the founders of this country. That is, the founding fathers declared that the citizens of this country shall be allowed to voice their opinions, right or wrong, good, bad or ugly. Is ZDASIUK fat? Let the Court decide and then contemplate the wisdom or folly of granting Plaintiffs the injunctive relief they seek."[80]

Naturally, both our appellant briefs became SLAPP Web sites. Orrick's opposition and our reply briefs followed, and in time, we dedicated an entire Web site to this appeals case. Mary included a URL to her opening brief in this Yahoo! VAR message to coincide exactly with our country's 4th of July celebration:

> **George Zdasiuk vs. the US Constitution** by: dantecristo
> To think that anyone would be such a dumbshit as to think
> they can oppress First Amendment rights:
> http://www.geocities.com/mobeta_inc/slapp/appealsmed.html
> Let freedom ring!
> Happy 4th of July 2000!

On July 17, someone who had bastardized my "million_dollar_mistake" alias and who was referred to as a "Varian loyalist" by Glynn because of his defamatory remarks in support of Varians' SLAPP, posted this on Yahoo! VAR:

> **mikey's smear campaign fails again**
> by: million_dollar_mistak (43/F/Los Altos, CA)
> Despite mikey's best efforts the cream still rises to the top,
> while mikey fell out the bottom. mary must be so proud.
> Monday July 17, 2:53 pm Eastern Time
> Company Press Release
> Varian Medical Systems Board of Directors Elects George
> Zdasiuk and Keith Krugman Corporate Vice Presidents
> PALO ALTO, Calif.--(BW HealthWire)--July 17, 2000—
> Varian Medical Systems (NYSE: VAR - news) today
> announced the election of George Zdasiuk and Keith Krugman
> as corporate vice presidents. Zdasiuk, 48, manages Varian's
> Ginzton Technology Center, including the company's research
> and development activities and emerging brachytherapy

---

[80]"Defendant's, Mary Day's Supplemental Brief Regarding the Lanham Act," filed February 2, 2000

business. Krugman, 54, manages global customer support and service for Varian's Oncology Systems business.

"The Ginzton Technology Center and our customer support and service businesses play important roles in our growth strategy," said Richard M. Levy, president and CEO of Varian Medical Systems. "George Zdasiuk and Keith Krugman are proven senior managers and significant contributors to our management team."

Zdasiuk, who has his Ph.D. in Applied Physics from Stanford University, joined Varian in 1980 as a staff member in the technical research laboratory. He began assuming management responsibilities in 1985 and became director of Varian's Healthcare Technology Laboratory in 1990. As director of the Ginzton Technology Center, Zdasiuk is responsible for Varian's breakthrough and start-up activities, including brachytherapy, biotechnology-based ventures, and the development and acquisition of new core technologies for the company. A native of Toronto, Zdasiuk has a masters degree in physics and a B.A.Sc degree in engineering science from the University of Toronto.

I can only wonder why Varian would promote Zdasiuk for any reason, but to do so in the middle of his then year and a half old defamation lawsuit, where damages are necessary, was inexplicable. Unless our Internet postings were found to be libelous per se:

"A libel which is defamatory of the plaintiff without the necessity of explanatory matter, such as an inducement, innuendo or other extrinsic fact, is said to be a libel on its face. Defamatory language not libelous on its face is not actionable unless the plaintiff alleges and proves that he has suffered special damage [i.e., all damages suffered in respect to his property, business, trade, profession, occupation] as a proximate result thereof."

a violation of the California Civil Code 45 requires the following:

"Libel is a false and unprivileged publication by writing, printing, picture, effigy, or other fixed representation to the eye, which exposes any person to hatred, contempt, ridicule, or obloquy, or which causes him to be shunned or avoided, or which has a tendency to injure him in his occupation."

While calling Zdasiuk a "fat liar" may have indeed subjected him to ridicule, the fact that it was true negated any and all liability. However, Whyte's Preliminary Injunction had prevented us from saying such truths. Now the threat of it being dissolved was unacceptable to Varian, so Hermle submitted her "Brief of Appellees," on July 31, 2000. I was actually surprised that she would submit anything challenging the Constitution:

"First, the November Order is not an unconstitutional prior restraint. Courts have regularly recognized that speech may be enjoined after a judicial determination that it is defamatory or otherwise unprotected, particularly where the defendant's defamatory conduct has been recurrent and is directed at private individuals....

Second, the November Order only prohibits Delfino and Day from making provably false statements of fact about Appellees; they remain free to express their opinions about Appelles.... messages accusing Felch and Zdasiuk of adultery, mental illness, incompetence, and chronic lying all contain provably false statements if fact.... they are classic examples of statements held in previous cases to constitute libel per se....

the November Order does not violate Appellants' First Amendment right to post anonymous Internet messages. To the contrary, it expressly permits them to continue using one pseudonym each when posting Internet messages about Appellees. To the extent the order can be construed to limit Appellants' right to anonymity, it is still valid because it is narrowly tailored, is justified by the compelling need to put a stop to Appellants' fraudulent use of multiple aliases when discussing Appellees on the Internet, and has not deterred Appellants from continuing to post daily Internet messages...."

The Grande Dame of SLAPP continued to vehemently argue against our right to use as many Internet aliases as we liked:

"Delfino posted messages almost every day under numerous different pseudonyms to create the appearance that his views were shared by many people ... Indeed, he often had his different Internet persona converse with each other to advance his goal....

On the issue of multiple aliases, the District Court observed that its "clear intent in issuing the preliminary injunction was to prevent

Delfino from using multiple user names on one bulletin board to create the false impression that multiple people were involved in Delfino's campaign of harassment against Varian and its employees.""'

From the earliest moments, Orrick had complained about my anonymity and use of multiple aliases to post Internet messages, even though neither practice was illegal. There was nothing wrong with what I was doing – Yahoo! in fact advertised, "Create up to six different Public Profiles with one account!" on their message board sign-in page, thus allowing seven aliases per email account. In her December 9, 1999 deposition Mary explained how and why she took advantage of their policy:

LIBURT: Why have you posted on the Internet, using at least 18 aliases about this lawsuit?
DAY: One of my primary reasons was somebody, and your firm was one of those, was deleting message-board postings, and I was doing a test to see in which there was some sort of pattern into why the -- those messages were being deleted. That was the primary reason.

In her appeals opposition brief, Hermle identified Orrick's view of my motivation for using multiple aliases:

"Appellees explained that Delfino had used multiple aliases in an attempt to deceive Internet users into believing that his bizarre views were held by a crowd of people...."

The use of an alias to post, either singular or multiple, was a longstanding issue that goes back to the original complaint. Therein, Orrick showed its frustration at my Constitutional Right to privacy and anonymity, as it forced them to connect me with a defamatory posting, something they were never able to do even with all their subpoenas. From the beginning, I had identified myself as the user of 6 aliases and the author of 60 postings. Although Whyte had found me in contempt for allegedly impersonating Stock-Talk postings that I had no involvement in. After my six-month hiatus in 1999 between February 24 and August 13, I was ready and raring to post. However, because of

Whyte's Injunction, I could only use one alias identified to Orrick and His Honor so that they could keep a watchful and unconstitutional eye on me. Reading Whyte's Order carefully and priding myself on always being able to "follow" the rules, I made his restriction more interesting than I think anyone anticipated. On that same day, Glynn faxed off this letter to Poppe and the court:

> "Pursuant to the June 21, 1999 "Order Granting Plaintiffs' Motion for Preliminary Injunction," at page 6, paragraph (4), please be advised that defendant Michelangelo Delfino, will be using the Internet pseudonym of "stents4me2". A copy of this letter is concurrently being forwarded to the court to comply with the notice requirements of the court's Order ..."

On August 25, Tom faxed another letter to Poppe and the court:

> "... please be advised that defendant Michelangelo Delfino, will be using the Internet pseudonym of "mark_twain_again" ..."

As soon as Orrick received it, Poppe, quite predictably reacted:

> "I write to inform you that Mr. Delfino has violated the preliminary injunction and is in contempt of court due to the fact that he is using more than one internet pseudonym to post messages about Varian and its employees. We intend to bring this violation to the attention of the Court ...We explained in our preliminary injunction papers that one form of deception used by Mr. Delfino on the Internet has been to post messages under multiple pseudonyms ... This conduct is deceptive, is harmful to Varian and its employees, and must come to an immediate halt.
>
> In a related matter, we note that Mr. Delfino has begun posting Internet messages specifically related to this litigation. We would advise you to caution Mr. Delfino that he should take care not to disclose any confidential information that is subject to the protective order entered in this case. Failure to abide by that order would also constitute contempt of court ..."

I pestered Glynn to fax off another letter to Poppe on August 30:

> "... and will be currently posting under the one Internet pseudonym ("alias") of "million_dollar_mistake". Mr. Delfino continues to not

post using more than one current alias, which is fully compliant with the Court's order and permits tracking of his actual postings. A copy of this letter is concurrently being forwarded to the court ..."

Poppe was POOPed, he had had enough. On September 1, he wrote the Honorable Ronald M. Whyte a rather lengthy letter:

"We write to request your attention and guidance in responding to Mr. Delfino's continued violations of the preliminary injunction entered in this case....

An important element of the preliminary injunction entered in this case is an order barring Mr. Delfino from posting Internet messages about Varian, Ms. Felch, Mr. Zdasiuk, or other Varian employees under more than one alias. A copy of the preliminary injunction order is attached.... The purpose of this order is twofold: it permits the tracking of Mr. Delfino's messages, and, even more importantly, prevents Mr. Delfino from continuing his pattern of deceiving other Internet users by leading them to believe that multiple persons are posting negative messages about Varian, Ms. Felch, Mr. Zdasiuk, and other Varian employees.

Mr. Delfino has violated this order by posting messages about Varian and its employees under at least three different aliases to date: "stents4me2," "mark_twain_again," and "million_dollar_mistake." Copies of these messages are attached.... Mr. Delfino has continued the tactic of posting under multiple aliases as a way to deceive Internet users, as shown by at least two facts.

First ... Mr. Delfino's different aliases talk to and respond to each other, thus continuing the pattern of deception. For example, in a message posted on August 25, 1999 under the alias "stents4me2," Mr. Delfino wrote: "[This lawsuit] is serious enough that Richard 'Dick' Aurelio the CEO of VSEA may be one of those deposed!" The next day, under the alias "mark_twain_again," Mr. Delfino wrote: "Dick Aurelio deposed??? WOW! HOLY COW! UNBELIEVABLE! DICK? WOW! NOT DICK!?... Any other Dicks to be deposed?"

Second, Mr. Delfino has created a public profile for each alias that gives the impression that different people are posting messages. The profile for "stents4me2" states that the person posting under that alias is a male. The profile for "mark_twain_again" states that the person posting under that alias is a 27-year old male from Elmsford, NY. The profile for "million_dollar_mistake" states that the person posting under that alias is a female from Menlo Park whose marital status is "single, and looking" and whose occupation is "esquire." Copies of the profiles for each alias are attached ...

Notably, a summary of a user's Yahoo! profile appears in each message posted by the user next to the user's alias. For example, the messages posted under the "mark_twain_again" alias contain the following by-line: "mark_twain_again (27/M/Elmsford, NY)." Thus, any Internet user who reads one of the messages posted by Mr. Delfino can see a summary of the deceptive profile information without actually having to download the full profile sheet.

On Aug 26, 1999, I wrote to Thomas Kotoske, counsel for Delfino, to inform him that Mr. Delfino was violating the preliminary injunction by posting under multiple aliases ...`

Mr. Delfino and his counsel ignored this letter. Four days later, I received a letter from Mr. Falcon, Mr. Delfino's other attorney, informing me that Mr. Delfino intended to begin posting messages ... creating the impression that multiple individuals are criticizing Varian and its employees.

It also appears that Mr. Delfino has posted or has encouraged the posting of an additional message about Varian, Ms. Felch, and Mr. Zdasiuk under a fourth alias, "siztheday." The message entitled "VARIAN, FELCH & ZDASIUK SUE SINGLE MOM!" was posted on August 30, 1999. A copy of the message is attached ....

Although Mr. Delfino will undoubtedly claim that the message was posted by his co-defendant, close friend, and business partner, Mary Day, it is clear that Mr. Delfino had a hand in its posting. The style of this message is identical to that of the other messages. In addition, like most of the recent messages posted by Mr. Delfino, it contains the qualification "[i]n my opinion..." And like several of the recent messages posted by Mr. Delfino, it ends with the statement "Note: This is in no way intended to advise anyone to buy VAR & VSEA stock." If Mr. Delfino is indeed responsible for this message, in whole or in part, he has further violated at least three provisions of the preliminary injunction: ...

We believe that these incidents provide further grounds for holding Mr. Delfino in criminal contempt of court. At a minimum, Mr. Delfino and his counsel should be informed in no uncertain terms that his recent conduct violates the preliminary injunction.

Mr. Delfino should also be ordered to post a message on the Yahoo! message boards for Varian and Novellus under the pseudonym "stents4me2" explaining that he was responsible for the "mark_twain_again," "million_dollar_mistake," and "siztheday" postings and that in the future he will only post under the "stents4me2" pseudonym.

We further ask that you schedule a hearing, either in person or by telephone, to address Mr. Delfino's continued violations of the preliminary injunction."

I hadn't violated any order, anything, but I sure as hell was going to make my point. And so on September 28, I asked Glynn to notify everyone that I had changed my alias again:

> "... please be advised that defendant, Michelangelo Delfino, has discontinued the use of any previously disclosed aliases ("stents4me2", "million_dollar_mistake" and "mark_twain_again") and will be currently posting under one Internet pseudonym ("alias") of "gino_in_torino". Mr. Delfino continues to not post using more than one current alias, which is fully compliant with the Court's order ..."

and on October 20 again:

> "...please be advised that defendant, Michelangelo Delfino, has discontinued the use of his previously disclosed alias "gino_in_torino" and he will be posting as "ima_posta2" as his Internet pseudonym ("alias")."

This is my religion and I practice it regularly: if you are going to push -- then push. My intent was to show how ridiculous the court's order was both in substance and phraseology. I focused on Whyte's wording in the original June 21, 1999 order:

> "... a pseudonym may be used after identifying the pseudonym to plaintiff's counsel and the court in writing ..."

Clearly, his own words had allowed me to change my alias repeatedly as long as I used only *one* alias at a time and disclosed it before using it. Glynn agreed with my logic, but always a bit more cautious than me, worried that Judge Whyte might find me in contempt anyway. Glynn was convinced this judge didn't like me.

Irrespective of all that on November 19 Judge Whyte said, in open-court, "I'm going to give Mr. Delfino the benefit of doubt," and rewrite the order to include Mary and explicit rules:

> "... each defendant may use only one pseudonym for the duration of this injunction. Each defendant is specifically enjoined from changing his or her pseudonym...."

In spite of the severe restriction, it was an early victory for us and one that annoyed Orrick a great deal. Hermle explained her frustration at not being able to silence me in her July 31 brief:

> "Delfino did worse than play procedural games; he danced on the border of contempt. In bad faith, Delfino took advantage of a technical ambiguity in the original preliminary injunction to violate the obvious intent of that order and force the District Court to issue a clarification...."

and refused to acknowledge that Whyte had modified his order:

> "This Court lacks jurisdiction over Delfino's appeal of the November Order. Delfino claims the Court has jurisdiction under 28 U.S.C. ... which confers jurisdiction on the courts of appeals over appeals from orders "granting, continuing, modifying, refusing or dissolving injunctions, or refusing to dissolve or modify injunctions...." ... the November Order does none of the above; it merely clarifies one provision of the original preliminary injunction entered against Delfino. It therefore is not an appealable order...."

On August 16, Glynn educated Hermle about the Constitution:

> "It is only the Appellees who are trying to "clarify" the Modified Preliminary Injunction. Everyone else can clearly read that this Order not only "supercedes the Preliminary Injunction," but that it adds a new party (Mary Day) to the equation, changes the relationship of the parties, and denies Dr. Delfino the lawful use of anonymity via serial or multiple Internet aliases, or to post anything whatsoever on the Internet using a second alias, regardless of content, whether specifically enjoined or not.
>
> Moreover, in the modification, each defendant was enjoined from ever changing their Internet alias. These are not trivial modifications, but constitute a vast change to the existing legal landscape covered by the injunction.... Day was added to the mixture, and Delfino and Day were enjoined from using multiple Internet aliases, and from ever changing their alias - - - period. It did not matter to the District Court that the use of multiple alias by defendants to lawfully discuss any aspect of Varian's business was also being curtailed by its "Modified" injunction. It did not matter to the District Court that anyone and everyone in the world, except these defendants, were free to discuss

any aspect of Varian's business on the Internet using any number of aliases.... By including Mary Day as a party, it effectively joined Delfino and Day by the hip, even though there was no substantial evidence that Day and Delfino were acting in concert....

This was more than a mere "clarification." It changed the status and relationship of the parties, instituted new restrictions on Delfino's ability to communicate freely over the Internet, and imposed content and view-based restrictions on his messages...."

Following Whyte's Modified Preliminary Injunction Order, Mary continued to use "dantecristo" and I used "ima_posta2" to post. Several months later, on March 6, 2000, Yahoo! deleted my account altogether. It was funny to discover that this happened by reading about it on the Yahoo! VSEA message board. Someone knew about it before I did. I called Yahoo! to inquire how this was possible. Sue Florimonte, of Yahoo!'s customer care, assured me it wasn't. On pointing out this March 6, 2000 Yahoo! VAR message to her, she had no explanation:

> **ima_posta2's screen name is leaving** by: <u>globix_rules</u>
> Yahoo has confirmed this tonight

I told her about my legal predicament and alias dilemma. Forbidden by Whyte from changing my alias anymore, I could only resume posting using my real name. She offered to help. Together we activated a new Yahoo! account using, "dr_michelangelo_delfino" to post.

I was back in business that very same day. But not everyone was happy and six weeks later on April 18, all 122 of my "dr_michelangelo_delfino" Yahoo! message board postings were instantaneously gone – censored! But it would take more than that to shut me up. And so I immediately set-up another Yahoo! account using "mr_michelangelo_delfino" and still another using "michelangelo_delfino_phd". Running out of lawful variations, hopefully, Orrick or whoever was responsible for deleting my postings from Yahoo!'s message boards had gotten the hint that I was not quitting:

> **Recoup your VSEA losses - take the bet**
> by: michelangelo_delfino_phd
> $1,000,000 CASH - enough to have someone buy your
> groceries at a Safeway supermarket for the rest of your life!
> Read the fascist Varian (VAR & VSEA), Susan B. Felch and
> George Zdasiuk 'Appeals Brief' & bet against ME and the
> United States Constitution!
> Be as dumb as your Dick - and maybe -as rich too!

The SLAPP was now a year and a half old. By August 2000 we had paid $236,000 in legal fees to our three attorneys. And I still had a $20,000 contempt bill hanging over my head. MoBeta, Inc. was alive and kicking but no longer the medical R&D start-up company we had intended it to be. Instead, Mary and I were devoting almost all our time to this lawsuit. We were more than ever determined to beat these bastards into the ground, no malice intended. And we posted every single day, and updated our "removed postings" Web site as quickly as our messages were censored. In some ways, we were working harder than we had ever done before, and being hyperactive, that's saying something.

Periodically, Yahoo!, and to a lesser extent other Web portals such as Silicon Investor, would email us to inform us that we had allegedly violated some rule. On Silicon Investor, a paid per use message board host, a violation would sometimes be explained, and if ignored, lead to a temporary suspension of posting privileges. I, of course, managed to be permanently banned from ever posting there again and was unable to even sneak by using someone else's credit card for payment. Mary has come close to joining me in exile, but continues to post as of this writing. On the other hand, Yahoo! never provided any reason for censoring a message and very often simply deleted the message or the free account altogether. Mary and I have had dozens of accounts deactivated by Yahoo!. One consequence of this is that those aliases can never be used again by anybody. Ordinarily when a user retires an alias, it may be reactivated by a new user after a few months waiting period.

Mary, always looking for reasons to celebrate, commemorated our first-year posting anniversary with this on Yahoo! VAR:

Happy Anniversary to Me! by: <u>dantecristo</u>
Yes, folks today marks the one year anniversary of my first Internet message board posting. As you know the Varian (VAR & VSEA), Susan B. Felch & George Zdasiuk SLAPP lawsuit is based on 60 message board postings from one defendant. After being named the second defendant in this frivolous and malicious lawsuit, I began posting on August 13, 1999 and collectively the two named defendants have posted on over 100 message boards over 10,000 messages dedicated to the truth about the despicable plaintiffs and their unethical Orrick Herrington & Sutcliffe SLAPP attorneys.
I have been constantly and unabashedly inspired to gleefully post every single day over this last year. The plaintiffs and their attorneys have been more than generous in providing the material to publish such as the secret bathroom videotaping, a SLAPP witness running away in the middle of her deposition, two court-ordered CEO depositions, conflicting testimony, "I don't recall", lies from attorneys, etc. Of course, least we forget, there is the Grande Dame of SLAPP and Orrick partner Ms. Lynne C. Hermle and her misguided musings to fight the First Amendment of the Constitution of this here Untied States of America. So please join me in celebrating a most prosperous and fruitful year. I look forward to so many more years of posting to come.
And remember...Be careful who you SLAPP!
Regards,
Mary E. Day

On September 11, 2000, the United States Ninth Circuit Court of Appeals issued a memorandum for our case No. 00-15059. Appellate Judges Wallace, Fernandez, and McKeown ruled unanimously that Judge Whyte's preliminary injunction was "dissolved as a matter of law." Why did Whyte ignore U.S. law?

We were once again free to express our opinion on the Internet using whatever alias we wanted. Moreover, just like the Varian loyalists, we could resume posting messages anonymously and use as many aliases as we liked. Grinning like a toothless kid in a candy store, I grabbed another one pound bag of jelly beans and parked myself in front of the computer. I would have been found in contempt had I done this September 24 Yahoo! VAR posting just two weeks earlier:

> **Re: George Zdasiuk is a FAT LIAR!**
> by: <u>gina_in_torino</u> (39/F/Bella Sicilia)
> MAMA MIA! I knew it!
> Da sunamagun anda hissa scareeee Susy Felcha causa alotta
> truble fora my Gino!
> Disa fatso, heeza gonna tella da trutha abota disa SLAPPa
> messa and how heeza he causa sucha messa for hisa Dicka
> anda anudda Dicka!
> Da sunamagun dinka weeza stupida?
> Fugettabout it!

We welcomed the return to the world of multiple aliases with a vengeance. The Orrick had made it all too clear that their clients didn't like it at all, which only motivated us to use more and more aliases. This was not going to be tolerated by Varian. And so we found it necessary to constantly create new aliases as both messages and accounts were deleted. As of the writing of this book, the number of aliases we had used on Yahoo! alone would exceed 500. This press release almost two years after beating Varian and the Grand Dame of SLAPP yet again, happily concluded our second victory in Federal Court:

"MoBeta, Inc. President & CEO Awarded Appellate Court Costs

LOS ALTOS, Calif.--(BW HealthWire)--Jan. 28, 2002--MoBeta, Inc. announced today that The Honorable M. Margaret McKeown, a Ninth Circuit Appellate Judge ordered Varian Medical Systems, Inc. (VAR) et al., to pay undisclosed costs to Mary E. Day, the President of MoBeta, Inc. following her successful appeal. The Federal Court Order, case no. 00-15059, filed on January 24th of this year, grants Day's "opposed motion for taxation of costs" and states that "the taxation of costs on the mandate will be allowed to stand." Ms. Day was pleased with the decision. She was represented by Randall M. Widmann, Esq., a Palo Alto, CA attorney in private practice. Orrick, Herrington & Sutcliffe's Menlo Park, CA law partner Lynne Hermle, Esq. represented Varian in this US Court of Appeals loss.

MoBeta, Inc. is a pre-IPO R&D start-up company located in Los Altos, California. MoBeta, Inc. owns one US patent and has another US patent pending for manufacturing radioactive medical devices like stents as used in balloon angioplasty."

- 10 -

SLAPP BY ANY OTHER NAME

We had been in the California State Court for four rather uneventful months following Judge Whyte's remand. While it was Mary's first visit, for me it was a return engagement. Then, on August 11, 2000, following what seemed to be just another court hearing, the Honorable William F. Martin issued an order that would delay the SLAPP trial for another year.[81] Although, Hermle had boasted she was "pleased to be moving towards trial," she didn't. Instead she added another year's litigation. Judge Martin allowed Varian to file their "Third Amended and Supplemental Complaint," which they did ten days later. It was very similar, but not identical to what they had filed in Federal Court just before the remand. Amending the complaint once again would delay any trial as it would necessitate responses from both our attorneys. In State Court, for example, a complaint may be attacked by a "demurrer" on the basis that its claims do not have sufficient grounds to justify

---

[81]"(1) Plaintiffs' Motion for Leave to File Third Amended and Supplemental Complaint is GRANTED. Plaintiffs shall file and serve their Third Amended and Supplemental Complaint within thirty (30) days after entry of this order.

(2) Defendants Michelangelo Delfino and Mary Day shall file their respective responsive pleadings within thirty (30) days (or such larger time as may be permitted by the California Code of Civil Procedure) after service upon them of a file-endorsed copy of Plaintiffs' Third Amended and Supplemental Complaint.

(3) Plaintiffs' Motion for Summary Judgment Re Defendant Delfino's Counterclaim is DENIED without prejudice to refile the motion after this case is at issue again."

legal actions. So of course we filed demurrers. Glynn's demurrer summarized why the latest complaint was lacking:

> "There are two individuals and two corporate plaintiffs in this action. The corporations are using their power over their employees (the 2 individual plaintiffs) to incorporate them into an obvious SLAPP lawsuit in a futile attempt to hide behind those individuals to avoid detection of the fact that this is just a SLAPP suit bought and paid for, in fact controlled by, the two corporate giants in order to impose their view of the world, and upon defendants, and to suppress defendants' right of free speech.

> They have failed, for the fourth time, to file a clear, intelligible and legally cognizable complaint. Instead, they re-file the same tired old SLAPP allegations that has lost for them, both in the federal district court and, now, before the 9th Circuit Court of Appeals. Plaintiffs enjoy playing "hide the ball" with their allegations, leaving defendants to guess what it is they are to defend against. But in final analysis [as well be shown in defendants special motion to strike this SLAPP lawsuit] plaintiffs are, in effect, attacking defendant's First Amendment rights, and this court should sustain these demurrers, without leave, and put this puppy to rest."

Amending the complaint opened the door for us to ask the court to strike the lawsuit. We invoked the California Anti-SLAPP Statute CCP § 425.16, which calls for immediate dismissal:

> "A cause of action against a person arising from any act of that person in furtherance of the person's right of petition or free speech under the United States or California Constitution in connection with a public issue shall be subject to a special motion to strike, unless the court determines that the plaintiff has established that there is a probability that the plaintiff will prevail on the claim."

Mary and I had been proclaiming this lawsuit a SLAPP on the Internet for over a year. And as far back as September 10, 1999, Poppe asked and was denied sanctions for our doing so:

> "Delfino loudly proclaims this to be "SLAPP lawsuit" designed to oppress free speech ... describes defendants as "despicable corporate bullies" in conjunction with the SLAPP allegations ...

Delfino is incorrigible. Indeed, he seems empowered by the Court's Order prohibiting him from his unlawful and improper actions.... Delfino has continued to amass an all-out internet assault against plaintiffs.... Delfino has described defendants as "despicable corporate bullies" ... Delfino persists in describing this as a frivolous "SLAPP" suit designed only to oppress defendants and to impair their First Amendment rights. His co-defendant Mary Day has entered the fray, stating that plaintiffs are "unscrupulous" and "despicable."...."

And postings like this one on August 16, 2000 on Yahoo! VSEA were done with more regularity than I brushed my teeth:

> **From my cute butt to your ugly Dick!**
> by: michelangelo_delfino_phd
> Be careful who you SLAPP!
> Hee, hee, hee!

Yet it was only now that we were able to take advantage of the anti-SLAPP statute. On September 26, 2000, Randy filed Mary's special motion to strike as a SLAPP suit. Mine was filed on October 5, and while similar to Mary's in spirit, had a different basis. I, for one, had posted Internet message board criticisms of Varian and its executives for several months before being sued. As Glynn later wrote:

"Delfino's postings concerned public issues over 1) Varian's corporate split-up, product direction, and management team; 2) the EDD [Employment development Department] and CUIAB [California Unemployment Insurance Appeals Board] proceedings and determinations; 3) Internet reporting and commenting upon this lawsuit...."

In contrast, Randy simply noted:

"[Mary] did not even start to post anything, as the undisputed facts reveal, until August 13, 1999, after she was sued by Plaintiffs and eight (8) months after Plaintiffs filed an action."

Irrespective of the differences, the significance of either of us having our motions granted is that besides immediately winning the lawsuit, the California statute guarantees "a prevailing defendant on a special motion to strike shall be entitled to recover his or her attorney's fees and costs." This would have amounted to a significant windfall. At this point we had paid Glynn and Randy collectively, a whopping $283,395.

Victory was not to be ours, and on November 1, 2000, following an October 26 Court Proceeding, the Honorable Conrad L. Rushing issued the following minute order:

> "The Demurrers to the 7th cause of action is sustained with leave to amend. The demurrers are overruled in all other respects. The motion to strike is denied. The Motions to Strike A SLAPP suit are denied."

We were devastated, not so much by the demurrer ruling, but by Rushing's dismissal of our two anti-SLAPP motions. Prior to the hearing, we were all convinced this judge would at least declare the two publicly traded corporations SLAPPers. He didn't. But more to our amazement, the judge queried, "What makes you think the Internet is a public forum?"[82] Speechless at his naivety or stupidity we were unable to respond. On exiting the courtroom our attorneys were probably more dismayed by Rushing's unfamiliarity with technology than Mary or I. This was our first real setback in Superior Court, and just a taste of what lay ahead.

On November 7, Glynn filed a "Notice of Appeal" and the SLAPP made its debut in the California Sixth District Court of Appeals. The Sixth District has jurisdiction over some 2.4 million people living in California's Monterey, San Benito, Santa Clara, and Santa Cruz counties.[83] Because we appealed Rushing's decision, the governing 425.16 statute requires that all Superior

---

[82]"Cases construing the term "public forum" as used in section 425.16 have noted that the term "is traditionally defined as a place that is open to the public where information is freely exchanged.... While newspapers exercise editorial control over access to their pages that feature is not shared by the Web sites [Raging Bull] involved here. We therefore conclude defendants made a *prima-facie* showing that the Web sites [Raging Bull] involved in this case were public forums for purposes of section 425.16." *ComputerXpress, Inc. v. Jackson* (2001) 93 Cal. App. 4th, 993.

[83]The year 2000 U.S. Census.

Court proceedings come to a halt until the appeal is finalized.[84] But Rushing did not recognize this California law and refused to halt the proceedings. And so on the 16th, Glynn was forced to file a "Petition for Writ of Supersedeas"[85] in the Court of Appeals, thereby requesting an immediate stay of discovery. He noted that the money it would cost to file would be the "best investment I would ever make." Certainly a higher-court would recognize the need to follow the law, he reasoned.

> "Petitioner and appellant, Michelangelo Delfino, petitions this court for a writ of supersedeas to stay further proceedings ... The appeal was timely filed ... The granting of the special motion to strike would have resulted in the immediate end of litigation between the parties, without further discovery, motions or trial.... It is inconceivable how further proceedings in the Superior Court after Notice of Appeal was given would not affect or embrace the matters appealed from, in as much as the whole of the complaint (the very heart of the litigation) is subject to the special motion to strike. If the Court of Appeal reverses the trial court, in whole or in part, then the appeal will have been for naught because the Superior Court intends to rush this matter to trial, even with the appeal now pending.... the Superior Court has refused to consider that a stay of proceedings exists.... the court advised that it would not consider the case stayed unless, and until, the Court of Appeals directs it to do so...."

An appellate decision didn't take long. The stay was denied the following day by two Republican Sixth District Court of Appeals appointees, Associate Justices Eugene M. Premo and Patricia Bamattre-Manoukian. Moving quickly, on the 27th of November, Glynn smirked and upped the ante. The California Supreme Court received not only his request for an enforcement of the automatic stay but also a petition for review. Basically, Glynn was asking the State's Supreme Court to reconcile the conflict

---

[84] "All discovery proceedings in the action shall be stayed upon the filing of a notice of motion made pursuant to this section. The stay of discovery shall remain in effect until notice of entry of the order ruling on the motion. The court, on noticed motion and for good cause shown, may order that specified discovery be conducted notwithstanding this subdivision."

[85] A court order that halts a legal proceeding.

between the legislature and the judiciary. The California 425.16 statute became law in 1992, yet not a one of these judges was recognizing it. Worse, yet they had no precedent of their own to challenge it. The court record was transmitted to the Supreme Court the same day via overnight mail.

At the same time, Poppe, eager to add fuel to the fire, wrote Glynn and Randy first on November 17:

> "The Court never issued a formal order on the demurrers and SLAPP motions. Accordingly, we have prepared the attached proposed order. Please let me know if you approve of the form of the order:"

PROPOSED ORDER

> "The [anti-SLAPP] motions were untimely because they were not submitted within 60 days of the service of the complaint... The Court does not deem the late filings to have been proper. The Court also finds that the causes of action in the Third Amended and Supplemental Complaint do not arise from "any act of [the defendants] in furtherance of [their] right of petition or free speech under the United States or California Constitution in connection with a public issue,"... Plaintiffs have established that there is a probability that they will prevail on their claims ...

> The Court finds that the defendants' respective SLAPP motions are frivolous and are solely intended to cause unnecessary delay.... Filing the unmeritorious motions at such a late date has delayed the completion of discovery and the setting of trial and has increased litigation expenses, all to Plaintiffs' prejudice.... Plaintiffs shall be awarded attorney's fees in the amount of $12,555.00 jointly and severally against defendants Delfino and Day and their counsel, Glynn Falcon and Randall Widmann, to be paid by 60 days from the date of this order.

> With the exception of the order granting attorney's fees, this order is issued *nunc pro tunc*[86] as of November 1, 2000, the date of the minute order regarding the above matters...."

It got no reaction, so ten days later a pesky Poppe wrote Rushing:

---

[86]Literally "now for then," this requests that the order be made effective earlier than the time dated.

"Enclosed is a proposed order denying the defendants' SLAPP motions ... the Court issued a written minute order ... we believe it would be appropriate for the Court to enter a formal order, particularly in light of the fact that the defendants have filed an appeal in connection with the SLAPP ruling. The Court has the authority to enter a formal *nunc pro tunc* order despite the filing of a notice of appeal....

We wish to draw the Court's attention in particular to the portion of the proposed order granting Plaintiffs' request for attorney's fees. The Court has not expressly ruled upon this request. We request a ruling and believe an award of attorney's fees to Plaintiffs is appropriate under the circumstances of this case ...

When I provided Mr. Falcon with an earlier draft of the proposed order, however, he expressed opposition to the order in general and to the request for attorney's fees in particular...."

Randy calmly wrote Rushing the next day:

"Ms. Day opposes entry of the proposed order on numerous grounds. First of all, your Honor never made any specific findings as to the reason for denial of Ms. Day's SLAPP motion. Ms. Day argued that she was only named as a party Defendant long after the original complaint had been filed against Mr. Delfino and that all of her comments were directed to the proceedings brought against her. Ms. Day also argued that her SLAPP motion was timely in that the Federal Courts did not allow the filing of SLAPP motions until late 1999 by virtue of a 9th Circuit decision and that in any event SLAPP motions were allowed even as to amended pleadings, again with a cited reference by Ms. Day to a District Court proceeding.

... emphasize that Ms. Day's position is far different than Mr. Delfino's with respect to the SLAPP motion.... what Mr. Poppe is trying to do by virtue of the order he is asking the Court to sign is to create a record which does not exist...."

And Glynn, even less concerned followed with a letter to Rushing on December 1, 2000:

"While I understand the court was not inclined to grant the special motions, thinking that the "delay" deprived the court of jurisdiction to rule on a SLAPP motion, it is also true that the 60 days is discretionary with the trial court, and as here, where the circumstances justify the "delay", the courts have not hesitated to grant CCP§425.16 motions to strike.

We have now asked the 6th DCA to review our anti-SLAPP motion de novo,[87] and have asked the California Supreme Court to review the automatic stay issue ... We firmly believe the stay should exist, especially now since we have directly appealed from your Minute Order of November 1, 2000. To change that Order now would affect the appeal and are embraced by the matters appeal from. A granting of sanctions would look vindictive for our pursuing our client's legal rights, including the right to appeal and to petition for review of your decisions.

Equally important, our claims are not frivolous, and there should be no finding that our motives were frivolous. There was never any suggestion by you that they were frivolous.... If this truly is a SLAPP suit, then a granting of sanctions plays right into plaintiffs' hands in that they achieve the objectives of curtailing defendant's speech and right to petition while concurrently taking away his limited financial resources to combat the SLAPP and to defend himself."

So much for Rushing. Once again not recognizing California law,[88] he signed Poppe's proposed order on December 1, 2000:

"... the defendants' respective motions to strike the third Amended and Supplemental Complaint pursuant to... (the "SLAPP" statute) are DENIED. The motions were untimely because they were not submitted within 60 days of the service of the complaint, as required.... The Court does not deem the late filings to have been proper. The Court also finds that the causes of action ... do not arise from "any act of [the defendants] in furtherance of [their] right of petition or free speech under the Untied States or California Constitution in connection with a public issue, as required.... Plaintiffs have established that there is a probability that they will prevail on their claims...."

At least he denied the sanctions. After all, this judge is a Democrat. It is perhaps ironic that a year later California Governor

---

[87]Literally "anew" or "fresh," a request to consider the matter as if it had never been heard before, as if no decision had been previously made.

[88]"... the term "complaint" implicitly encompasses "amended complaint"...[the defendants] could have filed their motion at the outset of the case... We nevertheless conclude...that [the defendants'] motion was timely filed within 60 days of service of the third amended complaint." (*Yu et al. v. Signet Bank/Virginia et al.* (2002) 103 Cal. App. 4th 298

Gray Davis[89] would announce the appointment of Rushing as an Associate Justice of the Court of Appeal, Sixth Appellate District. And in November 2002, the 65-year-old Rushing would be elected to a 12-year term.

Adding to our collapse, on December 15, 2000, the California Supreme Court too denied the petition for review and the application for stay. The rulings were made *En Banc*.[90] The Courts' denials were not as bothersome as was the omission of any explanation. They simply said, "denied." Losing is always bad enough, but not knowing the reason why seems unconscionable. There was just no accountability; so much for our "... government of the people – by the people – for the people ...".

Meanwhile, our anti-SLAPP appeals had begun. On January 18, 2001, the Grande Dame of SLAPP wrote Glynn and Randy demanding that our appeal be dismissed:

> "On behalf of the Respondents, we request that each appellant dismiss the appeal in the above matter. If the appeals are prosecuted and not dismissed, Respondents will seek monetary sanctions against you and your respective clients ...
>
> Appellate sanctions are authorized by C.R.C. 26(e) where an appeal is frivolous or taken solely for purposes of delay. The appeals meet both these standards....
>
> Both Appeals cannot possibly serve any purpose other than bringing about delay and unnecessary expense given that trial court proceedings will almost certainly conclude before the appeals are decided. There is no reason to proceed with the appeals.... the appeals are frivolous.... only filed the motions as a last resort to delay the inevitable trial...."

Hermle had her usual effect. On February 15, Randy filed Mary's "Opening Appellate Brief" along with a fifteen volume Appendix of 4,345 pages. On March 19 Glynn filed mine:

> "The Superior Court had the wool pulled over its eyes when it accepted plaintiffs' argument that Delfino's special motion was not

---

[89]The Governor of California from 1998-2002 just re-elected to a 2nd term.
[90]Refers to court sessions with the entire membership of a court participating rather than the usual quorum, i.e., "by the full court" or "full bench."

timely filed.... As soon as plaintiffs filed their third amended complaint, Delfino timely moved to strike it pursuant to CCP§425.16.... The special motion to strike was brought at the earliest possible moment ... The Superior Court not only had the discretion to permit the special motion, but under the statutes clear imperative that "[t]o this end, this section shall be construed broadly," it had the obligation to permit the motion, especially since it was being brought against the recently filed third amended complaint."

Ten days before Glynn's opening brief, The Orrick grew more pungent. They filed an "Association of Attorneys" officially adding Gerald Z. Marer to Hermle's stable. Marer, an elderly Palo Alto, California lawyer in private practice who specializes in appellate law, had been assisting the Grande Dame for some time. On November 28, 2000, he had lent a helping hand co-authoring with Hermle and Poppe a letter to the California Supreme Court:

"A stay would now only serve to postpone the date when Delfino has to face a jury, which is undoubtedly the true purpose of his request...."

I found this falsehood irritating enough to post about it the following day on the Yahoo! law board that I had long ago created:

Gerald Z. Marer joins Orrick's SLAPP
by: mr_michelangelo_delfino
team as the Varian (VAR & VSEA), Susan B. Felch and George Zdasiuk SLAPP looks to the Supreme Court. Click & enjoy:
http://www.geocities.com/mobeta_inc/slapp/supreme.html#marer
Q: How many lawyers does it take to win a SLAPP?
A: I won when I said I would post forever.

The hyperlink in my message allowed the interested reader to see the Supreme Court letter in its entirety and helped introduce Marer as the latest SLAPPer. Thereafter, Mary and I would rarely post about him as he seemed to be passively involved at best. However, now on 9th of March with our anti-SLAPP appeals moving forward, he became a formal member of the Orrick SLAPP team.

That very same day Marer asked the Appeals Court permission that his clients be allowed to file a single reply brief instead of one for Mary and another for me. The intent, of course, was to maintain the illusion of a conspiracy so the court would not differentiate between us. Randy filed the requisite opposition:

> "The problem with lumping DELFINO and DAY together is that it blurs the issues and attributes anything that DELFINO did to DAY as the plaintiffs would like to see happen."

Glynn having predicted the court's denial emailed me:

> "As a personal favor, I would appreciate it very much if you would eliminate reference to Mr. Marer. I met with him yesterday to serve the brief on him. He is suffering from a nerve disease [multiple sclerosis] and is wheelchair bound. Apparently, his mind is still keen, and contracts out to write appeal briefs. He is not a target, and any attacks upon him will only backfire with the courts, as they know and respect him, and must know of his plight. Thanks"

While Mary and I felt the same way, we respected Glynn's wishes and did not post about Marer anymore, not that any of our postings about his actions were particularly scathing anyway. Our messages were simply intended to communicate our outrage with the addition of yet another officer of the court joining this attack of our Constitutional Rights. Marer, in spite of his physical condition, is not a victim – he chose to unlawfully try to shut us up and to do so for money. He was no different than the fascist Italian and Rumanian soldiers accompanying the German invaders at Stalingrad – all deserved the same fate.

On April 27, 2001, Varian filed their respondent's brief. It included a five volume Appendix of which two were sealed, i.e., not available to the public. Randy concluded with Mary's reply brief on May 16. A month later, because of the death of a close family member on June 18, 2001, Glynn filed mine at which point the case was now fully briefed. Typically, this meant that six months or so would pass before the Appellate Court would make a ruling. While it wasn't clear whether the trial would occur before an Appellate decision, the notion that I ever wanted to avoid a trial was perhaps one of my biggest buttons. The Orrick had indeed pushed it more than once. If anything, I was looking forward to facing the "Gator"[91] at trial. I still seethe over the memory of having to sit in silence when first deposed by her.

Prompted by a Fourth District California Appellate ruling on August 21, 2000, Glynn wrote our court requesting the matter be expedited:

> "Last week, the case of Tony Lam v Ky Ngo ... was decided ... Two of the three issues raised in Delfino's appeal were addressed ... (1) whether an anti-SLAPP motion can be filed within 60 days of an amended complaint, (2) whether the prior granting of a preliminary injunction is collateral estoppel[92] or res judicata[93] on the issue of whether a plaintiff is likely to prevail.) were decided in favor of defendant, and the 4th DCA then decided, *de novo*, the merits of the anti-SLAPP motion....
>
> This letter is to request an early submission of this matter for appellate decision, prior to the start of the October 22, 2001 trial date.
>
> Alternatively, this letter is to renew our request for a temporary stay of the trial pending the outcome of this appeal. This last alternative is addressed both to the Sixth District Court of Appeal, and to Team-Leader Judge (Judge Jacobs-May) in the exercise of her discretion to supervise the court trial schedule and resources. It would seem a shame to have the appellate decision come-in after the time and expense that will be expended at a trial (which raises the question of whether the anti-SLAPP motions provision for an award of

---

[91]Benjamin Howell, Deborah Rosenthal and Jeanna Steele, *California Lawyer*, May 2001: "Liti-gators": "With more than 15 trials and no losses under her belt, Lynne Hermle has established a reputation for being a take-no-prisoners employment lawyer ... Hermle is "particularly useful when we have a male attorney on the other side. She turns them into putty as far as I can tell." ... "She actually had the plaintiff's lawyer throwing up in the bathroom every morning, he was so freaked-out about the case, and this happened day after day, through all the motions. The plaintiff and her lawyer actually agreed to withdraw from the lawsuit after Hermle's opening statement."

[92]Once a court has decided an issue that decision may preclude relitigation of the same issue on a different cause of action.

[93]A final judgment on an action precludes relitigating any issue that could have been raised on that action.

attorneys fees contemplates legal fees generated by a trial - - - which [a trial] is what the anti-SLAPP motion statute is designed to avoid.)
... we will waive oral argument if that will help facilitate an early decision on the appeal...."

On September 6, 2001, Marer expressed his opposition:

"We have just learned of an August 27, 2001 letter to this Court from counsel for appellant Delfino. The letter requests an "early submission" of the above-entitled case ... Opposing counsel suggests that *Lam* resolves in appellants' favor certain issues in this appeal. It does not.... Opposing counsel, as an alternative, "renew[s]" an earlier request for a stay of the October 22, 2001 trial pending a decision in this appeal.... This "request" is without merit procedurally and substantively. It has been made before and denied by this Court. It has been made before and denied by the Supreme Court...."

And on September 18, 2001, Acting Presiding Judge J. Bamattre-Manoukian ruled against us again – "Appellants' request for calendar preference and/or stay of the trial court proceedings is denied."

On June 28, 2002, another of California's six Appellate Courts published a ruling holding that an automatic stay pending an appeal was indeed the law.[94] Adding to the enforcement of this ruling, on August 29, 2002, the State's Supreme Court said it was not up to its judges to act otherwise.[95]

---

[94]"in enacting section 425.16, it was the intent of the Legislature to provide for an early resolution of the special motion to strike in aid of vindicating an appropriate exercise of free speech rights of defendants ... the trial court was divested of jurisdiction upon perfection of the appeal and it acted in excess of jurisdiction by setting a trial date." (*Mattel, Inc. v. Luce, Forward, Hamilton & Scripps* (2002) 99 Cal. App. 2nd 1179, 1190)

[95]"When on previous occasions we have construed the anti-SLAPP statute, we have done so strictly by its terms ... and no reason appears why we should proceed otherwise in this case.... When interpreting statutes, "we follow the Legislature's intent, as exhibited by the plain meaning of the actual words of the law.... 'This court has no power to rewrite the statute so as to make it conform to a presumed intention which is not expressed.'"..." (*Equilon Enterprises v. Consumer Cause, Inc.*, (2002) 29 Cal.4th 53, 65.)

- 11 -

SLAPP HAPPY

After Superior Court Judge Rushing, Appellate Court Justices Premo and Bamattre-Manoukian, and Chief Justice Ronald M. George of the California Supreme Court all had denied the stay that the state legislature demanded, there was nowhere left to appeal. There was no ombudsman. We would now get ready for our Superior Court trial.

On December 19, 2000, Glynn took aim and fired the first volley as he redirected the case toward discovery:

"... pursuant to CCP 2025 Defendant will take the depositions ...:

J. Tracy O'Rourke	January 4, 2001 at 10:00 a.m.
Susan Felch	January 5, 2001 at 10:00 a.m.
George Zdasiuk	January 8, 2001 at 10:00 a.m.
Richard "Dick" Aurelio	January 9, 2001 at 10:00 a.m.
Jeffrey Wright	January 10, 2001 at 10:00 a.m.
Martin Klausmeier-Brown	January 11, 2001 at 1:30 p.m.
Kathy Hibbs	January 12, 2001 at 10:00 a.m.
Carl Herrera	January 16, 2001 at 10:00 a.m.
Juanita Sonico	January 17, 2001 at 10:00 a.m.

Each of these depositions may be videotaped ... Each deponents is requested to bring and produce any and all statements, declarations, affidavits, verified discovery answers, or any other document that they have executed at any time in connection with this case ..."

Randy quickly added a few more names to the schedule – our version of an anti-SLAPP blitz. Recognizing their predicament, · Orrick immediately balked at having their witnesses deposed and filed Motions to Quash. J. Tracy O'Rourke, the former Chairman of Varian Associates, was the man in charge when the lawsuit was first filed. Then Levy and Aurelio's boss, he now had the distinction of being the first scheduled deponent, and was the first to seek protection. On December 29, Poppe replied:

> "... object to the deposition notice on the following grounds: ... O'Rourke is unavailable on January 4, 2001.... O'Rourke is a top executive without personal knowledge of relevant facts.... In light of the holidays and O'Rourke's position in his company, Delfino did not serve the deposition notice sufficiently in advance of the deposition.... Delfino did not confer with Plaintiffs' counsel prior to serving the notice.... notice is intended solely for the purposes of burden, oppression, and harassment.... videotaping of the deposition is intended solely for the purposes of oppression and harassment.... The location of the deposition is not within 150 miles of O'Rourke's residence.... The notice does not provide for sufficient time to gather the requested documents.... The document request is vague and ambiguous.... improperly purports to require that O'Rourke, an individual, produce corporate documents...."

Poppe's objections were quite typical and certainly not unexpected. While an attorney has the responsibility to protect his client and to prevent the discovery of damaging evidence, with Orrick the truth was rarely a priority. The multi-millionaire O'Rourke was still a resident of Los Altos Hills, California the same affluent town that housed Felch and Aurelio.

A month later, on January 18, Randy, frustrated with Orrick's stonewalling, issued Mary's Trial Setting Conference Statement:

> "It is evident that while the Plaintiffs are claiming that they desire an early trial date, their actions belie their words as they have done everything possible to stall and frustrate Defendants' discovery in this matter ...
>
> DELFINO noticed nine depositions.... To date, not a single one of those depositions has gone forward due to the Plaintiffs' actions....

They have brought: Motions to Quash as to the depositions of O'Rourke, Zdasiuk and Aurelio, have simply objected to producing the remainder of the witnesses on various grounds.... Plaintiffs have objected to the taking of the deposition of Ms. Hibbs.... on the grounds that Ms. Hibbs has no relevant knowledge of the underlying facts and that since the deposition notices went out in December and that Ms. Hibbs is so highly placed in the company, the deposition notice was untimely.... They simply refused to submit the witnesses.... Plaintiffs have ... objected that Mr. Herrera has no relevant knowledge of the underlying facts and again shouldn't be burdened with a deposition. These claims are absolutely false.... Plaintiffs filed an Initial Disclosure setting forth the witnesses and the testimony they expected them to provide in this matter.... Ms. Hibbs and Mr. Herrera are both listed in the initial disclosure....

the deposition of the person(s) most knowledgeable regarding Plaintiffs' damages was actually a deposition ordered in Federal Court several months prior under Rule 30(b)(6). Rather than produce the witness on the date noticed, Plaintiffs notified Defendants' counsel that Felch, whose deposition was objected to, and Mr. Wright, another deposition noticed by Mr. DELFINO, were the two designees on the damages issue, offering just one day for each of these witnesses, days on which both defense counsel were not available. As to the remaining four depositions of Mr. Fair, Ms. Niehaus, Ms. Mustonen and Mr. Powell, while Ms. DAY's counsel has not yet received objections, there is little doubt he will be in receipt of same....

The short and the long of the issues presented here are that while the Plaintiffs say they want an early trial date, they have completely stonewalled the Defendants' efforts to move discovery along quickly and expeditiously ... the earliest available time for a trial in this matter would be late June...."

After much bickering, discovery Judge Neal Cabrinha granted Orrick's Motion to Quash O'Rourke and Aurelio's depositions. Aurelio would later resurface at trial, but O'Rourke, who never testified, retired to Flagstaff, Arizona never to be heard from again.

Federal Court rules had given Judge Whyte the authority to arbitrarily restrict the number of depositions that each side might take. He allotted the defense 10 and we had used all but one. Orrick had completed 6 of their 10 depositions, including two

Stock-Talk witnesses located in Florida. In their haste to overwhelm us, and fully aware of the 10-deponent restriction, on October 8, 1999, Varian provided a list of 26 people they intended to call against us at trial:

> "Pursuant to Rules 26(a)(1) and 26(e) of the Federal Rules of Civil Procedure and Local Rule 16-5, plaintiffs ... submit the following Amended Initial Disclosure.... with a list of the following individuals likely to have discoverable information relevant to disputed facts alleged with particularity in the pleadings:
>
> ... Susan Felch ... George Zdasiuk ... Jane Crisler ... Kathy Hibbs ... Jim Fair ... Ron Powell ... Michael Haswell ... Paul Williams ... Justin Marino ... Scott Lebredo ... Maria Mustonen ... Jessica Niehaus ... Dave Humber ... Dayton Cheatham ... Linda Hester ... Fred Ahoorai ... Matt Goeckner ... Glynn Reynolds ... Juanita Sonico ... Carl Herrera ... Jack Holihan ... Jim Hennessy ... Archie Everett ... Kevin Felch ... Matthew Poppe ... Elizabeth Banker ..."

Although I knew the names of everyone on Orrick's list, I was at a loss to predict what relevant testimony some of these people might provide. Carl Herrera, a manic-depressive-like former machinist who for many years worked for Dave Humber and then Felch was one such person. On February 22, 2001, we got a hint of his value:

> FALCON: Are you claiming that Mike Delfino somehow posed as you, say, on the Internet?
> POPPE: Objection; vague and lacks foundation.
> FALCON: Well, counsel, I'm just reading -- So you know where I'm coming from on this -- you've been disclosed as a witness by Varian and Susan Felch and George Zdasiuk about, quote, your areas of knowledge, misconduct of Delfino at Varian, and Delfino's misappropriation, which means taking without permission, of your identity. That's why I'm asking the question. If it's vague and unclear, it's because that's the way that plaintiff's counsel phrased it.
> ...
> HERRERA: Somebody used my name, I guess not -- I can just say my name, I guess, on the web.
> ...
> FALCON: Okay. And to the best of your recollection, what did it say?

HERRERA: Oh, something about Choo-Choo Carl, about --
something about Varian. I don't remember.
FALCON: You have to go a little slower. I missed that. It said
something about what?
HERRERA: Saying Choo-Choo Carl.
FALCON: Choo-Choo?
…
HERRERA: Choo-Choo Carl.

…

FALCON: Did you take it as humorous or as threatening? What was
your take on seeing that web page?
HERRERA: Truthfully?
FALCON: Yes.
HERRERA: Bullshit.

A number of others on Orrick's list, I thought, would intentionally be helpful to me. However, if someone has not been deposed prior to testifying at trial, there is no way of knowing what evidence they will provide. Thus, there is little chance of impeaching them. Now that the case was back in Superior Court there was no limit to the number of depositions allowed.

Martin Klausmeier-Brown, one such addition, was a Varian employee who Orrick had identified when they subpoenaed his Yahoo! alias "Singin_InTheRain" which Varian alleged posted defamatory messages. As soon as The Orrick realized it was not I, they tried to hide the subpoena. Why? This computer programmer had an office adjacent Felch and I and, like me, was one of those who urinated and defecated and showered in the restroom she videotaped. When noticed for deposition, Martin had moved to Indiana, and so, we did not depose him.

For more than a year, Randy had been attempting to take the last deposition allowed by Federal Rules – the deposition of "person(s) most knowledgeable" for the corporations. Defamation requires proof of damage to property, business, trade, profession or occupation and we needed to examine Varians' "proof" before trial:

"... pursuant to ... Magistrate Trumbull's Order dated January 28, 2000 ... Defendant MARY DAY, will take the deposition(s) of ...

officers, directors, managing agents or other persons most knowledgeable about the amount of the damages alleged to have been sustained by each of the corporate Plaintiffs as a result of any actions taken by Defendant, MARY DAY and about how the damages alleged to have been sustained by each of the corporate Plaintiffs as a result of any actions taken by Defendant, MARY DAY, were calculated ..."

When the February 14, 2000 Federal trial was on hold, Poppe only then disclosed who those witnesses would be:

"We anticipate having Susan Felch, George Zdasiuk and Jeff Wright testify on behalf of Varian Medical and Varian Semiconductor at the 30(b)(6) deposition. Ms. Felch is available in the morning of March 2, and Mr. Wright is available in the afternoon. I do not yet know Mr. Zdasiuk's availability...."

As the year passed, Zdasiuk, succumbing to the stress of litigation, dropped out as an "expert" leaving Wright as "Varian Medical Systems Most Knowledgeable Witness." Wright who had declared on January 7, 2000 that "Varian employees came forward and informed me ... that they were concerned about their safety" was already on Glynn's deposition list. After all, we had a right to find out who was so fearful of us. Of course, there was no one and this was just another ploy to inflame the court.

The Orrick delayed again and again, fighting vigorously to keep Wright's testimony secret. On March 23, 2001 McMahon wrote:

"Defendant Michelangelo Delfino's ongoing campaign of harassment on the Internet has caused the targets of his attacks to feel real fear for their personal safety....

Delfino and Day have served Plaintiffs with requests to produce many security-related documents.... The information should not be disclosed to Delfino, who is the primary reason why security measures were implemented in the first place. Nor should the information be disclosed to Day, who is Delfino's girlfriend, business partner, neighbor, and co-harasser....

Delfino's Internet messages ... show that Delfino feels extreme hatred toward Plaintiffs. In his messages, he calls Plaintiffs liars, fascists, and cowards ... accuses them of such things as homophobia, sexism, and infidelity. ... The frequency with which Delfino posts on the Internet--dozens of messages every week on many different message boards--suggests an unhealthy and possibly dangerous obsession ...

Delfino is not merely a voice on the Internet.... He has posted about attending Varian stockholder meetings and he and Day have actually shown up at one meeting...."

The ploy worked, Cabrinha took the bait and on June 7 he ordered:

"Mary Day and Michelangelo Delfino shall not attend either the deposition of Jeff Wright or the deposition of Varian Medical Systems, Inc. Nor shall their counsel discuss with them what is disclosed in the depositions; ... Glynn Falcon and Randall Widmann shall keep their copies of the Jeff Wright and Varian Medical Systems, Inc. deposition transcripts and any documents produced in connection with those depositions separate from their other files related to this case, in a locked room or cabinet to which Michelangelo and Mary Day have no access;"

Even with us barred from facing our accusers, Wright's deposition did not proceed smoothly. The first attempt ended after ten minutes with Hermle's flatulent histrionics taking center stage.

Finally, on August 17, 2001 Wright, represented by both Hermle and Poppe, completed his deposition with Mary and me *in absentia*. It was the only one out of more than two dozen that we did not attend. Moreover, to this day we have no idea what he said. Even when he testified at our trial we were not allowed to remain in the courtroom:

WRIGHT: It's an invoice from Security by Design to Varian Medical Systems for security consulting. The amount is $2,359.50.
POPPE: Does this amount represent anything other than consulting related to the perceived threat from Mr. Delfino and Ms. Day?
WRIGHT: No, it does not.
POPPE: What were the specific additional security measures that Varian Medical implemented in reliance on Security by Design's advice?
WRIGHT: We implemented additional hardware within the building that would summon assistance in the event of an intrusion or prevent intruders from gaining access in the first place.

POPPE: And what measures were these?

WRIGHT: One is a series of duress alarms that are located at various areas within the building that, once deployed, link with a response plan, including video. The other is interior barrier doors beyond the lobby so, once past the receptionist, there's additional doors that require card access to gain entry into the building.

POPPE: Were there any additional video systems implemented?

WRIGHT: Yes. Tied in with the duress alarm system.

POPPE: Absent the perceived threat from Mr. Delfino and Ms. Day, would any of these three security systems I've just identified have been implemented?

WRIGHT: No, they would not.

...

WRIGHT: The first page is an invoice -- actually, it's the application for payment from James R. Griffin, which is the general contractor for the door installation in a total $49,346 total contract sum. The next page is an invoice from Pierce and Associates for project management. The dollar amount on the first invoice is $180. There's another invoice that will come in. Next invoice is from APEX Communications for a dollar amount of $10,111.36. There are supporting documents that include the change orders and the backup to arrive at the $10,111.

...

POPPE: And looking at the sum of the various amounts that we've discussed for the shareholder meetings, the additional security around the Palo Alto site, the consulting costs and the hardware costs, what is the total amount approximate of security costs related to measures that were implemented as a result of Mr. Delfino and Ms. Day?

WRIGHT: I believe it's in the low $90,000 range.

Because of another Orrick bevue, we, along with the rest of the Internet world, did get to see Wright's testimony in its entirety on July 8, 2002. It was clear why they had fought so hard to prevent it from going public – Varian had sustained no damage whatsoever. And even when two of our Yahoo! accounts were deleted, it did not stop us from lawfully advertising Wright's testimony on the Web. Two days later, Orrick demonstrated their impotence again:

"TO THE CLERK OF THE COURT ...

The purpose of the motion was to preserve the confidentiality of certain portions of the [November 9, 2001] trial testimony of Jeff Wright concerning security measures implemented by Respondent

Varian Medical Systems, Inc., in order to preserve the effectiveness of those security measures. However, it has come to Respondents' attention that Appellant Michelangelo Delfino already obtained a copy of the Jeff Wright transcript and published it on his Internet web site. He did this even though (1) he had been excluded from the courtroom during the testimony; (2) the transcript contains a court order stating that the testimony was confidential and should not be disclosed outside the courtroom; and (3) Respondents' counsel had informed Delfino's appellate counsel that Respondents intended to file a motion to seal the transcript. Unfortunately, it appears that Delfino's bad faith actions have rendered Respondents' motion to seal moot.

Accordingly, that motion is hereby withdrawn...."

and we immediately made it available to our readership.

Although Felch and "her group" worked no more than three miles from our house, the VSEA facility is located in Gloucester, Massachusetts. So I presume they believed because of the distance we weren't a credible threat to their security or likely to attend their annual meeting. Not to be outdone by their sibling, they conjured up an almost surrealistic argument and used Frau Felch to deliver it. On March 28, 2001, she was chosen to represent VSEA in detailing the damage our Internet postings had allegedly caused:

FALCON: When did you get the assignment as the representative from VSEA to be the person most knowledgeable?
FELCH: I don't remember.
FALCON: In the last month?
FELCH: No.
FALCON: More than three months?
FELCH: Yes.
FALCON: More than a year?
FELCH: I don't remember whether it was more or less than a year.
FALCON: Who gave you that assignment?
FELCH: I believe that it came from Gary Loser.
FALCON: And who is Gary Loser?
FELCH: He's the general counsel for VSEA.

How appropriate, I thought, to be a Loser. Gary Loser was Varian's 50-year-old Vice President, General Counsel and Secretary, someone who should know better than to assign this critical task to someone with no accounting background. Perhaps you had to be delusional to accept this assignment:

> WIDMANN: The amount of damages set --
> FELCH: Sustained by Varian Semiconductor Equipment.
> ...
> WIDMANN: What are the amount of the damages it sustained?
> FELCH: As of Tuesday, March 27, 2001, it came to $38,000 -- $38,947.
> WIDMANN: What are you referring to, ma'am?
> FELCH: Lost work time for various employees.

Felch then described a day in the life of a hard-working VSEA employee.

> WIDMANN: All right. Now, in this -- under the first heading, you've got down here "Lost Work Time for S.B. Felch; Read, discuss, and contemplate Internet postings: 146 hours." How much is that worth?
> FELCH: I would have to multiply it out.
> WIDMANN: How did you -- in other words --
> FELCH: We --
> WIDMANN: -- what hourly rate did you use?
> FELCH: That is shown, we used an hourly rate of $86.28 per hour.
> WIDMANN: For every employee?
> FELCH: Except for Mr. Aurelio.
> WIDMANN: What did you use for him?
> FELCH: You can see that was basically $2,292,321 divided by 2,080 hours.
> WIDMANN: That's how you got his hourly rate?
> FELCH: Yes.
> WIDMANN: Okay. In this heading here, "Read, discuss, and contemplate Internet postings: 146 hours," did you include time you spent on issues concerning you personally? You follow me?
> FELCH: No, I don't know exactly what you mean.
> WIDMANN: You're a plaintiff, an individual plaintiff. You understand that?
> FELCH: Yes.
> WIDMANN: And you had personal and individual claims against my client and Mr. Delfino. You understand that?
> FELCH: Yes.
> WIDMANN: On the other hand, the corporate defendants -- the corporate plaintiffs have claims against Mr. Delfino and Ms. Day.
> FELCH: Yes.

WIDMANN: All right. And this 146 hours, did you include any time in work on your personal portion of the lawsuit?
FELCH: This was time that Varian Semiconductor lost out of my normal workday when I was not productive -- a productive employee doing other work-related matters and was spent relating to the postings. So it was a damage to the company.
WIDMANN: And it was postings that had to do with you personally, you're claiming that defamed you; correct?
FELCH: Myself and the company.

This was by far the most laughable deposition in the case. At least Crisler had the sense to drive off in the middle. It was bizarre to think that Loser would base his company's defamation claim on the notion that its employees should be compensated for time spent reading our postings or pursuing a personal lawsuit. As Glynn would put it on March 11, 2002: "... [VSEA] claimed lost productivity for the time the corporation actually permitted its employees to look at the Internet postings! (Self inflicted damages - much less no mitigation efforts). ..." Can you imagine, publicly traded companies claiming the right to sue message board critics because they believe that their employees may have been reading Internet critiques while getting paid by the corporations? Not a bad way to make money!

True to form, a jury later found that neither Varian corporation had sustained any special damages. And of course, Felch and Zdasiuk never claimed any.

From time to time, Varian would add to their witness list. On January 31, 2000, Orrick, provided this answer to one of Randy's interrogatory questions:

> "Varian Medical believes that the following persons have knowledge regarding the amount of damage to Varian Medical's reputation resulting from actions that Varian Medical believes were undertaken by Day and that form a basis for this lawsuit: Richard Levy, Richard Aurelio, George Zdasiuk, Sue Felch, Julie Fouquet."

naming Dr. Julie Fouquet a percipient witness. In keeping with Orrick's penchant for picking seemingly arbitrary names out of their SLAPP pond, this product of Harvard and Stanford

Universities would later say under oath, "I am not an employee of Varian, so I don't consider myself an expert on the extent of any damage." Hardly pretty, her value to Varian Medical Systems was never apparent. She in fact worked for Agilent Technologies, Inc. in neighboring Palo Alto and was unknown to us at the time. Even when she would later be revealed to be Zdasiuk's wife, which of course made her a more interesting deponent, it never made sense why VAR named her as a witness.

Little did we know that the service of a subpoena notice, usually a fairly mundane event, would take on a life of its own with Fouquet and her husband. A first attempt was made to subpoena her at her place of employment on June 4, 2001. She refused to meet the server in the lobby, having instead a company attorney ask him to leave the premises. This, of course, required the server to try to serve her at her million dollar-plus estate in Portola Valley's rural hills. The next day's attempt to lawfully serve Fouquet resulted in this sworn statement:

"PARTY TO BE SERVED: JULIE FOUQUET
Home: 48 HILLBROOK DR, PORTOLA VALLEY, CA 94028 as enumerated below: 06/05/2001 08:25 pm

A MALE, IN HIS EARLY 40'S, 5'11 WITH DARK HAIR, TOLD ME TO "GET THE FUCK OUT OF HERE". I ASKED HIM IF THE PLACE WAS HIS PROPERTY, HE PAUSED FOR A MOMENT AND THEN SAID "GET OFF MY FUCKING PROPERTY". I EXPLAINED THAT I HAD SOME LEGAL PAPERS FOR JULIE FOUQUET. HE JUST LOOKED AT ME AN TOLD ME "GET THE FUCK OUT OF HERE". I COULD SMELL ALCOHOL ON HIS BREATH.

BRET MAZZOCCO (EXP-01/2002) REGISTERED INDEPENDENT CONTRACTOR (signed)"

An intoxicated and vulgar male?

The very next day, a second attempt at servicing Fouquet by yet a different process server resulted in this even more disturbing account of a percipient witness married to a Varian Medical Systems Executive Vice President, a man with a problem:

"PARTY TO BE SERVED: JULIE FOUQUET
Home: 48 HILLBROOK DR, PORTOLA VALLEY, CA 94025
as enumerated below:

06/06/2001 04:53 pm
PLEASE SEE ATTACHED DILIGENCE
PERSONAL SERVICE OF SUBPOENA

STAKEOUT JUNE 7, 2001

"06/06/2001 11:52 AM I called from lobby [Agilent Technologies],
only got her voicemail. I talked to her administrator and she said the
subject is not in.

06/06/2001 4:45 PM I could hear subject in the house after I rang the
doorbell. I also called out her name. Then I called her home number.
Again, I could hear the phone ringing from the porch (where I was
standing). I put tape on the garage and put a penny on back tire of
vehicle.

06/07/2001 6:45 AM Stakeout started per client. No cars in driveway.
Yesterday there was a Maroon and Grey Ford Bronco in driveway but
the vehicle was not here today. I parked on the street so I could have
a good look at the garage and front of the house. I noticed there was a
current newspaper at the bottom of the driveway. At 7:45 am, a male
came out of the garage, walked down to the end of the driveway and
picked up the newspaper, then walked out to the street. He walked
past my car and started to write down my license number and asked
me, "Can I help you?" I said, "Yes, are you the person who gave
another process server a very hard time 2 days ago?" He answered
"No", and then he said, "you can not come on my fucking property."
At that point, I got out of my car, followed him onto his driveway and
said "I have every right to be here, I have a subpoena with Julie
Fouquet's name on it, can you get her to come out and accept this
subpoena, and then I can leave." He just kept saying, "Get the fuck
out of here, my attorney has already worked this out." I could tell he
had been drinking. I could smell alcohol on his breath. Then he said
he was calling the police. I said, "I wish you would." He then closed
the garage and I went back to my car. A few minutes went by and
then he opened up his blinds above the garage. In the living room I
could see a female standing next to him. At that point I walked back
on the property, announced service, and left the documents on the
door, I also announced that I would be waiting for the police. At
about 8:06 am, a Sheriff drove up. I explained what had transpired.
They asked me for my process server's registration number and

driver's license. After we talked for a few minutes, they handed me back my card and license. The man who had called them was standing in his driveway as the Sheriff and I were driving away. They never even talked to the erratic man!!. I left the scene at 8:15 am.

I declare under penalty of perjury under the laws of the State of California that the foregoing is true and correct.
Date: June 29, 2001
Greg Vartanian (*signed*)"

Intoxicated and vulgar *again*? Zdasiuk's violent and rather ugly outbursts at his spacious home made for wonderful postings. Even before we had these sworn statements in hand, the *two* process servers' oral reports alone provided sufficient credibility to post the story. We knew Zdasiuk. He had often displayed childish emotional tantrums at work. And so, I posted this message on the Yahoo! VAR board on June 7, 2001 shortly after hearing about the incidents from Niloofar Poorooshasb, Randy's pixie-like paralegal:

Mr. Zdasiuk - Pleeeeeeeeez get help!
by: varian_videotapes_bathrooms (F/Palo Alto, California)
George Zdasiuk has complained of anxiety, sexual problems, sleeplessness, high blood pressure, mouth cankers, etc.
But is George Zdasiuk a violent & dangerous man too?
I have been informed and therefore I believe that George Zdasiuk, the fascist pig SLAPPer and despicable Varian Executive Vice President has made a threatening and violent display of rage and anger when confronted by an innocent man serving a deposition subpoena on his wife Julie Fouquet, a man earning a living by just legally doing his job. I am informed that this very scary behavior has occurred on at least two occasions this week in lovely Portola Valley, California as his wife had apparently tried more than once to avoid being served at Agilent Technologies, her place of employment. I pray that no one has been harmed by this unfortunate set of events and that Mr. Zdasiuk get whatever psychological or psychiatric help that he himself has sought publicly. And, of course, there are the children, innocent ones that should not be subjected to such loud noises. Violence and rage against our American legal system is unacceptable! Mr. Zdasiuk, please harm no one, including yourself. Follow the law and just let your wife speak the truth as the law demands!

Mary exercised her poetic license in this June 20, 2001, Yahoo! VAR posting:

> **Is Zdašiuk just a dumbshit?** by: be_careful_who_you_slapp
> There once was an Executive VP at Varian who may have broken the law;
> He went into a such a rage while trying to stop a legal subpoena, now that's a flaw!
> He asked a Federal judge to prohibit the free speech of describing him fat;
> And he repeatedly violated company policy, what do you think of that?
> That's what SLAPP plaintiffs are like when they act as though the First Amendment wasn't a law.

The seriousness of Zdasiuk's drinking and baseness at home was not something Varian's Dick Levy wanted publicity about. Consequently, Mary and I posted about this repeatedly.

For more than six months, Zdasiuk had successfully avoided his third day of deposition. Unlike his first two, this one was going to be videotaped. Glynn's June 13, 2001 declaration, gives some idea of why Orrick fought so hard to prevent it:

"I took Mr. Zdasiuk's deposition ... last on November 11, 1999 ... Mr. Zdasiuk is probably the worst witness I can ever recall seeing at a deposition. By that I mean he repeatedly looked over to his counsel before answering any pointed questions, repeatedly looked over to his counsel for approval of his testimony, repeatedly took long breaks before answering tough questions ... and squirmed and delayed repeatedly when giving his answers, was evasive, illusive, delaying, and non-responsive to my questions.... it took 23 minutes just to get a straight answer from Mr. Zdasiuk as to whether or not he is actually overweight (he claims in his lawsuit he was libeled for being called "fat," "overweight," or "fatso"). The cold, typewritten transcript does not reveal the antics of this witness, or the aid he attempted to get from his counsel, and does not do justice to the mannerism differences displayed by Mr. Zdasiuk's face and movements when he answered "easy" questions compared to those questions going to meat of his accusations against my client. Of the 918 questions asked him, Zdasiuk only answered 673 of them (public record portion). Of those answered, Mr. Zdasiuk asserted responses of "I don't recall" approximately 125 times, "I don't know" 97 times, and "I don't remember" 25 times. Moreover, his counsel's role there seemed to be mainly to delay and slow down the deposition by repeated objections (approximately 178 objections appear in the public portion of the transcript, alone. That is about one per page) and 14 instructions not to answer the pending question.

... plaintiffs have videotaped all five (5) sessions of Mary Day's depositions, and have videotaped all three (3) deposition sessions of my client, Michelangelo Delfino. The reasons they give for taking defendants' depositions by videotape are precisely the same reasons why I desire to take Mr. Zdasiuk's deposition. I believe that videotaping Mr. Zdasiuk will keep his antic in check and will prevent, to some extent, the interruptions by his counsel. It will allow the trier of fact a better record to determine, from the written, audio and visual records, whether Mr. Zdasiuk is telling the truth or is lying....

It is imperative that my client be in the deposition with me, as he was present at all of the other depositions, and he was a participant to many of the subject matter areas that I will be deposing Mr. Zdasiuk upon. My client's help is critical to me, for his note taking, oversight, and for his information on whether Mr. Zdasiuk is truthful or not, and if not, what information is available that I could use to impeach him on the record....

Plaintiffs are so nervous about having their client appear on videotape, that they tried to convince me that their client would prefer to answer questions by written interrogatories (purportedly to save expense) instead of live deposition. They know that their client gives the appearance of lying under oath, and they definitely do not want any video record preserved that might possibly reveal what an awful witness Mr. Zdasiuk truly is. For me, videotaping of Mr. Zdasiuk is of paramount importance, as it reveals him for what he truly is. It is critical for comparison to the jury later in the case when he gives smooth and polished answers to them, and when I show the video cuts from his deposition on the same facts or issue...."

Unaware of the sworn statements by two different and unrelated process servers that were in our possession, Zdasiuk was deposed and videotaped on July 25, 2001:

FALCON: Were you present when a process server attempted to serve a subpoena on your wife to appear at a deposition?

...

ZDASIUK: I don't know if a process server attempted to serve a subpoena to my wife.

FALCON: Okay. So nothing like that rings a bell?

...

ZDASIUK: Well, an individual came to my house.

FALCON: Okay. Tell me about that individual that came to your house. What happened?

ZDASIUK: Can you tell me what time you're referring to?

FALCON: The one that you were just referring to.

ZDASIUK: An individual came to my house and asked to see my wife.... I asked him to get off my property.

FALCON: Why did you tell him to -- ask him to get off your property?

ZDASIUK: Because I didn't wish to have my privacy invaded.

FALCON: How did you know your privacy was going to be invaded?

...

ZDASIUK: This person was an agent -- I believe was an agent of Mr. Delfino.

...

FALCON: Okay. So as I understand it, they asked to -- that person asked to see your wife, and then you next then ordered that person off your property?

ZDASIUK: That's correct.

FALCON: And what happened next?

ZDASIUK: He said something to the effect that "I'm a contractor."

FALCON: "I'm a contractor"?

ZDASIUK: Yes.

FALCON: Okay. Then what did you say in response to that?

ZDASIUK: I said, "Please get off my property or I will call the police."

...

FALCON: And did you call the police?

ZDASIUK: No.

FALCON: Did the police come out?

ZDASIUK: No.

FALCON: Was a police report made?

ZDASIUK: No.

FALCON: What time of day or night was this?

ZDASIUK: This was in the evening.

FALCON: Was it night or was it dark?

ZDASIUK: No.

FALCON: Approximately what time?

ZDASIUK: 7:00, 8:00 o'clock, something like that. I don't know exactly.

FALCON: Had you had a suspicion that someone may try to serve a subpoena on your wife?

ZDASIUK: Yes.

...

FALCON: Is there a reason that you did not want your wife to be subpoenaed?

ZDASIUK: No.

FALCON: Did you feel like you were blocking or obstructing justice?

ZDASIUK: No.

FALCON: Was your wife home?

ZDASIUK: Yes.

...

FALCON: Had you had anything of an alcoholic nature to drink that evening before the process server or this agent or contractor showed up?

ZDASIUK: Yes.

FALCON: Were you intoxicated?

ZDASIUK: No.

FALCON: How much had you drank?

ZDASIUK: One to two glasses of wine.

FALCON: During how long of an interval?

ZDASIUK: Probably several hours.

FALCON: Was this a work day?

ZDASIUK: Yes.

FALCON: What time did you get home that day?

ZDASIUK: Probably 6:15, 6:30, something like that.

FALCON: Okay. Again, you think this was around 7:00 or 8:00 that the person came to your door?

ZDASIUK: Around 8:00.

FALCON: Around 8:00 now?

ZDASIUK: I'm not sure exactly, but around -- it was after dinner, after dinner was finishing up.

FALCON: So you had had the wine with dinner?

ZDASIUK: That's correct.

FALCON: And you don't believe that you demonstrated any signs of intoxication to this person?

ZDASIUK: No.

FALCON: I mean -- that answer could be interpreted either way. Let me make it clear, clarify. Do you feel that you demonstrated any signs of intoxication?

ZDASIUK: No.

FALCON: Now was this the only attempt that was made to subpoena

your wife for deposition that you're aware of?
ZDASIUK: I don't know if this was an attempt to subpoena my wife.
A guy came to my door.
...
FALCON: Do you feel that you were in any way obstructing service
of process by refusing this person to have access to your wife?
ZDASIUK: No.
FALCON: And why is that?
ZDASIUK: I consulted with my attorneys prior to this particular --
these incidents and was informed --
POPPE: Well, instruct you not to answer.
FALCON: You don't have to tell me what you were informed, but
you were basically acting in conformance to whatever advice you
received from counsel; is that correct?
ZDASIUK: That's correct, yes.

Don't you wonder what The Orrick advised him to do?

FALCON: Okay. Did you ever threaten any of these process servers -
-
ZDASIUK: No.
FALCON: -- with physical harm?
ZDASIUK: No.
FALCON: Did you ever say anything to the effect that "I'll kick your
ass"?
ZDASIUK: No.
FALCON: "Get off my property or I'll" -- in some way do physical
harm to them?
ZDASIUK: No.

Later that same day, this Varian Executive Vice President was
given yet another opportunity to set the record straight:

WIDMANN: You talked under questioning -- under examination
rather by Mr. Falcon about these two individuals who came to your
home. With respect to the first individual, the male that came to your
home in the evening hours --
ZDASIUK: Yes.
WIDMANN: -- did that person tell you that he had legal papers for
your wife?
ZDASIUK: I don't recall exactly what he said other than he wanted to
see my wife.
...

> WIDMANN: All right. Did you tell that individual to "get the fuck out of here"?
> ZDASIUK: No.
> WIDMANN: Did you use -- did you say the word "fuck" to that person at that time?
> ZDASIUK: No.
> WIDMANN: And am I correct that when you -- when you spoke to this individual, you had had one or two glasses of wine prior to that conversation?
> ZDASIUK: Most probably, yes.

Once again, Zdasiuk had proven himself to be a liar, although at this point he was no longer quite as a fat.

> WIDMANN: Since the last session of your deposition back in November of '99, has your suit or sport coat size changed?
> ...
> ZDASIUK: I stated that I lost between twenty and thirty pounds.
> ...
> WIDMANN: Okay. Well, tell me what your suit size was in November of '99 and tell me what your suit size is now, if you know?
> ZDASIUK: I believe that my suit size was in the vicinity of 46, and I believe that now it's in between a 44 and a 42, but I'm not actually -- I mean different people have different opinions.

If Zdasiuk intentionally lied during his deposition about his encounters with the two process servers, then he was also guilty of perjury.

After what seemed like an eternity, the Fouquet deposition was scheduled for June 28, 2001, but did not occur as the day before Randy's parents house in Sacramento burned down. We had to wait until September 19, 2001 for Fouquet to finally be deposed. And yes, it was worth the wait.

> WIDMANN: Okay. Now we talked a little bit about the process server or servers who came out to try to serve you with process. Did you understand they were process servers trying to serve you with papers while they were located where you could see them from your residence?
> POPPE: Objection; assumes facts.
> FOUQUET: I knew there were process servers trying to serve me

with papers from this case, or at least had a good reason to believe
that was the case once my boss, Steve Newton, read on the Internet
that that was what was supposed to happen.
WIDMANN: Okay. And after you read that on the Internet, did
process servers appear again at your residence to try to serve you with
papers?
FOUQUET: I believe so.
WIDMANN: Did you try to avoid service of process?
FOUQUET: No.
WIDMANN: Okay. I understand from your husband's testimony, he
was out and talking with them or dealing with them at various times.
During any of those times, had your husband consumed alcohol
immediately prior to that?
...
FOUQUET: Yes.

Fouquet displayed as much veracity as her husband; they were indeed a match. How is it that she knew we were trying to serve her notice of deposition yet her husband, the plaintiff advised by Orrick, had no idea. Not until after her deposition, did Niloofar tell us how the third process server had her daughter assist her in getting the elusive Fouquet to answer a few of our questions:

> **Girl Scouts help subpoena FOUQUET!** by: reall123
> I just got this off the web.
> Apparently this Julie Fouquet was subpoenaed with the help of
> the Girl Scouts of America.
> If this really on the level, I'm doing more than just buying
> cookies,
> I'm contributing a little extra.
> How about you?

Fouquet was videotaped just like her husband and most everyone else now that the case was in Superior Court. Realizing the mileage we got from videotaping Varians' Dicks and showing excerpts on the Web was all Orrick needed to complain. On June 27, 2001, Judge Cabrinha issued another order:

"Plaintiffs' motion is GRANTED IN PART. The parties are hereby
ordered not to post on the Internet, in whole or in part, the transcript
of Mr. Zdasiuk's deposition or the transcript of any other deposition

or portion therof not already published on the Internet. The parties are further ordered not to post on the Internet, in whole or in part, the videotape of Mr. Zdasiuk's deposition or the videotape of any other deposition or portion therof not already published on the Internet. This order does not bar the parties from posting commentary. This order will remain in force even if the testimony is submitted to the Court in connection with motion or other proceeding...."

preventing us from publishing *any* of Zdasiuk's pending deposition on the Internet. It did not, however, stop us from putting Fouquet's transcript and video testimony on the Internet. And of course we did. Orrick reacted as expected and complained bitterly that we had violated his order and should be found in contempt.

In support of trying to put us in jail, Fouquet made this declaration on September 28, 2001:

"... At the very bottom of the web page is a button labeled "SLAPPer Video Excerpts.".... Toward the bottom of the second web page is a hyperlink labeled "More SLAPPer Video Clips".... The third web page contains two buttons labeled "Julie Fouquet & her family values" and "Wife Impeaches George Zdasiuk." When I pointed my cursor at these tabs and pressed the mouse button, a RealPlayer window appeared on my computer screen and displayed video clips from my deposition on September 21, 2001. In the video clips, I could hear Mr. Widmann asking me questions and I could see and hear me answering them.... I had not seen these video segments before today and was not aware before this evening that they had been placed on the Internet...."

so that Poppe could once gain lay out his specious argument:

"Defendants Michelangelo Delfino and Mary Day have once again demonstrated ... their willingness to go to any lengths to harm plaintiffs and those associated with them, regardless of the costs.... Several days ago, Delfino and Day announced their intention to post video clips from the depositions of Julie Fouquet ... and Kevin Felch ... on the Internet....

Beginning twelve days ago, Delfino and Day let it be known that they intended to violate Judge Cabrinha's order. On September 19, 2001, Day's counsel took the deposition of Julie Fouquet, Zdasiuk's wife. ... Delfino and Day were present.... The deposition was videotaped....

After the deposition concluded, Delfino asked the videographer to provide him with a copy of the videotape in digital format and agreed to pay extra to have it sent to him on an expedited basis.... over the next 24 hours, Delfino and/or Day posted two Internet messages on Yahoo! message boards announcing that they intended to post video clips from the Fouquet deposition on their web site....

Plaintiffs responded to these announcements by immediately faxing a letter to counsel for Delfino and Day warning them that Delfino and Day were threatening to violate a court order and attaching copies of the defendants' Internet messages, the court order, and the corresponding Notice of Entry of Order.... Plaintiffs requested their "written assurance that no such violation will occur," but no response was ever received....

It was clear that Delfino and Day saw the letter and the attachments because a copy thereof appeared the next day on the Internet web site Delfino and Day have admitted operating.... Among the messages containing a link to the pertinent web page was one posted under Delfino's admitted alias, "michelangelo_delfino_phd." ... In the message, Delfino mocked Fouquet's testimony and then joked , "Seems VAR's attorneys would like to keep that quiet -- too bad for them this is America!" ... following this comment was a link to the web page containing a copy of the letter from Plaintiffs' counsel.... The web page prints the letter verbatim, followed by a snide comment ... At the bottom of the page, in large font, Delfino and Day made the following promise: "Julie Fouquet Video - coming soon - guaranteed!" ...

On September 25, 2001, Delfino and Day announced the creation of a telephone "hotline" that would provide information about this lawsuit.... Two days later, Plaintiffs' counsel called the hot line.... He heard a recording ...

"Welcome to the Varian, Susan B. Felch and George Zdasiuk SLAPP trial hot line where you will hear only the truth and our Constitutionally protected opinion. Today's SLAPP news is September 26th, 11:30 am PST. The trial remains on schedule for an October 22nd start, just 26 days away. Here is the latest POOP. SLAPPer spouse Julie Fouquet, the famed Agilent Technologies innovator completed her video taped deposition last week on the afternoon of September 19th. She is a great witness. Video excerpts of her testimony are coming to the Internet as soon as available. In brief, she helps reveal the nature of SLAPP plaintiff, George Zdasiuk.

295

It has long been an undisputed fact that George Zdasiuk is sick as he testified. Paranoia, mouth cankers, sleeplessness, and gastrointestinal problems are but a few of his many ailments. As he is also a liar, he may not be all that sick. We the ever-so-cute stockholders of MoBeta, Inc. in order to determine the truth have offered a psychiatric session with our Dr. Martin Blinder for Mr. Zdasiuk and his scary "friend" Mrs. Felch. Lastly, there were no reports of loud screams coming out of Los Altos Hills, California last night. We hope Kevin Felch and the boys were not woken up by any nightmares that his present wife, SLAPP Plaintiff Susan B. Felch, may have had. That is all for now and remember - Be careful who you SLAPP! Call back for regular updates as fascist SLAPP news is made. God bless America!"

... the Court is authorized to impose the following civil penalties for each act of contempt charged; a fine of up to $1,000; monetary sanctions payable to the county of up to $1,500; imprisonment of up to five days; and payment of the reasonable attorney's fees and costs incurred by the parry initiating the contempt proceeding...."

Zdasiuk's and Fouquet's family values were of great interest judging by the number of visits to her testimony Web sites:

WIDMANN: All right. In observing him and how he responded when these events occurred, was he more upset in your observation with his father's death or with these postings?
...
WIDMANN: Right, I am, and I want you to put all those together, and we've got one set of circumstances -- his father unfortunately had a lingering illness with cancer and then passed away, and during that time, he was upset obviously, and then we have these postings and this lawsuit which have been going on for quite some time, too, and I want you to compare those two events in your husband's life and tell me as you observed him, which one, to your observations, upset him more?
...
FOUQUET: Probably this, if you just take it all over time, probably this.
...
POPPE: I assume you're referring to the World Trade Center disaster?
WIDMANN: I am. I'm sorry. I'll clarify it. The terrorist activity that occurred last week and people passing and the plane crashing and all those things we have been watching on TV now, did he appear to you to be more upset about those events or the postings?

FOUQUET: The postings -- taken over time, not necessarily on that particular day, over all time, yes, the postings.

How callous! But perhaps not so shocking for the hundreds of Agilent employees who viewed this testimony. Alas, all this came to an end on October 3, 2001, when Cabrinha ordered:

"Plaintiffs application for an order to show cause re contempt against Delfino and Day is DENIED. Although the Court's intent in issuing its Order of June 27, 2001 was to prohibit the parties from posting on the Internet the deposition of any person whose deposition had not already been posted on the Internet, the Court finds that the Order may have been ambiguous in its scope, and would not support a finding of contempt for non compliance.

... the Court hereby MODIFIES its Order of June 27, 2001 to read as follows: The parties are ordered not to post on the Internet, in whole or in part, any of the following: (1) the transcript of Mr. Zdasiuk's deposition taken in this action on July 25, 2001; (2) the transcript of the deposition of any other person whose deposition was taken in this lawsuit, provided that such transcript had not already been published on the Internet prior to June 27, 2001; (3) any audio or video recordings of Mr. Zdasiuk's deposition taken in this action on July 25, 2001; and (4) any audio or video recordings of the deposition of any other person whose deposition was taken in this lawsuit, provided that such audio or video recording had not already been published on the Internet prior to June 27, 2001.

This order will remain in force even if testimony described above is submitted to the Court in connection with a motion or other proceeding. This order does not bar the parties from posting commentary about any person's deposition or testimony, nor does it bar the parties from posting on the Internet the transcripts, audiotapes, and videotapes of the depositions of Michelangelo Delfino and Mary Day. The term "transcript" as used in this paragraph, refers to the official transcript as well as to any unofficial or draft transcript prepared by the court reporter...."

forcing us to deactivate Fouquet from the Internet. But Mary and I are most resourceful and not easily discouraged. Just because we couldn't publish deposition excerpts on the Internet did not mean that a more interested public couldn't learn the truth:

WIDMANN: No, not yet. You said that in previous testimony when I was asking you questions, you mentioned threats by Mr. Delfino. What threats were you referring to, sir?
...
ZDASIUK: Threats of selling the videotape associated, for example, with this deposition.

I didn't threaten to sell his videotaped deposition-- I *did* sell it, and others too. Mary and I created a SLAPP home shopping page [http://www.geocities.com/mobeta_inc/slapp/shop.html] where one could purchase VHS and CD-ROM copies of everyone's video recorded deposition. It advertised the sale of memorabilia as non-profit and because of the small number of orders actually placed, we were in fact non-profitable. Nonetheless, it had the desired effect of keeping our spirits high while adding to the SLAPPers' consternation.

Cabrinha's order did not allow us to publish on the Internet the deposition of Kevin Felch, Julie Fouquet, or Zdasiuk's third-day. Because this book includes those excerpts, it cannot be published on the Internet either. Lastly, any image from these videotaped depositions, including the picture of Zdasiuk on the jacket back cover, are also banned from the World Wide Web.

Most people, I think, given the choice of having their own words, or our commentary on the Web, would probably not opt for the latter. But life is good, and so following Cabrinha's order, their "deposition" Web sites featuring eye-witness commentary made their debut. While all were quite popular, one stood above the rest:

"WIDMANN: Were you intoxicated when you broke the law?
ZDASIUK: Uh, I like to drink, but I am not a habitual drinker, yea, PHHHT! When I have put down a couple, two, three, four, Julie or Jules or whatever the hell she calls herself drives. Carlo Rossi Paisano? I can't recall, but I had few when I cursed that process server, alright yea, two process servers? Wow! Yea, I, I, I just can't recall, but uh, two glasses a wine seems right, I'm I just got home from work. Dropped my trousers, and uh, opened a bottle, I guess, uh. Geez, PHHHT! Give me some time here, uh, PHHHT! Can I have something to drink or uh, eat?
...
FALCON: Mr. Zdasiuk, how long did you prepare for today?

ZDASIUK: Uh, today, uh, well I wasn't drinking, uh, but PHHHHT! That was yesterday, uh, I, I can't recall, uh, can I ask uh, my uh poop, I mean Mr. Poppe, uh.
POPPE: I object. Six. What the hell kind of question is that. Six. This is an outrage. Six. I have a good mind to end this deposition. Six. Mr. Zdasiuk, you may answer as well as you can under these oppressive circumstances. Six, dumbshit!
ZDASIUK: I, I, PHHHT! I can't recall exactly, PHHHT! but I think I spent, uh six, PHHHT! six days, no, no. Strike that. Six, yea, six hours yesterday. Ok?
…
FALCON: Mr. Zdasiuk are you intoxicated?
POPPE: I object on attorney work product.
FALCON: Counselor you know that's part of this lawsuit. You can answer.
ZDASIUK: Uh, I like Dick, but uh, I'm not a homo. Joe Phair's not a homo either. Joe does live in Frisco, but I live in Portola Valley. Sure I made a couple of jokes, and I do travel to Frisco, and well yea, I like Dick. I, I can't recall what I said to Jim Fair, but uh, PHHHT! He liked Dick too, so uh. Could you, uh, PHHHT! repeat the question?
…
FALCON: Do you have a history of violence and using vulgarity?
ZDASIUK: Fuck no, I'm just sick! What did I say? Geez, uh, I, I, can't recall, uh, well when I broke the law, I, I, said, uh. I mean someone, yea, someone said, "I'll kick your ass!" and PHHHHT! "Get the fuck out of here" "You can't come on my fuckin property" and I said, I mean someone, Jules, yea that's it, Julie said "My attorney has already worked this out". No I don't have a gun at home, on me? Can you repeat the PHHHT!! fucking question?
POPPE: George, just shut up. Smack! Shut the fuck up!"

On March 11, 2002, Poppe filed another *ex parte* application for placing us in contempt arguing this time to a different judge that our long standing commentary was now an impersonation:

"Fouquet is then misquoted as saying such things as "You want to know about my present husband? Well, he's a real SICKIE." …"

He was denied.

- 12 -

YOU DON'T KNOW JACK

"The American jury trial system has, with rare exceptions, been played out in the public eye for over two centuries. But the Internet has added a whole new dimension of visibility to the legal process.

In the case of Varian ... not only are Internet message board postings the focus of the plaintiffs' lawsuit, the two co-defendants have also set up a Web site that gives their version of a daily trial update. [http://www.geocities.com/mobeta_inc/slapp/trial3.html]

These updates are not full of dense legalese, nor are they for the easily offended.

... the defendants described Felch as, "the scary yenta bitch," and repeatedly suggested that Zdasiuk has a "gastrointestinal problem" that keeps people from sitting near him in the courtroom. The defendants gave one of the plaintiffs' attorneys, Matthew Poppe, the scatological nickname, "POOP," and refer to the plaintiffs' lead attorney, Lynne Hermle, as the "Grand Dame of SLAPP." ...

James Chadwick, an expert on free speech law, said the First Amendment protects any person's right to disseminate information on his or her own trial.

"California law also protects this right, even if the information is not accurate," said Chadwick. "If someone makes an allegation in a trial proceeding that is untrue, that allegation can be reported as long as it is an accurate reporting of the allegation made."

As long as Delfino and Day report what goes on in the courtroom, their speech is protected, he said. "Things that might be construed as defamatory or invasive of privacy, that does not matter, as long as it is accurate."

Chadwick said defendants' use of derisive nicknames for plaintiffs' attorneys, while insulting and juvenile, probably are not something they could be sued for.

"Calling someone "POOP" is not actionable, because no one would believe they are calling him excrement. The "Grand Dame of

300

SLAPP" could go either way, but it more likely would be found to be hyperbole or inflammatory language," he explained. "A good part of what could be considered "opinion" is context."[96]

Our daily trial updates Web site is reproduced here.

"Day 1 - October 22, 2001

A Preemptory Challenge[97] and a Reassignment[98] gave the Honorable Jack Komar authority as judge in this our nation's first Internet trial. At approximately 9:10 a.m. Judge Komar got his first introduction to the fascist Varian (VAR & VSEA), Susan B. Felch and George Zdasiuk SLAPP attorney, Lynne C. Hermle, Esq. the Grande Dame of SLAPP herself, an Orrick, Herrington & Sutcliffe law partner. She was accompanied by no less than three attorneys. Neither Felch nor Zdasiuk were in attendance.

Representing the lovely Ms. Day and the good Dr. Delfino, both smartly attired, were famed anti-SLAPP attorneys Randall M. Widmann, Esq. and Glynn P. Falcon, Esq.

Judge Komar spent much of this first day trying to settle the matter in chambers. Alas, around 2:30 p.m., the judge announced the case would not settle and the trial was to begin.[99] All parties were ordered to return the following morning for In Limine arguments and jury selection.

Day 2 - October 23, 2001

Hermle and her Orrick subordinate Matthew H. Poppe aka POOP, spent most of the morning trying in vain to get Varians' In Limine

---

[96]Michael Bartlett, *Washington Post Newsbytes*, November 12, 2002.

[97]The rules allow each side to disqualify one judge. When the case first began, Falcon had Superior Court Judge Mary Jo Levinger disqualified and now Judge Cliff was disqualified by Hermle: "Judge Frank Cliff is prejudiced against the interests of plaintiffs, and so I believe plaintiffs cannot have a fair and impartial hearing before Judge Frank Cliff."

[98]Joseph Biafore, Jr. was first assigned trial judge by Judge Jamie Jacobs-May, but having already been transferred elsewhere, Komar became our judge.

[99]There could never be any settlement because no plaintiff was present!

Motions[100] approved by Judge Komar. The judge made it clear that he favors seeing evidence before precluding the option of discussing an issue. Delfino's In Limine Motion to have non-party witnesses be excluded from the trial until after they have testified was adopted but his other Motions followed with similar success to Varians'. On the other hand, two of Day's eight Motions In Limine, the Preclusion of Alter Ego Assertions[101] and the Bifurcation of Punitive Damages[102] were immediately granted.

Judge Komar is allowing Defendants to claim this lawsuit is a SLAPP and to allege that Varian is trying to steal MoBeta, Inc. patent technology. He is also permitting the presentation of Varians' spoliation of bathroom videotaping evidence during the trial. And he ordered the timely deposition of Dr. Blinder,[103] the

---

[100]A hearing on a specific legal point that relates to matters of jurisdiction and not the merits of the case.

[101]"... exclude evidence of the alter ego liability of a non-party, a company in which they are shareholders named MoBeta.... In their Third Amended Complaint Plaintiffs allege that "On information and belief, MoBeta is the alter ego of Day and Delfino." ... MoBeta, despite over two years of litigation, has never been joined as a party Defendant."

[102]"... requests that the issues of punitive damages be tried separately and only after liability is established...."

[103]Doctor Martin Blinder, M.D., a practicing psychiatrist and a Fellow of the American Psychiatric Association, author of 6 books and 100 plus journal articles had prepared a psychiatric opinion for Glynn on October 25, 2001:

"Today I reviewed the multi-volumed depositions of Susan Felch and George Zdasiuk, with particular attention to any psychiatric disabilities they may have sustained as a consequence of disturbing messages posted on the Internet by the defendants and other inappropriate and harassing defendant conduct. My view of this matter will be a narrow, clinical one having to do with the presence or absence of a compensable psychiatric disorder or loss.

Both plaintiffs report that they have suffered "loss of reputation and standing in the community, humiliation, embarrassment, hurt feelings, mental anguish and suffering...",

DEPOSITIONS OF SUSAN FELCH: Mrs. Felch reports: Lost work time due to time spent reading these messages; Emotional energy spent after reading; "Emotional side effects. When I read such messages my heart goes faster, I breathe faster, I'm sometimes short of breath, I lose my concentration on what I was doing before, I find myself distracted, grinding my teeth. I've had some trouble sleeping, waking up in the middle of the night, sometimes having trouble going to sleep..."; Loss of one to two hours per week of work time; Headaches that are "a little more frequent" since the Internet postings, going from once a month to as many as three times per month; Avoiding certain Internet websites; General anxiety; Pre-deposition nightmares; Fear for her physical safety which caused her to secure the doors of her home.

Mrs. Felch states that she has received no treatment for these conditions, save taking the occasional Tylenol for headache. She also states that her wish to avoid Internet postings is counterbalanced by her need to know what is being said about her.

DEPOSITIONS OF GEORGE ZDASIUK: Mr. Zdasiuk reports: "High blood pressure," although, this has never been diagnosed or treated; Headaches; Sleep problems; "Paranoia"; Despair, sadness and anger; Forgetfulness, distraction, memory loss, and lack of concentration "Gastrointestinal complaints" (which on further inquiry appear to be, limited to.. occasional episodes of heartburn); Canker sores; Loss of libido; Overeating; Loss of self-confidence.

Mr. Zdasiuk has mentioned some of these symptoms to his treating physician but apparently has not received any specific diagnostic workups or treatment for them, save the taking of an over-the-counter antacid. Neither has he received any counseling or psychiatric treatment, although he states that he would like to at some future time.

He, had difficulty in tying any of these symptoms, such as heartburn or headache, specifically to, viewing the Internet postings, and in fact he did not know exactly what brought these symptoms on.

He states that he bad stress-related symptoms in the fall of 1980 when his sister was killed in a traffic accident at the same time he was preparing for his Ph.D. oral exam, but the Internet postings have been far more stressful than the events of 1980.

COMMENT: As explicated in ... my textbook, *Psychiatry in the Everyday Practice of Law*, ... "emotional distress" is a vague legal term for which there is no clinical equivalent, but is generally ... below the threshold of a diagnosable mental disorder. Such are the complaints of the two plaintiffs in this case. Both report a variety of decidedly unwelcome but modest, transient symptoms that together have not caused any demonstrable disability, loss of income, or a, need for psychiatric intervention. Rather, their symptoms appear to reflect inordinate vexation as a consequence of what are described as distinctly unpleasant events, coupled with an extremely problematic relationship with the defendants.

Compensation for psychiatric damages is a relatively recent phenomenon. Decades after the routine awarding of substantial sums for bodily injury, the courts remained reluctant to explicitly recognize psychic trauma as a cause of action because of its supposed indefinability and subjectivity. And admittedly, though one can readily visualize a hairline fracture of the femur, even with the psychiatrist, who is slated to provide expert testimony about the mental health of Felch and Zdasiuk. Wow!

The day ended around 4 pm with the judge developing jury protocol with the attorneys. Plaintiffs were denied use of their written jury questionnaire. Jury selection is scheduled for tomorrow. Felch and Zdasiuk were again *in absentia*, as Mary Rotunno, Esq., a VAR attorney sat in the courtroom taking copious notes throughout the day.

Day 3 - October 24, 2001
Today marked the first appearance by Susan B. Felch and George Zdasiuk at the trial. The two SLAPPers were accompanied by

---

enormous, advances in psychiatric diagnostic techniques over the last 50 years, the psychiatric profession has yet to come up with demonstrable diagnostic evidence equal to that routinely provided by the other medical specialties.

Nevertheless, it is now well established that in certain situations, psychological symptoms do coalesce into the form of a disabling, crisply defined, immutable psychiatric disorder comparable to physical injury or loss. When such occurs as a consequence of another's negligence, that psychiatric disorder may well be every bit as compensable as a physical one.

In my more than three decades of work in this field, I've come to appreciate the two implicit criteria the courts apply to determine whether or not such psychic trauma is compensable.

First, the psychological symptoms afflicting the plaintiff must gather into a recognized, definable psychiatric pattern or *diagnosis*, as distinguished from the diffuse emotional discomfort one may suffer from the slings and arrows attendant to living in a less than perfect world.... a headache or stomachache here, some loss of appetite or sleep there probably do not constitute compensable psychiatric conditions. By contrast, someone who develops ... a *post-traumatic stress disorder or a major depression* can be just as grievously injured and disabled as someone who has lost the use of a hand or a leg. But such psychiatric diagnoses require an enduring and specific set of symptoms, not merely some vague psychological discomfort and a scattering of complaints which come and go.... neither plaintiff meets this first criterion.

Second, to be compensable, the diagnosed psychiatric condition must produce an occupational or significant social disability--again roughly comparable to that generated by some physical ailment. Here, both plaintiffs clearly fail this criterion as well...."

Hermle, POOP, and a juror expert. VAR's Rotunno returned to court in the afternoon to take notes.

Judge Komar's clerk began the jury selection process at 9 am explaining the court rules to a pool of 90 American residents living in Santa Clara County, California. First, hardship arguments were presented to the judge who excused all but 28 of the potential jurors. Hardship was granted mostly because of the length of the trial. Next, a random selection of 18 remaining citizens was queried by the judge followed throughout the afternoon by friendly questioning from Hermle, Falcon and Widmann. At 5:00 p.m. the judge ended the day and met privately with the attorneys. The jury selection process continues tomorrow.

During the lunch break, an Orrick courier delivered to Hermle a couple of freshly published Internet postings that were ascribed to the anti-SLAPP Defendants. For reasons unclear, the postings were brought to the attention of the judge and the famed anti-SLAPP attorneys. No apparent reaction was noted 'cause this is America!

Day 4 - October 25, 2001
With all parties promptly in attendance Judge Komar resumed jury selection. Almost immediately a potential juror asked and was granted an excuse for hardship. Next followed a disqualification and a dozen preemptory challenges[104] from both sides leaving the court with the requisite 12 jurors, but only 2 alternates. Just before ending at noon, one of the chosen 14 alluded to being yet another potential hardship excuse. Seemingly dismayed at the notion of beginning this 8 week SLAPP trial with perhaps a single alternate, the Court adjourned till 9:00 a.m. tomorrow.

Day 5 - October 26, 2001
This morning the Grande Dame of SLAPP assisted by more than five Orrick SLAPPers delivered Varians' Opening Statement. It

---

[104]Limited number of disqualifications each side in a trial can use to eliminate potential jurors without stating a reason.

took an hour, not too surprising when you have nothing to say. In contrast, Falcon using half as much time disclosed that VAR's perennially novice CEO and President, Richard 'Dick' Levy had in fact already lied under oath, and his Executive Vice President, George Zdasiuk had unabashedly violated Varian company policy. Falcon's brief mention to the jury of Varians' five weeks of continuous 24-hour-a-day invasive bathroom videotaping may have alarmed Craig Anderson a reporter for the *San Francisco Daily Journal* as it set the tone for the trial.[105]

The VAR entourage in the audience today included SLAPPer Zdasiuk, and for the first time, multi-millionaire Joe Phair, the VAR Corporate Secretary and General Counsel accompanied by the highly paid Mary Rotunno at his side. A number of Varian stockholders were said to exclaim, "My oh my, how much is this trial going to cost us!"

Shortly after dismissing the jury for the day, The Orrick submitted a Motion for Non-Suit that included a multi-page brief in this their 4th attempt to dismiss VAR's Breach of Contract Liability. Judge

---

[105]"Trial has begun ... with the company's attorney attacking the defendants as "obsessed with harming" the company and its executives.

"This is not a case about a simple expression of opinion," said Lynne Hermle, ...

Attorneys for Delfino and Day defended the posted missives, saying the messages they have admitted to writing can be proved accurate when considered in context. While they may be offensive, they are not defamatory, defense attorneys argued in opening statements.

"You're going to find some of these postings [that] you're not going to like," said Randall Widmann, a Palo Alto attorney who represents Day. "That doesn't mean there's liability attached to that."

... the Varian case has always been in a class by itself, in part because of the company's persistence and also because Delfino and Day have refused to back down. They continue to post messages ... and they created their own Web site devoted to their legal battle with the company.

While the case may have some broader implications concerning the limits of online free speech, Hermle did not address those in her opening statement....

"The main purpose was to defame," Hermle said. "The secondary purpose was to promote [Delfino and Day's] new company...."

Komar, with look of disgust, allowed oral arguments before denying the plea and wishing everyone a happy weekend.

Day 6 - October 29, 2001

The morning began at 9:10 am with the Grande Dame of SLAPP calling it's first witness, the scary yenta bitch[106] Susan B. Felch. Hermle began by asking her to demonstrate the Felch Telephone Gesture which was claimed to have occurred more than 100 times yet was never witnessed.[107] Felch followed this with her newly introduced Yapping Gesture that she alleged Delfino did once.[108] Hermle then attempted to downplay the hiding of a special video camera in Felch's office that for weeks violated the privacy of people including children going to the bathroom. Lastly, Felch was walked through hundreds of allegedly defaming Internet postings, none of which were authenticated and as of yet allowed as evidence.

Just before 2 p.m., anti-SLAPP attorney Falcon began his cross-examination. Felch was asked to read aloud from her log journal, the work diary she kept to record alleged acts of harassment and misconduct. To no surprise here, she could not explain why any of her allegations were never substantiated by anyone. While she did disclose for the first time the details about her nightmares, Felch

---

[106]On December 14, 2002, Poppe wrote: "Delfino and Day should be enjoined from stating that Felch is a "yenta" or a "scary yenta bitch." As the defendants have testified and as the Court has observed, "yenta" is synonymous with "gossip" and thus conveys a false statement of fact. Alternatively, the phrase is clearly harassing and serves no legitimate purpose." His request was ignored.

[107]FELCH: Yes. It looked like this with the thumb pointing up towards the ear and the pinky pointing down kind of like a mouthpiece and the fingers curled up looking like the rest of the telephone, and then he would wiggle them back and forth for maybe a few seconds. (Demonstrating)

HERMLE: May I describe that for the record, Your honor?

KOMAR: I think she just did.

[108]FELCH: Sure. It's kind of like this, with your fingers kind of forming a V, going back and forth, imitating somebody being in a conversation. (Demonstrating)

claimed that no Internet posting had ever caused her any damage. One has to wonder then, what her SLAPP is really all about. Later, Hermle inexplicably exclaimed: "Do you have a problem with Dick?" causing some onlookers to guffaw. Among those spending the entire day in the courtroom were Zdasiuk and VAR attorneys Rotunno and Phair. The judge adjourned for the day at 4:30 with Felch's cross-examination far from complete.

Day 7 - October 30, 2001
Cross-examination of The Felch by famed anti-SLAPP attorney Falcon resumed at 9:20 and continued 'till a scheduled noon recess. Felch wearing glasses for the second time in memory and who has admitted to being a liar when previously deposed was now trying to qualify what remains of her veracity in terms of white lies vs. blatant lies. Momentarily caught off guard she testified that message board postings must be interpreted within the context of the previous 10 or 20 messages. Falcon responded by having her go through such a sequence of Yahoo! VAR messages to show in fact that an allegedly defaming Internet posting was but a truthful dialogue of Varian managerial incompetence involving a number of investors.

While this SLAPPer in fact admitted having special treatment that included reduced work hours, she was most unease accounting for an incident of alleged PLAD laboratory sabotage, wherein dangerous toxic gases could have been released.

Conspicuously absent in today's court room were VAR attorneys Joe Phair and Mary Rotunno. Could it be George Zdasiuk's gastrointestinal problem was the culprit? If it was, it didn't prevent Gary Loser, the Vice President, General Counsel of VSEA from being an expensive substitute having flown in from Gloucester, Massachusetts where he is headquartered.

Day 8 - October 31, 2001
Felch's third day of cross-examination continued with Falcon having her admit that allegedly defaming postings upset her so

much that she's had to take a few extra Tylenol per month.[109] She then added that supposed impersonations of her on the Internet were believed by no one other than her; talk about damages!

Next came Widmann's cross-examination of Felch. She began by telling him she had spent 10 to 20 hours reviewing her declarations, her depositions and countless message board postings in preparation for testifying at this trial. Not too surprisingly, the scary yenta who testified earlier about her knowledge of the sleeping habits of the MoBeta, Inc. stockholders informed the court that she knew some of their birth dates as well. She concluded her first days on stand by admitting to the jury that videotaping a public bathroom would in fact be an invasion of privacy. No kidding!

Returning from lunch, George Zdasiuk began his direct testimony under the Grande Dame of SLAPP. It would last but 2 hours and 15 minutes and although he would acknowledge that he was sick there would be no cross-examination by either anti-SLAPP attorney at this time. A dumbfounded Hermle and her POOP, unprepared for their next witness pleaded for any early dismissal, which the benevolent Judge Komar graciously granted.

During the afternoon break just outside the courtroom, Varian General Counsel, Gary Loser, Esq. accompanied by Rotunno flew into an unprovoked rage wagging his index finger at anti-SLAPP defendant Delfino, and yelling, "Don't fuck with me asshole!" This unfortunate and frightening event was witnessed by several trial participants, one of whom exclaimed, "What do you expect, he *is* a LOSER." Judge Komar was made aware of Loser's out of control

---

[109]Felch declared on January 26, 2001: "Felch attributes headaches and sleeplessness to the conduct of Delfino and Day ... Felch responds as follows: (1) headaches, with varying frequency and severity over time; (2) sleeplessness, with varying frequency and severity over time; (3) nightmares, with varying frequency and severity over time.... Felch experienced headaches, sleeplessness, and nightmares from time to time before Delfino and Day began the conduct alleged...."

emotional outburst, [but declined to take action] and the court bailiff is ready.

Day 9 - November 1, 2001

Three SLAPP witnesses testified in succession today. First, Craig Moro was examined by the Grande Dame of SLAPP. After being cross-examined, POOP brought on Juanita Sonico followed by Carlo Herrera. Of these three Varian employees, Moro's testimony was the most damaging as it highlighted Varian's legendary hostile work environment under Richard 'Dick' Levy.

Moro first confirmed that the camera he was authorized to hide in Susan B. Felch's office did indeed secretly videotape a Varian men's bathroom and a Varian women's restroom for a number of weeks. Then when shown several photographs he produced from one of the invasive bathroom videos Moro verified that at least two dozen images had been destroyed by Varian. Among those that survived and were now submitted to the jury as evidence was at least one photograph showing an employee inside the bathroom, causing one court room observer to exclaim, "Oh my dear God!"

Alas, there is more to this infamous May 28, 1998 day. The time stamps on the Varian photographs actually show the duration the employee was in the bathroom urinating or defecating or performing some other normally private act!

Adding credence to the long-held assertion that Susan B. Felch is a "liar and/or hallucinator," Moro confessed that Varians' weeks of invasive bathroom video surveillance disproved her harassment allegation causing both anti-SLAPP attorneys to say, we're finished with this witness."

Seems a courthouse is not a place for Loser's like Gary, as Mary Rotunno was the only Varian corporate attorney in attendance. With Herrera still on the stand, the judge was forced to recess the court midday as Varian once again failed to be prepared for their next witness. Delay, delay, delay!

Day 10 - November 6, 2001
The day began with Judge Komar supplementing his earlier order forbidding jurors to access certain Internet sites with an order that they do not read newspaper articles on this SLAPP. Returning to Felch's subordinate Carl Herrera, questioning about Varians' hostile work environment resumed. Under cross-examination, he said Felch pointed at the men's bathroom from her windowed office to show the camera's field of view. Herrera acknowledged using the bathroom and added that there were mirrors along the bathroom's inside wall facing Felch's office where the camera was hidden. Believe me, it's going to get worse!

Yahoo!'s Cathy McGoff was the next witness called. She said that while Yahoo! was interested in maintaining controversial and tantalizing message boards they collected identifying information so that Yahoo! could easily comply with the daily supply of corporate subpoenas. Shown several subpoenas, McGoff noted how easy it was for The Orrick to delete Internet message board postings compared to the originator. Subject to a 48 hour recall, Judge Komar excused her for the day.

POOP then called their Internet expert Stephen Melvin to testify. Inexplicably, this SLAPPer for hire was asked to identify the operators of this anti-SLAPP web site and to read aloud the following into the record:

"This Web-Site was created by Michelangelo Delfino & Mary E. Day, who believe that FREE SPEECH is not for sale, and TRUTH is the only answer to Varian's fascist SLAPP!" He was then ordered to read this: "Disclaimer: This Web-site contains information largely provided to us in documents produced by others and we can in no way validate the accuracy and totality of their contents. We have made every effort here to be truthful and to reproduce these documents accurately and as completely as reasonable. Our opinions, are just that, our opinions."

Confused? So are we!

Day 11 - November 7, 2001

Just before Melvin resumed testifying, Felch moved away from her fellow SLAPP plaintiff to sit next to the VAR attorneys, Phair and Rotunno. This left Zdasiuk alone and isolated at the opposite end of the courtroom. As the day progressed, some distant onlookers speculated that Zdasiuk's gastrointestinal problems were responsible for her move but none to quick to test their hypothesis; sad, but true.

Melvin, who has worked on this SLAPP case since early 1999, testified that he was unable to ascribe any Internet posting to a person, no less a particular computer and for this Varian paid him as much as $230 per hour. For reasons unknown, he submitted this highly-popular deleted message board postings web page [http://www.geocities.com/mobeta_inc/slapp/rempost.html] that he ascribed to the anti-SLAPP defendants but was unable to explain why or by whom they were censored. Falcon's cross-examination of this so-called expert was a thing of beauty, unless of course you're a SLAPPer.

Next came Maria Mustonen, who had been in the courthouse since 8:30 this morning, finally getting the call to testify at 2:00 pm. She, an innocent witness caught in this SLAPP testified that POOP and an Orrick paralegal, Jessica Niehaus Beane visited her Kinko's store in Cupertino, California and watched several video surveillance tapes. She could not account for how many Kinko's videos nor which videos were subsequently handed over to The Orrick. Niehaus, the ninth witness to testify, enthusiastically identified the anti-SLAPP defendants on excerpts of an Orrick produced copy of the May 5, 1999 video. The Orrick tape was played before the jurors as Niehaus, who had never met Day, and had seen but one minute of Delfino in an Orrick lobby before her Kinko's visit said she was sent to the stores to identify the defendants. Niehaus reluctantly confessed that an earlier visit to the Kinko's in Mountain View, California failed to show either defendant on any tape.

Day 12 - November 8, 2001
The Kinko's manager April Shelton was the only witness called today. She viewed what was purported to be an Orrick produced copy of a May 18, 1999, Mountain View, California, Kinko's video surveillance tape. Like Niehaus, she did not identify any customers on the excerpts she watched. While she admitted handing over two tapes to subpoena, she had no record of which tapes were surrendered and to whom they were given. And she had no recollection of ever meeting Niehaus at her store, only POOP. The day ended at noon with POOP reading excerpts from the deposition of Florida's Paul Williams, the owner of the Stock-Talk message board. Boring!

On a sad note, Zdasiuk remained alone and isolated as Felch sat with Rotunno at the opposite end of the courtroom. Onlookers queried: A lingering gastrointestinal problem?

A juror was dismissed at noon because of hardship leaving this first Internet SLAPP trial with but a single alternate.

Day 13 - November 9, 2001
The day began with POOP continuing to read excerpts of William's out-of-state deposition into the record. Falcon followed suit, followed by more POOP, at which point almost everyone was fast asleep. Finally at 11:30, after having waited outside the courtroom for more than 3-hours, Orrick's Peter McMahon became the day's first live witness. Acknowledging he personally represented the SLAPP plaintiffs and several of their supporters in numerous depositions and had filed a number of declarations on their behalf, McMahon spent almost an hour on the stand identifying a number of locations on an Orrick produced Kinko's surveillance video only to confess under Widmann's cross-examination that he had never even been in the store. Caveat emptor!

Then at 2:30 p.m., the good Dr. Delfino took the stand and came face to face with the Grande Dame of SLAPP and her POOP. The polemics began almost immediately with Delfino answering that he only posted the truth, his opinion, or hyperbole. Volunteering he had never knowingly made a false statement, he freely admitted that while he had used but 4 aliases to post 60 messages before being SLAPPed, he and the lovely Ms. Day have since posted more than 13,000 messages using dozens of aliases. A happy witness, Delfino did not turn to putty, he did not throw up, he did not wet, and he will return next Tuesday for more of the Gator.

The afternoon courtroom was unusually crowded with Hermle assisted by several Orrick, perhaps a dozen onlookers in attendance, the Felch, Phair and Rotunno trio clumped together, and you know who, characteristically alone off to the side.

Day 14 - November 13, 2001
A Washington Post article on Richard 'Dick' Levy's company's SLAPP trial set the tone for this morning's testimony as the good Dr. Delfino returned to the stand. After first confusing the whole court room as to who used which aliases, the Grande Dame of SLAPP next spent the better part of the morning dwelling on the infamous quote the famous L.A. lawyer Megan E. Gray, Esq. stated in her legal brief submitted in this very case: "Felch is a female executive who acquired semen stains on her clothes from oral sex with a supervisor ..." Hermle then asked "Do you have any idea Felch and Dick Levy were having a sexual affair?" whereon an astonished Delfino replied quite quizzically, wow!

When queried why he posted messages with "Come clean you dirty, filthy Dick", Delfino said in the example shown that he was referring to Levy, the CEO of VAR who had in fact lied under oath and that this Dick will certainly get the opportunity to come clean when he testifies at this trial. A pink faced Hermle immediately brought up the question of Levy committing perjury, but Delfino cautioned that he was unable to make such a legal conclusion.

The court room was unusually crowded this morning with Felch and Rotunno amidst a few newspaper reporters and you know who off to the far side of the room all by himself. Some onlookers have begun to wonder about the seriousness of George Zdasiuk's gastrointestinal problems. For those less familiar with this SLAPP, Zdasiuk claims, among a host of ailments, GI damages from voluntarily reading message board postings at work.

The court was recessed at noon due to an ailing juror.

Day 15 - November 15, 2001
After briefly inquiring about Felch likening herself to Monica Lewinsky, the Grande Dame of SLAPP spent the rest of the day asking questions about message board postings that reported Zdasiuk's paranoia and sexual problems, Felch's recurring nightmares, and the company's history of videotaping children using Varian's public bathrooms. When asked which children might have been recorded urinating or defecating in Varian lavatories with Felch's hidden video camera, an emotionally outraged Delfino responded: his son, Day's daughters, Felch's sons, the janitor's children, and those boys and girls invited to Varian's Take Your Child to Work Day - all under Richard 'Dick' Levy's nose!

The blotchy-faced Gator, now seemingly wanting to get out of the toilet, redirected her questioning onto a number of allegedly defaming postings that covered Varians' legendary hostile work environment under Levy, the company's perennially novice CEO. One of Levy's directly reporting Directors, Ron Powell, was identified as another Varian manager who used hidden surveillance cameras to watch employees, while Jim Fair, his subordinate used company equipment for such things as producing this entertaining letter [*see* footnote 59].

With the day finally ending at 4:30 p.m., and the good Dr. Delfino still on the stand, one had to wonder what was the point of the Grande Dame of SLAPP showing the jury literally dozens of one-time anonymous Internet postings none of which have ever been shown to be false or damaging. The exposure certainly did not appear to please Felch who sat glumly next to Zdasiuk suggesting, at least for today, that his GI problem was under control.

Day 16 - November 16, 2001

The good Dr. Delfino stepped down from the stand a few minutes past 11:00 a.m. having completed his testimony and without benefit of any direct examination by the anti-SLAPP legal team. The Orrick, frustrated in not having broken this proud law-abiding American, demanded twice to know if he intended to "post forever and ever".

Be Careful Who You SLAPP, never had more meaning.

> [HERMLE: In this posting you were saying it's going to cost big time, and you go on to say, "I have a lot of money, more than some of you clowns can imagine," that will make this fight the best investment you've ever made?
> DELFINO: That's part of what it says.
> HERMLE: "In my opinion, it's just a question of time, and I have all the time in the world," right?
> DELFINO: That's exactly what it says.
> HERMLE: And you've posted several postings saying you plan to post forever and ever, isn't that true?
> DELFINO: I plan to follow the Constitution of the United States of America, yes, I do.
> HERMLE: You plan to post forever and ever, right, sir?
> DELFINO: As part of my First Amendment privilege, yes, I do.
> HERMLE: And in your view, your First Amendment privilege covers all of the postings that you've done?
> DELFINO: In my view, the First Amendment thank God, God bless America, yes, it does.
> HERMLE: And you plan to post till you die?
> DELFINO: As long as I'm an American citizen, I plan to follow the Constitution and the laws of this country, yes, I do.
> HERMLE: You plan to post forever and ever, right?
> DELFINO: I plan to have the privilege to post the truth, my opinion, or hyperbole. That is the answer to your question, yes.
> HERMLE: And you think you've posted the truth?
> DELFINO: I believe you have not shown a posting by me that is not the truth, my opinion or hyperbole. And I stand by that and I will prove that before this trial is over, yes.]

Waiting outside the courtroom, was the next witness dirty Richard 'Dick' Aurelio, the impotent Chairman of VSEA. He had just flown in from the Gloucester, Massachusetts headquarters to testify and was emotionally distraught as soon as he took the stand. What effect has this near 3-year-old multi-million dollar SLAPP suit had on him? Well, with a tear in his eye, this dirty, filthy Dick, said that at one time he wanted to "go out and buy a gun" but after calming himself down, he installed an electric fence around his horses on his spacious "other" home in lovely Los Altos Hills, California. Moreover, his wife Linda, has pictures of those ever so cute stockholders of MoBeta, Inc., the two who seemingly enjoy posting the truth about him and his company on the Internet, just in case!

[HERMLE: Did any family members, other family members, contact you about the postings?
AURELIO: Yeah, they did.
HERMLE: And who was that?
AURELIO: My father.
HERMLE: And what did he tell you?
FALCON: Objection; hearsay.
AURELIO: Hearsay? It's my father.
KOMAR: All right. Hearsay --
FALCON: Relevance.
KOMAR: Hearsay is a legal concept. Do you want to make an offer on that?
HERMLE: Yes. Not offered for the truth, Your Honor. Offered for the publicity and to prove --
FALCON: He's not a plaintiff in the case.
KOMAR: He's the chairman and a CEO of the corporation, which is a plaintiff. I will overrule the objection and I will advise the jury, again, this testimony about what somebody told Mr. Aurelio is not being offered for the truth of what they said, but merely to show what they said and the effect that it had on him. All right. So you may answer the question.
HERMLE: And what was communicated to you?
AURELIO: Well, let me paint the picture for you here. My father is 82 years old. He and my mother don't have a clue what I do. It's beyond their imagination what I do, how I could have possibly gotten to the position that I'm in. So for his birthday present, he gets a computer. And this crap is what he sees.

317

HERMLE: And did he tell you about that when he called you?
AURELIO: He was distraught. He couldn't believe that this was possible in this country. My father was a construction worker and I worked with him -- I suppose Mr. Delfino will post about my father now because it's obvious that this has a severe effect on me personally, so tomorrow we'll probably read about this on his website.]

[This Yahoo! YHOO posting was among a dozen or so posted that afternoon that survived deletion.]

> **I don't have a gun** by: go_gat_help
> VSEA's CEO Richard Dick Aurelio brought new meaning to Nirvana's song
> when he testified at the First Internet SLAPP trial:
> http://www.geocities.com/mobeta_inc/slapp/trial3.html#yoohooyahoo

The lunch recess brought a more combative and perhaps slightly heavier Dick to the stand. The ruthless multi-millionaire who filed a false declaration earlier in this lawsuit, now claimed that his insider sale of millions of dollars worth of his company's stock at its near high was not detrimental, and there was not a single disgruntled employee among the 700 he recently laid off. After all, Aurelio stated proudly, it's 30% of our work-force and VSEA is located in a fishing town near the *Perfect Storm*.[110]

Aurelio acknowledged under cross-examination that Felch and Zdasiuk have paid no legal fees to perpetuate this SLAPP, adding that their salaries are paid while they're obligated to be at this trial. One onlooker gasped, "No wonder Felch and Zdasiuk like Dick so much!"

Day 17 - November 19, 2001

This morning brought two high-level Novellus Systems managers to the stand. First, Ron Powell a Novellus Director testified. He

---

[110]The year 2000 George Clooney movie about Gloucester, Massachusetts fishermen caught in "the greatest storm in modern history."

was followed by his former Varian subordinate, Jim Fair, now also a Novellus Director. On this day there was brief testimony about Fair's mismanaged government funded contract, with Powell unable to recall if he had undertook any corrective action. He didn't. Judge Komar ordered the two Novellus employees to make sure they were available for further examination. "They'll be back!" exclaimed one exuberant courtroom observer.

While waiting for their next witness to arrive, POOP read a few excerpts of the Scott Pritchard Stock-Talk deposition that took place back in 1999 in Jupiter, Florida. Shortly before lunch as POOP was droning, Steve Henderson a long-time Zdasiuk subordinate and lunch partner arrived and was ordered to take the stand. His testimony would focus on the Varian men's bathroom that was secretly videotaped when he was one of its more frequent users. Henderson testified that there were two inside doors in the mirrored men's bathroom, but was caught off guard when shown bathroom photographs surrendered by Varian showing no such doors. Flustered, he then confessed that the men's and women's lavatory entrances were quite visible from Felch's windowed office, and he should know, since he occupied the office circa 1982. The judge ordered Henderson subject to recall too.

Last but not least, Jeff Wright was called to testify. Unfortunately, we have no idea what he said. The day ended at 4:30 p.m. with Zdasiuk sitting next to Felch and at least one onlooker sighing, "Well at least today no Varian witness said they had wanted to buy a gun!"

Day 18 - November 20, 2001
Beginning a few minutes past 9 a.m., the lovely Ms. Day was the twentieth witness called by The Orrick in support of their SLAPP. Like her cute codefendant, Day was periodically made to view excerpts from her videotaped depositions as the Gator repeatedly tried to impeach her. Other than showing how well Day had aged the last 3 years it only proved her veracity. And evidence like Day's declaration only reinforced today's testimony about her

charitable donations and her responsibility as an officer of MoBeta, Inc. Several hours were spent on the relationship of Felch and semen, Zdasiuk's issues with homophobia and pregnancy, and Aurelio's publicly-disclosed $12M stock-dump. Frustrated in her attempt to twist the truth, Hermle introduced two napkins with "Julie & George" printed on them as part of an argument that Day knew who Julie Fouquet really was prior to posting about her. Showing Day in Fouquet's 1987 wedding video, her lone encounter, was supposed to infer some memory of the name Fouquet. Instead it induced some chuckling in the courtroom as Day completed her examination at 4:15 mouthing the words, "I will continue to post forever!"

With the day almost over, the first SLAPPer spouse, Julie Fouquet stepped to the stand. She immediately shocked a number of courtroom observers confessing that like Linda Aurelio, she too has pictures of the anti-SLAPP defendants. Fouquet's brief examination ended with her describing her present husband, as having anxiety, nervousness, sleep loss, headaches, being preoccupied and crabby, sometimes overeating, and having gastrointestinal problems and canker sores. The judge raising his eyes recessed the somewhat rapidly emptying courtroom.

Day 19 - November 21, 2001
The cross-examination of Fouquet began with a rerun of the "Julie & George" wedding video. If nothing else, it proved that not everyone ages well. Returning to the present day, an emotionally charged Fouquet described this message board posting as upsetting. So much for prayer, this trusting soul was simply convinced her husband's company wouldn't do such a horrible and despicable thing. Agilent maybe, but this was Dick Levy's Varian!

A half hour later, Kevin Felch, the other SLAPPer spouse took the stand. Rating his marital bliss as a "B" at best, he testified that while his wife has long been smitten with nightmares that even wake him up, as a couple they "were ignored" when they shared Varian's invitational-only hospitality suite with Day and Delfino at a 1998 pro-basketball game in San Jose, California. "But weren't they afraid!" quipped one court room observer.

Saving the best for last, Susan B. Felch returned to the stand as "Person Most Knowledgeable," a designation which for many of us is an oxymoron. On cross-examination, this scary yenta bitch resurfaced as the liar or hallucinator that her secret video camera has so conclusively proved her to be. Felch concluded her testimony by describing her company, in general, and her group, in particular, as one where employees voluntarily "read, discuss and contemplate" message board postings during the work day. And for this, she said, VSEA claims damages!

The day ended at noon with Judge Komar wishing everyone a happy Thanksgiving.

Day 20 - November 26, 2001
Following the long Thanksgiving break, the day began with a new In Limine argument by the Orrick. While the motion was granted by Judge Komar, it did little to protect the former VAR corporate counsel Kathy L. Hibbs from embarrassing Varian. For starters, Hibbs was asked about her monumental February 25, 1999 declaration filed on behalf of the corporate plaintiffs, wherein she included as an exhibit 213 allegedly defaming message board postings by Delfino and those acting in concert with him. Unfortunately, for her Orrick subpoenas of Yahoo! showed that near 100 of those postings were not authored by anyone named as a defendant in this case. Wow, did you say malicious, frivolous, SLAPP? Hibbs, the 24th witness called by the Orrick then admitted Varian did destroy evidence confessing that at least 200 images were missing from a "minute and 12 sec" segment of a Felch bathroom video. Accounting for what the trusting employee was doing, "No gastrointestinal problem here," exclaimed one courtroom observer.

Returning from lunch, the anti-SLAPP team would begin it's defense calling Hibbs as it's first witness. Hibbs reluctantly admitted she never witnessed any harassment of Felch by Delfino prompting one onlooker to say, "Gee, Felch is a liar or a hallucinator!"

Zdasiuk followed at 2:15. First, this fascist pig SLAPPer unabashedly admitted repeatedly violating Varian company policy and not seeming to think that being more than a year late on performance reviews meant he was incompetent. Then, he supported the widely held contention that Felch is indeed a dogged harasser of employees. Finally, he reaffirmed that his sister's untimely death in a car accident is less upsetting to him than reading message board postings about him and this lawsuit. Mary Rotunno's expression said it all: Oooooooooooh, how callous!

Day 21 - November 27, 2001
Zdasiuk completed his mostly uneventful examination in a few minutes setting the stage for Jane Crisler, the former Varian Human Resources Representative. Crisler, a joy to behold, quickly identified Zdasiuk as a manager who ignored doing annual performance reviews, a violation of Varian company policy, adding that this was a common practice anyway. Flustered by an apparent conflict of interest she had as a Varian employee with a catering company that she is now the CEO of, Crisler not only impeached herself a number of times, but managed to impeach Juanita Sonico and Kathy Hibbs, both of whom had testified earlier in the trial. It only got better. Crisler then verified that Felch's hidden video camera was intentionally pointed toward the men's bathroom adding at no point did she ever witness Delfino harass anyone.

Next, Dave Humber, a 25 year plus Varian employee testified how Felch rudely interrupted a work conversation he was having with Day and Delfino back in 1998 and how she later tried without success to get him to support her scheme to destroy the good doctor. The Gator flying into a rage, attempted to discredit this witness accusing him of being a friend and confidant of the anti-SLAPP defendants. Steadfast in his honesty, Humber answered under blistering cross-examination that he had had no contact with the defendants since this lawsuit began and was simply telling the truth.

Passing his former colleague, the good Dr. Delfino returned to the stand to begin his direct examination. Famed anti-SLAPP attorney Falcon after first laying a foundation for his client's integrity and veracity began the more arduous task of establishing the message board context of Delfino's original 60 postings that formed the basis for this SLAPP. Boring, but essential for explaining the Internet message board culture to the jury, the review of postings would last all day and certainly continue through tomorrow.

Day 22 - November 28, 2001
Delfino's direct examination was briefly interrupted as Judge Komar allowed James Hennessy, the former Varian Director of Human Resources to testify. Hennessy, who had been Crisler's supervisor confirmed that Zdasiuk had indeed violated company policy and verified that Varian had no facts with which it based its decision to terminate Delfino's employment. In fact, Hennessy added that at Varian he personally interviewed three eye witnesses none of whom, not a one who corroborated any of Felch's bogus harassment claims.

Delfino welcoming the opportunity to follow Hennessy's 25 minute testimony spent the rest of the day being walked through his early posting days on the Yahoo! VAR message board. Sequentially viewing more than 200 postings from 1998, Delfino, grinned like a Cheshire Cat when asked to explain this posting [since deleted]. And the jury also got a glimpse of a few of the falsely accused postings that the Orrick SLAPP attorneys used to illegally suppress the free speech of two law-abiding Americans. Adding to the defendants glee, the inclusion of postings by a number of Varian employees like Felch's one time supervisor, Reuel Liebert, and Martin Klausmeier-Brown, a Zdasiuk direct report, only raised the Grande Dame's ire.

As the day ended one could see expressions of despair on the faces of the fascist pig SLAPPers Zdasiuk and Felch, while dollar signs danced above POOP and his Gator.

Day 23 - November 29, 2001
Delfino, still on direct, continued to explain his 60 postings within the context of the dialogue on the October 1998 to February 1999 Yahoo! VAR message board. Then he was walked through some of the thousands of postings he authored since August 13, 1999, none of which have ever been shown to be defaming. Delfino testified that while Felch did admit to being a liar when deposed, two weeks before the SLAPP even began, a Judge had already ruled that Susan B. Felch was a liar and in effect a dogged harasser of her fellow employees.

Hermle, looking more and more like Shirley Stoler[111] began her cross-examination at 2:45 by asking more details about the men's bathroom that was videotaped by Varian. Yes, Felch's hidden camera could record an occupant urinating or defecating. Just as the dialogue heated up, Delfino's testimony was interrupted by a 40 min recall of Cathy McGoff, who came to provide additional Yahoo! subpoena documents and verify user accounts. On returning, Delfino was more than pleased to describe in great detail how Richard 'Dick' Levy lied under oath when he was compelled by a Federal Judge to testify in this SLAPP.

Throughout the day, Felch and Zdasiuk sat as far apart as the courtroom seating allows causing a few observers to wonder if the gastrointestinal problem had returned.

Day 24 - November 30, 2001
The good Dr. Delfino continued to battle the Grande Dame of SLAPP through the early morning hours. Every attempt to discredit this witness failed miserably as jurors seemed to

---

[111] The Nazi commandant in the 1976 film classic, *Seven Beauties*.

intermittently give smiles of approval to Delfino's answers that were in effect a defense of everyone's free speech privilege.

A change of anti-SLAPP combatants at 10:25 am would bring the lovely Ms. Day to the stand to begin her direct examination by famed anti-SLAPP attorney Widmann. Day first testified that she was one of the women to shower in the men's bathroom that was secretly videotaped for five weeks by Varian. She noted this was the only such facility for joggers in the building. Then she explained how Zdasiuk once told her, "I never would have hired you back had I known you were going to get pregnant." Forced to end her 15 plus year career at Varian because of Susan B. Felch's unchecked harassment of her, Day's parting words to the Varian HR Representative Crisler were, "I want out of this company!"

Day returned from the lunch break to take the stand a few minutes past 2 p.m., complete her direct, and face the Gator. Belly up, the Gator was unable to impeach any of Day's all too vivid description of Varian's hostile work environment under Richard M. Levy, a workplace fraught with pornography, employee harassment, invasive bathroom videotaping, destruction of evidence, and repeated violations of published company policies, oh my.

The Orrick then called back Kathy L. Hibbs. A mistake, a big mistake, this former Varian attorney did no more than impeach just about every other SLAPP witness she was supposed to corroborate, including the boss, Richard 'Dick' Levy. Who says Christmas comes only once a year!

The day ended at 4:50 p.m. with Mr. Falcon having read into the record excerpts of the deposition transcript of dirty, filthy Richard 'Dick' Levy, the perennially novice CEO of VAR. Several smiling courtroom observers laughed aloud on hearing how this Dick claims to have watched unsuspecting people holding hands in a neighborhood public park during what he called his normal work hours. Not too surprisingly, Felch and Zdasiuk were not among them.

Day 25 - December 3, 2001

The jury had today off as Judge Komar decided which exhibits would be admitted into evidence. The Orrick argued for their more than 230 exhibits, among which was the unexpected submission of the anti-SLAPP defendants' 998 Settlement Offer.[112] Its inclusion

---

[112]"Defendants Michelangelo Delfino and Mary E. Day offer to compromise and settle the pending actions ... pursuant to Section 998 of the Code of Civil Procedure on the following terms:

1. Judgment for Defendants on Plaintiffs' Complaint. Defendants will waive recovery of their court costs and attorneys' fees as against Plaintiffs.

2. Defendants will not file malicious prosecution or abuse of process actions against plaintiffs, or any of them, their heirs, employees, agents, or assigns, providing however this shall not inure to the benefit of, or release therefrom, the Orrick Law Firm or any of its attorneys.

3. Defendant Delfino shall dismiss his cross-complaint with prejudice. Plaintiffs agree to waive costs, attorney fees, and rights to bring a malicious prosecution or abuse of process action(s) against defendants.

4. Plaintiffs Varian Medical Systems, Inc. and Varian Semiconductors Associates, Inc. shall pay to Delfino and Day the total sum of Twenty-Four Million, Nine Hundred and Ninety-Nine Thousand, Nine Hundred and Ninety-Nine Dollars ($24,999,999.00). Said sum shall be payable in five (5) equal annual installments, the first installment of $5,000,000 due and payable at the time of acceptance of this offer.

5. Plaintiffs shall forthwith publish, once, in the *San Jose Mercury* and in the *San Francisco Chronicle* newspapers a full page ad containing substantially the following text:

"Varian deeply believes in the Constitution of the United States and in that of the State of California, and in the civil rights contained therein and in the Bill of Rights. Varian deeply regrets the actions it has taken since February 1999 in which it sought to silence free speech on the Internet. Varian apologizes for any harm it may have caused others, and promises that it will never again engage in any efforts to restrain free speech in the future."

6. Day and Delfino agree to cooperate and assist Varian in the future by, namely, agreeing hereby to assign to plaintiffs an exclusive license and right to use the patent attached hereto (and identified as U.S. Patent 6,264,595 B1, issued on or about July 24, 2001.) Day and Delfino shall be entitled to a 10% royalty on the profits of all accumulated sales after Varian, or its agents, assigns, licensees, etc., has profited by the amount of $25,000,000 (using generally accepted accounting procedures) from sales or earnings resulting from the use, in whole or in part, of that Patent.

caused a grinning Falcon to exclaim, "I've never seen this before," and a perplexed judge to add, "Neither have I!" Following a short break, the famed anti-SLAPP attorneys argued for admission of their 60 or so exhibits, most of which were allowed by the judge.

Next came defendants' non-suit motions against the False Advertising & Corporate Libel claims among others contained in the third amended complaint. In discussing the Yahoo! Third Party Beneficiary Claim, Falcon warned of the possible implications, i.e., "3 billion defendants," to which Judge Komar gaily replied, and "3 billion plaintiffs." Orrick then tried their hand at directed verdict requests including yet another attempt to dismiss Delfino's cross-complaint. To no ones surprise, no pleas were granted.

Felch, Zdasiuk and Rotunno were conspicuously absent, causing those who know that gastrointestinal problems are not contagious, to wonder if Zdasiuk were intoxicated or out of control again or simply back at Varian violating company policy.

Day 26 - December 4, 2001
Today's action took place inside chambers wherein attorneys for both sides submitted jury instructions to Judge Komar for presentation to the jury. These trial proceedings were not open to

---

7. Day and Delfino will agree not to refer to Felch or Zdasiuk, or any of their known relations, on the Internet, and will remove any such reference(s) on any web site maintained by them. However, this is a voluntary provision on their part, which they will honor, but not guarantee, nor permit any alleged future violation of this provision to, in any way, defeat this Compromise agreement, nor shall it result in sanctions, breach, contempt (whether civil or criminal), nor give right to any remedy at law or equity to any plaintiff herein, which remedies plaintiffs hereby waive and release.

8. Plaintiffs waive and release any and all claims they may have, known or unknown, against defendants, including a Civil Code §1542 waiver.

If plaintiffs accept this offer, please date and sign the accompanying notice of acceptance, and file the offer and notice of acceptance in the above-entitled action prior to trial or within 30 days after the date that this offer is made, whichever occurs first, or else it will be deemed withdrawn....

Dated September 19, 2001"

the public. Reading Bernice Young's article in the *San Francisco Weekly*[113] gave us all pause for reflection: "Was it worth it?" Dr. Martin Luther King said it best:

---

[113]"It is a crisp fall afternoon in early November, and Michelangelo Delfino takes a seat on a bench in San Jose's seedy St. James Park, across the street from the Santa Clara Superior Courthouse. For about three weeks, since the trial for a libel lawsuit against him began, Delfino has been seeking fresh air in the park during court recesses.

A scientist and engineer in his 50s, Delfino, along with his co-defendant, Mary Day ... breathes deeply, glad to be away from Courtroom 22, where they have spent the past 15 days under accusations of defamation, invasion of privacy, and "Internet terrorism," .... The couple are being sued by ... Varian ... the company they used to work for, because they allegedly conspired on libelous postings to Internet message boards in 1998 and 1999.

The postings that inspired the lawsuit are critical of the company....

Delfino and Day admit to making *some* postings -- using aliases such as "oh_no_dirty_dick_levy" and "felch_makes_me_vomit" -- but they deny penning the overtly libelous ones. They say they have been wrongly accused, and the real issue at hand is freedom of speech. Indeed, Delfino and Day claim to be champions of the First Amendment, and have become skillful at employing its rhetoric.

"This is truly a First Amendment fight," Delfino insists....

Delfino and Day, who are using their 401(K) plans to pay their household bills and court costs, say that though they are emotionally and financially exhausted by the lawsuit, they "refuse to be silenced." "We're pushing that line [of free speech], and we intend to push that line," Delfino says. "We are obsessed, consumed. We are determined. We are relentless. We believe we have the right to post, and they can never stop us from posting. We will post until we die." ...

But the Internet postings are overwhelming on their own. ... Delfino and Day are accused of using about 200 aliases to post an unspecified number of defamatory messages. Delfino and Day, however, admit to using only 78; they say other ex-Varian employees are behind the libelous postings. Though Yahoo! provided identity information on some aliases when subpoenaed, there are some aliases behind the alleged defamatory postings that are still unaccounted for. As a result, Delfino has been called to the stand to testify whether or not he admitted to using particular pseudonyms, a process that lasts several hours.

"I'm not sure if it's "dick_on_tape" or "dicks_on_tape" [that I used]," he says earnestly when asked about a particular alias. "The problem is, there are so many variations." To complicate things further, Delfino and Day continue to make postings, and Varian's attorneys continue to use them as evidence....

"There is nothing in all the world greater than freedom. It is worth paying for; it is worth losing a job for; it is worth going to jail for. I would rather be a free pauper than a rich slave. I would rather die in abject poverty with my convictions than live in inordinate riches with the lack of self respect."

Day 27 - December 5, 2001

The jury instruction arguments continued for the second day behind closed doors and out of public scrutiny. Meanwhile, the ever so cute anti-SLAPP defendants resumed posting the truth,

---

As Delfino's questioning continues, Varian's attorneys ask if he is proud of himself. "I am extremely proud of the postings," he says, swiveling in his chair to face the jury directly. "I am proud of the Web site, and of speaking up and defending myself and printing the truth. I'm proud of Mary's spunkiness and her determination to fight this incredible injustice."

As soon as Delfino and Day have their coffee in the morning, they begin posting. They post again at Internet cafes during the lunch break. And in the evening, when they've returned home from court, they are likely to be found at their iMac, crafting more searing commentary. But for all their prolific message posting, Delfino and Day are not the only ones lurking on the ever-shifting threads of the Internet dedicated to the Varian case.

The couple has, in fact, attracted a number of detractors ... One anti-Delfino poster, who uses the alias "crack_smoking_jesus," has even likened Delfino to "the Internet bin Laden." ...

It is the noonday break, and Delfino reclines on a park bench to evaluate the morning's legal proceedings. Wearing a business suit and a shit-eating grin, he recalls a particularly amusing anecdote that he was able to slip into his morning testimony -- that [Jane Crisler] the human resources manager at Varian had burped into a microphone when introducing herself at a company meeting. "I get very giddy with that kind of stuff," he told the jury; some members laughed aloud.

Delfino describes himself as an honest and "incorrigible" person with a good sense of humor. As a result, he says, he is also the "perfect target" for this lawsuit. "If you ask people about these statements, people would say that it sounds like something I would say," he says. "But I mean, who the hell are we?"

Delfino continues, as if philosophically. "In the whole grand scheme of things, we are totally insignificant. We know where we are in the food chain. But these are two near-[b]illion-dollar corporations. If you called up Varian, we'd get dismissed as clowns or lunatics. Why would you spend all this money on clowns posting to message boards?""

their opinion, and hyperbole on countless Internet message boards and with a newly found vigor!

Day 28 - December 6, 2001
Judge Komar began the day by granting Orrick's Directed Jury Verdict in dismissing Delfino's cross-complaint. Not a good start for the anti-SLAPP team. He then called for the return of the jury from their unduly long recess. To much surprise, the Judge struck Felch's testimony wherein VSEA tried to claim litigation expenses as damages, and ruled against Varian that there would be no inference of impersonation or defamation from there having been a preliminary injunction, long since dissolved by a unanimous ruling of three fine Federal Judges. The morning was looking better already!

This set the stage for the Grande Dame of SLAPP to begin her closing statement. Starting at 10:00 am with SLAPPers Felch and Zdasiuk accompanied by his present wife Julie Fouquet and what appeared to be a life-time supply of Kanka. Rotunno and her notebook were in attendance too. The morning would be multi-media display of Internet messages, Kinko's videos, and some of the biggest charts ever shown in a court room, I'm sure. Hermle argued, if the jury were to find liability for postings such as this one [I did on Yahoo! VAR on October 2, 2001]:

> **Does GEORGE ZDASIUK terrorize** by:
> george_zdasiuk_intoxicated (49/M/Portola Valley, California) you?
> Harassed?
> Are you GAY and a victim of Varian SLAPP terrorism?
> In 20 days and 10 hours the SLAPP trial will begin and the truth about GEORGE ZDASIUK and his puny Dick will SHOCK the living shit out of you!
> REMEMBER: Buying and selling stock in a company that faces a 5 to 8 week jury trial is not without risk!
> Hee, hee, hee!

and this one [Mary posted on Yahoo! VSEA on March 13, 2000]:

> **I DID throw up!** by: <u>dantecristo</u>
> I made an attempt to avoid the ruthless millionaire novice
> CEO at my Los Altos Safeway on Saturday and drove to
> another grocery store only to run into VSEA Director Susan B.
> Felch. I was so disturbed and frightened for my children that I
> literally threw up after seeing her in another Los Altos grocery
> store miles away from her town!
> Am I being stalked?
> I am truly frightened of this woman and her novice CEO as
> they have shown the moral turpitude to do anything in my
> opinion.
> Damages? You bet!"

among the more than 13,000 available, and determine by clear and convincing evidence the defendants had acted with "malice, fraud *or* oppression," then $2,000,000 would be a reasonable punitive award.

Beginning at 3:25 p.m., famed anti-SLAPP attorney Falcon parked himself on a desk directly across from the jurors and began his closing argument. Waving MoBeta, Inc.'s first patent in the air, he said now you know why Varian is asking for really big bucks, money they know Delfino and Day don't have. The jury was suddenly awake. Shifting gears, Falcon said there had been no evidence of defamation per se, and as such, no reason to award punitive damages to anyone. Adding that bathroom videotaping, destruction of evidence, alleged lab sabotage, and the pitiful attempt to charge for security at a VAR stockholder meeting were proof enough of Varian incompetence. Judge Komar recessed the court at 4:30, as Falcon had only just begun.

Day 29 - December 7, 2001
On this day that would live in infamy, Mr. Falcon continued with his oral defense of everyone's free speech privilege. At ease with the jurors, he cited the conditional privilege jury instruction, wherein a defaming posting can be made as long as their is a good faith belief in the truth of the statement and it is not motivated by hatred or ill will.

["And unless you do it knowingly false – (counsel indicating) – conscious disregard of the truth or designed to do it with malice, it's privileged. End of case. This case is over. You walk into the jury room, you go to the last page, you sign your name on it, put the big zero, and out. That's what happens."]

"Pox on both of their houses," ["Even if you were to find something *was* defamatory ..."] responded this emotionally charged free speech advocate to the notion of damages.

Famed anti-SLAPP attorney Widmann began his closing argument at 10:55 and ended with the lunch break. Describing Varian he stated "That company has a strange view of the world." Referring to his client first posting only months after being named a defendant, he said "You sued me, I'm fighting back!" and I will post "until you leave me alone."

["Today is Pearl Harbor Day.... it's a very important day. Many men and women died on this day for the First Amendment.... That is why people fight and that is one of the reasons that Ms. Day took to using the posting and fighting back."]

Hermle returned from the lunch recess to give her shrill like rebuttal at 1:45. The fattened Gator presented another high-tech pyrotechnic display of message board postings like this one [I did on Yahoo! VAR on February 26, 2000]:

> **Does Orrick know about Kathy Hibbs Dick**
> by: ima_posta2
> I mean really know?
> Perhaps, they will the next time Orrick SLAPP Attorney
> Lynne C. Hermle and Hibbs 'socialize'.
> Can you imagine a female that says it is ok to capture on video
> unsuspecting men, women, and children going to the
> bathroom!
> Urinating or defecating!
> Such impeccable integrity!
> Great company - Richard 'Dick' Levy - tell us all about it at
> trial!
> Ha, ha, ha, ha!

and this one [I posted on Yahoo! VAR on Christmas Eve 2000]:

> **Calling George Zdasiuk a FAT LIAR**
> by: felch_sees_things_or_is_a_liar (F/Los Altos Hills)
> the truth, pure and simple. Sure these two fascist SLAPPers
> can sue, and in fact they are suing, but they will lose.
> Similarly, statements about videotaping the INSIDE of at least
> one Varian bathroom, the repeated violations of Varian
> company policy, the production of pornography with Varian
> equipment, the hostile Varian work environment, etc. are all
> true, therefore not libelous, and both despicable Varian
> companies suing will also lose.
> Why do you think it has taken almost two years of fighting
> and still no trial? Both sides know exactly what's going to
> happen at the SLAPP trial, and after all the Orrick games that
> is why we are still trying to complete our depositions - the
> sooner the better!

and this one [I did on Yahoo! VSEA the following day]:

> **Do you see what I see?** by: varian_videotaped_a_bathroom
> Said Susan B. Felch the scaree SLAPPer to the judge and
> jureeeeee. An invasive bathroom video camera, a hidden video
> camera with a big long lens showed nooooooo facial gestures,
> noooooo hand gestures, and noooooooooo harassment, only
> images of urinating or defecating or showering!
> Do you you hear what I say? Said the jureeee of her peers.
> You Mrs. Felch are a CHRONIC LIAR or a NEUROTIC
> HALLUCINATOR. And you Mr. Aurelio are a puneeeee
> cowardly Dick on tape who should have known better!
> Do you know what I know? Said the anti-SLAPP defendants
> to the stockholders? You been duped, you been tricked, you
> suckers lost a lot of money on VSEA cause you didn't believe!
> MERRY CHRISTMAS!

in a last attempt to enrage the jury. Accounting for Felch and
Zdasiuk not having any out of pocket expenses she said, "We
presume damages because it is difficult to prove." Arguing for the
$2,000,000 plea for damages, she closed with, "Money talks for
some people ..." "But I fear not these two anti-SLAPP defendants,"

mused a few court room observers. The jury was dismissed at 2:50 p.m. for next week's instruction and deliberation.

Day 30 - December 10, 2001
Judge Komar began this day with a reading aloud of the 67 Jury Instructions to the jury. After which he swore in the bailiff, and ordered the jurors to enter the jury room and select a foreperson. With them out of the court room, he dismissed the alternate juror explaining that (s)he remain on call in case one of the twelve was discharged. Next, he explained why he had overruled defendants' objections to Jury Instruction no.'s 34, 43, 44 and 106, and plaintiffs' objections to no.'s 38 and 75. Lastly, Judge Komar rocked the Gator and her POOP with "there is no Federal contempt", at which point a few court room observers whispered, "Wowee, justice has finally been served!"

At 11:30 a.m., the jury returned to the courtroom, announced their foreperson, and were handed Orrick's 29 page Special Verdict Form, which Judge Komar explained briefly. Ten minutes later all parties and their attorneys were dismissed so that the jury could begin its deliberation in earnest.

Although it was a short day in court, a GI plagued Zdasiuk seemed to make an inordinate number of hurried trips to the men's room. The scary Susan B. Felch did not accompany him and no videotapes were found.

Day 31 - December 11, 2001
This first full day of jury deliberation commenced with the jury submitting written questions throughout the day. Responding "No." to *"Can we have a dictionary?"* questions like, *"Is monetary compensation for the plaintiffs a way (incentive) to make the postings stop? Or if we find the defendents guilty and say the defendents have sustained damages - enable the court to enjoin the defendents to stop posting?"* and *"If an individual person votes negative on sustaining damages but the group as a majority of 9 votes on sustaining damages does that individual cast a vote for*

334

the amount of damages and/or malice, fraud or oppression?" and, finally *"Do all questions have to have a majority (at least 9 votes)? If there is a deadlock on a question does it negate everything else?"* were cheerfully answered by Judge Komar with the jurors sitting back in the box.

At 10:50 a.m., Orrick's Prayer for Relief Injunction Hearing began in Judge Komar's open courtroom. Felch, Zdasiuk, Rotunno, and Joe Phair phonetically related to Jim Fair accompanied by an unidentified Dick were in attendance. POOP began his SLAPP argument with "MoBeta is a real company," whereupon a number of stockholders said, "No shit!" He then complained to the Judge that money is an inadequate remedy for "defamation, impersonation and harassment." especially with these people. But didn't his Gator say "Money talks!", whispered a court room attendant. Widmann and Falcon, waiting their turn, responded that Preenjoining Free Speech was Unconstitutional and certainly not based on any jury decision in this trial. The judge, not dissuaded, began with this is "one of the most unusual cases I have encountered" and I am "frankly at a loss" to explain the escalation, but that there has been "serious defamation and serious harassment by both defendants" and "without remorse." Since they would, "promise to do it until their dead." I will enjoin them, to which someone said, there is no injunction that will silence us. While the details are not yet known, Judge Komar warned that the ever so cute stockholders of MoBeta, Inc. would not be calling Susan B. Felch a liar, at least until his ruling was overturned by the Court of Appeals. Wow!

By the way, was that Ralph H. Baxter, Jr.?"[114]

---

[114]David Brown, *The Recorder*, September 12, 2002: "Orrick, Herrington & Sutcliffe and its employees have pumped more than $1.3 million into local and state political campaigns …in the words of chairman Ralph Baxter Jr., [The Orrick] "expects nothing in return" for its contributions."

- 13 -

SLAPP YOU SILLY

Mary and I were chipper as ever. We weren't unduly concerned about losing either. At very worst, losing could only cost more money and we were nearly broke anyway. We had demanded a jury trial and had long anticipated one. Instead, the inclusion of Komar's jury instruction no. 34:

> "You must determine whether each statement allegedly made by the defendants is or is not defamatory on its face. If you find that a statement is not defamatory on its face, then you must determine whether in light of all the circumstances it constitutes a defamatory statement.
>
> A statement is defamatory on its face if the natural and probable effect on the average reader is to defame the plaintiff without the necessity of considering the surrounding circumstances.
>
> A statement, if untrue, is defamatory on its face if it assets or implies as a fact any of the following:
>
> 1. That a person committed a crime;
> 2. That a person has a personal trait or engaged in conduct that would tend directly to injure the person in respect to his or her profession, trade of business, either by imputing to him or her general disqualification in those respects which the profession, trade or business peculiarly requires, or by imputing something with reference to his or her profession, or trade or business that has a natural tendency to lessen its profits;
> 3. That a person is impotent;
> 4. That a person is an adulterer, that is, that he or she engages in sexual affairs outside of marriage;
> 5. That a person has attained his or her professional position by having sex with a supervisor;

336

6. That a person is a liar or chronic liar, or has committed perjury;

7. That a supervisor discriminates against other persons on the basis of race, gender, pregnancy, sexual orientation, or similar characteristics;

8. That a person has engaged in sabotage or intentionally caused damage in the workplace;

9. That a person engaged in sexual harassment;

10. That a person has created a hostile work environment due to sexual misconduct;

11. That a person has caused another person to be videotaped inside a company bathroom;

12. That a person has stalked another person; when a statement is defamatory on its face, plaintiff can recover damages including general and presumed damages without proof of special damages, so long as plaintiff establishes by the required standard of proof that he, she or it is entitled to recover. If a statement is not defamatory on its face, but nonetheless under all circumstances is defamatory, plaintiff must establish that he, she or it has sustained special damages in order to also recover general damages."

made this jury impotent. Glynn, in fact told Komar:

"We believe that that deprived our clients to the right to the jury trial to have the jury determine what is or was not defamatory. When the Court took that, in effect, from the jury without getting the specifics from the jury as to was Susan Felch a liar, was there a sexual slur or something to this effect, we don't know. So we have this huge chilling on free speech, because we don't know.... When the Court decided that was defamatory, then that deprived us the right to a jury trial, a jury finding."

By telling the jurors what language is defamatory *a priori*, Komar made it impossible for them to evaluate whether our postings were false and had actually caused damage. In particular, they were not allowed to evaluate our words within their message board setting, as is required by law. Thus we did not expect to win. Still, while waiting for the jurors to deliberate, our most depressing scenario showed us as financially ruined, but gleefully posting away.

Before the trial began, the irascible Komar after first being introduced to our attorneys told them that he intended to enjoin our speech. And periodically throughout the trial he reminded Glynn and Randy that we *would* be silenced, and we therefore should simply agree to an injunction. For us, this was never an option. We were confident he could never succeed.

> KOMAR: This is certainly one of the most unusual cases that I've heard requesting an injunction complaining of conduct. We have some extraordinarily intelligent and bright, very capable people here including the defendants. And frankly, I'm at a loss to understand what would really motivate Mr. Delfino and Ms. Day from engaging in the course of conduct that they've engaged in.
>
> I can understand their being angry. I can understand their being unhappy. I can understand their disagreeing with what their employer did. I can understand their disagreeing with the basis for their termination.
>
> But I cannot understand how that type of disagreement could possibly escalate into the course of tenuous, repetitive attacks on people with whom they have no further contact. I don't understand that....
>
> But I certainly find that there has been a very serious defamation, a very serious harassment in this case by the defendants, by both of them. It is without remorse or repentance.
>
> There's a promise and a commitment to do it until they're dead as they both said both on the messages that were introduced into evidence as well as from the stand under oath. And I take them at their word.
>
> And irrespective of what the jury may do regarding the damages I think because of the repetitive nature of their conduct over the last two years as well as their commitment to continue that type of conduct that the Court has no alternative other than to enjoin improper conduct by them in the future....
>
> So I'm going to at the outset issue an injunction against further defamation whether it be on the Web Site postings or otherwise of any Web Site. And that includes the MoBeta Web Site which I have found in effect is in the nature of a public journal. You can't defame somebody in the newspaper, you can't defame somebody in a public journal, you can't defame them with impunity on any Web Site....
>
> I'm going to enjoin them from continuing to post those statements in any way, shape or form on the Internet or otherwise....
>
> There's no question that what a person earns when he works for a corporation as the Chief Executive Office is of public record, and it's available to anybody that wants to find it. But providing that information along with information about the address, the residence address of the individual I think creates a real danger.

And I think that's wrong. And I think it's wrong legally, and I think it's wrong morally....

Certainly the orders that I've made concerning the defamation against the individuals, because this all occurs in connection with the business at Varian, it attacks their business and is put in the context at least on the MoBeta Web Site as being in support of their business but not so on the Yahoo Web Site, it seems to me that there's a question about whether or not this is enjoined under Section 17200. And I'm going to take another look at that before I make any decision about that.

It seems to me that there is a conditional privilege available as I've indicated to you previously when we were talking about the instructions as to both the Yahoo Stock-Talk and other stock related Web Sites and the MoBeta Web Site which requires that it be a report of litigation, that it be a fair and accurate report of the litigation. So that things said in the litigation can be posted in their entirety. But they can't be posted as fact, they have to be posted as a statement of what the litigation was and what was said during the litigation. And that's one of the failures that I think has occurred on the MoBeta Web Site. Because -- well, I won't go into that at this point....

HERMLE: May I be heard on just a few additional issues which fit into this portion?

KOMAR: Yes.

HERMLE: You said that you're going to enjoin the defendants from stating that Susan Felch is mentally ill or unstable or hallucinates.

And we'd request in light of the postings that label Mr. Zdasiuk as "sick," "What a sicky" and similar comments that you enlarge that portion to include no postings alleging that Mr. Zdasiuk is mentally ill or disturbed or sick....

KOMAR: This is a statement of intended decision. And that's obviously subject to final form. But that's what my intended is at this time.... if the vice-president of a corporation makes a decision to do something or not to do something with the corporation and an employee or former employee or a competitor or whatever says "that's just sick," that is not per se defamatory, certainly not defamatory on its face. And I don't think you can enjoin that type of statement by somebody even though it may be uncivil, it may be done with the worst of motives, but it is not defamatory. It's not defamatory and cannot be enjoined on that basis.

... when opinions exceed truth and they're demonstrably untrue, then the court has an obligation to do whatever it has an obligation to do. So I will take a look at the rest. I might well ask for further argument I'm not sure, with regard to the harassment and other issues. I ultimately will want input from all counsel in terms of the form of the injunction even though you may not agree with the substance. I think that as with any other orders of court it really has to be considered approved as to form. With that we still have a jury deliberating. I'm going to recess at this time and we will talk further about both the form of the order as well as these other two areas.

"Day 32 - December 12, 2001

The jury completed its third day of deliberation. Elsewhere, the lovely Ms. Day and the good Dr. Delfino returned to their favorite keyboards and gleefully resumed posting lawful messages on some of the more popular Internet message boards. On this day outside the court house, calls to the SLAPP HOTLINE[115] were unusually heavy. Talk of this SLAPP and its lasting effect on free speech on the Internet was in the air. Could you call someone a LIAR? While rumors of dirty Richard 'Dick' Levy scurrying about San Jose's Saint James Park in search of his purported booster seat could not be substantiated, Zdasiuk's lingering GI problem remained a threat to the community at large.

Day 33 - December 13, 2001

Word of Judge Komar's intent to impose an injunction began to spread as the newly empowered anti-SLAPP defendants posted message after message after message, all of them lawful and well within any attempted court restriction. Noting that injunctions against these defendants' free speech have been overturned by a

---

[115]The SLAPP HOTLINE was a telephone service we offered in which an interested party dialed 650-207-4297 and was greeted with a Mary Day voice message: e.g., "Welcome to the Varian, Susan B. Felch and George Zdasiuk SLAPP trial hot line where you will hear only the truth and our Constitutionally protected opinion. Today's SLAPP news is dated October 28th, 12:20 p.m. PST. Last week marked the first week of the trial. On Friday the jury heard opening arguments. Lynne Hermle's Opening Statement included her first public demonstration of the Susan B. Felch Phone Gesture. As memorable as it was watching the Grand Dame of SLAPP stick her finger in her ear, her demonstration did not seem to amuse the judge or jury. Hermle, not dismayed reminded the court that the B in Susan B. Felch stands for Benjamin. Of course, a number of witnesses in this case believe the B stands for something else. That is all for now and remember - Be careful who you SLAPP! Call back for regular updates as fascist SLAPP news is made. God bless America!"

higher court once before, Day mused, "The jury hadn't even decided the case yet!" to which Delfino quipped, "There is a Supreme Court, *n'est pas*?" Meanwhile, the really cute anti-SLAPP statistician noted that the defendants had passed the 14,000 message board posting milestone. Congratulations!

> "... as jurors toiled ... a bigger struggle -- over the type and extent of any injunctive relief -- may lie ahead for the lawyers and the judge.
>
> The unusual case, marked by defendants who continue to post messages that criticize and insult the plaintiffs, their witnesses and their lawyers during the trial, has become an expensive test of wills with no easy way out.
>
> Depending on the outcome ... Komar could end up writing a wide-ranging injunction that may add a new and important precedent to the growing body of Internet law....
>
> "There is no easy way out because they are not going to silence us," Day said Tuesday. "I believe there is no injunction that will silence us." ..."[116]

At 2:15 p.m., the jury did return from more than three days of deliberation to issue its verdict. Sitting tall in Judge Komar's rather crowded court room, were the lovely Ms. Day and the good Dr. Delfino, accompanied by their famed anti-SLAPP attorneys, Randall Widmann and Glynn Falcon. Judge Komar, looking a bit weary, directed the reading of the verdict into the record by the clerk. It would take but one hour.

Following the judge's instructions, the jury found liability for defamation, impersonation, breach of third-party contract, and conspiracy and awarded $425,000 in damages as follows: $150,000 for Felch; $125,000 for Zdasiuk; and $75,000 each for VAR & VSEA despite no plaintiff having any out of pocket expenses whatsoever. Not a dime, oh my!

While the Grande Dame of SLAPP seemed to be waiting for someone to throw up or for that long awaited GI eruption to take place, someone asked a news reporter, "Geez, so how much does it

---

[116]Shannon Lafferty, *The Recorder*, December 12, 2002.

cost to post one of these Internet messages?" "Looks like 30 bucks a piece," was today's verdict.

> "Day said she hopes to appeal Thursday's decision.
> "There's a list of things I can still say about this company and these people so I'm not sure what Varian got out of this case. I got ... the right to continue posting and the right to continue exercising my First Amendment rights, Day said.""[117]

Day 34 - December 17, 2001
Reacting to last Thursday's jury verdict and SLAPP award for $425,000, the ever-so-cute anti-SLAPP defendants noted: "we're broke, but we can still post." Varian, having spent the better part of three years and upwards of five-million dollars had clearly succeeded in destroying MoBeta, Inc., and in motivating its founders to post 'till they're dead!

Today marked the end of this our nation's first Internet SLAPP trial, the punitive damages phase [KOMAR: "Because defendant ... was guilty of malice,[118] oppression,[119] or fraud,[120] you may ... award punitive damages ..."]. The Gator would ask for "$20 million" going so far to suggest that the good Dr. Delfino had hid money in Hong Kong. Not Los Altos?! The jury, already duped into believing the two SLAPPed families have anything financially left to lose was instructed and told to award more and more money to Susan B. Felch, George Zdasiuk and their corporate sponsors for SLAPPing. At 5 p.m., the jury taking less than 45 minutes to deliberate, awarded another $200,000 to Felch, $150,000 to Zdasiuk, and not a dime to the corporations! A few Varian stockholders were heard to say, "Geeez, what perennially novice CEO's spend so many millions and wind up with this?" [Yahoo! VAR posting dated December 16, 2001]:

---

[117]Mercury News, *San Jose Mercury News*, December 15, 2002.

[118]The publication of defamatory material with knowledge that it was false or a reckless disregard of whether it was false or not.

[119]Causing physical or mental distress.

[120]Intentionally or by omission stating as fact something that is untrue.

done by: <u>kill_delfino</u>
Agree with you both (harv, oh_no). I've had it.
This SOB and his bitch have ruined this and other boards for their purpose. They will not stop posting their gibberish. I really don't care what they have to say. As I said a long time ago, the right to free speech (which this is NOT about) does not mean we have to listen. But butt-wipe Delfino insists we do, no matter what.
Here's a message for Delfino: ok, asswipe, you can post all you want- it's all boring crap that only you and your stupid woman care about. Everyone else knows you're lying and how much. And we know which new aliases are you. (Harv- he has two impersonations of you if you haven't noticed.)
But think about this, Sledge: I travel out to the valley, hate it as I do, as required. You don't know what I look like, but I know you, where you live, where Mary lives, where you drink to excess, and with whom. When I visit, you won't know, but you will remember afterwards.
As I see it, I'm 10-15 years younger, taller and bigger than you, and most importantly much meaner when I'm pissed off. And you've done that. So keep posting your drivel- one day you'll see the light. And you won't even see it coming when I give you the proper tribute for the 'wonderful' things you've done.
OF COURSE, just like your crap is about free speech, by the same token I'm not talking about physcial violence. In the same way you have a SLAPP suit, I am NOT talking about beating the living sh*t out of you. And the following contain the same veracity: you don't defame people, I don't make their lives a living hell in person, upclose and personal.
And I would never use mace or pepper spray to disable the both of you before NOT hurting you. THAT WOULDN'T BE FAIR!!!
See you soon, waste-of-life.

SLAPPers Felch and Zdasiuk, who were conspicuously absent as Delfino and Day thanked the jurors for their civil service, were thought to be house hunting. Meanwhile, Lynne C. Hermle and her POOP left without comment!

Day 35 - December 18, 2001
This last court day in 2001 began with Varian's first press release:

"Varian Wins $775,000 Jury Verdict in Internet Libel Case Jury Orders Former Employees Michelangelo Delfino and Mary Day to Pay Varian Damages for Defaming and Harassing Company Managers and Their Families

PALO ALTO, Calif.--(BUSINESS WIRE)--Dec. 18, 2001-- Varian Medical Systems, Inc. (NYSE:VAR - news) and Varian Semiconductor Equipment Associates (NASDAQ:VSEA - news) have won a major jury verdict before the Santa Clara County Superior Court today in an Internet defamation and harassment case filed against former employees Michelangelo Delfino and Mary Day. The jury verdict in Varian v. Delfino, 780187, followed a six week trial. The jury awarded Varian Medical Systems, Varian Semiconductor Equipment Associates, Inc., and two of their managers $775,000 in compensatory and punitive damages. In addition, Santa Clara Superior Court Judge Jack Komar, who presided over the case, issued an injunction that prohibits Delfino and Day from continuing to post defamatory and harassing statements on the Internet.

The jury of eight women and four men found unanimously that Delfino and Day acted with malice, fraud, and oppression through some 14,000 Internet postings on 100 message boards and their own web site since 1998 when Delfino was terminated and Day resigned from research positions with Varian Associates. In these messages, Delfino and Day falsely accused various members of Varian management of being homophobic, discriminating against pregnant women, having sexual affairs, and secretly videotaping employees while in office restrooms. Delfino and Day were also charged with impersonating Varian managers on Internet message boards.

"We are thrilled with this result," said Lynne Hermle, a partner in Orrick, Herrington & Sutcliffe LLP, which represented Varian in this case. "Delfino and Day have terrorized and threatened Varian managers and their families. It is a relief that this campaign of defamation and harassment must stop now. Both the judge and the jury have made it clear that the Internet is not a safe haven for defamation." …"

The lies hurt. Threats? Harassing families? We had harassed no one. Everything we had done in this case was done with one purpose – to lawfully pursue justice. Malice, fraud *and* oppression? Mary and I had never ever knowingly made a false statement. Any stress suffered by the SLAPPers was self-inflicted. Seeing us

344

maligned this way was too much. But no matter how untrue, it pained. Somehow being printed in the newspaper made it all too real. And if that weren't enough, our family members and our neighbors got to read it as well. In spite of all the well-wishing we received that weekend and in the weeks that followed, reading the Varian press release that morning was truly upsetting.

Extremely wired, I didn't need my usual dose of French Roast and loud polyphony to wake up that December 18 morning and make the 30-minute drive to San Jose. When Mary and I arrived at the courthouse a few minutes before 9 a.m. and entered the courtroom, I don't think I ever saw Hermle more "thrilled," as her all too exaggerated grin was more in tune than ever with her bouncy step. At 10 minutes past the hour, a highly-agitated Komar entered the courtroom. And almost immediately, he came down on the two of us almost as if he just read the Varian victory speech:

KOMAR: Well, let me just tell you some things that I'm concerned about here. It seems to me that the defendants have misperceived what it is that the Court has ordered with regard to the injunctive relief. And I think that has perhaps been made very obvious by the postings that are reflected … in the second phase of the trial, the punitive damage phase.

And I'm looking right now at that exhibit…. a message … which is entitled, "Varian videotaped a bathroom," by "oh no dick". Well, the difficulty here is that the posters of this message are trying to skirt the law, but they've stepped over the line. It's false that Varian videotaped a bathroom, certainly the inside of a bathroom, that Varian videotaped people within a bathroom.

If you read this message in conjunction with the prior postings, it's very clear what it is that is being communicated. In the first instance, if you knew nothing else about it, if there had been no postings, it continues to be defamatory of Varian.

The second page of this exhibit, which says, "Varian videotaped two lavatories with a camera hidden in Dick Levy's direct report's office," is just more of the same. If you look at it in combination, it is more defamation, it is more of a reference to what has been said here for the last three years.

And if you go to the next page, by "megan e gray is a liar," presumed alias, and the language it says there is, "no injunction current or otherwise will ever keep the victims of Varian's secret bathroom videotaping from posting, posting lawful messages every single day, I'm sure." Again, making a very clear reference to the previous allegations and statements of fact which were untrue.

And if you go to the next page of this exhibit, by Mr. Delfino, referring to Mr. Levy lying, having subordinates that violate company policy, secretly videotaping a men's bathroom, videotaping a women's restroom, force pornography on a subordinate -- the list goes on and on – "did I forget the destruction of evidence and hostile work environment?" close quote.

Again, the next one, Varian, "Varian under Richard Dick Levy videotaped over and over" – "and even destroyed the evidence that might have shown," etc. etc.

The next one, "Varian videotaped two lavatories hidden in Dick Levy's direct report's office."

And the last one by, quote, "varian videotaped lavatories", it says that the weeks of invasive – "invasive men's and women's restroom videotaping pornography, etc."

These are defamatory messages. They all relate to the previous defamation. They are probably defamatory on their face as it is. They state as a fact that certain things have happened. The Court has found them to be untrue....

Now, this is not a contempt hearing. This is an attempt to clarify the Court's injunctive order, so that we don't have to go into a contempt hearing at some later time regarding these postings. And I don't think anybody wants to have to do that. And I'm going to try and make it real clear so we don't do that.

Postings which have been found to be defamatory -- and I've outlined some of those -- are not to be posted. They are not to be posted in the body of the message, they are not to be posted in the title of the message, they are not to be posted as an alias. So   when you post an alias, "varian videotaped bathrooms," you are posting a defamatory statement. That is prohibited. It is enjoined.

There are a number of other related kinds of postings that are wrong in the way in which they are done.... It would be false to state that pornography was forced upon a subordinate at Varian. That is not a true fact. The postcard that was introduced into evidence is not pornography. Pornography has a real clear definition in the law. That does not constitute pornography....

Use of the names of the various employees, the attorneys on this case, attorneys referred to in this case, witnesses referred to in this case, their families, Varian Medical, Varian Semiconductor and Varian, Incorporated, or Varian Associates, or any play on those words, shall not be used as an alias by the defendants in this case, nor shall they be used as a title in conjunction with any of the statements that have been demonstrated to be false....

346

It would be very difficult -- it would be impossible for the Court to make an order that says you can no longer defame somebody, in generalized terms. What is defamatory in the future is different than what has been demonstrated to be defamatory today. I'm talking about the conduct and the statements that have been adjudicated in this proceeding and this proceeding only....

You may not go over the line. This is not a playground. This is not something that you can try to taunt the other side with by going as close to the line as you can. If you go over the line, you're going to be in violation of the Court's order. If you stay on the proper side of the line and make rational postings, there is no interference at all with your desire to do that. Now, you can express whatever opinions you wish. Do not state facts that are false.

I'm going to order that the defendants remove prior defamatory statements, those statements that the Court has determined have been defamatory. That includes the language, whether it be in the title or whether it be in the body or whether it be in an alias. Those are to be removed ... looking at my notes and looking at the various postings here that say that Varian managers repeatedly violated company policy -- there is one company policy that was established by the evidence that may have been violated, and that was the annual reviews....

I want the defendants -- and I know they're going to continue to post, and they have a right to post just as anybody else does -- but I want them to maintain a list of their aliases that they use. They can provide a copy of that to their attorneys, so there's no doubt about what they're using and who is posting various messages....

I'm going to make these orders also within Business and Professions Code 17200. And the reason for that is that these are false statements attacking the corporation, the value of its products and its shares. I think that this is the kind of conduct that is contemplated by 17200 of the Business and Professions Code and is designed to damage the reputation of the corporations and the value of their stock and their business and their products....

Now, I've told counsel about this. I gave them a copy of an e-mail that I received unsolicited on my computer. How somebody got my e-mail address, I don't know. I know it wasn't Mr. Delfino. This is an e-mail that I will make part of the record here, because I have a copy of it here. But essentially, it's an individual in Louisiana by the name of Vince Castille, C-a-s-t-i-l-l-e, who sends me an e-mail telling me that he has been monitoring the Internet postings and discussions about this case and the jury's award and rulings of the Court. And he encloses a copy of an e-mail from somebody using the alias of "rjm2" to "dantecristo", suggesting that they can e-mail them to me and I will post them. The quote, "Screw the judge," close quote. Well, that can happen, I suppose, but I think this needs to be part of the record. And I'd just tell the defendants in this case that you're not to cooperate. It would be a violation of this order to do indirectly what you can't do directly.

All right. Now, what I'm going to do -- and I also want to issue a no contact order here. I don't want Mr. Delfino or Ms. Day to contact any of the plaintiffs, plaintiffs' employees who are not their friends, anybody that's been referred to in this case who would not consent to that contact, either by mail, e-mail, by personal contact or otherwise. I'm hoping that will not be a problem.

FALCON: Will that be mutual, Your Honor?

KOMAR: No. It will not be mutual. And it's not funny.

DAY: It's scary.

And while it *was* scary, Mary and I and our attorneys were the *only* ones ever threatened in this case:

"The FBI is investigating online death threats against two Internet gadflies who've been locked in a bitter legal battle for years with their former Palo Alto company over their own inflammatory Web postings.

In a strange twist to an already heated cyberspace conflict, investigators expect to file charges against the author of several months' worth of threatening e-mails and message-board postings directed at Los Altos residents Mary Day and Michael Delfino, according to federal law enforcement officials. The suspect has not been identified, but usually goes by the Internet name "crack_smoking_jesus'" in his Yahoo messages and e-mails.

The threats have been linked to a court case brought against Day and Delfino by Varian ...

Since April ... a Yahoo user has delivered graphic threats to Day, Delfino and their ... lawyers, including specific threats to kill Delfino.

Day and Delfino believe that all the threats have come from the same person, although different online names have been used, including "here_comes_the_scythe,'" who warned: "It will be hard to post when you're DEAD.'"

Both federal and state law make cyber-stalking a crime. "Hopefully, they'll get to the bottom of this craziness,'" Delfino said Thursday.

The threats are an ironic turn to the case because it is Varian that has complained that Delfino and Day have crossed the line for years in what they post on the Internet, much of it caustic and often very personal criticism about company officials and their attorneys....

Day and Delfino ... maintain their comments are protected free speech and nothing more than "opinion and hyperbole as Day put it Thursday. Day and Delfino continue to maintain and update a detailed Web site devoted to bashing Varian, vowing on it to "post until we're dead.'"

Day and Delfino say their Web site is different than the threats they are receiving, which have included references to their children as well. "These threats have ranged up to the point of being pretty scary,'" Day said....

Lynne Hermle, who ... is harshly critical of Day and Delfino's past conduct, said she was unaware of the FBI probe and could not comment further....."[121]

No matter how hard The Orrick tried to vilify us, nothing we had ever posted was of a criminal nature – we followed the law. But our adversaries, the Varian loyalists, crossed the line.

"What started out as an offbeat Internet libel suit over inflammatory message-board postings has escalated to a full-scale Web war involving death threats....

Mr. Delfino sees the irony in arguing for the right to post what he wants but draws a line. It is one thing, he says, "to go onto a message board and say Mike Delfino is a horse's ass. In that case, I respect your opinion. But saying you're going to kill me ... that's different.""[122]

Not longer limited to just threatening to kill Mary and me in Yahoo! message board postings, beginning April 12, the perpetrators started emailing me directly via Yahoo!:

"It's coming, motherfucker, and you won't see it. I seriously hope you have health insurance because you're going to get your ass stomped by me and some friends. The best part will be you won't be able to prove it was me- I already have proof I was somewhere else.

You can look forward to all of your fingers getting broken, several kicks to the ribs and mouth, break some teeth, and a cracked head.

---

[121]Howard Mintz, *San Jose Mercury News*, August 1, 2002.
[122]Allyce Bess, *The Wall Street Journal*, August 8, 2002.

Also, your car will be trashed and your computer destroyed. Maybe set your place on fire so you can be evicted. If your cunt is there, she'll take a little ride to the parts of San Jose where they don't speak english, and she can walk home from there- naked. You'll be left somewhere equally unpleasant but much farther away.

You think this is all clever little games- but your mommy and your lawyer won't be around to save you from this. And remember: you can't be on guard 24 hours a day. You won't always have whatever weapon you think will protect you. And you'll never know when the hammer is coming down on YOU.

Die, motherfucker. You'll wish you had."

Die, motherfucker? Emails like this really do scare the bejesus out of me. This same lunatic even went so far as to send a number of life-threatening emails directly Glynn – we alerted the police.

Komar's absurd notion that we are a threat to Varian and Varian not a menace to us and our families made me smirk and Mary gasp, "It's scary." This parochial-minded judge didn't like us and we had certainly come to realize the danger of his prejudice.

KOMAR: It's not funny. And I don't appreciate your attitude. I'm trying to make an order here that preserves your freedoms and your rights and also preserves the rights of the other parties to that action. And I think that you're far better off if you treat this with some level of seriousness. And you've not done that thus far, either in your testimony or otherwise.

... the Court will reserve jurisdiction to modify the terms of the judgment, including the no contact order, in the event that there's a further need for enforcement or modification of that in any way. Even to the extent that if somebody can demonstrate to me that there's a need for a reciprocal or mutual restraining orders, I would certainly entertain that.

...

FALCON: Just on the clarification. You're requiring the defendants to remove prior defamatory statements. Are you talking about to Yahoo or –

KOMAR: Anywhere.

FALCON: That includes their own website reporting this litigation?

KOMAR: If there is something that is defamatory, if they have stated something as a fact as opposed to a fair and accurate report of what

was said in a proceeding, then that should be removed.
FALCON: Some of the things -- as we saw in the evidence -- like a removed posting page, which those are removed postings, some of those became evidence in this case. And so, it brings some problems. And I have a couple of other things. I'm not trying to be -- because I appreciate the spirit of the Court and what it's trying to accomplish here.

One of the problems -- it gets back to that issue of as to whether the jury should have been provided specific statements to make a determination of false or defamatory -- both sides had a right to a jury trial. Both requested a jury, and I think it was reserved by both defendants in the case.

And I had asked that that specific language be submitted to the jury. So we're in this position right now not having to second guess whether or not that was a false statement that the jury found or not a false statement.
KOMAR: The injunction is not based on the jury's findings. The injunction is based on the Court's findings of falsity....
FALCON: And I understand -- my dilemma, of course, is a right to a jury trial on those issues, I think, was reserved and preserved.
KOMAR: I'm not quarreling with your right to a jury trial. I'm telling you that the Court has other obligations other than the jury's obligations.
FALCON: I understand. As respectfully as I can put this, it puts us in a dilemma that the jury could have found statements like -- and talking to some of the jurors previously yesterday I think they were of mind that, most of what the plaintiffs were claiming were false statements, were not.

For instance, the videotaping of the bathroom, the comments that I received were that, "How come we didn't have a wrongful termination case?" ...
KOMAR: The jurors' state of mind obviously is not something the Court can take into consideration about what a juror says is right or wrong about what he or she was thinking.
FALCON: I understand that. I'm just bringing that up. But it's possible that they found that one statement was defamatory and based it on that. Especially in light of the numbers that were requested versus what they gave back. And so, it's just –
KOMAR: Mr. Falcon, I understand your consternation. The difficulty is that, if somebody says a company videotaped a bathroom, that is not in and of itself defamatory. But when somebody says that a company videotaped a bathroom and in the bathroom people were urinating and defecating, the implication is that they were taped while they were doing that, that is defamatory if it is not true....

FALCON: ... That's a good example. There was substantial evidence that went into evidence that the video camera was focused towards the men's and also caught the entrance to the men's room.

There was testimony that, when the door was opened, you could peer inside.

There was testimony that, when standing at the urinal, you could look in the mirror –

KOMAR: That testimony was not believed.

FALCON: By the Court?

KOMAR: That's right.

FALCON: But we don't know whether that was believed or not by the jury.

...

KOMAR: Here's the interesting part of this thing. Posting repetitively about that bears no relationship at all to any issue that Mr. Delfino has or that Ms. Day has. This is pure unadulterated harassment of both the company and its employees. The fact that it's false is what permits it to be enjoinable.

But the difficulty is -- and that's where you have the malice aspect -- the difficulty is there's no justification for doing that. If there's a violation of law, you report it to the proper authorities and let them do something about it. Well -- I'm not going to argue with you, Mr. Falcon.

...

FALCON: Just on that removal aspect. Assuming that there are 14-, 15,000 postings, there's a 10,000 plus website, is there a timeframe in which the Court envisioned this being accomplished?

KOMAR: I'm trying to remember the phrase that you used in Brown versus Board of Education. With all deliberate speed. Whatever that means.

FALCON: And then one last issue. On the company policies, there was another policy that came into evidence. And that was the fair treatment plan. As a matter of fact, I think Mr. Widmann argued that it was called the -- in his closing -- the treatment plan, as opposed to the fair treatment plan. And whether or not that was followed through with both his client and my client.

KOMAR: There can be reasonable differences of opinion about that. It depends on how you characterize it. If you post something that says I don't believe that I was fairly treated by the fair treatment plan –

FALCON: Correct.

KOMAR: -- that is probably a true statement. It's an expression of opinion and it relates to the personal perceptions, and the subjective evaluation. Let me ask you this, Mr. Falcon. Why are we looking for ways to say bad things?

FALCON: I'm not, Your Honor. I'm trying to avoid being down here three weeks -- in three weeks on a contempt order.

KOMAR: You may, Mr. Falcon. But I have an impression that your clients are. And I hope that's not true. But I have that impression. And every time somebody tries to skirt the line as close as they can without going over the edge, there's something about the state of mind of the person doing that that causes me to question why he would do it. What's the point?

FALCON: My only point is by maximizing the clarification -- we already know they're going to post. The Court has found that they're going to post, and what have you. Post lawfully is what they want to do. My job is to make sure that the order is clear, understandable, and can be followed.

KOMAR: ... I don't understand what would motivate somebody to do -- to want to do that. Most of the time we find those things in the criminal courts. We see them with some degree of constancy in the criminal courts. I don't expect to see that in this type of a context. But I have seen it here. All right.

POPPE: Your Honor, two very small points of clarification. With respect to the list of aliases the defendants are to provide to their attorneys, will that be provided to the plaintiffs' counsel or to the Court or how will that be dealt with? Is it just to be –

KOMAR: I just want them to have it. I want them to maintain their own list and share it with their attorneys. It's not going to be given to you. I mean, we're not in the business of censoring everything that somebody might say. We're not going to do that. I'm not going to do that. And you're not going to do that. To the extent that your clients are injured or defamed, to the extent that this court's order is not complied with, I will deal with that.

POPPE: And the other point -- I believe it's implicit -- but the prohibitory aspects of the Court's order that's being announced is effective immediately?

KOMAR: Yes.

Could this government employee really silence us?

"On of the more intriguing issues surrounding the trial is what happens if Delfino and Day lose. What sort of injunction can be crafted to protect Varian and its executives while preserving the defendants' free-speech rights?

And what if they violate the order? Will they be thrown in jail? ...

"I have confidence that should [Superior Court Judge Jack Komar] find there to be violations, he will fashion an order that protects legitimate First Amendment rights and stops the defamatory harassment that their people have engaged in for years," said Lynne Hermle...."" [123]

While the Grande Dame sounds rather reasonable, the reality is she had to hope we'd violate the injunction, be found in contempt, and get carted off to jail. Once in jail and becoming a part of the criminal system, our ability to fight back in the courts would be severely curtailed. Mary and I certainly had no intention of going down that route. We were mindful that Varian had us under surveillance even before the lawsuit and how The Orrick had produced a mountain of apocryphal evidence to argue for contempt in Federal court. Now, the stakes were higher than ever and Varian was running out of options.

On the morning of January 16, 2002, all four trial attorneys returned to Komar's court room with the specific notion of signing off on the final judgment and ironing out the details of restricting our Internet posting repertoire. The roguish Poppe once again sensing a kill, submitted a declaration in support of the form of the judgment with yet another futile undertaking:

> "Attached ... is a ... printout of an Internet message posted on the Yahoo!/VAR message board ... along with a printout of the web page to which the message links. I believe that the message was posted by Michelangelo Delfino and/or Mary Day. The message, posted under the alias "semen_on_my_mind," implies that Dick Levy and Susan Felch have engaged in sexual activities with each other. It also includes the name of a Varian officer (Richard Levy) in the title...."

Although Mary and I had never seen any such posting on the Internet, we had had enough of POOP's lunacy and not being believed by this judge. We did not attend the hearing, and remained at home doing what we do best -- posting messages on the Internet. We continued to post like bunnies using the guidelines from Komar's yet to be finalized injunction. Uncertain about the injunction's impact on our SLAPP Web sites, we created new sites

---

[123]Craig Anderson, *San Francisco Daily Journal*, November 27, 2001.

that we believed complied with his censorship. This posting I did on the Silicon Investor VSEA board on January 15, 2002 included a hyperlink to our newly created "dicketal" Web sites:

> **VSEA's Chairman talks about wife!!** from: ima_posta2
> Linda Aurelio has a picture of another man, oh my!!
> http://www.geocities.com/dicketal/aurelio.html

This Web site juxtaposed Adolph Hitler's picture with Aurelio's trial testimony. Other "dicketal" Web sites used color still-photos from Felch's and Levy's videotaped depositions coupled with images of toilets and urinals to communicate the truth about Varians' bathroom videotaping exploits. The photograph of Felch was especially entertaining in that it showed her sticking her finger in her ear demonstrating her infamous telephone gesture while being deposed.

Our favorite [http://www.geocities.com/dicketal/yenta3.html], titled, "Urinating or Defecating in VARIAN is Not Without Risk!" included a deposition photograph of Dick Levy and a larger black and white photograph of a Nazi soldier with an apparent gastrointestinal problem squatting in an open field captioned, "Varian's hostile work environment." Since our speech was being censored, we figured that like Kathy Hibbs, a picture was worth a thousand words.

From what little we were later told by Glynn and Randy, nothing much was accomplished that January 16 morning in Komar's court room and another hearing was scheduled for the first week of February.

On February 4, two days before this second Komar final "final judgment" hearing, Glynn wrote Poppe expressing my good faith offer to settle this remarkably acrimonious litigation:

"My client, Michelangelo Delfino, has authorized me to convey to you and to your clients the following settlement offer:

Varian Medical Systems will call a press conference and issue the following statement:

"Varian Medical Systems, Inc., CEO and President Richard M. Levy accepts full responsibility for the hostile work environment that blossomed under him as then Executive Vice President of Varian Associates, Inc. On behalf of his company, Mr. Levy deeply regrets the actions that occurred under him and that it has taken against Mary E. Day, the President and Michelangelo Delfino, the Vice President of MoBeta, Inc. in which it sought to silence their truthful reporting of such events on the Internet. Varian Semiconductor Equipment Associates, Inc., and its Chairman Richard A. Aurelio join Mr. Levy and Varian Medical Systems, Inc. in this expression of regret and together with Varian Executives George A. Zdasiuk and Susan B. Felch, and Lynne C. Hermle, Esq. and Matthew H. Poppe, Esq. of the Orrick, Herrington & Sutcliffe law firm apologize for all harm they may have caused, and promise that they will never again engage in any efforts to restrain free speech of anyone in the future. All deeply believe in the Constitution of the United States and of the State of California, and in the civil rights contained therein and in the Bill of Rights."

Said statement will immediately appear on Business Wire and on the Orrick Home Page for one year. It is to be contained in the Annual Stockholders Report of both Varian corporations in the form of a full page display with the following commentary:

"Ms. Day and Dr. Delfino forgive the two Varian corporations, their chief executives, the Felch and Zdasiuk families, and their highly-paid attorneys for violating American civil liberties and only hope that they have learned from their unfortunate mistakes. It is time to move on, a time for a better corporate America."

In return, Delfino/Day ask for no money, will stop posting 30 days after issuance of the press conference, and remove all Internet web pages within their control. Plaintiffs will not execute or attempt to collect on their respective judgments. After one year, plaintiffs will file a satisfaction/waiver of judgment.

I believe Mr. Widmann will also be conveying the same offer from his client, Ms. Day."

Actually, Mary had no interest whatsoever in settling, always quick to say, "They have nothing I want." In any event, my settlement offer was not even seriously acknowledged until March 12, 2002, when Poppe finally wrote Glynn, "... Plaintiffs have rejected Delfino's offer and do not intend to consider it further...." All four plaintiffs?

Assuring ourselves that Felch and Zdasiuk were made aware of my settlement letter we posted it. And it certainly helped make for entertaining dialogue on the Yahoo! VAR board:

> **and really deluded** by: <u>youarenutzzz</u>
> Dude, and Mary, you are really nuts! If you lawyer wrote that
> without a gun (or a sledgehammer[sic]) aimed at his head you
> should fire him and sue for malpractice! If you wrote it for
> him, most likely given your recent correspondence about your
> poverty, check yourselves into the nearest mental home and
> get on a lithium drip, fast 'cause you are both clearly crazy!!!!!

On that same day, Glynn's February 4 letter to Poppe gave
some indication of how well Komar's final judgment was coming:

> "You should be proud of your work; so, too, with your proposed
> judgment. So, please don't play hide the ball with me. What are the
> changes? What is different than what the judge wanted or said? What
> is your reasoning for the additions, deletions, modifications, etc.?
> Send me the redline version together with your explanations.
> You could have easily sent me this, it is common with all word
> processors to redline and compare versions. Otherwise, we should put
> Feb 6th off for another week so I can have time to do what you
> should have done for us. Please give the information requested...."

This judge was having his problems. Komar's third final "final
judgment" hearing took place on the morning of February 6. And it
turned out to be as productive as his January 16 hearing where he
and the attorneys argued the critical language of this ever-
regressing free-speech injunction. Once again, the grumpy Komar,
signed nothing and told all four attorneys to return a week later.

Randy explained part of the problem in this February 11, 2002
letter to Poppe:

> "I simply do not understand why you are insisting on including
> things in the judgment that Judge Komar has not authorized. In your
> cover letter to Mr. Falcon and me you again state you are inserting
> things the Judge has not authorized or ordered.
> Please remove items from the judgment or at least identify them
> in some manner so that Judge Komar, Mr. Falcon and I will have the
> opportunity to see precisely what you are doing....
> There are other provisions I would address, but those are
> primarily for Judge Komar to take a look at. I would suggest that if
> you would stop trying to include things that weren't ordered by the
> court, this process would have been over by now."

On the afternoon of February 13, a mentally drained Komar signed the judgment and it was finally filed. We did not see it until the following afternoon. It was given to us in sealed envelopes by Varian's *miles gloriosus* Craig Moro as we entered the company's annual stockholder meeting:

> "This cause came on regularly for trial on October 22, 2001, in Department 22 of the above-entitled court, the Honorable Jack Komar, Judge, presiding. Plaintiffs Varian Medical Systems, Inc., Varian Semiconductor Equipment Associates, Inc., Susan B. Felch, and George Zdasiuk appeared by their attorneys Lynne Hermle, Esq. and Matthew Poppe, Esq; defendant Michelangelo Delfino appeared by his attorney Glynn Falcon; and defendant Mary E. Day appeared by her attorney Randall Widmann, Esq.
>
> A jury of twelve persons was regularly impaneled and sworn to try the action. Witnesses were sworn and examined. After hearing the evidence, the arguments of counsel, and instructions of court, the jury retired to consider their verdict, subsequently returned to court, and being called, duly rendered their verdict in writing, in words and figures. The jury's verdict, signed by the foreperson and dated December 13, 2001, is attached hereto ...
>
> Following the rendering of the verdict, a second phase of the trial was held related to punitive damages. Witnesses were sworn and examined. After hearing the evidence, the arguments of counsel, and instructions of the court, the jury retired to consider their verdict on punitive damages, subsequently returned to court, and being called, duly rendered their verdict in writing, in words and figures. The jury's verdict on punitive damages, signed by the foreperson and dated December 17, 2001, is attached hereto ...
>
> WHEREFORE, by virtue of the law, and by reason of the premises aforesaid, IT IS ORDERED, ADJUDGED, and DECREED that:
>
> 1. plaintiff Susan B. Felch have and recover from defendant Michelangelo Delfino the sum of $75,000.00 in compensatory damages and $100,000.00 in punitive damages;
> 2. plaintiff Susan B. Felch have and recover from defendant Mary E. Day the sum of $75,000.00 in compensatory damages and $100,000.00 in punitive damages;
> 3. plaintiff George Zdasiuk have and recover from defendant Michelangelo Delfino the sum of $75,000.00 in compensatory

damages and $100,000.00 in punitive damages;

4. plaintiff George Zdasiuk have and recover from defendant Mary E. Day the sum of $50,000.00 in compensatory damages and $50,000.00 in punitive damages;

5. plaintiff Varian Medical Systems, Inc. have and recover from defendant Michelangelo Delfino the sum of $50,000.00 in compensatory damages;

6. plaintiff Varian Medical Systems, Inc. have and recover from defendant Mary E. Day the sum of $25,000.00 in compensatory damages;

7. plaintiff Varian Semiconductor Equipment Associates, Inc. have and recover from defendants Michelangelo Delfino the sum of $50,000.00 in compensatory damages;

8. plaintiff Varian Semiconductor Equipment Associates, Inc. have and recover from defendant Mary E. Day the sum of $25,000.00 in compensatory damages;

9. plaintiffs Susan B. Felch, George Zdasiuk, Varian Medical Systems, Inc., and Varian Semiconductor Equipment Associates, Inc. have and recover from defendants Michelangelo Delfino and Mary E. Day their costs of suit;

each said amount with interest theron at a rate of ten percent (10%) per annum from the date of the entry of this judgment until paid."

The Orrick even tried to order that our SLAPP bill be phrased as "jointly and severally." This would have meant that if one of us had died, the other would be accountable for the total amount due. The fact that I am 6 years older and a male who is statistically predicted to die 5.4 years earlier than Mary did not stop us from joking -- now we really were joined at the hip. But the ever-equitable Judge Komar didn't buy that line, and at the February 6 meeting, he voided "jointly and severally" from the judgment.

Prior to this SLAPP, we were by any standards a financially well-off couple. As of February 19, 2002, we were broke having paid our attorneys $822,000. Maybe Edmund Burke, the famed 18th century British politician, gave it some rationale when he said, "The only thing necessary for the triumph of evil is for good men [and women] to do nothing."

On February 28, The Orrick added $134,246.88 in legal costs. The stick-like Poppe summarized the cost breakdown as follows:

Models, blowups, and photocopies of exhibits	$66,525.84
Deposition costs	$30,087.11
Service of process	$19,718.51
Court reporter fees as established by statute	$ 6,930.36
Jury fees	$ 6,463.35
Other	$ 2,030.75
Witness fees	$ 1,395.96
Filing and motion fees	$ 1,095.00

This brought the total judgment against us to $909,246.88. We were long past the point where the amount of money we owed had any meaning. The 10% interest alone was beyond our means. Considering that neither of us had had any earnings for more than three years and our prospects for making serious money ever again were gone, the whole situation once ludicrous, was now tragic.

Nine months into the SLAPP, a then deflated Hermle told a news reporter, "... the cost of pursuing cases against individuals is probably more than companies could hope to recover."[124] So then why do it?

It was widely rumored that Varian had paid the Orrick, Herrington & Sutcliffe law firm more than $5,500,000 in legal fees alone. This bill too could have been added to the judgment but it would have required an itemization of all the monies Varian had spent on Zdasiuk and Felch's personal lawsuits – something I suspect the IRS would find useful as well as the VAR and VSEA stockholders.

As of this writing, Orrick's clients have not collected a dime. And Mary and I continue to post on the Internet every single day. The SLAPP had failed. It was still not clear what anyone had won.

On March 12, 2002, a befuddled Glynn wrote Poppe:

"I have wondered why a firm would use legal tactics that drain all of defendants' financial resources, yet all the time seeking vast monetary awards which they know they have no hope of ever being

---

[124] Craig Anderson, *San Francisco Daily Journal*, November 30, 1999.

able to collect? I have no answer. I have also wondered how a multi-million dollar legal campaign justifies a $775,000 piece of paper. I have no answer...."

After creating a million dollar piece of paper, Herr Komar ordered:

"WHEREFORE, by virtue of the law, and by reason of the premises aforesaid, IT IS FURTHER ORDERED, ADJUDGED, and DECREED as follows:

1. Michelangelo Delfino and Mary Day may not publish, post, or otherwise disseminate, directly or indirectly on the Internet or elsewhere, any written statement that is untrue, expressly or by implication, with regard to any person identified in subparagraphs (a)-(w) below in any of the ways specified therein, which the Court finds are untrue, except that this paragraph 1 does not prohibit Michelangelo Delfino or Mary E. Day from making statements about matters that may occur after the date of the trial:

a. that Susan Felch or George Zdasiuk is or was a liar or chronic liar;
b. that Susan Felch, George Zdasiuk, Richard Aurelio, Richard Levy, or any of their spouses has engaged in adultery or extramarital affairs or is or was sexually promiscuous;
c. that Susan Felch, George Zdasiuk, or James Fair is or was a danger to children or others;
d. that Susan Felch, George Zdasiuk, Varian Associates, Inc., Varian Medical Systems, Inc., or Varian Semiconductor Equipment Associates, Inc., or any of their officers, directors, employees, agents, or representatives videotaped children or videotaped any bathroom, restroom, lavatory, or similar place, or videotaped any person inside any such place, or videotaped any activity inside any such place (including but not limited to statements that any person was videotaped "going to the bathroom" or using the bathroom" or "performing bodily functions");
e. that James Fair is or was homosexual;
f. that Susan Felch or George Zdasiuk is or was mentally unstable or mentally ill or suffers from hallucinations;
g. that Susan Felch sabotaged a PLAD experiment or process or any other experiment or process at her employment;
h. that Susan Felch had a semen stain on her dress or other clothing or had sex with a supervisor;
i. that Megan Gray said that Susan Felch had a semen stain on her dress or other clothing or had sex with a supervisor;

361

j. that Susan Felch or George Zdasiuk stalks other persons, including but not limited to Michelangelo Delfino and Mary Day;

k. that George Zdasiuk is or was homophobic;

l. that George Zdasiuk discriminates on the basis of gender or pregnancy;

m. that George Zdasiuk has stared at or regularly stares at female employee's breasts or chests in the course of his employment;

n. that Varian Associates, Inc., Varian Medical Systems, Inc., Varian Semiconductor Equipment Associates, Inc., or any of their present or former officers or supervisors produced pornography in the workplace or downloaded from the Internet, or that they allowed others to produce pornography in the workplace or download pornography from the Internet;

o. that any present or former Varian officer, director, or employee of Varian Associates, Inc., Varian Semiconductor Equipment Associates, Inc., or Varian Medical Systems, Inc. sent pornography to or forced pornography on any of those companies' present or former employees, including but not limited to Michelangelo Delfino;

p. that Richard Levy or Richard Aurelio has lied under oath or has committed perjury or is being or has been investigated for perjury;

q. that Megan Gray is or was a liar;

r. that Varian Associates, Inc., Varian Medical Systems, Inc., Varian Semiconductor Equipment Associates, Inc., managers, past or present, violated company policies, except that certain written performance reviews were not timely prepared by some managers;

s. that Varian Associates, Inc., Varian medical Systems, Inc., Varian Semiconductor Equipment Associates, Inc., or any their present or former officers, directors, employees, agents, or representatives destroyed evidence in this case or wrongfully reused the tapes used in connection with the camera that was placed in Susan Felch's office in 1998;

t. that George Zdasiuk is or was an alcoholic or a drunk, or that he habitually drinks or is intoxicated, or that he was drunk or intoxicated at work or during any deposition or other court proceeding;

u. that George Zdasiuk was not upset by the death of his sister, or by the death of his father, or by the World Trade center disaster on September 11, 2001;

v. that Varian Associates, Inc., Varian Medical Systems, Inc., Varian Semiconductor Equipment Associates, Inc., or any their present of former officers, directors, or employees, created, fostered, supported, or permitted the existence of a hostile work environment, or that a hostile work environment existed at that Varian Associates, Inc., Varian medical Systems, Inc., Varian Semiconductor Equipment Associates, Inc.; or

w. that Susan Felch or George Zdasiuk harassed Michelangleo Delfino, Mary E. Day, or any other person, either in the workplace or elsewhere.

This paragraph 1 shall not be construed as a general prohibition on defamatory statements. Only written statements that defame any person identified in subparagraphs (a)-(w), above in any of the ways specified therein, all of which were shown to be false and defamatory, are prohibited by this paragraph 1. In addition, this paragraph 1 shall not be construed to prohibit Michelangelo Delfino and Mary E. Day from publishing fair and true reports of the proceedings in this action or other statements that are privileged under California Civil Code section 47."

Mary and I were stunned by this injunction. Not only did it prohibit us from posting demonstrably true statements, like "Felch videotaped two public restrooms," it also prevented us from posting about issues that were undisputed at trial. For example, no one refuted my December 29 trial testimony:

DELFINO: ... And then there was reference to all these accusations about people having sexual relationships.
FALCON: Were those your accusations?
DELFINO: I never made any accusations about that.

Not in our wildest dreams did we ever believe we would be prohibited from saying the Dicks' wives, Susan Levy and Linda Aurelio, are not engaged in extramarital affairs. Neither had been tried for adultery. If Komar actually knew who at Varian was fornicating whom that in itself was probably more interesting than this book. However, Komar's chastity announcement became an incredibly popular subject for the Internet. Mary posted this on the Raging Bull VAR board on March 13, 2002:

> **Susan Levy is not an adulterer** by: hayca
> according to a California judge. Now THAT is good news.
> But what does she think about her SLAPPing Dick?

And no one ever denied that pornography was produced at Varian under Dick Levy's nose:

WIDMANN: Now, this is a posting you made, ma'am?

DAY: I believe so.

WIDMANN: When you used the phrase "pornographic material," what did you have in mind? What were you referring to?

DAY: Because it says Varian equipment, which is relating to Kwok Lai, K-w-o-k L-a-i, printing pornographic material on Varian equipment.

WIDMANN: We won't go through that testimony again. But did you hear Mr. Delfino testify [Nov 29] about that, ma'am?

"There are two issues with pornography. Ron Powell, during his deposition, showed the pornography that he forced on me when he was my boss. That's the first thing. The second thing is there was a guy named Kwok Lai who printed pornography using Varian equipment. It was all over -- I mean, one day it actually got ludicrous, because he left the printer on -- and I'm not exaggerating -- it was a stack coming out like this (indicating several inches). And it was Mary Day, Ferdinand Engayo, Steve Henderson and myself. And one of us jokingly said, "Is there any way you can stop the computer?" And Henderson went, "No, I can't.""

DAY: Yes.

WIDMANN: Did you witness what you consider to be pornographic material being printed by that?

DAY: I was the one that complained. I went to see if Henderson could get access to the printer. We both went over to the printer, because it would get jammed, and nobody could use it. So he dealt with it.

And Henderson was never allowed to testify about the seriousness of Varians' pornography problem:

FALCON: From time to time when you would be called in to fix computer problems within the lab, within the research center, did you ever discover that people had downloaded pornography on to their computer?

HENDERSON: On the computers?

FALCON: Yeah.

McMAHON: Objection. It's not reasonably calculated to lead to the discovery of admissible evidence. It could potentially violate someone's privacy. The question is completely irrelevant to the lawsuit, Overbroad, It's vague. It's a ridiculous question. So do not answer.

364

FALCON: From time -- certify that. From time to time, did you discover that people were using their computers to either download or store pornography?

McMAHON: Same objections. Don't answer the question.

FALCON: Were you aware of anybody using Varian equipment to print pornography?

McMAHON: Objection. Same objections. Don't answer the question.

FALCON: Do you know of anybody either printing or downloading or storing pornography on their computers or were ever subject to any investigation?

McMAHON: Same objection. Don't answer the question.

FALCON: We're not trying to get to any particular identification. We're just generally looking at the practice and procedures and fairness of Varian's --

McMAHON: As far as we're aware, no issue before the Court regarding fairness of Mr. Delfino's termination, so that is an irrelevant matter, not reasonably calculated to lead to the discovery of admissible evidence. The questions are solely designed to harass and embarrass and annoy Varian in general, other employees in general, so we're not going to permit there to be any response.

FALCON: Did you ever find any pornographic material on any computer of George Zdasiuk?

McMAHON: Objection. Don't answer the question. Same series of objections.

FALCON: Did you ever find pornographic material or printouts connected with Susan Felch's computer?

McMAHON: Same objection. Don't answer the question.

Why not? Hermle knew all along she had a problem with her clients. In her December 7 closing argument, she struggled mightily to justify Zdasiuk's shortcomings as a Varian executive:

> "Well, the claim was he's [Zdasiuk's] incompetent because he didn't do annual reviews....There wasn't even any testimony that every manager at Varian does performance reviews.... At Varian it wasn't an important issue to ensure that they were timely."

She was even less skillful at masking his truly callous nature. Zdasiuk's baby sister Barbara J. Zdasiuk had been tragically killed by a drunk driver in a 1980 car accident just two weeks before her marriage. During his July 25, 2001 videotaped deposition, this soulless executive shocked everyone in the room when he

365

confessed that the personal lawsuit that he had initiated and was continuing to perpetuate was in fact more stressful than her death:

> FALCON: So this -- I want to make sure I'm perfectly clear on this. You're saying that the stress caused you by this Internet case has caused you more stress than the death of your sister?
> ZDASIUK: I believe so.

What a horribly pathetic creature!

Although his insensitivity to the loss of his five-and-a-half-year-old younger sister was for all of us unfathomable, it was news that was worthy of this loathsome SLAPP plaintiff That same evening I posted this Yahoo! VAR message:

> **SLAPP causes ZDASIUK more**
> by: michelangelo_delfino_phd
> stress than the untimely death of his baby sister!
> Is this the kind of person we want as a Varian Executive? Well, my fellow VAR stockholders that is what he said today under oath. Excuse me
> while I vomit in disgust at witnessing such a callous and unsensitive remark!

At Komar's trial, Orrick's well-rehearsed Zdasiuk acted a different role. He now played the part of the aggrieved and caring older brother:

> HERMLE: How did you feel about this posting?

> **Re: Isn't George Zdasiuk's sister dead?**
> by: zdasiuk_and_ripple
> If so, she will be saved from hearing his lies.

> ZDASIUK: I felt that this posting just sort of ripped open wounds that healed many years ago, or at least I thought they'd healed. And in here, it's just ripping this thing apart open in a really vicious manner. I don't know what else to say, but that's the way it feels, like a wound that's healed over and you think it's okay, and then somebody comes along and grabs it and just rips it open again, and it's there, it's bare. I don't know any other way to describe it.

Several witnesses had talked about Varians' hostile work environment under then Vice President Levy:

WIDMANN: Mr. Fair testified about your hitting Mr. Bennett, striking a Mr. Bennett.
POWELL: I see. What did – what was that testimony?
WIDMANN: He said he heard about it.
POWELL: Oh.
WIDMANN: What happened, did you strike Mr. Bennett?
POWELL: You mean Alan Bennett, my former boss?
WIDMANN: Correct.
POWELL: Well, that story is a gross exaggeration of facts. And --

Dr. Bennett, who reported directly to Levy soon left Varian's hostile work environment. He never testified; he never needed to testify. We had Ron Powell.[125]

---

[125]"Missing from the REC Lab computer. Administration staff have experienced problems with their computers suggesting tampering, the shed behind building 7 was broken into and expensive garden tools taken. "I reported these events to Varian security and asked for their advice on what to do. They recommended temporarily placing a surveillance camera in a high risk area. The REC Lab is such an area, borders HPM corridor used by contractors, TFS and TEL, recently has a high level activity such as M2000, DPVD and BST reactors, could be damaged by a theft or improper use of computer or hardware. I then asked Tom Boutwell to install the camera as part of the facilities work he was doing" away in that area – "doing anyway."

"I want to be clear that whenever this topic was discussed, I stated clearly that I did not believe anyone in GRC was responsible for these thefts.

Periodically GRC has experienced thefts. In fact the large bubble camera outside of my own office was a response to series of major thefts a year ago. I am particularly sensitive since as some of you know my own office was robbed of Christmas gifts and other administrative staff lost money or personal possessions as well as VCRs and camcorders from the training department. Also past history has taught me that petty thefts often escalate to major thefts if they are not quickly dealt with.

I therefore have asked Tom Boutwell to have a camera installed which was done around March 11. I wanted it to cover the area where our tools are in heaviest use. The cameras has been in place two weeks now and to my knowledge there have been no other reports of theft within GRC. I have never seen any of the video footage. In fact, the camera film to my knowledge has only been looked at once by Tom for the week of March 11-12.

But like so many things in Komar's trial, the truth of our postings was either not refuted in court, or not allowed in as evidence.

> "2. Michelangelo Delfino and Mary Day may not publish any written statement that uses any play on James Fair's name (including, but not limited to "Fairy") to suggest that he is homosexual."

We never suggested Fair was homosexual, and Fair never testified he wasn't homosexual.

> "3. Michelangelo Delfino and Mary Day may not publish any statement prohibited by paragraph 1 or paragraph 2 in any part of an Internet message, including but not limited to the body, the title, and the alias. For example, the alias varian_videotapes_bathrooms is prohibited.

> 4. Michelangelo Delfino and Mary E. Day may not use the names of Susan Felch, George Zdasiuk, or any other present or former officer, director, or employee of Varian Associates, Inc., Varian Medical Systems, Inc., or Varian Semiconductor Equipment Associates, Inc. (including but not limited to, Richard Levy, Richard Aurelio, James Fair, Ron Powell, James Hennessy, Jane Crisler, Jeffrey Wright, Craig Moro, Kathy Hibbs, Carl Herrera, Juanita Sonico, Joseph Phair, Gary Loser, and Steve Henderson), or any other person who testified as a deposition or trial witness in this case or was identified as a

---

Since we thought that someone might have taken tools out of the REC Lab that weekend following Mike's report of missing tools from his own lab that Friday. While nothing suspicious was seen, I still wanted to alert you to the possibility of additional thefts or computer tampering. I therefore e-mailed everyone at GRC on March 13 to take extra precautions. "I am obligated to protect Varian's property and feel a strong personal responsibility to protect your own property as well. Since this was a security investigation, I didn't want to broadcast where the camera was or make the thefts more of an issue than they were. Since there have been to my knowledge no other reports of missing items since the camera was put up two weeks ago, I have asked Tom to take it down....

My -- my recollection now is that there were in fact – and I think I indicated that I was concerned about thefts ... in the REC lab.... And so I think my statements earlier are a little misleading in that regard and I apologize for that. It's – I indicated that I didn't want what was going on the white board to go into the lab. But it looks like there were thefts going on in the lab and -- yeah"

potential deponent or trial witness in this case (including, but not limited to, Kevin Felch and Julie Fouquet), or any attorney who participated in the trial of this case or was referred to in connection with this case (including, but not limited to, Lynne Hermle, Matthew Poppe, Peter McMahon, Joseph Liburt, and Megan Gray), or any family member of any such person, in an alias or part of an alias in such a way that it appears to be a posting by any such person or otherwise a misappropriation or unauthorized use of such name, on the Internet or elsewhere, without the person's prior written permission, nor shall Michelangelo Delfino or Mary E. Day use any such person's name in the title of an Internet message if the message contains any statement that defames any person identified in paragraph 1(a)-(w) in any of the ways specified in that paragraph. Michelangelo Delfino and Mary E. Day may not impersonate the persons identified in this paragraph in any other way without their express prior written permission, including but not limited to impersonation by attributing to such persons, expressly or by implication, statements which they did not make.

5. Michelangelo Delfino and Mary Day may not use the names "Varian," "Varian Associates, Inc.," "Varian Medical Systems, Inc." or "VMS," or all or part of an alias, on the Internet or elsewhere, without prior written permission from an officer of Varian Medical Systems, Inc. Michelangelo Delfino and Mary Day may not use the names, or any play on the names, "Varian," "Varian Associates, Inc.," "Varian Semiconductor Equipment Associates, Inc.," or "VSEA" as all or part of an alias, on the Internet or elsewhere, without prior written permission from an officer of Varian Semiconductor Equipment Associates, Inc. Michelangelo Delfino and Mary E. Day may not use any such name in the title of an Internet message if the message contains any statement that defames any person identified in paragraph 1(a)-(w) in any of the ways specified in that paragraph.

6. Michelangelo Delfino and Mary Day may not post statement about the financial condition or any financial transactions of any present or former officer, director, or employee of Varian Associates, Inc., Varian Medical Systems, Inc., or Varian Semiconductor Equipment Associates, Inc. in the same place or on the same web site or message board where they have posted or will post any of the following:

a. a statement about the location of the person's residence;
b. a statement about where the persons' residence address can be found (such as the page and line location in the phone book);

c. a statement about the name of the person's spouse or child; or
d. a statement about where the person's spouse or child can be located.

Michelangelo Delfino and Mary Day may not post any statement listed in subparagraphs (a)-(d) above in the same place or on the same web site or message board where they have posted or will post any statement about the financial condition or any financial transactions of any present or former officer, director, or employee of Varian Associates, Inc., Varian Medical Systems, Inc., or Varian Semiconductor Equipment Associates, Inc.

7. Michelangelo Delfino and Mary Day shall remove all statements existing on any web site under their control (including but not limited to any web site whose address begins "http://www.geocities.com/mobeta_inc/slapp ...") that are untrue with regard to any person identified in paragraph 1(a)-(w) in any of the ways specified in that paragraph. This paragraph 7 shall not require the removal of statements that the Court has not found to be untrue, with the exception of the statements addressed above by paragraph 6. In addition, this paragraph 7 does not require the removal of fair and true reports of the proceedings in this action within the meaning of California Civil Code section 47(d).

8. Michelangelo Delfino and Mary Day shall take all steps needed to cause the removal of all messages containing one or more statements that defame any person identified in paragraph 1(a)-(w) in any of the ways specified in that paragraph from all Internet message boards, including but not limited to those operated by Yahoo, Raging Bull, Stock-Talk, Silicon Investor, and Motley Fool, whether such statements appear in the body of the message(s), the title of the message(s), or the alias(es). For purposes of this paragraph 8, an Internet message is "removed" when it is no longer publicly accessible. Michelangelo Delfino and Mary E. Day shall provide their current counsel (as defined below in paragraph 15) with a copy of all written correspondence between themselves or their representatives and the Internet message board operators related to their efforts to comply with this paragraph 8 within (10) days after sending or receiving the correspondence, and current counsel shall serve a copy thereof upon Lynne Hermle, Esq. and Matthew Poppe, Esq. via U.S. mail and/or facsimile within ten (10) days after sending or receiving it. If Michelangelo Delfino and Mary E. Day have no current counsel (as defined below in paragraph 15), they shall send a copy of all such correspondence directly to Ms. Hermle and Mr.

Poppe via U.S. mail and/or facsimile within ten (10) days after sending or receiving the correspondence.

9. In complying with paragraphs 7 and 8 hereof, Michelangelo Delfino and Mary Day shall act with all deliberate speed.

10. Before Plaintiffs file a motion for contempt or seek other assistance from the Court in connection with defendants' compliance or non-compliance with paragraphs 7 and 8 hereof, Plaintiffs' counsel shall meet and confer with current counsel (as such term is defined below in paragraph 15) for Michelangelo Delfino and Mary Day in an effort to resolve the dispute. All counsel shall meet and confer in good faith. If Michelangelo Delfino and Mary E. Day has no current counsel at the time of the dispute, Plaintiffs may comply with their meet-and-confer obligations under this paragraph 10 with respect to such defendant by sending a written demand for compliance directly to such defendant's last-known address and allowing him or other ten (10) days to respond to the demand.

11. Michelangelo Delfino and Mary E. Day shall maintain a written list of all aliases that either of them uses after the date of entry of this judgment to post Internet messages that make direct or indirect reference (whether in the body or title of the message or in the alias) to any person or company identified in paragraphs 4 and 5, along with all corresponding passwords (if any) and the dates during which they used or reserved the use of each such alias. Michelangelo Delfino and Mary Day shall update the list immediately upon using a new alias and/or password. Michelangelo Delfino and Mary E. Day shall within (10) days after creating or updating any such list, provide a copy of the most current version of the list of aliases (but not passwords) to their current counsel (as defined below in paragraph 15) or, if they have no current counsel, to Ms. Hermle and Mr. Poppe via U.S. mail and/or facsimile. Current counsel shall maintain each list for at least five years after receipt, except as provided below, and shall produce the lists to the Court and/or to Plaintiffs' counsel upon order of the Court. If current counsel's representation in connection with this case is terminated prior to the expiration of the five-year period, current counsel shall provide each list in his or her possession to new counsel (as defined below in paragraph 15), or, in the absence of new counsel, to Ms. Hermle and Mr. Poppe via U.S. mail and/or facsimile, and having done so shall have no further obligation to retain the lists. Any list provided to Ms. Hermle and Mr. Poppe under this paragraph 11 shall be deemed confidential and for attorneys' eyes only. If Plaintiffs wish to use the information in any such list in

connection with any proceeding in this Court, Plaintiffs shall lodge
the lost with the Court under seal in accordance with the applicable
rules of court."

It wouldn't take long even for this judge to realize the sophism
in his own injunction and in just a few weeks on March 26 he
would already be forced to face it:

WIDMANN: There is one point Your Honor hasn't addressed. And
that's the affirmative act Your Honor required of keeping a list of
aliases and turning those over to counsel. Now, Mr. Blackman is here
to represent the defendants on that on the OSC....
KOMAR: I think that could well be problematic in looking at that.
I'm just wondering whether the parties ought to be required to lodge
those aliases directly with the Court, rather than sending them to
counsel.... So I'm frankly inclined to modify that judgment to require
the parties, Mr. Delfino and Ms. Day --
BLACKMAN: Before the Court does that, may I speak to that?
KOMAR: Let me finish what I'm saying, Mr. Blackman. I'm inclined
to consider modifying the judgment in order to require that they lodge
the list of their aliases that they use with the Court in a sealed
document. That is, not to be opened other than by order of the Court.
    And the reason for that is to avoid putting counsel in the position
where they feel that they are violating some privilege or some right
that belongs to the parties or the attorney-client relationship. And as I
indicated to you, I thought -- apparently incorrectly -- that counsel
were agreeable to the process. In fact, I thought that was something
that had been essentially worked out by the parties. Apparently it was
not.
    Now, Mr. Blackman, you want to address that?
BLACKMAN: Yes. Thank you. I've been asked to offer some
comments to the Court on the questions in the civil litigation that
essentially fall into the criminal law area.
    From my perspective, my advice to my clients from a criminal
perspective is to object and to advise them to not, in fact, provide the
alias list, because to do so bridges their privilege against self-
incrimination...
    These individuals have a privilege against self-incrimination as to
whatever testimonial thrust there would be in providing this
information. They would also have a privilege against self-
incrimination as to the production of the alias names, which would be
essentially a document which would, at least under the plaintiffs'
theory, incriminate themselves. So it gets into a very complicated,

very difficult area as to a privilege against self-incrimination that clearly applies as to a contempt proceeding.

We're sitting here under certainly no surprise by the plaintiffs who, by seeking to pursue an OSC in re contempt, are inviting the Court to essentially undertake a criminal prosecution. They become prosecutors. Criminal court rules apply; proof beyond a reasonable doubt, each of the elements.

And there's clear authority for the proposition that, as to Ms. Day and Mr. Delfino, they each have privileges against self-incrimination, both testimonial and the production of documents, each of which is brought into effect when the Court specifically orders that these alias lists be produced. And additionally, to make the situation even more complicated, in our view, that represents something that the Court is affirmatively requiring that they do. And it gets back into the area of is it mandatory or prohibitory. And our view is it is clearly mandatory and it is stayed by operation of law because of the filing of the appeal.

And these issues strike in a particular way -- this case as a civil case -- but they strike, in my view, in a dramatically different way if the Court accepts the invitation by the plaintiffs to convert this into a criminal action because of the operation of the privilege against self-incrimination, and also the operation of the rules that deal with whether a judgment is stayed by operation of law when an appeal is filed.

...

KOMAR: I understand that, Mr. Blackman. And I'm not necessarily disagreeing with you. For example, in this type of a situation, that if the plaintiffs were to subpoena the hard drive of your clients' computer, that your clients are subject to the authority of the Court and the subpoena power and would be required to turn that over. And obviously an expert can go into that hard drive and get whatever information they want....

The ever accommodating judge had no qualms about inviting Orrick into our homes and into our computers. No longer naïve enough to believe Komar fair and impartial, we had Jim Blackman, a well-respected Palo Alto, California criminal defense attorney and long-time buddy of Randy, add to our representation.

"12. Michelangelo Delfino and Mary E. Day may not engage in any of the following conduct toward Susan Felch, Kevin Felch, George Zdasiuk, Julie Fouquet, Richard Levy, Richard Aurelio, James Fair, Ron Powell, James Hennessy, Jane Crisler, Jeffrey Wright, Craig Moro, Kathy Hibbs, Carl Herrera, Juanita Sonico, Steve Henderson,

Stephen Melvin, Ph.D., Joseph Phair, Gary Loser, or any such person's family member, without such person's prior permission:

> a. contacting, molesting, harassing, threatening, following, stalking, or attacking any such person;
> b. knowingly going to within 100 yards of any such person's place of residence, employment, or schooling, except that Michelangelo Delfino and Mary E. Day may go to and be at Mary Day's children's schools, but must comply with the other provisions of this paragraph 12;
> c. communication or attempting to communicate with any such person in any manner, including, but not limited to, via mail, email, facsimile, or telephone; or
> d. dialing the telephone number of any such person.
> In addition, Michelangelo Delfino and Mary E. Day shall stay at least thirty (30) yards away from each such person at all times, except for peaceful contacts related to court proceedings.

13. Michelangelo Delfino and Mary Day may not:

> a. approach within 500 yards of any Varian Medical Systems, Inc. or Varian Semiconductor Equipment Associates, Inc. facility without prior permission from an officer of the pertinent corporation; or
> b. dial any Varian Medical Systems, Inc. or Varian Semiconductor Equipment Associates, Inc. telephone number without prior permission from an officer of the pertinent corporation or the person whose number is dialed, except that Michelangelo Delfino and Mary E. Day may telephone each corporation's designated investor relations number, if any, with legitimate investor concerns or questions if they own stock in the corporation in question at the time of the telephone call."

Before Mary and I attended the VAR 2002 stockholder meeting on February 14, we notified the Palo Alto police. We told them of the Court's tentative order and they said they would not get involved unless there was an incident. The officer gave Mary her cell phone number just in case. With all this in hand, we entered the Sheraton Hotel and took our seats like the other attendees. Other than Zdasiuk being so rattled that he bumbled through his five minute slide show, the meeting was unremarkable. But Randy still had to write Poppe the following day:

"I am in receipt of your latest letter accusing my client of violating the judgment of the court. That is patently untrue. My client has not violated any judgment of the court nor has she ever violated any orders of the courts. Please be sure of your facts before making such accusations in the future.

Of greater concern to me is the fact that the judgment you had Judge Komar sign does not conform with what was discussed in chambers. Just taking a quick look at the judgment when I saw it yesterday morning, I noticed you didn't change the 500 yards to 100 yards [On September 2nd Poppe made the change] as was discussed.

It also doesn't include a provision for Ms. Day's attending and Mr. Delfino's attending business meetings and seminars and, of course, shareholder meetings, again, all of which was discussed in chambers with Judge Komar. Why aren't these provisions included and why did you not make the changes that we have discussed at length with Judge Komar?

Also of concern is the fact that my clients were informed that the police department was informed that they were going to attend the shareholder meeting and that you clients were intending to enforce a thirty (30) yard stay away order of some sort. As you know, my client is entitled to go to shareholder meetings. The judge made that very clear. The reason my client contacted the police in the first place was to make sure that nothing untoward would happen...."

Herr Komar's incomprehensible restrictions, prohibitions, and commands seemed endless.

"14. Michelangelo Delfino and Mary Day may not do indirectly what they are prohibited in paragraphs 1, 2, 3, 4, 5, 6, 12, and 13 from doing directly. Michelangelo Delfino and Mary Day may not encourage, aid, abet, or conspire with any other person to engage in any such conduct. In particular, Michelangelo Delfino and Mary E. Day may not communicate any message that would violate this order to another person for the purpose of having the other person post it on the Internet or with the expectation that the other person will do so.

15. For purposes of paragraphs 8, 10, and 11 hereof, "current counsel" initially shall mean Glynn Falcon, Esq. and Randall Widmann, Esq. If Mr. Falcon and/or Mr. Widmann ceases to represent Michelangelo Delfino and Mary E. day in connection with this case, "current counsel" shall mean the attorney(s) who most recently have agree to represent Michelangelo Delfino and/or Mary E. Day in connection with this action, provided that said attorneys

have agreed to execute and have executed a Substitution of Counsel form in the form attached hereto as Exhibit C and have provided a copy of the executed Substitution of Counsel form to their predecessors, to Plaintiffs' counsel, and to the Court. Each such attorney shall be deemed "new counsel" with respect to his or her immediate predecessor, if any.

In addition, the Court granted the motion for directed verdict brought by cross-defendants Varian Medical Systems, Inc. and Varian Semiconductor Equipment Associates, Inc. with respect to cross-claimant Michelangelo Delfino's cross-complaint for breach of contract. In accordance with that ruling, a verdict was entered in favor of cross-defendants Varian Medical Systems, Inc. and Varian Semiconductor Equipment Associates, Inc. against cross-claimant Michelangelo Delfino on the cross-complaint.

WHEREFORE, by virtue of the law, and by reason of the premises aforesaid, IT IS ORDERED, ADJUDGED, AND DECREED that judgment is entered in favor of cross-defendants Varian Medical Systems, Inc. and Varian Semiconductor Equipment Associates, Inc.; that cross-complainant Michelangelo Delfino have and recover nothing against cross-defendants Varian Medical Systems, Inc. and Varian Semiconductor Equipment Associates, Inc. on his cross-complaint for breach of contract; and that cross-defendants Varian Medical Systems, Inc. and Varian Semiconductor Equipment Associates, Inc. have and recover from cross-complainant Michelangelo Delfino their costs of suit...."

Who exactly is Jack Komar?

"Santa Clara County Superior Court Judge Jack Komar's response to being a victim of a hate crime this summer was to hide his Jewish past. And he got the *Mercury News* to help....

The judge is angered and upset that the firebombing incident is about to bring to light an obscure and little-known fact, a detail from his "personal life" that he tried to keep out of media reports: Jack Komar was born Jewish. The child of a Jewish mother, he converted to Roman Catholicism in 1962, when he was 25 years old.... The *Mercury News*, the lead media organization covering the crime, was aware of Komar's background during its coverage of the firebombing and aftermath, but deliberately omitted this detail from news stories at Judge Komar's request." [126]

---

[126]J. Douglas Allen Taylor, *Metro*, December 23, 1999.

How sad, I thought, to fear disclosing who you really are.

Komar viewed Mary and I as reprehensible for airing Varians' secrets. He made it very clear that he believed our Internet presence immoral. But morality was not on trial. He treated us as criminals and not as civil defendants. And he didn't like our legal defense. Randy, who was immediately admonished by Komar for warning the jurors they would hear the word "fuck," later said:

> "My clients believe quite strongly that the Constitution of the United States provides that you may not like what people say, you may not agree with what they say and some of the language may be offensive and profane, but it's your right to speak out."[127]

When confronted with real criminals, the perpetrators of the death threats, Komar still couldn't make the distinction between lawful and unlawful behavior:

> "I think anybody who is making the kind of threats that are being made here deserves to be tracked down and prosecuted and handled appropriately....
>
> I think that anybody who is the subject of those kinds of threats is entitled to take whatever reasonable action needed to take to protect themselves and others who may be affected by the threats....
>
> I am appalled at the messages that have been sent in this case. I'm appalled at the messages that you have received or that indirectly you've received that reference you and your clients. I have been appalled, if you will, as I have reviewed all of the record in this case from the very beginning.
>
> I think what is happening now is an extreme, and it's worse, because it is a physical threat. And if I had the ability to do something about it, I would. I don't."

As soon as the Komar Chill was official, the press reacted:

> "A Santa Clara County judge has ventured into unchartered territory by issuing a sweeping permanent injunction ...
>
> He began crafting the order even before a jury awarded $775,000 in damages ...

---

[127]Shannon Lafferty, *The Recorder*, November 5, 2001.

The order is unusual on several counts.... it was rare for such a case to reach a jury.... it prevents the pair even from posting information within the public record under certain circumstances....

According to ... Lynne Hermle, the defendants already are testing Komar's order....

"Unfortunately, it appears from the postings that it is unlikely [Delfino] is going to obey the judge's order," said Hermle ...

Nevertheless, she said she was pleased the judgment is in place and "confident Judge Komar will enforce it."

Delfino, interviewed Thursday, said he has posted on the Yahoo message board since receiving a copy of the injunction....

"My intent is to post every day, period," he said. "The injunction is in no way going to stop me from exercising my First Amendment privilege."

Komar's order bars Delfino and Day from making a long list of statements, such as calling 19 Varian employee liars, sexually promiscuous or mentally unstable....

Delfino and Day are prohibited from posting information from Securities and Exchange Commission documents concerning Varian "in the same place or on the same Web site or message board" as information about executives' home addresses or family members.

Komar also ordered the defendants to remove posts containing any statements he has found to be false.

Delfino said Komar never identified a single libelous post and has overstepped his legal bounds. One of the forbidden topics is an allegation that Varian videotaped an employee bathroom. The company acknowledges setting up a camera ... but says it never taped anyone inside the bathroom. Delfino argued the device did indeed peek inside the facility and says Komar's order prevents him from merely telling the truth.

He sees that as grounds for appeal.

"The injunction is only as good as your weakest link," he said. Delfino said he has written Yahoo and other companies that operate message boards asking that all of his and Day's posts be deleted. He said that meets their legal obligation...."[128]

Almost immediately and to no surprise, Orrick did what we all knew they had to do in order to try and win this SLAPP -- shut us up once and for all. In the weeks that followed the injunction, Orrick would search our Web sites and monitor the message boards looking for anything that might be used to lay a foundation

---

[128]Craig Anderson, *San Francisco Daily Journal*, February 15, 2002.

for finding us in contempt. Their four-year long hunt for that one defaming posting continued and on March 1, 2002, Poppe formally complained to Glynn and Randy:

> "We have begun the process of reviewing your clients' "SLAPP" web sites to determine whether those web sites are in compliance with the permanent injunction issued by the Court. Our initial review has uncovered dozens of violations.... Enclosed ... are printouts of web pages ... that contain statements prohibited by the permanent injunction. We have indicated with a red pen the language that must be stricken.... The violations are too numerous to discuss them all individually, but we will address several specific examples:
>
> (1) On several web pages, including the "check1" page, Delfino and Day purport to comply with the permanent injunction by replacing certain words, such as "bathroom" and "children" with asterisks. This does not constitute compliance. The web page still conveys false messages that must be deleted in their entirety.[129]
>
> (2) Numerous web pages, like the defendants' continuing stream of Internet postings, repeated refer to George Zdasiuk as "sick" or "sickie," often in conjunction with links to or description of Dr. Blinder's expert report[130]....
>
> (3) Several web pages impersonate depositions witnesses, attributing to them words, thoughts, and sentiments that were not expressed at their depositions.[131]....

---

[129]"Despicable SLAPP terrorist Susan B. Felch who a judge has found not to be mentally unstable nor having a semen stain on her dress or other clothing or had sex with a supervisor hid a special video camera that recorded continuously 24 hours a day, 7 days a week, two Varian public ********* - ******* used by unsuspecting Varian and Novellus employees, their customers, and even their ******** - Varian actually produced from 800 hours of secret video taping B&W still photos of an employee INSIDE a ******** - this invasion of ******** privacy, and other heinous acts in Varian's ******* work environment - like the dogged harassment of employees, allegations of lethal laboratory sabotage, the production of ********** with Varian equipment ..."

[130]*See* Day 2 in Chapter 12.

[131]"KEVIN FELCH, was examined and testified as follows:

Yea, I used to work at Varian, and boy am I glad to be doing what I'm doing. I'm a good ballplayer you know, but ok, ok, we're here to discuss Susan, Susan B. Felch. It's bitch, I mean Benjamin. Is this being recorded?

(4) The defendants' daily trial journal on the "trial3" web page contains many false statements that are covered by the permanent injunction. They also are unprivileged because they are not fair and true reports of the proceedings and they were done with malice.[132]

(5) The "vtape" web page selectively quotes from a Varian court filing in a false and misleading way in order to convey a false message that would not be conveyed by a fair representation of the document.[133]

Semen? I don't know anything about semen. Oh, oh, well, Susan, well yea, Susan is kinda scary. Actually, from time to time she scares the living shit out of me and the boys, geez. Her boys Collin and Trevor. Mine too, oh? What did you say? How? Well you, you a know about her nightmares. Geez! How do I say this. Seems, uh, after she got caught videotaping public restroom at work she began grinding her teeth and having trouble sleeping. Well, it has taken its toll. I close the door when I go. The boys go at school. Her pussy, uh, I mean, her cat's a mess too, a real bitch. You go to bed. Close your eyes, fall asleep, and a few hours late. AAAAAAAAAAAAAAAAAAAAAAAAAAAAAAAAAAAAH!

You want her to see a Dr. Blinder? He's a psychiatrist. Great, fine with me, geez, I need to get a good nights sleep. Mike Green, he's got questions, uh. I told Susan this is never going to end, geez, I told her, AAAAAAAAAAAAAAAAAAH! Sorry, I'm ok. The water is getting to me. Is it ok to pee here? I mean, she's not here, right?

NOTE: This is eye witness commentary."

[132]"**Day 38 --February 13, 2002**

On this long day, Judge Komar would lose his cool in chambers and exclaim, "If this were England or France I'd put them both in jail!" Famed anti-SLAPP attorney Widmann gently reminded His Honor to close his eyes and click his heels while muttering, there's no place like California, there's no place like California ....

Returning after lunch, the Judgment was finally signed. Immediately, its factual & legal basis was called into question, and its survival through appeals queried.

Safe at home, the ever so cute Ms. Day and Dr. Delfino having just passed the 15,000 posting milestone notified the Palo Alto, California police that they would in fact attend tomorrow's VAR stockholder meeting and feared for their safety. Indeed, they would be protected by Palo Alto's finest, "'cause this is America, Jack!"

[133]"Delfino alleges that he was videotaped during his employment at Varian while "in and/or coming out of the restroom at Varian." ... a witness [Crisler] stated that a video camera was placed in a <u>hallway</u> <u>outside</u> a bathroom at Varian.... The alleged videotaping previously formed the basis of Delfino's ... claim for violation of California Labor Code section 435. Section 435 bars

If the text marked with a red pen has not been removed from the defendants' web site by Friday, March 8, 2000, or we have not otherwise resolved these issues ... we will appear before Judge Komar *ex parte* ... to seek an order to show cause why Delfino and Day should not be held in contempt for these violations and for other violations contained in Internet messages they have posted since the judgment ... We will also seek an order requiring that Delfino and Day disclose whether the aliases used to post certain messages are theirs...

we have only begun our review of the defendants' web sites. We expect to find additional violations as we continue our review. Indeed, because our review to date indicates that Delfino and Day have not attempted in good faith to review and correct all of the web sites under their control, they should undertake their own comprehensive review as well...."

On April 2, 2002, Orrick subpoenaed Yahoo! requesting identifying information for 54 aliases – thinking them all, of course, us. They were wrong.

** Subpoenaed by Varian ** by: <u>stockholder09</u>
I KNEW there was a reason that I didn't like Varian!!!
I've just been notified by YAHOO that all information related to my user account at YAHOO has been subpoenaed by Varian.
Let me make it clear that I don't know Delfino or Day and have absolutely nothing to do with their case. However, I have expressed some disapproval of the actions of Varian and their lawyers.
This has certainly reinforce my negative opinions of Varian and their slimebag lawyers. So much for freedom of speech on the internet! Maybe I'll get SLAPPed next since I have said some things that Varian didn't approve of.

---

employers from videotaping employees in a restroom unless authorized by court order. However, Section 435 was enacted in September of 1998 and therefore did not take effect until January 1, 1999 ... Delfino cannot complain about alleged conduct that did not become unlawful until a later date.... Delfino does not allege facts showing the seriousness and gravity necessary to support an invasion-of-privacy claim. He does not allege, for example, that he was videotaped while urinating, undressing, or engaging in other private activities... Rather, he was allegedly videotaped while in *or* coming out of the restroom. ...."

A number of anonymous Internet posters on learning their privacy was being invaded by the Varian SLAPPers expressed their outrage on the Yahoo! VAR message board:

> *** **I'll POST TIL I'M DEAD** *** by: var_sucks
> The subpoena from Varian and their "fascist pig SLAPP attorneys & highly-paid legal terrorists" isn't going to intimidate me!!!
> I'll fight for freedom... you can go back to Afghanistan you varian fascists!! We believe in freedom here in America!!!
> Varian, YOU CAN KISS MY ASS!!!!
> God bless America!!!

Unlike back in 1999, Yahoo! now notified users their privacy was being invaded,[134] thus accounting for these patriotically irate posters. The experience is alarming. The once anonymous critic is now forced to deal with the legal ramifications and costs of defending their Constitutional Rights. Likely identified and harassed into submission by one helluva powerful corporate bully – there are not a lot of choices. Can we tolerate a society where only those with wealth and power decide who speaks?

Once again Poppe got to relive his never-ending fantasy of having Mary and I, his two favorite Internet gadflies, "forced to trade their keyboards in for orange jumpsuits:"[135]

> "... the Court is authorized to impose the following civil penalties for each act of contempt charged: a fine of up to $1,000; monetary sanctions payable to the county of up to $1,500; imprisonment of up to five days; and payment of reasonable attorney's fees and costs.... will ask that the Court impose the maximum permissible civil penalties upon Delfino and Day ..."

---

[134]"Yahoo says they changed their subpoena policy in April-after revealing the identity of "Aquacool_2000," but before he sued them. Previously, Yahoo immediately turned over identities without notifying the user.... Aquacool_2000's lawsuit, however, claims that Yahoo had a policy of handing over members' real names without any legal requirement to do so.... The right to anonymity lies at the heart of the Internet and other forms of speech...." Brian Livingston, *Tech News - CNET.com*, May 26, 2000.

[135]Shannon Lafferty, *The Recorder*, March 25, 2002.

- 14 -

SLAPP ON ICE

On February 1, shortly after our anti-SLAPP case had been to be assigned to a Sixth District Appellate panel, the handicapped Marer somewhat hurriedly submitted a brief:

"Respondents hereby move this Court for an order dismissing Appellants' appeals from the order of the Superior Court denying their special motions to strike Respondents' Third Amended and Supplemental Complaint under Code of Civil Procedure Section 425.16 (the "SLAPP motions"). Respondents make this motion on the grounds that this action has proceeded to trial in the Superior Court; the jury has rendered a verdict in favor of Respondents; the Superior Court has issued a permanent injunction against Delfino and Day; entry of final judgment is imminent; and therefore this appeal is moot...."

Glynn quickly answered Marer's rush to judgment with a declaration on the 13th of February requesting a 60-day extension:

"... trial proceedings have not concluded, no judgment has been entered, nor has any post trial motions been decided, filed or even scheduled. Until the case is finally decided, and the various motions have concluded, and the ultimate decision of the trial court is known the respondents' motion to dismiss is both premature an improper because respondents' underlying premise (conclusion of the trial and related proceedings) has not occurred."

The court did not listen, and on February 28, 2002, our anti-SLAPP appeals were involuntarily dismissed by the Sixth District as moot, meaning "without legal significance." Associate Justices

Eugene M. Premo and William M. Wunderlich, two Republican appointees, ended our anti-SLAPP appeals before we had even begun to exhaust our right to appeal the trial. So much for California's anti-SLAPP statute.

But just as the Nazis had underestimated the stalwart defense of Stalingrad, The Orrick hadn't a clue as to our resolve. Our devastating trial defeat was not the end of our war of words on the Internet. As Glynn had dryly noted, "This is just the first stage ... it's not an unexpected result."[136]

Wasting no time, Glynn filed a "Notice of Appeal" of Komar's trial with the Sixth District on March 8. We had just hired Horvitz & Levy LLP, the largest, and we hoped, the best civil appellate law firm in California to represent us. Glynn, Randy and the Horvitz & Levy attorneys, Jon Eisenberg and Jeremy Rosen, argued that since the final judgment was being appealed, we could not be found in contempt:[137]

> "Plaintiffs contend the injunctive portion of the judgment is not automatically stayed upon defendants' appeal. This is contrary to Code of Civil Procedure section 916 ... it is well-settled that a mandatory injunction is stayed on appeal, while a prohibitory injunction is not....
>
> An injunction is mandatory if it requires affirmative action and changes the status quo.... The pivotal question is whether the injunction requires or precludes conduct in such fashion that it materially alters the status quo.... Since the injunction is mandatory and stayed by appeal, there is no basis for a finding of contempt.... even if this court concludes the injunction is prohibitory, there is no basis for a finding of contempt at this time because defendants' good faith belief that the injunction is mandatory precludes a finding of the intent required for contempt...."

Our counter-attack had begun. This new and unexpected legal wrinkle caught The Orrick and their judge totally by surprise.

---

[136]Shannon Lafferty, *The Recorder*, December 14, 2001.

[137]"Defendants' Opposition to Plaintiffs' Motions to (1) Require an Undertaking to Stay the Injunction and (2) Set an OSC Hearing Re Contempt," filed March 20, 2002.

Mary had been searching for an appellate attorney to represent us in our appeal as soon as the jury was dismissed. She phoned the appellate specialist Jon Eisenberg, who works out of Horvitz & Levy's Oakland office. Jon had read about our case and was enthusiastic about representing us. He was astonished at the language of the injunction even before he learned of the facts. He said that Jeremy Rosen, an associate in their Encino, California headquarters would work with him on our appeal. So on March 18 Mary and I and 31 boxes of legal documents, compliments of Glynn and Randy, made the 400-mile trip to meet Jeremy. Although he had minimal phone conversations with Mary, Jeremy was surprisingly familiar with the case having spent time surfing our SLAPP Web sites. Much to our delight, this young conservative attorney treated us to burgers, fries, and onion rings while expressing enthusiasm for the case between each bite.

When on April 10 we drove across the bay to meet Jon for the first time, he reiterated his amazement at how broad the injunction was over a Vietnamese lunch. With tofu in hand, we hardly needed to remind this Lenny Bruce[138] fan that we would not be silenced.

Poppe's hearing requesting the court issue "an order to show cause [OSC] why Delfino and Day should not be held in contempt for continuing to post defamatory Internet messages in violation of the permanent injunction" had been delayed to March 26:

> "Santa Clara Superior Court Judge Jack Komar initiated contempt proceedings Tuesday against two defendants found to have libeled their former employer on the Internet.

---

[138]The brilliant satirist (1925-1966): "four naval psychiatrists worked me over at Newport Naval Hospital: 1st officer:"Lenny have you ever actively engaged in any homosexual practice?" Lenny: "No sir." An active homosexual is the one who does the doing, and the passive is the one who just lies back. If you were a kid and you were hitchhiking and some faggot came on with you and you let him do whatever his do was, he was an active homosexual, and you are a passive homosexual. You'll never see this in an AAA manuel, but there it is. 2nd officer: "Do you enjoy the company of women?" Lenny: "Yes sir." 3rd officer: "Do you enjoy intercourse with women?" Lenny: "Yes sir." 4th officer: "Do you enjoy wearing women's clothing?" Lenny: "Sometimes." All four: "When is that?" Lenny: "When they fit.""

Komar said attorneys for Varian ... had presented enough evidence to move forward with an order to show cause hearing in July that could result in jail time for defendants Mary Day and Michelangelo Delfino....

Jon Eisenberg, a partner at Horvitz & Levy representing Day and Delfino on appeal, has called the injunction an unlawful prior restraint, and said he would file a habeas writ[139] if Komar orders his clients jailed at the July 11 contempt hearing."[140]

Komar's March 26 OSC hearing certainly did little to clarify what was the supposed violation:

WIDMANN: Right. I mean, in terms of the automatic stay, in terms of past conduct, whether that's going to come in in terms of contempt. That's a possibility. And I'm just concerned.
KOMAR: I'm certainly not issuing an order to show cause with regard to that. All I'm issuing an order to show cause with regard to is the future postings at this point.
BLACKMAN: And that would be the postings from the day of the judgment forward?
KOMAR: Yes. Actually, from the date of the order, because there was an oral order made prior to the judgment being entered. It was made in open court. The defendants were present. Counsel were present. And it was on the record. And that's part of the order.
...
POPPE: You've said that the scope of the order to show cause will be limited to the new defamatory postings. If the websites continue to be unaltered to remove defamatory materials that are currently on there, will the Court entertain a supplemental request for an order to show cause with respect to that?
KOMAR: If the websites continue to be unaltered. At this point let's stick with what I've indicated the order to show cause will relate to.
HERMLE: And I presume you mean, Your Honor, defamatory and impersonations.
KOMAR: Yes. Or unfair competition, as the case may be.

Five days earlier we met had with Jim Blackman, Glynn, and Randy as part of our Palo Alto strategizing meeting. Jim warned

---

[139]A judicial mandate that an inmate be brought to court to determine if he or she was lawfully imprisoned.

[140]Shannon Lafferty, *The Recorder*, March 27, 2002.

that it was possible that all four of us could be found in contempt and jailed. Randy quipped, "Glynn, make sure you bring a tooth brush to the next hearing." At this point, five different attorneys were defending Mary and me. Ka ching!

Early the morning after the hearing, I received an unexpected phone call from two old friends and former colleagues in New York, Gabe Loiacono and John Zola, who told me they heard this on the local *National Public Radio* station while driving to work:

"SHOW: MarketPlace Morning Report
DATE: March 27, 2002
KAI RYSSDAL, anchor: Two former employees of a California company are facing possible jail sentences for making what their former bosses say are libelist statements on the Internet. Chris Richard reports.
CHRIS RICHARD reporting: Three months ago, Michelangelo Delfino and Mary Day were found guilty of libeling officers of their former employer, Varian Medical Systems. A judge ordered them to stop. But since then, Delfino and Day have allegedly posted a storm of Internet messages claiming, among other things, that some Varian executives are having affairs, and others are videotaping employees in office rest rooms, the same kind of accusations that led to the judge's injunction. Now the judge will decide whether to jail Delfino and Day for defying his order.
JON EISENBERG: That would be absolutely unprecedented.
RICHARD: Defense attorney Jon Eisenberg.
EISENBERG: I don't think anyone in this country has ever gone to jail for violating a prior restraint on speech.
RICHARD: Varian officials say they only want reasonable protection from unfounded personal attacks. I'm Chris Richard for MARKETPLACE.
RYSSDAL: And this is PRI."

On forwarding an audio copy of this radio broadcast to my son Michel, he replied by email, "You're bigger than Jesus!" While we all knew that I couldn't shine Jesus' shoes on a good day, the SLAPP silence was truly deafening. We now had to prepare for this July 11 contempt hearing, ironically, my mom's birthday.

Typically, the winner of a near million-dollar damage award would make some effort to collect their money. But this was no ordinary victor and we showed no signs of surrender. The weeks passed and nothing happened. Then, inexplicably, on March 8, Varian added to their arsenal of legal ruffians. Thomas Loran III, a highly-paid partner of the Pillsbury Winthrop LLP, a 900-attorney San Francisco firm joined the 600-attorney Orrick conglomerate in trying to shut us up. Normally, the collection of a civil damages award is quite straightforward and certainly something within Orrick's stable of specialties. But these were two near billion dollar corporations and we had long ago vowed: "We'll post until we're dead!" And so, Mr. Loran issued a subpoena on behalf of his now cash hungry SLAPPer clients requiring us to produce all our financial records at a debtors' exam. Mary and I had as of now paid $1,061,324 to our growing list of attorneys and were living off early withdrawals of what remained in our pension plans. Thankfully, the Dow Jones had been good to us and this money, our only asset, was exempt from collection. If need be, it would be used to keep us fed and armed to fight the SLAPP to the very end.

Our debtors' examination was scheduled for the morning of April 2. While we paid to park Mary's '93 Honda, the impatient Komar signed an order granting Varians' request to begin contempt proceedings. The ink not yet dry, Mary and I were served with it as we approached the old San Jose Court House steps:

> "Defendants Michelangelo and Mary E. Day are ordered to appear on July 11, 2002 at 9:00 a.m., or as soon thereafter as the matter may be heard, in Department 17 of this Court, located at 191 North First Street, San Jose, California, then and there to show cause, if any they have, why they should not be adjudged in contempt of court and punished accordingly for willfully disobeying [the injunction]"

Had Orrick and their judge made a mistake trying to place us in contempt *before* a debtors' examination? Orrick could have easily completed this inquiry on the day of the final judgment or shortly thereafter. Because they failed to do so, Glynn would later explain their SLAPP quandary:

> "There is no question that the privilege against self-incrimination may be asserted by a civil defendant who faces possible criminal

prosecution based on the same facts as the civil action.... the 5th Amendment privilege may be properly invoked in a judgment debtor's examination (OEX) when an Order to Show Cause Re Contempt is hanging over the debtor's head.... Plaintiffs even concede that the 5th Amendment objection is proper..."

Our debtors' examinations were to take place in Komar's courtroom, although he would remain in his chambers during questioning. Having spent so many weeks at a crowded trial all dressed up, it was refreshingly weird for us to return in Tevas, t-shirts and jeans to an empty courtroom.

Mr. Loran, who was saddled this day with an uncontrollably runny nose had insisted I be deposed first. Renee A. Jansen, another Pillsbury Winthrop attorney, assisted him, I assume, by sitting and glaring at me. Mary and Randy sat nearby along with the dutiful Mary Rotunno, the VAR attorney who had spent almost everyday at trial.

Glynn was especially sharp this day. It did not go well for the new kids on the block:

LORAN: Sir, I am going to show you what has been marked as Exhibit 1001 and ask you to look at it. Your counsel has already received a copy. You recognize that document, don't you?
DELFINO: Do I recognize this document?
LORAN: Yes, sir.
DELFINO: I think I have seen something similar to this.
LORAN: You were served with a copy of this document on or about March 27th at 8 p.m. at 854 Carmel Avenue, were you not?
DELFINO: I may have if that's what you're saying.
LORAN: Do you have an independent recollection of being served with papers at your residence on the evening of March 27th?
DELFINO: I have recollection of being served, but I have been served so many times I don't keep track.
FALCON: Don't volunteer information.
LORAN: Okay. Have you been served any time after you received this document?
DELFINO: Yes.
LORAN: Okay. In response to this document, sir, that is Exhibit 1001, have you brought any documents with you here to court?
FALCON: I'm going to object here. This document was not served according to the statutory time requirements in advance of the hearing

date by your own signature March 27th on the proof of service showing March 27th so we're not responding to any of the requests pursuant to Exhibit 1001 at this time.

LORAN: Well, Counsel, what is your contention with respect to the time for service of this document?

FALCON: My contention is it was not timely served in advance of the hearing.

LORAN: So you have failed -- your client has failed to produce any documents in response to the subpoena requesting them with him here today?

FALCON: No. You failed to serve the subpoena in advance of the hearing date with sufficient time in order for the documents to be gathered and prepared and reviewed by me and organized in time for this hearing date.... Why don't you proceed ahead with your questions.

LORAN: Okay. Are you prepared to produce documents in response to this subpoena at some time?

FALCON: We will cross that bridge when we get there.

LORAN: So you're not prepared to commit to produce any of the documents responsive to this subpoena now or any other date?

FALCON: We will take a look at a properly served subpoena and give you a proper response at that time.

...

LORAN: I am asking you, sir, if you would help me to understand what the nature of your objection is.

FALCON: Did you serve this ten days before the hearing date?

LORAN: And what is the source of the ten-day requirement that you're relying upon, sir?

FALCON: California law.

LORAN: What California law?

FALCON: Look it up.

LORAN: Okay. Okay. So you're not going to tell me what statutory requirement --

FALCON: I am not here to educate you on the law.

LORAN: Okay.

FALCON: I am sure you looked at the code sections before you prepared this and served it. This is a subpoena that was served weeks after the original subpoena for an OEX that did not require any document production. If you wanted the documents, you could have changed the date, you could have changed the examination date. You could have served it earlier.

LORAN: Okay.

FALCON: I am not telling you what to do. I am telling you my objection.

390

LORAN: You brought no documents here and you are not prepared to say what your position is with respect to any documents listed in this subpoena. Is that correct?

FALCON: Objection. Compound.

LORAN: Is that correct?

FALCON: Sir, please move on with your questioning.

…

LORAN: I am happy to brief the law to the Court and discuss it with the Court. I am happy to discuss the law or if you would like to discuss that. I asked you that question; and as I heard it, you were unwilling to address that issue.

FALCON: You are the proponent of this document. What is your position regarding the time limit?

LORAN: That it was served within a reasonable time before the hearing. The witness had ample opportunity to contact me, as did you apparently, if there was some problem with responding to it within the time frame contemplated by the service. I am happy to talk to the Court about that. I am also just trying to work with you to find out what your position is.

FALCON: No. That's my -- my position is it was not timely served. You need to do whatever you need to do.

LORAN: Okay. I guess what I would like to do is reserve that issue until we -- there may be some other issues that will come along before the hearing is over, and we will discuss those with the Court at the same time…. Sir, do you have any bank accounts?

FALCON: The witness is instructed not to answer the question on the grounds of the Fifth Amendment. Let me say when you asked him earlier whether he had been served with any other documents, as you know, Mr. Loran, as he entered the court today he was served with an OSC re contempt by your client and their agent for contempt hearings, I think, it's July 11th this year. Based on the criminal nature of those proceedings, we took the Fifth Amendment.

…

LORAN: Mr. Delfino, you're familiar with the name MOBETA, are you not?

FALCON: You can answer that question.

DELFINO: Yes.

LORAN: And is that a corporation that you helped to form?

FALCON: We're getting close to an area, but I will permit him to answer that question.

DELFINO: Yes.

LORAN: When did you help to form MOBETA, sir?

FALCON: You can answer that question

DELFINO: I believe it was incorporated on January 4, 1999; so it would be formed on January 4, 1999, yes.

LORAN: Okay. And what was your role with respect to the incorporation of MOBETA at that time, sir?

FALCON: You can answer that.

DELFINO: It was -- what was my role? I don't know. I'm not sure I understand what that means.

LORAN: I asked you previously if you had assisted in the incorporation of MOBETA. You said that you had. I am asking you, sir, what you did with reference to the formation of MOBETA in or about -- on or about January 4th, 1999.

DELFINO: I am not sure I understand your question. I asked to form MOBETA, to form a corporation.

LORAN: Who asked you to form MOBETA, sir?

DELFINO: Me.

LORAN: You asked yourself about forming MOBETA. What was your purpose in forming MOBETA?

DELFINO: I wanted to start a business.

LORAN: And in what business is MOBETA engaged, sir?

FALCON: Now we're into an area here not designed either to elicit information regarding matters subject to collection enforcement of the judgment and starting to get into the area protected by the Fifth Amendment. Instruct the witness not to answer.

LORAN: So you are instructing the witness not to answer the question, In which business is MOBETA engaged; is that correct?

FALCON: That's what I just said.

…

LORAN: Do you own a computer?

FALCON: Objection. Fifth Amendment.

LORAN: Do you use a computer?

FALCON: Objection. Fifth Amendment.

LORAN: Do you have access to a computer?

FALCON: Objection. Fifth Amendment. Relevancy.

LORAN: It's tangible personal property.

FALCON: Having access to a computer that he does not own?

LORAN: Well, I don't know if he owns it or not. We haven't established that, have we?

FALCON: I understand what you are trying to do. Again, Fifth Amendment.

My deposition with Loran ended quickly and Mary's never began. Komar was called back to open court and asked to resolve this "question and answer" problem. Notwithstanding a rather unsightly pile of used Kleenex on the table, he ordered:

"Now, as to the Fifth Amendment privilege, I'm going to ask you to have a transcript prepared of the questions and the assertions of the privilege. And you can present that to the Court on the [April] 11th as well."

Two days before the hearing, Glynn quite convincingly explained why I was invoking my Fifth Amendment privilege for the second time in this SLAPP:

"While seemingly innocuous, Plaintiffs' questions of defendant seek answers that are "*links in a chain*" of evidence that may tend to establish guilt of a criminal offense or violation of a court order or judgment.

For instance, seeking other names that Mr. Delfino may have used, which if answered, could disclose aliases that he could have alleged used on Internet postings.... Mr. Delfino was asked about the whereabouts of his parents and siblings, which would then lead to whether they had computers, Internet access, and allowed his use of such computers.

Disclosure might provide the link to find potential family witnesses who might provide incriminating evidence .... compelling Delfino to disclose his present and past addresses could lead to the location of potentially incriminating evidence, such as Internet computer, telephone access accounts, files, papers and eye witnesses.

Forcing Mr. Delfino to disclose his present and past employers could also lead to location of incriminating evidence such as computers, Internet access, accounts, papers, and witnesses....

Seeking an admission of prior felonies, which would also be an element of any criminal prosecution and enhancement charge, and might be used to invoke Evidence Code §1101, evidence of other crimes.

While seemingly innocuous on its face, questions that seek information from Delfino about his accounts and dealing with third persons are actually conduits for plaintiffs to subpoena the business records of those parties (just like the Yahoo and AOL SDT's that were just recently requested by plaintiffs), which could lead to, or tend to lead to, evidence of Mr. Delfino's Internet use and access, including access names and aliases."

When we returned to Komar's courtroom on the 11th of April this SLAPP Q & A conundrum was further exacerbated. His Honor, in particular was not happy:

> KOMAR: Leading to a problem and being a problem are two different things, Mr. Falcon. At this point you've provided the Court with no basis for concluding that the questions are asked, the specific questions, will tend to incriminate Mr. Delfino or lead to evidence that would tend to incriminate. Therefore, as I've indicated to you, your objections are overruled.
> And the way you have articulated, Mr. Falcon, is that you have in effect made essentially a blanket objection and assertion of the privilege. I have looked at each one of the questions, and I do not believe that there is any basis for the Court being able to conclude that his answers would tend to incriminate him.
> Now, there may well be some very specific follow-up questions that would give rise to an assertion of privilege. And that's what you have to deal with as an attorney advising your client.
> FALCON: I understand, You Honor. In effect, the Court's order -- can we request a stay of that order so we can seek appellate relief?
> KOMAR: I'll give you five days to seek relief to seek a stay.... This order of examination is going to proceed on the 17th of April. That's five days.

Komar's scowl was unusually marked. Pleasantly making my morning, I got to sit next to a rather jittery Joe Phair, VAR's 54-year-old General Counsel. When we got the respite, he mumbled "Oh shit!" and ever so quietly farted. Quickly, I got up and left the court room with Mary and our attorneys.

The five days were welcome, but not a lot of time given the circumstances. Faced with this ever-growing threat to incarcerate us, Jon and Jeremy, our Order of the Coifs,[141] filed a writ of supersedeas the very next day:

> "Defendants have appealed the judgment. Nevertheless, the trial court has gone forward with proceedings to hold defendants in contempt of the injunction, in spite of legislation effecting an automatic stay of an appealed mandatory injunction....

---

[141]A prestigious national honor society based on grade point average for law school graduates who have attended member schools.

A petition for supersedeas must show that "substantial questions will be raised upon the appeal [citation]." ... Here, the issues for appeal are more than just "substantial." There are compelling and irrefutable grounds for reversal of the underlying judgment on which contempt proceedings are scheduled. The injunctive portion of the judgment must be reversed as an unconstitutional prior restraint on speech. The entire judgment must be reversed because the case was wrongly tried on a theory of libel rather than slander....

the writ *may* issue – if petitioners would suffer irreparable injury absent the writ. Here, the defendants would indeed suffer such irreparable injury. They are threatened with discovery of proprietary and privileged information, incarceration for contempt, and a denial of their First Amendment rights. In contrast, the plaintiffs will sustain no injury if writ relief is granted....

This case is *extraordinary*, both in the narrow sense of that word for purposes of writ relief and in the broader constitutional sense. Defendants are about to be incarcerated for purportedly violating a prior restraint on speech. In America, imprisonment for speaking one's mind is a relic of the 18th century – one of the evils that led to the American Revolution and, ultimately, the First Amendment to the United States Constitution. Our Founders would be appalled by what is about to occur in this case. This court should put a stop to it now...."

By now, Mary and I had come to love those late Friday afternoon filings. For one, they made for great weekend Internet postings. This weekend, however, was special and a bit more busy than usual. With us now facing the prospect of going to jail at the following Wednesday's debtors' examination, Jeremy and Jon filed a hurried "Supplemental Petition for Writ of Supersedeas, Prohibition and/or Other Appropriate Relief" on Monday the 15th:

"In a writ petition filed last Friday, April 12, 2002, defendants Michelangelo Delfino and Mary E. Day have asked this court to stay contempt proceedings in enforcement of the *injunctive* portions of a libel judgment.

As the April 12 petition was on its way out the door for service and filing, the trial judge scheduled a judgment debtor examination hearing for April 17, 2002, in connection with enforcement of the damages portions of the judgment. At the scheduled April 17 hearing, defendants risk a finding of contempt if they continue to invoke the Fifth Amendment and the attorney-client privilege.

This supplemental petition, as a companion to the April 12 petition ... seeks a stay of all proceedings to enforce the damages portion of the judgment as well as the injunctive portions. Absent such stay, defendants risk incarceration on April 17.

What is happening in this case is remarkable. A major hi-tech corporation now has four of Northern California's top litigation, collection, and appellate attorneys billing a combined rate of perhaps $1,600 per hour in their race to have defendants incarcerated and to execute on a six-figure judgment before the judgment can be reversed on appeal. The corporate plaintiffs seem willing to do anything, and to spend unlimited sums of money, in order to silence the defendants. The defendants believe so passionately in their right of free speech on the Internet that they are willing to risk incarceration in defense of that right. The trial judge is understandably exasperated.

There is now an urgent need for this court to step in and say: "Everyone stop. Calm down. Wait until this court decides the merits of the appeal."

Otherwise, Michelangelo Delfino and Mary Day – two middle-aged scientists whose professional careers and finances have already been destroyed by this dispute – will end up somewhere they surely do not belong: in jail...."

The day after the filing of our second writ, a seemingly desperate Loran III, having at least beaten the flu, wrote the Honorable Justices of the Court of Appeal:

"Petitioners have obstructed the completion of a routine debtor's examination on the basis of contrived objections asserting the constitutional right against compelled self-incrimination.... The superior court properly characterized both petitioners' legal positions as asserting a "blanket objection" to answering any of the questions that were propounded at the exam related to petitioners' assets, income, support and debts....

the court below properly overruled petitioners' blanket objections, ordered the debtor's examinations to resume on April 17 and directed petitioners, at the resumed proceedings, to "evaluate each question and make a determination" as to whether they can make a more particularized showing that a Fifth Amendment privilege is properly implicated as to each and, if not, to answer the question....

The parade of horribles advanced by petitioners is thus a pure fiction. The debtor's examinations will resume tomorrow in the court below. Petitioner Delfino will be asked again whether he "ha[s] any bank accounts"...

The only area of examination as to which Petitioners raise even a colorable Fifth Amendment objection is the first, which concerns property transfers ... Due to their blanket refusal to answer, however, petitioners prevented any inquiry into the types of transfers about which examination was sought and likewise prevented any possible limitation of questions to transfers not presenting concerns related to Penal Code section 154 in their legal memoranda ... it was not error for the for the trial court not to have sustained a particularized objection that was never made....

... the Supplemental Petition should be seen for what it is: a transparent attempt to circumvent the filing of a bond to stay enforcement of the $775,000 money judgment ....."

When I spoke with Glynn the day before the hearing, he told me he was still very concerned about my pending debtors' examination. He was insistent that Jim Blackman attend my deposition too, saying, "Komar will put you in jail. You need a criminal attorney!" This was not what I wanted to hear.

Mary and I, anticipating Wednesday's possible trip to the Santa Clara Big House, had made all the necessary childcare arrangements for her two teenage daughters, who were purposely kept unaware of what was going on and what might happen. We had all long been willing to pay a big price for our free speech privilege, and for us it would have been worth losing our freedom to achieve a greater good.

"This is an imminent threat of jail time," said Eisenberg ...

"My clients have chosed to disregard what they believe to be an unconstitutional prior restraint on speech. The First Amendment precludes prior restraint on speech. You can be sued for defamation and required to pay damages but no court can tell you that you may no longer speak ...""[142]

---

[142]Shannon Lafferty, *The Recorder*, March 27, 2002.

While the prospect of being a forgotten Susan McDougal[143] did not sit well with either of us, I still couldn't comprehend how calling the deceitful Felch and Zdasiuk liars on the Internet could end this American dream. Perhaps my mom was watching out for her eldest son, because before I could contact Jim, around 3:50 p.m., I clicked on the Appellate Court's Internet "Docket Entries Page" and was delighted to see this:

"BY THE COURT:
To permit further consideration of the issues raised by the petition and supplemental petition for writ of supersedeas, all contempt proceedings and related discovery enforcing the injunctive portion of the trial court judgment as well as all proceedings to enforce the damages portion of the trial court judgment are stayed until further order of this court, including but not limited to the order of examination set for April 17, 2002, and enforcement of the subpoenas issued to Yahoo! Inc. and Pacific Bell Internet Service, Inc.

Real parties in interest may serve and file on or before May 1, 2002 points and authorities in opposition to the petition and supplemental petition for writ of supersedeas. If real parties in interest file points and authorities in opposition, petitioners may reply to the opposition within 5 days after it is filed in this court...."

Justice Franklin D. Elia, another Republican Governor George Deukmejian[144] appointee, had literally put the SLAPP on ice. Later elected to a twelve-year term, this judge saw the injustice. Mary and I couldn't contain ourselves – we were not going to jail!

Immediately, we called our five attorneys and, one by one, we read aloud Elia's order. They were ecstatic. Jim, so much so, he asked that I read it twice. It seemed so reminiscent of the Stalingrad Kessel where 60-years before, the 300,000 strong Nazi Sixth Army got trapped in a Russian pincer – and was ordered to stay and accept their fate. No one had any idea that this entrapment would forever turn the war around. No one thought that no more than 5,000 Nazi's would ever see home again.

---

[143]Susan McDougal served 18 months in prison for refusing to answer questions about President and Mrs. Clinton before the Whitewater grand jury.

[144]The New York born and raised Governor of California from 1983-1991.

The next morning, Marer, Varian's immobile Hessian, wrote the Honorable Justices of the Court of Appeals:

> "We request that the Court vacate a portion of the temporary stay issued yesterday.... We request that the Court vacate the temporary stay solely with respect to the contempt related discovery proceedings, specifically including the subpoenas served upon Yahoo! Inc. and Pacific Bell Internet Services, Inc.
>
> As shown in our Opposition to the stay filed this morning, but after the stay was issued, Real Parties will be irreparably harmed by a stay ... The main issue in dispute in the contempt proceedings below is whether it was Petititioners who posted certain defamatory Internet messages in violation of a permanent injunction ...
>
> Real Parties are seeking documents ... that may identify the authors of the messages ... Real Parties need the information now, before it disappears forever...."

Jon immediately pointed out the obvious:

> "... plaintiffs can easily avoid any danger of loss of the desired material by asking Yahoo! Inc. and Pacific Bell Internet Services, Inc., to preserve the material during the pendency of the writ petitions. Evidently plaintiffs have not taken, or even thought to take, that simple measure of self-help...."

And so the SLAPPing wheelchair-bound hireling hurriedly wrote another letter to the court and on the very same day:

> "... concern is not that Yahoo and Pacific Bell Internet Services will fail to preserve responsive documents. The concern is that the documents may identify other Internet companies that Real Parties will have to subpoena to discover the identity of the authors of the contemptuous Internet messages...."

Justifiably, everyone ignored Marer, and so the courts' stay stayed. Our reaction to this SLAPP breather was one of unbounded euphoria. And we were not alone in our exuberance, judging by the reaction in the press. First, *Bloomberg's* Pham-Duy Nguyen wrote:

> "Varian Medical Systems Inc. can't collect a $775,000 jury award from two former workers who are appealing the ruling that they

defamed the world's largest maker of cancer-therapy radiation machines....

Under the temporary stay granted by a California appellate court, Day and Delfino can continue to post comments about Varian officials on the Internet, Delfino said.

Varian's attorney did not immediately return a call seeking comment."

No comment? Well, the *San Francisco Daily Journal's* Craig Anderson had something to say:

"Two ex-employees who regularly post insulting comments about the company win one round.... The victory for Michelangelo Delfino and Mary Day ... blocks the efforts of Varian Medical Systems, Varian Semiconductor Associates, and two company employees from collecting a $775,000 jury verdict. "We're blown away that they granted this stay," Delfino said during a telephone conversation late Tuesday, shortly after he learned of the court's order.

Delfino and Day faced a July contempt hearing for allegedly violating ... Judge Jack Komar's permanent injunction ... the ruling was a good surprise for Delfino, who was trying to ward off efforts by Pillsbury Winthrop attorneys representing Varian to question him about his assets so the company could collect the damage award. Delfino had balked at answering questions, asserting his Fifth Amendment rights, but Komar ruled he must respond....

Delfino and Day also have been threatened with jail time if found in contempt of Komar's order. Jon Eisenberg ... said Komar's injunction amounted to unconstitutional prior restraint of his clients' free speech rights.

"We're likely to get this judgment reversed," Eisenberg said. "It would be tragic for these people to go to jail for violating an injunction that was declared unconstitutional." ...

The case is believed to be the first lawsuit to go to trial against people who post caustic commentary on Internet message boards...."

And the *The Recorder's* Shannon Lafferty was also aroused:

"The two defendants ... won't be going to jail anytime soon. On Tuesday, the Sixth District Court of Appeal granted a temporary stay of contempt proceedings and an injunction aimed at Michelangelo Delfino and Mary Day.

The court also stayed efforts to collect damages and ordered briefing.... "It's good news to the extent it means that all of us -- the

400

judge, counsel and litigants -- can take a deep breath and pause while the court of appeal decides the petitions," said Eisenberg ...

In the writs ... Eisenberg argued that the injunction, entered after the jury returned its verdict in December, is an unconstitutional prior restraint on speech.

He also argued that the damages verdict should be reversed because the case was wrongly tried on the theory of libel versus slander, adding that special damages can't be recovered under California's slander statute."

And finally, the *Washington Post's* Michael Bartlett finished the news of our triumph over Varian fascist oppression with this:

"A California appeals court has granted a temporary stay ... Jon Eisenberg ... told Newsbytes he asked for the stay until his clients' appeal is heard. Eisenberg said he believes the lower court's finding was unconstitutional and will be overturned ...

According to Eisenberg, Delfino and Day continue to post on the Internet after the trial, both on their Web site and on various Yahoo boards. He said plaintiffs contend the Web site violates the injunction and asked for a hearing. If found guilty, he said, the defendants could be jailed.

"The injunction tells Delfino and Day there are certain things you must stop saying on the Internet," said Eisenberg. "The First Amendment says there can be no prior restraint on speech. If speech is defamatory, then the speaker can be sued for damages, but the government can't stop people from speaking."

"In this case, the defendants were told they had to shut up." ... "The appeals court agreed to stop the proceedings temporarily," said Eisenberg. He said a hearing will be held to determine if the contempt hearing will be stayed until after the appeal of the case is heard.

"I believe the appeal has a good chance of winning, and if I'm right, they have no lawsuit because they went to trial on the wrong theory of defamation," he said...."

So significant was this free speech victory that Varians' SLAPP cadre filed two opposition briefs on the afternoon of the 1st of May, the last day allowed by the court. First came Marer, the Gator and her POOP's rather ambitious 54 page brief:

"The court took Petitioners at their word when they made the boastful and vindictive "promise" to continue ... "until they are dead." ...

postings ... which have continued in existence for all the world to read, 24 hours a day, 365 days a year for almost three years. ... Petitioners now seek, by petition for a writ of supersedeas, the interruption of ... discovery and the aid of this Court in keeping their promise ... Petitioners have no legal or constitutional right to defame and tortiously hurt Real Parties [all four Varian plaintiffs]. Petitioners will not suffer any cognizable legal harm if they are not permitted to continue to hurt Real Parties, but Real Parties will suffer real harm if, by a writ of supersedeas, Petitioners are allowed to continue their course of misconduct. ... there are no substantial legal issues for appeal raised in the petition, as the injunction does not constitute an invasion of Petitioners' constitutional rights."

Then followed Loran III, Jansen and Craig E. Stewart, an appellate specialist, all of Pillsbury Winthrop. They argued in but 26 pages that our supplemental writ was simply "a transparent attempt to circumvent the filing of a bond, which is required to stay enforcement of the $775,000 money judgment," finishing that "[T]he debtor's examinations should be permitted to resume immediately."

Five days later, as was our right per the Appellate Court's April 16 order, Jon and Jeremy responded:

"... the principal purpose of the injunction is to stop defendants from posting messages on the Internet.... The threat of incarceration is demonstrated by plaintiffs' statement of intent to ask the trial court to "impose the maximum permissible civil penalties," which include "imprisonment of up to five days" for each of dozens of claimed acts of contempt.... The threatened denial of First Amendment rights is demonstrated by the injunction itself.... The threatened discovery of privileged and confidential information is demonstrated by the subpoenas issued to Yahoo! Inc. and Pacific Bell Internet Services, Inc.....

It is ludicrous to suggest that this mega-corporation, which is now enjoying the greatest success of its 50-year history at a time when other high-tech companies are struggling, was harmed by defendants' pre-judgment postings or will be harmed by post-judgment postings.... The Orrick firm contends defendants should have asserted challenges below to the subpoenas issued to Yahoo! Inc. and Pacific Bell Internet Services, Inc.... at the hearing of March 26, 2002, the trial court expressly invited the discovery of defendants' computer records.... It would have been futile for defendants subsequently to ask the judge to stay the very discovery he had invited....

The Orrick firm concedes, as it must, that prior restraint on speech are highly disfavored and presumptively unconstitutional.... The injunction in this case does not merely "prohibit...speech that was found to be libelous...." ... the injunction prevents defendants from posting *truthful and publically available* information regarding "the financial condition or any financial transactions of any present or former officer, director, or employee of Varian" on the same web site where they have posted equally *publically available and truthful* information such as "the location of the person's residence" and reference to the "page and line location in the phone book" where "the person's residence address can be found." ... the injunction prevents defendants from expressing their *opinion* that Varian and its employees "created, fostered, supported, or permitted the existence of a hostile work environment, or that a hostile work environment existed at Varian." ...

Ever since Fox's Libel Act of 1792, there has been "a right to a jury determination as to the libelous nature of speech." ... "the jury provides a safeguard against judicial censorship of speech." ... The jury in this case did not make specific findings that any particular statement made by defendants was defamatory. ... while the jury never found any *specific* statement or category of statements to be defamatory, the injunction proscribes defendants from speaking on *twenty-three* separate categories of statements.... It was too late at the close of trial, and is far too late now, for plaintiffs to try to revive their abandoned theory of slander per se. Thus, the absence of special damages   which plaintiffs do not dispute   precludes plaintiffs' recovery for defamation of any sort....

The Pillsbury firm's primary argument is that defendants may not obtain supersedeas from this court because they did not first ask the trial court for a discretionary stay of enforcement of the money judgment.

... the Pillsbury firm complains there is no evidence that defendants lack the financial wherewithal to obtain an appeal bond, ... We assumed plaintiffs' counsel would concede that defendants are not millionaires.... Evidently, plaintiffs' counsel will concede nothing.

We therefore attach to this reply brief the evidence plaintiffs demand – declarations by Delfino and Day stating that they lack assets in the sum of $1,162,500 necessary to provide security for an appeal bond.... responding to the supplemental petition's Fifth Amendment arguments, the Pillsbury firm contends defendants must demonstrate "probable error" in the debtor examination order of April 11, 2002, in order to obtain writ relief.... But the Pillsbury firm overlooks the larger question, briefed in defendants' April 12 writ petition: whether there was probable error *in the judgment*. If there was, the debtor examination order which is based on the judgment is undermined and must fall with the judgment. As we have demonstrated, there are compelling arguments on the merits for reversal of the judgment."

Jon and Jeremy also highlighted Varians' SLAPP bungle:

"The Orrick firm recognizes that the broader issue is ... invalidity of plaintiffs' trial theory of libel ... that is just another way of saying the judgment should be reversed because there is no substantial evidence of libel - a point we have already said will beat issue in this appeal...."

Acknowledging all our other appellate arguments, on May 7, the now overwhelmed Poppe wrote yet another whiny letter in a last-ditch attempt to stop a stay:

"... request permission to supplement their opposition with this two-page letter.... [W]hile Petitioners once stated below that the libel/slander issue was "a basis for granting judgment NOV," the statement appeared *only* to their opposition to the motion for an undertaking ... it would still have been untimely because all of the parties had already tried the case on a libel theory...."

The truth being what it is, we had no need to further respond and once again Orrick's Inspector Javert[145] was ignored.

Feeling empowered by the temporary stay, we began restoring our SLAPP Web sites to their pre-injunction states. This heading:

"This Web Site has been censored by order of Superior Court Judge Jack Komar and is now in full compliance with his Honor's chill on Free Speech!"

was replaced with this:

---

[145]The morally-flawed relentless antagonist in Victor Hugo's *Les Miserables*.

"This Web Site, no longer censored by order of Superior Court Judge
Jack Komar is in full compliance with United States Law!"

on the dozen or so of our SLAPP Web sites that we had reluctantly
modified per the Komar Chill. And as the weeks passed, we
continued posting. Our messages grew to exceed 17,000, and on
June 9, 2002, an impotent Komar celebrated his 65th birthday, 10-
days before I would turn 52. Two days after Judge Komar passed
retirement age this anonymous Yahoo! VAR message board
posting appeared among a slew of others as a gentle reminder that
there would be no July 11 contempt hearing:

> **ORRICK_&_VARIAN_-_DIVORCE!!** by: slapping_penis
> It's official folks, the once prestigious law firm of Orrick,
> Herrington & Sutcliffe having milked VARIAN out of an
> estimated $4,200,000.00 no longer lists the SLAPP
> TERRORIST COMPANY as a client!!
> Rumor has it that the VARIAN CEO, RICHARD M. LEVY
> has hit his panic button and is now SHITTING!! With the
> SLAPP CONTEMPT HEARING no more, Mr. LEVY is
> expected to SHIT again and again and again. Ditto for Mrs.
> LEVY!!
> Stay tuned for more SLAPP NEWS!

Finally, on June 25, the Sixth District Court of Appeals
granted both writs:

"The petition and supplemental petition of appellants Michelangelo
Delfino and Mary E. Day for a writ of supersedeas, in the matter of
Varian Medical Systems, Inc., et al. v. Delfino, et al., H024214 is
granted as follows: Let the writ of supersedeas issue, staying, pending
this appeal, enforcement of the trial court judgment, including all
contempt proceedings and related discovery enforcing the injunctive
portion of the trial court judgment as well as all proceedings to
enforce the damages portion of the trial court judgment. This court's
temporary stay order of April 16, 2002, is vacated as moot."

Justices Premo and Wunderlich participated in this decision.

In spite of all this judicial exuberance, the ever-recalcitrant
Komar refused to take our scheduled July 11-12 contempt hearing

off his Santa Clara Complex Civil Litigation Internet calendar. Not until the late afternoon of July 9 did he cancel the hearing that was supposed to lock-us away. Poppe had finally run out of ways to try and put us in prison. The fascist SLAPP was stayed and our free speech was not.

Appellate justice had warmed Komar's Chill. It was now unenforceable, and yet paradoxically, The Orrick continued as if they had achieved something. The ever engorged Hermle still advertised her Varian SLAPP victory on her company's Web site:

> "In the recent high-profile trial of *Varian v. Delfino and Day*, one of the first cases to go to a jury on the question of defamation and harassment on the Internet, Ms. Hermle obtained a $775,000 verdict for her clients, who sued to stop defamation and harassment by an ex-employee. She also obtained a comprehensive permanent injunction prohibiting further harassment and defamation. She also obtained a comprehensive permanent injunction prohibiting further harassment and defamation."

Did no one notice that soon after the trial ended, the Orrick, Herrington & Sutcliffe Web site no longer listed Varian as a corporate client?

Varian and Orrick are never going to have the last word. On August 28 at 10:14 pm, MoBeta, Inc. published this, my favorite press release:

> **"MoBeta, Inc. Beefs Up Security as 2nd Patent Issues**
>
> LOS ALTOS, Calif.--(BUSINESS WIRE)--Aug. 27, 2002--MoBeta, Inc. announced that U.S. Patent Number 6,440,487 for radioactive transition metal stents was assigned to the company today. This second MoBeta, Inc. patent addresses the therapeutic and diagnostic applications of implantable medical devices like stents in which the placement of transient radiation is deemed beneficial.
>
> MoBeta, Inc. is a privately owned R&D company specializing in the creation of novel medical technology located in Los Altos, California. Incorporated in January 1999, it maintains a web site at http://www.mobetainc.com. Almost immediately after filing their first patent, the company founders were named defendants in Varian

Medical Systems, Inc. (VAR), et al.'s., Strategic Lawsuit Against Public Participation (SLAPP), a lawsuit that is presently in the California 6th District Court of Appeals.

Michelangelo Delfino, Vice President of MoBeta, Inc. and co-inventor said, "For months now, the FBI has been investigating a plethora of Internet death threats linked to this SLAPP and directed at the MoBeta, Inc. officers as well as a number of their attorneys. The FBI has since identified and made contact with two of the perpetrators, both of whom expressed "remorse" shortly after being caught. The case is in now in the hands of a United States Attorney."

Mary E. Day, President of MoBeta, Inc. and co-inventor added, "We are very pleased in the awarding of this second patent and are hopeful that this reign of Internet terror has come to an end. We look forward to the appeals process moving forward so that MoBeta can best return to serve the needs of the community.""

Remarkably, for a period of several hours over the next week, our third press release was the second most widely viewed news article on Yahoo! Finance. And even though no one offered us any money for our patented technology, we were doing just fine.

We had survived 1278 days of litigation and had paid a $1,366,884.79 legal bill. FBI Special Agent Sean Wells and United States Attorney Jeff Nedrow had assured us and our attorneys that we were all safe and in no immediate danger, this despite some death threats traced to Agilent Technologies – Julie Fouquet's company!

Lucy and Rana, oblivious to all this craziness, slept through most of it -- I think. For good and bad, Mary and I were wide-awake through all of it. A bit scarred, perhaps, a bit tired too, yes, older but not necessarily any wiser, we slouched together on our leather couch finishing off a $4 bottle of Bordeaux Rouge, that I had picked up at our local Safeway. As Rachmaninoff came to a timely end on the CD player, we got ready for bed.

Our fate was now in the hands of a three-judge panel. While all of us on both sides of freedom would be made to wait for the process to unfold, Mary and I would not be idle. On September 20, 2002, Jeremy, the principle author of our 62 page "Appellants'

Opening Brief" asked the Sixth District Court of Appeals permission to make an exception and accept a longer than standard 14,000 word brief.

> "The record in this case is substantial, with a 35 volume Reporter's Transcript, more than 300 trial exhibits, and a 7 volume Appellants' Appendix. The appeal raises numerous constitutional and statutory issues as demonstrated in the accompanying proposed Appellants' Opening Brief and the prior supersedeas briefing."

Six days later, Presiding Justice Bamattre-Manoukian approved his request and all 17,294 words were filed:

> "The Court of Appeal for the Second Appellate District recently held that the perfection of an appeal from an order denying an anti-SLAPP motion divests the trial court of jurisdiction....

> According to the rule of *Mattel*, in the present case the trial court acted in excess of jurisdiction by setting and conducting trial of this action during the pendency of defendants' anti-SLAPP appeal ... defendants are at least entitled to an unqualified reversal of the judgment ...

> The anti-SLAPP motion previously asserted by Delfino and Day should be renewable on remand of this action to the superior court, so that Delfino and Day may seek to recover their attorneys fees and costs pursuant to code of Civil Procedure section 425.16..."

A new clock started ticking, and two Varian corporations, Felch, and Zdasiuk had 30 days to respond. But the law was not on their side. On the 25th of October all four plaintiffs asked for more time and we stipulated, providing us 50 days to reply to their opposition brief. Notwithstanding the extra month, the SLAPPers needed still more time. On November 20, Marer, called and asked for another 30 day extension. Jeremy graciously agreed – these SLAPPers would have no more excuses for when they lost.

In the meantime, like any other Americans, we are now free to post the **truth**: "Varian videotaped children going to the bathroom under Richard Meyer Levy's nose;" **hyperbole**: "Varian Executive George Andrew Zdasiuk is one sick mo-fo;" and our

Constitutionally protected **opinion**: "Susan Benjamin Felch, the scary yenta bitch, is a chronic liar or a neurotic hallucinator;" and to do so anonymously, and as frequently as we like, just like everyone else in this great country. And you know, of course, Richard Anthony Aurelio is still really just a Dick.

SLAPP, SLAPP, Hooray!

INDEX